Praise for *The Maverick M.D.*

D0609683

With a captivating narrative style—Mary Swander takes the reader on the intense journey which was the life and work of Dr. Nicholas Gonzalez. Every physician and any layfolk interested in health should know of this man, for if the medical science establishment was a true meritocracy, his name would be household. Thanks to Ms. Swander, we can open our mind's eye to his intellect and training—honed through classrooms, labs, hospital wards, meetings with remarkable mentors, athletic fields, and through life's lessons; And witness his dedication, integrity, and resilienc—all matched up against many of the perverting influences that have co-opted the medical profession, and science in general. To the very end—he faced them with resounding dignity and resolve, all the while continuing to heal the toughest cancer cases at an incomparable success rate. I am grateful to this physician scientist. This book allowed me to further and more deeply appreciate his life and contributions.

Faiz Khan, MD, Dual Board Emergency / Internal Medicine,
Former Chair of Emergency Medicine, Former Chair of
Medical Ethics, and Founder of CityMD Urgent Care

Mary Swander's biography of Nicholas Gonzalez, *The Maverick M.D.* is a brilliant portrayal of a man who devoted his entire life to finding an alternative cure for cancer. Yet, as we have witnessed, like many medical pioneers who dare to go against the grain of established theory, Gonzalez had to put up a fierce fight to have his research put to the test, and the door to his own medical practice kept open. In crystal clear prose, Swander has created a thriller, a vivid dramatization of the tension, roadblocks and intrigue this Ivy-League, conventionally trained doctor dealt with to the end. Anyone interested in discovering a different approach to cancer and other degenerative diseases should read this book.

Ty and *Charlene Bollinger*,
Founders of The Truth About Cancer

Nicholas Gonzalez was a very amazing person and physician. His life story is an inspiration. This book takes you on a journey beginning with his family origins in Mexico and Italy. His Mexican ancestors survived revolution, war, and very difficult circumstances but throughout all that they thrived as musicians and as a tight-knit family. The story of his Mexican ancestors just barely making it through Ellis Island is very moving, like many things in the book. These family strengths, courage and determination shine out in Dr. Gonzalez's creativity, persistence and brilliance as a cancer doctor. His legacy and his gifts to cancer patients live on in these pages.

Colin A. Ross, M.D., founder and President of
The Colin A. Ross Institute for Psychological Trauma

The Maverick M.D.

The Maverick M.D.

Dr. Nicholas Gonzalez and His Fight for a New Cancer Treatment

The Authorized Biography

By Mary Swander

Notice

This book is intended for general informational purposes only, not as a medical manual. The materials presented in no way are meant to be a substitute for professional medical care or attention by a qualified practitioner, nor should they be construed as such. Always check with your doctor if you have any questions or concerns about your condition or before starting or modifying a program of treatment. New Spring Press LLC and the author(s) are not responsible or liable, directly or indirectly, for any form of damages whatsoever resulting from the use (or misuse) of information contained in or implied by this book. Although the author and publisher have made every effort to ensure that the information in this book was correct at press time, the author and publisher do not assume and hereby disclaim any liability to any party for any loss, damage or disruption caused by errors or omissions whether such errors or omissions result from negligence, poor memory, accident or other cause.

For information address: New Spring Press, PO Box 14, Sanibel FL 33957 USA or email: custsvc@newspringpress.com.

Publisher's Cataloging-in-Publication Data

Names: Swander, Mary, author.
Title: The maverick M.D. : Dr. Nicholas Gonzalez and his fight for a new cancer treatment / Mary Swander.
Description: Includes bibliographical references and index. | Sanibel, FL: New Spring Press, 2020.
Identifiers: ISBN 978-0-9985460-8-7 (Hardcover) | 978-0-9985460-6-3 (pbk.)
Subjects: LCSH Gonzalez, Nicholas J., 1947-2015. | Physicians--United States--Biography. | Immunologists--New York--Biography. | Physicians--Diseases--United States. | Cancer--Alternative treatment. | BISAC BIOGRAPHY & AUTOBIOGRAPHY / Medical
Classification: LCC R154.G64 S93 2020 | DDC 616.99/4/0092--dc23

Book design by Six Penny Graphics
Indexing by Dr. Toni Briegel
Cover design by Six Penny Graphics

In Memory of Nicholas J. Gonzalez, M.D.
(1947–2015)

Table of Contents

Pray God to send a few men with what the Americans call "Grit" in them; men who when they know a thing to be right, will not turn away, or turn aside, or stop; men who will persevere all the more because there are difficulties to meet or foes to encounter; who stand all the more true to their Master because they are opposed; who, the more they are thrust into the fire, the hotter they become; who, just like the bow, the further the string is drawn, the more powerfully will it send forth its arrows, and so, the more they are trodden upon, the more mighty will they become in the cause of truth against error.

—Charles H. Spurgeon

(Quote found in a sterling silver frame with a picture of Dr. Nicholas Gonzalez and his wife Mary Beth. After her husband's sudden death, this was a gift to Mary Beth by a longtime patient and friend.)

I

1

1972. Nicholas Gonzalez descended into the New York City underground subway. Doors open, doors shut. Darkness filled the tunnel, the car jostling along, his fellow travelers seated beside him, staring straight ahead. His own vision widened out beyond the subway car. Nick, at 25 years old, was on his way to work at Time Inc., a great job for a young journalist—steady, reliable employment that provided enough money for him to live a life he enjoyed in a city he loved, and still have enough time at night to work on his novel.

His usually glistening blue eyes assumed the gray tint of the day. Of both Mexican and Italian heritage, a full shock of wavy dark brown hair framed his face, a pair of wire-rimmed aviator's glasses perched on his nose. His movements matched his stature: quick, powerful and tight with the musculature and alertness of a short stop on a baseball team, the game and position he had played from childhood to adulthood.

In reality, he was a journalist during the day, but an artist at night. His novel was his focus. He came from a family of famous musicians, artists who made beautiful classical music, appreciated great composers, painters, dancers, and writers. He knew that he was going to join those ranks. He was going to be a great writer. Writing was his art. He fit right into this creative family pattern.

He had never told anyone in his family, though, about his first revelation, his first insight into his own talents. He had been around fourteen years old, so young to experience this startling event. He was in his room in his family home in Queens, alone, about to fall off to sleep when he sensed a presence beside him, an apparition, a spiritual being, that's the only explanation for it—an angel. The angel was at once comforting and terrifying. Nick had no idea what was happening. The angel sat there for several minutes with Nick, then said, "One day you will write a great book that will change the world."

3

Nick filled with a charged energy, a focus and feeling of clarity that would carry him through his whole life. He fell asleep in a profound state of comfort and inspiration.

Nick had no idea at the time how this prediction would play out. His house was filled with classical music and great books, but this experience was so extraordinary that he couldn't tell his parents. They would think he was making it up, inventing the incident to get attention.

On the subway, he recaptured this same sense of inspiration and determination. He was going to write a book that would change the world. He was going to write the great American novel. That's why he was so disappointed to be going to Time, Inc. to meet with his boss. A rumor had spread around the office that his boss was going to assign him to the science beat. How was this happening? Why? The science beat was considered the booby prize of journalism. Here he was a young, up-and-coming well-credentialed journalist, a novelist, who was going to be forced to cover the dullest subject imaginable. What a grind. He didn't deserve this assignment.

Right after receiving his undergraduate degree from Brown University, Nick had launched his journalism career. Nick wrote about dozens of subjects, his interests broad and wide-ranging. This work had given him the time to read and research. He couldn't have been happier. His apartment, on the corner of East 72nd and 3rd Avenue, began to fill up with books. He secured a literary agent and got an advance for his novel. He worked on his journalism and his fiction, and in between, he read a book every day or two. His reading was eclectic but had begun to center around his love of natural history and ecology. His childhood days at Lake George and at the family farm in Vermont nurtured this interest. Now, removed from these natural environments, he schooled himself in the working of the natural world from his Manhattan apartment.

Ecology wasn't science, he told himself, at least it wasn't the formulaic, stifling stuff he'd had to suffer through in high school and college. Ecology was the study of the interactions of organisms within their environment, the relationship of humans and animals, animals and plants, plants and organisms, humans and organisms, and the whole cycle of nature. The study of ecology was fluid and creative. Ecology had great writers, artists, who could convey their ideas to lay audiences. Scientists couldn't relate to the real world. They were locked away in their own heads.

First, Nick had become fascinated with the cycling of nutrients. Rock broke down to soil, soil feeding plants, plants feeding animals and humans. Animals and humans then returned to the soil and the cycle repeated itself over and over again. The health of any ecosystem, including its plants and animals, depended upon the efficient cycling of nutrients. If the process broke down at any point with even any one nutrient—say calcium—the whole system and all its populations could collapse. The system failure first demonstrated itself as disease. Botanists and wildlife scientists accepted the idea that disease was not an inevitable state, but rather, an end point of a breakdown in nutrient cycling.

From his nightstand, Nick then picked up the works of the great agronomist Sir Albert Howard (1873–1947). In *An Agricultural Testament*, Howard discussed his work in India where he had observed farmers maintain a very nutrient-rich soil that produced very nutrient-dense food. Utilizing only organic compost, the farmers grew high-yielding insect and pest resistant crops without the use of herbicides, pesticides and other inputs that had become so prevalent in the post-World War II Green Revolution.

Howard noticed that the farmers and local villagers living off of these crops were also extremely healthy, generally free of the degenerative diseases so common in Western civilization. Howard concluded that healthy soil produced healthy food that produced healthy people. A simple principle, but one that was all but forgotten in the 1970s push toward an industrialized food system, when open pollinated crops had been replaced with hybrids and compost with anhydrous ammonia.

After reading Howard, Nick was beginning to formulate an idea that there was another medical model, one that wasn't part of the halls of the Ivy League, one not even understood by the professors in medical schools. Nick was convinced that health resided in nutrients, and that one's best defense against disease was in eating the right food. He explored this hypothesis further by picking up the work of René Dubos, the famed Rockefeller University microbiologist, who had a vision of human health that began with the microbial, then expanded to the interconnection of all beings:

> *Man himself has emerged from a line of descent that began with*
> *microbial life, a line common to all plant and animal species...[he]*
> *is dependent not only on other human beings and on the physical*

world but also on other creatures—animals, plants, microbes—
that have evolved together with him. Man will ultimately destroy
himself if he thoughtlessly eliminates the organisms that constitute
essential links in the complex and delicate web of life of which he
is a part.

Dubos challenged the twentieth century ideas about infection. The medical model looks at infectious disease through the lens of exposure. Exposure to a deadly or debilitating microorganism means you've "picked-up" an illness. Quarantines and isolation, hand-washing, sanitizing and sterilizing all helped reduce exposures. But Dubos demonstrated that susceptibility to infection and its severity depended not only on the level of exposure to the pathogen, but to the health and nutritional status of the individual.

The polio epidemic of the 1950s well-illustrated the concern over exposure to the exclusion of the notion of nutrition. During this period before the Salk vaccine, polio was one of the scariest viruses known. Pictures of children in leg braces and iron lungs were pasted all over March of Dimes tin cans asking for spare change to help fight polio. When there was an outbreak, swimming pools, theatres, churches, schools—anywhere where people congregated—were closed for weeks at a time. Neighbor children weren't allowed to gather, and every runny nose was monitored.

Dubos and his colleagues researched polio exposure in various locations including high density populations in urban areas. What they found surprised them. Ninety percent of children and adults living in cities carried antibodies for polio. They had been exposed to the virus, but only rarely had someone developed a full-blown case of the disease. Researchers believed that a person's nutritional state determined their susceptibility.

Polio hit the rural areas and small isolated towns of the country the hardest. The bias of the day believed that people on farms and rural areas were dirty, so they contracted the virus. Researchers found out that it was just the opposite. People in rural areas were in effect too clean. They hadn't bumped up against enough people who were carriers of the virus. They hadn't had the chance to develop antibodies to polio, and so they had no defenses. Again, the most nutritionally deficient were the most vulnerable.

Nick was amazed and had a hard time wrapping his head around this idea of nutritional susceptibility. His childhood had been one of intense fear of exposure to viruses—polio and others. And the go-to miracle drug for all ailments was an antibiotic, even though doctors and pharmacists knew antibiotics didn't work on viruses. They worked on bacterial infections. Antibiotics had saved millions of lives, but their great success created overuse and antibiotic resistance. Have a cold? Here's a shot of penicillin. Acne? Take tetracycline.

The next book on Nick's shelf was Weston Price's *Nutrition and Physical Degeneration*. Price's work was a revelation to Nick. Here was the tome that finally pulled together all of Nick's readings in ecology, wildlife biology, organic farming and microbiology.

The food people ate and the way that food was grown and processed mattered. Nick opened the 500-page book and was fascinated by the photos capturing the New Zealand Maori family of five siblings. The oldest sister who was raised on the native diet had a well-proportioned body with wide cheek bones and hips. The next two brothers who were raised on a Westernized diet had narrower faces, flat and club feet. The last two siblings, a sister and brother, revealed the results of the period when the parents returned to their native diet. Their faces and physiques were much more closely aligned with their older sister's.

Price documented isolated peoples and the physical changes they underwent when they changed from native to Westernized diets. He also noted the physical changes that occurred in groups like one he had visited in Ontario, Canada. They remained on their native diets but also suffered deformities when their soil became depleted. Price linked depleted soil, depleted Westernized diets, and physical deformities to other, often less obvious symptoms like fatigue, depression, mental illness, and even criminality. Price went on to link the economics of our food system—the price of food and the price of health care—to the price of incarceration.

Book by book, Nick's view of human health had become intrinsically bound to the health of the planet and the cycles of nature. It was difficult for him to shift away from the imprinting of the medical model—a pill for every ill—but he eventually assumed a more holistic perspective. Without courses, classes, internships or mentoring, he had taught himself the basics of the sophisticated connections of sustainable agriculture to epidemiology.

This conversion toward a more holistic view of health was one of a series of conversion experiences Nick experienced in his life. Changing one's paradigm toward any subject is a lonely, difficult experience. Often, you have to go against the grain of family, peer, professional and community pressure. And once you've slipped over to another point of view, it's difficult to return and resume your old stance or perception. You often stand alone.

Nick realized that attempting to convince others of your fresh insights smacked of evangelism, the enthusiasm of the convert, and a certain naiveté. He would have to be prepared for the raised eyebrow, the discounting comments and off-hand dismissals. There's something very threatening to have someone in the tribe disagreeing with a tribal ritual or habit. And changing your diet may be the most difficult paradigm shift of all. Food means connection to family and community. No one wants to sacrifice those bonds. It means familiarity and comfort. Who wants to abandon those pleasures?

Nick knew that he would be completely at odds with these traditional scientists that he would be assigned to interview. He would have nothing in common with these researchers. The job that he liked so much would become a bore. As involved as Nick was in the study of ecology, he didn't think of himself as a scientist. That was for those nerdy guys in high school with slide rules. Nick was angry when he finally arrived at Time, Inc. and took the elevator up to see his boss.

Nick waited anxiously outside his boss' office until the door opened and he was invited inside.

"I want you to take on the science beat, Nick."

No, no, no, not the science beat, Nick thought. None of the other journalists wanted to cover science. Most of them, like Nick, thought the subject uninspiring. Nick was impatient with the whole conversation. He wanted to just stand up and walk out of the office. Instead, he tried to talk his boss out of it.

"Don't you think I'd be more valuable on another assignment?"

But his editor was firm. "I'm sure you'll be really good at the science beat."

2

On December 10, 1914, in the midst of the Mexican revolution, Guillermo José González and Maria Luz Pimentel, Nick's grandparents, sat waiting impatiently at Ellis Island in New York to be processed as immigrants to the United States. Seated on hard wooden benches, they were anxious to be called up before the inspector who perched on a tall stool behind a high desk at the front of the room. The noise in the Great Hall packed with immigrants speaking hundreds of languages was earsplitting.

The couple had floated into Ellis Island on a steam ferryboat. The vessel was docked, the gangplank placed. Guillermo, carrying his cello, crossed into the United States with his young wife. They climbed the winding stairs that led to the Registry Room. Doctors stood on the second floor, eyeing each person, looking for any infirmity, any defect—a limp, shortness of breath—that could send the immigrant to the deportation room. A throng of other immigrants, some also from Mexico, but the majority from Eastern, Southern and Central Europe, pressed against Guillermo and Luz.

Guillermo longed for the opportunities the United States offered, but he also knew that deportation could cost Luz and him their lives. No, he couldn't turn back. He would be shot. But he also pined for his old life playing in Mexican President Francisco Ignacio Madero González's quartet. Then Guillermo had propped his cello between his knees, bow drawn across the strings, left hand posed against the neck of his instrument, waiting to join the other members of the group. Guillermo was an accomplished musician from a family of accomplished musicians. Guillermo's father had taught his son to play the cello. He was a stern teacher and hit Guillermo on the head when he didn't practice.

In the National Palace in 1913, Guillermo, dressed in white tie and tails, had gathered his composure, his dark hair swept away from his face, revealing a

9

high forehead, large round eyes, open wide. His mouth curved slightly upward on the right side of his face with the confidence of an artist at the top of his field. Music was what he loved and what he intended to pursue despite the political tensions surrounding him.

Guillermo was in good company. The quartet contained not only his brother Gustavo González, but the famed violinist Julián Carrillo who went on to become a composer, conductor, and developer of a theory of microtonal music that he called "The Thirteenth Sound." Guillermo was from a wealthy, landed gentry family in Córdoba, Veracruz, a city founded by the Spanish in 1618, replete with the Immaculate Conception Cathedral with its traditional Spanish colonial architecture. The church, the center of the Catholic community that included the González family, sat on the historic town square in the center of the city, Parque de 21 de mayo.

Guillermo's talent and passion for the cello had taken him to the Conservatorio Nacional de Música, founded in 1866, the oldest official music school in Mexico City. The conservatory, which celebrated its 150th anniversary in 2016, still boasts of producing famous alumni who leave its graceful concert halls through the front façade, the doors encased by a bank of windows topped with sculptures of ancient musicians. The campus sits in the upscale Polanco neighborhood, now often called the Beverly Hills of Mexico City.

At the Conservatorio, Guillermo met Luz Pimentel, a classically trained vocalist and harpist. When Guillermo graduated, he became first cellist in the Beethoven Symphony Orchestra conducted by Julián Carrillo. The couple lived a life of shared love of music, playing together and with others until all hours of the night, falling into not only the rhythm of the compositions but eventually into the rhythm of the life at the National Palace where Francisco Madero served as the country's thirty-third president.

The short rule of Francisco Madero (1911–1913) kicked off the long and complex ten-year Mexican Revolution. Madero had urged Mexican people to rise up against the entrenched President Porfirio Díaz. During his thirty-five-year reign, Díaz had created a stable but repressive government that consolidated wealth in the hands of the elite landowners and foreign investors while leaving the poor, rural *campesinos* unable to make a living. Madero, a moderate, met with other revolutionary leaders including Francisco "Pancho" Villa and José Venustiano Carranza. Madero hoped to overthrow Díaz without bloodshed, but

Madero's wishes weren't realized. The other revolutionaries went on attack. Díaz finally resigned and was exiled to Europe.

Madero, from an extremely wealthy family, hoped to bring a cultivation of the arts and culture to his office along with political reforms. He formed his official string quartet in 1911, including Guillermo and Gustavo González, and Julián Carrillo. He left the basic governmental power structures of Díaz in place, and while his quartet played in the palace, Madero introduced freedom of the press, an infrastructure program, a Department of Labor, and some agrarian reforms. But during his three-year rule, other revolutionaries found Madero's reforms too little too late. Madero spent most of his time putting down rebellions. He tried to prevent the country from cracking apart into regional factions led by other revolutionaries and guerilla fighters.

During this time, Carranza became governor of his native Coahuila in northern Mexico, and he instituted his own range of reforms to benefit the working class—from safety in the workplace, to addressing abuses in the company stores. His relationship with Madero deteriorated, however, and Carranza criticized him as weak and ineffectual. Carranza thought Madero's presidency would not last, and in February 1913 during La Decena Trágica (The Ten Tragic Days), Victoriano Huerta and other military generals overthrew and murdered Madero. Huerta assumed the presidency, established a harsh military dictatorship, and was immediately opposed by Carranza and other revolutionaries.

Meanwhile, Pancho Villa, who had once been condemned to death by Huerta, but escaped with a stay of execution by Madero, formed a tough band of military men called The *División del Norte* (Division of the North). In December of 1913, much to Carranza's dismay, Villa became governor of Chihuahua. Polar opposites in character and personality, Villa had never gotten along with Carranza, but joined forces with him to depose his old enemy Huerta.

Seventeen months of civil war and bloody fighting ensued. No one wanted to volunteer for Huerta, so thousands of homeless, political prisoners, and scores of indigenous men in southern Mexico were rounded up, some in chains, to fight for the Federal Army in a war that meant little to the "soldiers." Finally, in June of 1914, Villa won a significant victory at Zacatecas that polished off Huerta's forces. Huerta fled Mexico on a German ship on July 14, and the Federal Army collapsed.

In the lead, Carranza–tall, stately, wire rim spectacles balanced on his nose, a stogie hanging from his lips–entered Mexico City with Villa–a large sombrero on his head, bandoliers crisscrossing his chest. Two victorious revolutionaries. Carranza declared himself the new president of Mexico. Villa then joined forces with Emiliano Zapata and other revolutionaries to oppose him. The fighting continued, and the beat went on until Carranza was driven out of Mexico City and killed in the Sierra Norte de Puebla mountains in 1920. Álvaro Obregón was sworn in as president and the Mexican Revolution came to a close.

And during all this turmoil, what became of Guillermo González, the cellist in full evening dress, back at the Palace? The Gonzalez family album opens to a photo of Guillermo, a broad-brimmed hat plopped down on top of his head, his bangs peeking out from the rim, standing in the back of a cluster of military men gathered around Generalísimo Carranza. The general is in uniform, shiny gold buttons securing his jacket, his iconic mustache and white beard making him instantly recognizable. The family oral history suggests that Guillermo became a pay clerk in Carranza's army.

On the other hand, a 1937 article in the *North Shore Daily Journal* placed Guillermo with Pancho Villa's band when it had combined with Carranza's forces. "I joined the army because there was nothing else to do," Guillermo was quoted in the newspaper. "They made me an officer even though I didn't know how to shoot. And often we would play for Carranza, Villa's co-leader. But Villa didn't care for the music."

Nick Gonzalez explained his grandfather's role in the revolution this way:

> *When tyrannical forces in the military assassinated the then Pres-*
> *ident and installed a military dictatorship in 1913, many of the*
> *country's leading intellectuals, including my grandfather, abandoned*
> *their careers to organize a counter revolution against the military.*
> *My grandfather became a major in the revolutionary forces, who*
> *for a time were able to re-establish a democratic government. But*
> *when that collapsed, my grandfather, with his young wife, a classical*
> *singer, were forced to flee for their lives, ending up in the US.*

Bill Gonzalez, Guillermo's grandson and Nick's brother, remembered visiting the Castillo de Chapultepec museum in Mexico City with his grandfather. They had climbed the steep hill to the 18th century castle once designed for the local viceroy, then looked down on a sweeping view of the city below. Inside on the lower levels housing the National Museum of History, they studied the displays and dioramas depicting all the battles of the Mexican Revolution. Guillermo explained each phase of the Mexican Revolution and each successive leader. He spoke disparagingly of Pancho Villa.

"Villa was nothing but a common criminal," Guillermo said.

Bill distinctly recalled that his grandfather fought against Villa. One can only speculate that once Carranza assumed the presidency and Villa, his co-leader, turned against him, Guillermo remained loyal to Carranza. In a revolutionary war predicated on reversals, Guillermo may have once fought in Villa's band, but ended up fighting against "the bandit" in the end.

In any case, with Carranza's fall from power, Guillermo González fled Mexico, fearing for his life. I imagine him throwing a few pieces of clothing in a bag, stuffing some pesos in his pocket, then slowly making his way from Mexico City to Cordoba to Cancún, travelling at night. Finally, he caught a boat to Cuba where he hid, waiting for a break in the political turmoil. He then returned to Mexico to retrieve both his cello and his wife whose family members were also "Carrancistas," and their lives threatened. Finally, Guillermo and Luz took the first boat to New York City.

"Name?" the U.S. immigrant inspector asked. "Occupation? Marital Status? Amount of money you're carrying?"

Guillermo González had escaped Mexico with little money, not enough to convince the inspector that he and his wife would not become indigents. He tried to explain that he and Luz were fleeing for their lives from Mexican revolutionaries.

"But I was a famous musician in Mexico," Guillermo said. "I can make a good living in the United States."

The inspector rolled his eyes. "What kind of living can you make in America as a musician? You'll be on the street playing for spare change."

"No, Guillermo protested. "I am classically trained. I played in President Madero's string quartet in Mexico."

"You'll be panhandling here."

The inspector had no time to argue and was about to stamp the deportation papers when Guillermo slipped his cello and bow from its case. Guillermo lifted his arm, and began to play, his strokes bold but even, seductive, but loud enough to make all in the crowded, cavernous room stop and listen. Whole, clear notes spilled from the strings, a sound so intricate but soothing that it gave the other immigrants who had fled their homelands, who had been confined for weeks in steerage uneasy about their chances for a new life in a new place, a moment to pause. Tired, poor, struggling with their own traumas, they took in the beauty of the music, and received some hope, some solace.

"Welcome to the United States," the inspector said, stamping Guillermo's papers.

3

At the time that Guillermo González was learning the intricacies of classical music and performing for the leaders of the Mexican Revolution, another revolution was playing itself out across the Atlantic Ocean. In a rented apartment in a working-class neighborhood in Edinburgh, Scotland, a little remembered embryologist named John Beard (1858–1924) bent over his Zeiss microscope on his dining room table. Lumps of coal in the stove provided the only heat. The walls of the room were stained a dingy brown from the dense yellow fog blanketing the old medieval walled city built on hills whose church steeples rose up into a cloud of smoke. Coal particles spewed from every home, factory and incinerator chimney in the city that was nicknamed Auld Reekie. Heart and lung maladies were constant complaints of Edinburgh dwellers.

A shiver rippled through Beard's torso and he buttoned his suit jacket to hold in some of his own body heat. His muscles tightened in his neck, back and shoulders, but he forced his hands to remain steady. He heated a kettle of water for tea on the stove. He blew into his hands to warm them. In an era before the electron microscope, Beard made meticulous sets of slides of the anatomical development of the embryos of fish and mammals, developing a vast private collection of specimens. He prepared slides of trophoblast cells, cells that form the outer layer of the blastocyst, a structure that possesses an inner cell mass that later forms into an embryo. Trophoblast cells surround and nourish the embryo and develop into a large part of the placenta. These primitive and undifferentiated trophoblast cells, so similar to cancer cells, fascinated Beard.

Even though he knew that his discoveries were not winning him funding at the University of Edinburgh where he held a lectureship, his absorption with the trophoblast and the workings of the pancreas drove him forward to continue his research. Beard made the astute observation that "germ cells" as he called them, or stem cells as we now know them, escaped from the trophoblast surrounding the embryo and scattered themselves throughout the human body. In the right circumstances, these germ cells could become cancerous, and Beard recommended that these could be treated with pancreatic enzymes.

For a brief time during Beard's career, his research did reach beyond the walls of Edinburgh and was embraced by many in the medical world, garnering him a Nobel prize nomination. His trophoblast theory was studied and written about in both the scientific literature and the popular press. It was even debated in the House of Commons. Peer-reviewed articles appeared in publications such as the *Journal of the American Medical Association* supporting his arguments. In a survey of physicians in New York State in 1907, one out of six respondents were already utilizing Beard's research and treating cancer with enzymes. Who was this obscure John Beard? And what happened to pitch his research into the dustbin of medical history?

John Beard was born near Manchester, England, the son of a clerk. Beard lived with his parents in a rented house in a white-collar neighborhood, affluent enough to have a servant. But when Beard was only eight years old, his comfortable life ended. In 1866, his father suddenly died at age 31 and the family had to tighten its belt. Seven years later, Beard's mother remarried. His stepfather financed Beard's way through grammar and secondary school, then to Owens College where he took to the new field of evolutionary biology, and finally on to the University of London.

In 1878, Beard suffered more blows. Beard's mother died at the age of 40, and a couple of years later his stepfather also died. Beard's nuclear family dispersed, and Beard was left to make his way in the world. He appears to have enrolled in medical school, witnessing many surgeries, but finally decided upon a life of research rather than practice. In 1880 he attended the Royal School of Mines to apprentice himself to Thomas Henry Huxley, the famous biologist, who taught Natural History at the university.

A few years later, Beard found another mentor in August Weismann, the evolutionary biologist, at Albert Ludwig University in Freiburg, Germany. In 1884, Beard completed his doctorate there with a dissertation on the small parasites of echinoderms, organisms that remove food from grooves in the skin of their hosts. While in Germany, Beard married a German woman and the young couple returned to England. Beard's career was then on a linear trajectory to study the evolutionary development of sensory organs in fish.

On a research expedition, Beard travelled to the remote Black Lake near the St. Lawrence River in upstate New York seeking samples of *Lepisosteus osseus*, the American bill fish, or the long-nose garpike. There, Beard found abundant garpike in this fisherman's paradise and, his eye bent to the lens of his microscope, he made a discovery that changed his career and ultimately led to his theory of cancer.

Beard discovered that the garpike had sensory neurons located within the dorsal zone of the spinal cord. This early nervous system was later replaced by the dorsal root ganglia. Beard observed that the garpike essentially had two nervous systems—one that grouped outside the normal embryo, and one that developed inside within the embryo itself. The discovery of two fish nervous systems ran counter to all the evolutionary biology of the day. Beard was curious and flexible enough to explore his out-of-the-box finding, and not dismiss and discount his own discovery off-hand.

Instead, Beard theorized that what he was observing was metagenesis, or the "alteration of generations" in vertebrates. The concept is common place in the life cycle of plants. A sexual generation alternates with an asexual generation. For example, a pine tree is basically an asexual organism. It doesn't produce gametes, or sex cells. It produces female cones on its upper branches and male cones on the lower branches. The female cones may be fertilized by pollen blown on the wind from the male cones. Upon sexual fertilization, a zygote forms. These spores become seeds that eventually become the asexual generation, the pine tree.

In animals the sexual generation predominates, but in certain invertebrates the generations alternate. The jellyfish, an invertebrate, displays an alternation of generations. The jellyfish on the beach is the sexual generation. The males and female jellyfish produce gametes, sperm and ova, that combine to produce a small embryo that actually becomes the asexual organism, a polyp that embeds itself in the ocean floor. The polyp grows for a time and produces spores that become the sexual generation that grows up into the big jelly fish.

Beard was convinced that metagenesis took place in all animals, not just the lower invertebrates. This idea was not popular at the University of Edinburgh where in 1894 he had taken a teaching and research position in embryology.

He received a low salary with few grants and had to self-fund most of his own research. His office was cramped and noisy. He carried out his research in cold, bare-bones rented apartments and houses in the smoggy city where his wife died of pneumonia at age 34.

Despite his personal set-back Beard put his head down again as he had done after the deaths of his parents, and focused on his research, the only thing that seemed to matter. With his slides, he studied the trophoblast, intently, almost obsessively. He believed that the trophoblast was the larval or asexual stage of human development. He also noticed that the trophoblastic cells not only invaded the uterus, but also the embryo. As the embryo grew, the cells spread around and became part of every organ. Beard theorized that these cells were there for regeneration in case of damage, loss or injury to the organ.

Then Beard made another leap. He noticed that the "germ" cells nested in crevices and corners of the organ tissues just as cancer cells did. He saw a similarity between trophoblast and the way that cancer grew. Both the cells of the trophoblast and of cancer were primitive and undifferentiated. He knew that the placenta grew out of the trophoblast, and if the placenta kept growing unchecked, as it occasionally did, it turned into an aggressive cancer called choriocarcinoma with the potential to kill both mother and child. So, Beard asked the question: What causes the placenta to stop growing and remain an organ that nurtures the developing fetus?

Beard went to work again, looking for the turning point in the growth of mammalian placentae. Beard determined human placentae shifted from an aggressive to a noninvasive form on day 56 of fetal existence. What happened on day 56 to cause this phenomenon? Beard knew that there had to be a physiological process involved. Such a dramatic change didn't occur without chemical intervention. Beard spent years of his life unraveling this mystery. He knew that the answer might lie in either the mother or the fetus. He investigated the endocrine system of both the mother and the embryo. He examined the development of the fetal nervous system. He looked into blood supply and immune function.

Finally, in the late afternoon of December 8, 1904, Beard crossed the courtyard of Edinburgh University, the green dome high above him, the stone walls and arched windows of the ancient buildings surrounding him. He had a flash of insight familiar to creative thinkers. His feet tapping out their own steady rhythm on the cobblestones, Beard strode along, lost in thoughts of the trophoblast, when suddenly it struck him. On day 56 the pancreas becomes active in the fetus. Pancreatic enzymes must be responsible for halting the growth of the cancer-like placenta. Then why shouldn't cancer be treated with pancreatic enzymes?

Beard believed that cancer developed from those germ cells scattered throughout the fetus in its early development. He thought that any cancer, whether in the brain or the big toe, was a product of these germ cells. The undifferentiated germ cells received the stimulation to turn on and transform into cancer. Pancreatic enzymes—especially trypsin—kept this activity in check. If the pancreas or these enzymes failed to function for any reason, the germ/cancer cells could proliferate.

Beard presented his ideas in lectures and papers from 1902–1915. His theories flew in the face of the traditional idea that cancer was the result of fully formed cells regressing into undifferentiated, aggressive cells with the potential to kill their host. At this time, the only basic European treatment for cancer was surgery. If you couldn't cut out the cancer, the patient died. Surgeons developed more and more complicated and convoluted cancer surgeries. Internists tended to be more open to using less invasive treatments like enzymes, but surgeons more often believed that surgery was the only viable treatment.

Enzymes began to be endorsed and successfully used throughout Europe and North America, from Switzerland, Germany and Italy to the United States. But a flurry of push-back also hit Beard. Colleagues often responded to Beard's lectures and publications with scorn and hostility. Doctors argued that if the pancreas is filled with cancer arresting enzymes, how could the organ itself develop cancer? Others argued that enzyme treatments on their terminal patients had been a complete failure.

Beard stood up to the criticism and to another tragic loss—the death of his second wife who passed away at the age of 43. Once again, Beard attempted to push beyond his personal tragedies and remain focused on his research. Beard countered his critics with the fact that the pancreas does not produce trypsin, but only its inactive form trypsinogen that is channeled into the small intestine where it is converted into its active form. And he insisted that enzyme therapy should not be a last-ditch effort when a patient was in the final days of life.

Ultimately, Beard's critics and the discovery of radium by Marie Curie pushed Beard aside. Curie, a brilliant scientist, was the first woman to win not one but two Nobel prizes, in both physics and chemistry. Marie and her husband Pierre

Curie were responsible for launching the use of radiation in the treatment of cancer. Ironically, they both died of long-term radiation exposure. Marie Curie was exposed to unshielded x-rays machines during the war and carried vials of radioactive isotopes in her pocket, storing them in her desk drawer.

By 1920 Beard had married for a third time, but his scientific voice fell silent. His health began to go downhill from likely heart disease. He retired from the university and didn't have the energy to continue to counter his critics. Beard finally passed away in 1924, but not before he published *The Enzyme Treatment of Cancer and Its Scientific Basis*. He had only one known descendant, a son named Edgar. It would be decades later before his theory was taken up again with any seriousness.

4

In the United States, Guillermo González immediately took up his cello again in all seriousness. He stepped into New York City, leaving Ellis Island and the dangers of the Mexican Revolution behind. In this large metropolitan area with immigrants from all over the world fleeing everything from war to famine, he and Luz felt overwhelmed but safe, their lives no longer endangered. They were excited be in the United States. But they missed their families and their homes. They missed their food and culture. They missed the very geography of the place that they had known so well, the valley that held Córdoba in its hand, the rivers, mountains, and coffee plantations surrounding the city.

Guillermo carried with him the image of his grand house in Cordoba, where as a child he roamed through the hallways and explored vast open spaces. The tiny apartments and confined spaces of New York stood in contrast to the spacious multiple rooms of the elegant house where his parents raised their seven children. He missed the height and expanse of Pico de Orizaba, the volcanic mountain in Veracruz, its peak rising up into the clouds. In New York, one could climb to the peak of the Statue of Liberty and look out upon the bustling city. One view traded for another.

Guillermo missed his parents and siblings, the constant activity and closeness of his family. He missed the way that they understood each other and bonded together through classical music. In Mexico, Guillermo's father José had been a minor composer. He played an array of instruments including classical guitar, then thought to be more of a folk instrument.

"Segovia would, in the 20ᵗʰ century, of course change all that, elevating the instrument to the level of the violin or cello." Nick Gonzalez once reflected. *"But I am proud to say that my great*

21

*grandfather José had seen the beauty in the guitar, even composing
some lovely pieces specifically for the instrument."*

José González had raised all his children to be master musicians, driving
them toward perfection. Gustavo González, who performed with Guillermo in
the Madero's quartet, was Mexico's premier violinist at that time. Their brother
Pepe was a gifted flutist, their sister Eva, a superb classical pianist. Guillermo
brought the drive and ambition to the United States that had been instilled in
him by his father in Mexico.

Guillermo and Luz settled in New York City, then Hauppauge, Long Island.
Guillermo is known for having brought the Spanish folk song, *La Cucaracha* (The
Cockroach) to the United States. The marching song, adapted by the Pancho
Villa army, was originally sung in Mexico to poke fun at the governor of Sonora
who was addicted to drugs. The tune became very popular during the Mexican
Revolution, with political factions from all sides inventing political lyrics:

Ya se van los carrancistas,
Ya se van haciendo bola,
Ya los chacales huertistas
Se los trayen de la cola.

And the Carrancistas,
Are on full retreat,
And the Huertistan jackals
Have caught them by the tail.

In the United States, the tune took on a life of its own, with hundreds of verses
and variations, performed by such diverse musicians as Louis Armstrong to
Riders in the Sky.

Of course, classical music was Guillermo's true love and talent. He became
solo cellist of the former Russian Symphony in New York and San Carlo Opera
Company. He played under Arturo Toscanini in the NBC Symphony, and for a
time was the musical director of RCA Victor. He toured Spain, and North and
South America as part of the Spanish Classical Trio. He played with the National
Symphony of Washington, and for many years Guillermo was a member of the

Metropolitan Opera Orchestra. In his later years he turned toward conducting and composing. He organized the North Shore Symphony and served as its conductor for a time.

On May 5, 1918, Guillermo and Luz had one child named William. Born into two generations of famous musicians with tight family bonds, William was oddly isolated, and lived the life of a first-generation immigrant. He had no siblings and all of his grandparents, aunts, uncles and cousins were thousands of miles away in Mexico, in a different land and culture. Guillermo, his father, traveled constantly for work, performing with orchestras.

"My grandparents would often travel together," Nick Gonzalez had once told me. "My father would be left with nannies. Sometimes finding himself alone with one of them on Christmas Eve. And when my grandparents were home, they loved nothing more than to play music all night long with friends."

William was born into a world of rhapsodic, heavenly melodies, surrounded by extraordinary beauty. Yet he seemed more like a single quarter note on a staff, his life always a bit off rhythmically, without ties or slurs to the surrounding notes in the phrase. Following family tradition, William became a skilled musician, taking up the difficult challenge of the French horn, and studying under a well-known colleague of Guillermo's.

William's life seemed pre-ordained, the third generation of a famous family of musicians. He was studying for a musical career, when the United States began building up their armed forces for what seemed inevitable—its entry into World War II. Soon his studies were interrupted when he was drafted into the Army in early 1941, before the Japanese even bombed Pearl Harbor on December 7.

Testing showed my dad to be uncommonly intelligent, so he was hand-selected to go to a special training program at Cornell University, to study languages—he already spoke fluent Spanish—and intelligence gathering. At Cornell, he specialized in Italian, with the Army's intent to put him into Italy. He was for a time made head of an Italian prisoner of war camp on Long Island.

But the Army being the Army and war being war, my dad was then shipped not to Italy for intelligence work but to India, to help with the effort against the Japanese in Indo China—and to help ultimately with the planned invasion of Japan (that the atom

*bomb would render unnecessary). He was married in 1943, just
before he shipped out to Asia. My dad, by all accounts—was a very
good soldier, quickly promoted, and a good leader of men—though
the tropical Southern Asia climate was a long, long distance from
his dreams of a classical musical career.*

When the war ended in 1945, William Gonzalez returned home. Already married, he was anxious to begin a family. During the war, he had wed Marie Concetta Franzese, daughter of Italian immigrants, Nicole and Graziela, "Grace" (née Giacopelli) Franzese. Nicole had been born in Bari, in the Apulia region of Italy on the Adriatic coast. Grace was born in a small town near Palermo, Sicily, and she was fondly remembered by the whole family for her Italian cooking. She made little meat ball soup, fettuccini, and cucidati cookies, cookies stuffed with ground figs and dates, with pine nuts and "sprinkles."

William had been away from his music for four years and with children on the way, he decided not to return to the French horn. Instead, he continued his studies part-time at Columbia in business.

*In retrospect, the business world was about as far from his previous
interests and genetics as one could imagine, but he never complained, grateful for his family.*

*My father's generation, as has been often said, was a most
extraordinary generation, so many of them plucked out of college,
and careers, and marriages to fight a brutal war on two fronts.
My father, like most of his contemporaries, never once complained
about his bad luck, or the vicissitudes of fate, or the unhappiness of
his musical dreams lost to the insanity of the War. He was extremely
patriotic, knew the Japanese and Germans needed to be stopped
for the sake of the world and for the sake of civilization, and was
proud to have played a role, however small, in ultimate victory. He
was a true patriot, from a patriotic generation, who appreciated
everything about America, the liberty it provided, the freedom to
choose and form one's destiny, even in the face of obstacles, like a
World War. I never heard one word of regret from him, ever, instead
I was told as I grew up, how lucky I was to be born in America. He*

*had seen the world at its worst, and came home only more grateful
for the opportunity that is our country.*

Ultimately, at the age of forty, William left the business world for a life-long career as a language teacher. Marie taught language classes in high school, too. William was fluent in English, Spanish and Italian, Marie in English, Italian, Spanish, French, and Sicilian. Both William and Marie valued education and their children were surrounded with music, poetry, and books. They encouraged their offspring to know their own minds and follow their own pursuits, always there to support them in their passions. William, still haunted by the isolation of his own youth, did all he could to build a more connected life for his children. Teaching offered three months outside of the classroom in the summer, time to nurture and spend time with family.

A daughter, the oldest and only girl, came along first, and Nicholas, the oldest boy just 15 months later in 1947, born in Queens, New York. The two youngsters looked alike, resembling the Franzese side of the family, and people often mistook them for twins. A second son was born a few years later. The parents were going to name their oldest son "William," after his father and grandfather, but Marie's father Nicole had just died.

"Let's name him Nicholas," Marie had urged, in honor of her father.

The household of Nicholas James Gonzalez was bathed in classical music. Before he was five years old, he was familiar with the strains of the major composers: Beethoven, Bach, Brahms, Handel and Vivaldi. The family was Catholic, and Nick went through the usual progression of sacraments, from baptism, to First Communion, to Confirmation. But the war may have been one of the most influential aspects of young Nick's life. In the late forties and early fifties, a Baby Boomer boy inevitably rode the wake of his father's passage through the waters of World War II.

In 1952–53, Nick sat with his father on the couch every Sunday afternoon at 3:00 P.M. in their living room in Flushing, Queens, New York City. Father and son had developed a ritual of watching "Victory at Sea" documentaries on their small black-and-white console television set. The half hour series broadcast by NBC drew from World War II film footage of warring navies around the world.

Famed Broadway composer Richard Rogers and Robert Russell Bennett created the soundtrack with the NBC Symphony Orchestra performing the score.

During the segments, William Gonzalez told Nick about his own war stories on his tour of Asia, interjecting comments throughout the T.V. drama.

The music imitated a distress signal and a large white "V" rushed across the waves of an ocean, growing bigger and bigger until the words "Victory at Sea" appeared super-imposed upon the screen. A periscope poked up out of the waves, then the film cut to a torpedo shooting through the water and exploding a battleship. The vessel listed toward the left of the screen, rapidly sinking into the water.

"War has begun," the voice-over stated. "Ships are sinking. Men are dying. It is September, 1939."

5

1939. A scratchy, blurry black-and white video of Dr. Weston A. Price and his wife rolls across the screen. They are doing anthropological field work with indigenous people in a remote village. Price beckons to a boy, opening his mouth, revealing a full set of teeth without cavities.

The film cuts to a shot of a shirtless man.

"How old are you?" Price asks.

"Twenty."

Price pats the man on his well-developed, muscular torso. "You look like you're a giant. My, my…"

The film cuts to Price against a backdrop of trees. "The most universal disease in the world is the decay of the teeth. And unfortunately, we have not known the cause until we've gone to the primitive people to find out how they prevent tooth decay."

And so, Weston Arthur Price, a Canadian scientific researcher and dentist, urges his film audience to learn how to have a strong healthy body. He holds up and points to his seminal book *Nutrition and Physical Degeneration.*

Price had graduated with a dental degree from the University of Michigan in 1893, and by 1915, he had published 150 scientific papers. He was the first director of the American Dental Association's Research Institute with a team of 60 scientists working under him, and an advisory board of world-famous physicians including Charles Mayo, one of the founders of the Mayo Clinic.

During the first two decades of practice in Cleveland, Ohio, Price became more and more alarmed at the patients who climbed into his wooden dental chair, spittoon attached to the side, with crooked, decayed teeth. Children often presented with thin narrow faces and even deformed dental arches. The narrowness of their faces was pushing their teeth inward. These same patients often had accompanying serious medical problems.

Dental theory has always held to the belief that decay is caused by the residues of high-sugary, starchy and sticky foods that cling to the teeth—candies, sweets and fruits. In his animal studies, Price found that these residues do have a detrimental effect on oral heath, but at the same time, he found it was very difficult to induce tooth decay by introducing such bacterium.

"If not bacterium, then what?" Price asked.

Price hypothesized that there was something missing in the bodies of people who had tooth decay. He found evidence that there was a disturbance in those people in the way that they handled calcium and phosphorus.

"In order to figure out tooth decay," Price said. "I need to find people who don't have tooth decay." He wanted to discover what people without tooth decay were doing differently, to study them and determine why their bodies processed minerals correctly. He wanted to show that is was possible to have good health, health that was better than that enjoyed by the average American.

Price looked around Cleveland and couldn't find a single person without tooth decay. He wondered if he could find insular populations in the world who weren't plagued by the problem. In the 1930s Price and his wife set out on an anthropological world tour, visiting isolated, indigenous, or what he called "primitive" cultures throughout the world. Price hoped to compare and contrast the dental health of these indigenous cultures to American populations. He crisscrossed the globe, visiting all the continents except Asia where wars prevented access. He examined diverse cultures from Native Americans, to the Lötschental in Switzerland in the Swiss Alps, over to the Scottish in the Outer Hebrides, down to Africa to the Pygmies, and out to Polynesian South Sea Islanders in the Pacific, and down to the Aborigines in Australia and the Maori in New Zealand.

Price took extensive photos, slides and film strips documenting indigenous peoples, focusing on their teeth, dental arches, and the shape of their faces. He found that despite poor dental hygiene like brushing and flossing, most of these people had excellent teeth, free of serious dental decay. Their cheek bones were high, their dental arches round, their teeth straight, free from crowding. Perhaps even more importantly, they did not seem susceptible to tuberculosis that was ravaging Western cultures at the time.

Price discovered that these isolated populations were eating their native diets of whole, unprocessed foods. The diets varied from continent to continent, people to people, but they excluded the denatured stables of civilization: white flour, refined sugar, skim or low-fat milk, refined or hydrogenated vegetable oil, and of course, they excluded the more recent high fructose corn syrup, GMOs, or additives and preservatives. Price saw a link between the diet of these isolated people and their health, a connection that wasn't a particularly popular concept then or now.

Price concluded that populations who ate their native diets isolated from the influences of Western denatured foods, were largely in good health. Once they began eating like Westerners, their health declined, and tooth decay set in. Tooth decay, then, is primarily a nutritional disease. The underlying disturbance in the human body that causes tooth decay is caused by missing nutrients from a depleted diet of refined foods. Price thought that he could reverse tooth decay through a nutrient-rich diet.

At its publication, *Nutrition and Physical Degeneration* was hailed by some as a brilliant study. The Canadian Medical Association Journal called it a "masterpiece of research." As the years progressed, other supporters called Price the "Charles Darwin of Nutrition." Critics disagreed, claiming the dietary evidence of his findings insignificant. The *Journal of the American Medical Association* thought Price's study biased and more "evangelistic rather than scientific." Others accused Price of embracing the myth of "The Noble Savage."

Price realized that there were a lot of variables, or "confounders," to his theory of tooth decay, such as genetics, heredity, altitude, climate, rainfall, and soil. He needed to control for these variables, so first he looked for populations that had preserved their genetic heritage in pure form. Then he looked for populations at the point of contact with Western civilization. A point of contact might be a town that opened up a port, soon becoming a conduit for modern foods. The people in the port town began to deteriorate while the people in the next town, still in isolation, were thriving. The people in the first town had the same climate, racial stock and genetics, and soil as the second town. The only variable was the food.

White men from Western civilizations came to these port towns bringing pasteurized milk, jams and jellies, white flour, sugar, milk chocolate, and industrial seed oils, particularly cottonseed oil that didn't exist before 1900. With the foods

came the ability to build roads into these remote areas and the roads eventually
carried the foods to more villages with "pure" eating habits. The villagers who
adapted the Western diet had children with narrower faces and crooked teeth.
Tuberculosis was the next invader with villagers on Western diets becoming more
susceptible to the disease.

In these point of contact areas, Price found some astonishing results. The
Gaelics in the Outer Hebrides, for example, had a 1.2% rate of tooth decay.
The Inuits in the Arctic Circle had 0.09% rate of tooth decay. When the Gaelics
were modernized, they had 30% of their teeth attacked, and the Inuits had
13% of their teeth attacked. Price found that he couldn't easily compare one
group to another, however. He discovered that the Inuit had a genetic adapta-
tion that increased active Vitamin D production, putting more calcium into
their teeth. Other variables, of course, existed, like cultural norms and lifestyle
differences. It was impossible to sift out all the variables, so Price's study did
not prove cause and effect, but he could say that some native diets produced
consistent good health.

Price discovered that different tribes had different native foods, although
most contained fermented milk products, eggs, and some meat. Meat-eating
tribes ate the whole animal including the organs. They boiled the bones for broth.
Price also found that each one of these indigenous populations have "sacred"
foods. These were foods that were revered and eaten before conception of a child
to assure its fetal health, then eaten throughout childhood to promote strong
bodies free of disease.

In the remote Lötschental region of Switzerland, for example, the sacred
food was butter. The sacred butter was spring butter, high in vitamin content.
The tribe had a butter ritual in their church, inserting a wick in the butter
placed in a bowl. They lit the wick as a spiritual invocation. In the Outer Hebrides, a barren, wind-swept island that didn't support the raising of livestock or
vegetables, the people ate a diet of fish and seaweed, and some oats they were
able to grow for porridge. The sacred food was fermented cod head and cod's
liver. The Intuits, who lived on a high fat diet without grains, or vegetables,
chose fish eggs as their sacred food, stating that, "We need these eggs to have
healthy babies."

For the most part, the babies of peoples on native diets were born with
rounded faces and good dental structures. Their births were easy. Their mothers,

with equally wide dental arches also had wide pelvises, and childbirth tended to be non-traumatic. Mothers rarely died in childbirth and there was little infant mortality. The babies seldom cried and were alert, active, and even-tempered, a joyful addition to their families. Intuit women often gave birth in the middle of the night with their sleeping husbands beside them. In the morning, they woke their mates to present them with their new off spring.

6

Nick Gonzalez was born with a rounded face, high cheek bones, and a high forehead. His twinkling blue eyes showed his spirited and mischievous nature, but by the time he was a pre-teen, he had a mouthful of cavities. His mother had learned the art of traditional Italian cooking from her mother who had kept a large extensive garden in Italy, but the American post-war industrial food age had begun in full force in the 1950s. Nick, as most of the Baby Boom generation, grew up on a mixture of traditional foods and on canned, frozen and processed foods that were considered more "modern."

Most typically, Nick was sipping a Coke, sitting on the bleachers in the Yankees stadium with his father, the two of them sharing a box of Cracker-Jacks, dubbed the "original junk food," a mixture of molasses-coated popcorn and peanuts. The motto "The More You Eat, the More You Want" was stamped on the box of this snack, with a picture of a saluting Sailor Jack and his dog Bingo. Father and son squeezed together, surrounded by 58,000 other baseball fans caught up in the roar of the exhilaration with the ball sailing out deep into the right field, going, going, gone into the stands for a homerun.

Nick loved attending these games in the grand stadium, "The Cathedral of Baseball," its hard concrete designed by Thomas Edison, its sports history tied to Babe Ruth. He loved the rhythm of the vendors, moving up and down the aisles yelling out their wares, "Peanuts, popcorn…" He loved the whole ritual of the game, all the players finding their positions, taking their parts, from the batters warming up in the box, to the umpires making their calls at the bases. He loved the pitcher's wind up, the release of the ball from his fingertips, the sound of the crack of the bat, the ball skidding across the field, scooped up by the short stop. He especially loved the position of the short stop.

By age four, baseball had become Nick's passion. One of his earliest memories was in 1951, his father bent over their brand new T.V. console, watching a Yankee's game, fixated on the center fielder.

"That's the famous Joe DiMaggio," William told Nick. "One of the greatest ball players of all time."

William told Nick about the Yankees and why they needed to support them, their home team, located right there not far from where they lived in New York City. William enjoyed bonding with his son over baseball, yet never encouraged his son to take it too seriously. But Nick had already begun a life-long habit of taking all his interests very seriously. The attention he gave baseball in his youth was indicative of the focus he gave his passions in the years to come.

> *By age six, I could quote the batting averages of the current Yan-*
> *kee team, their opponents, and by eight years old, I could recite*
> *the batting averages and slugging percentages of the extraordinary*
> *1927 Yankees, with Babe Ruth in right field, Bob Meusel and*
> *Earl Combs, all great hitters though overshadowed by the Babe,*
> *completing the outfield. Of course, Lou Gehrig was at first, in 1927*
> *in his extraordinary prime. There were Frank Crosetti at shortstop,*
> *an extraordinary fielder, who was in many respects a hero to me,*
> *since shortstop was my goal even then, Tony Lazzeri steady at third.*
> *Lazzeri, had he played for any other team of the time, would have*
> *been a triumphant hero, but on those Yankees, he was just another*
> *superb player among a team of the best of superb players, who did*
> *his job well. Bill Dickey behind the plate was probably the finest*
> *fielding catcher of all time, and could hit with power.*

Nick began playing short stop, considered to be the game's most demanding defensive position, when he was finally big enough to hold the bat. He recognized the position's importance as the lever that could make or break the game. At his son's request, William took Nick to the park on hot summer afternoons and hit fungoes to him, the ball arching up into the air, then smacking into his son's mitt. William hit drives to Nick who scooped them up with ease. Nick knew that as a short stop, moving fluidly between second and third base, he would have to constantly field the ball. More balls are hit to short stops than other positions. Most batters are right-handed and pull the ball toward left field. Short stops need to be agile, pivoting quickly between the bases, with a strong arm to throw the ball to first base.

William also taught his son to bat. Nick became an excellent hitter, very hard to strike out, able to make good contact with the ball. He had always been small and slight, but he had always had good vision and could smack the ball with great strength and control. Although he was never able to hit the ball "out of the park," he was very good at line drives.

> My heroes were many, but particularly for hitting, Roger Hornsby of the Cardinals, and Ted Williams of the Red Sox, each of whom had perfect vision, and could see the ball hitting the bat. Hornsby was so protective of his sight that while he played, he never went to the movies, or read newspapers.

Eventually, Nick played Little League. In uniform, he stood at the plate, his short fingers wrapped around the wooden bat cocked over his right shoulder. A traditional baseball cap held his hair out of his face, the bill shading his forehead. His lips parted in intense concentration, he glanced to his left to track the ball moving toward him, his eyes squinting, focused, biceps flexed, ready for the swing. Through William's coaching, Nick also became a talented bunter. More than once he confounded the other team. Anticipating another line drive, they were caught off guard with Nick's drag bunt for a hit, and sometimes even a run scored from his teammate on third base.

One day on the Little League field, when Nick was eleven years old, his love for his father merged with his love of baseball.

On a Saturday, the parents of the opposing teams had gathered in the stands. William Gonzalez, a man still very fit from his military training but standing barely 5'6" tall, was there on the sidelines, as usual to root for his son. He cheered for Nick at the bat, and applauded when he fielded the ball as shortstop. The mother of one of Nick's playmates sat in the bleachers. She and her husband were going through a brutal divorce, their son caught in the middle between the warring parents. The boy lived with his mother who encouraged his baseball. Simply feeling out of control, the father was enraged by his son's playing and told the coach to kick him off the team. The coach sided with the mother and continued to allow the son to play.

Then suddenly the father raced his car at high speed right through the outfield toward second base, barely missing Nick. The team's pitcher dodged out of the way, the car charging toward the mound. Finally, the car came to a screeching halt at home plate. The father, over six feet tall, jumped out of the car and picked up a bat, heading toward the coach. The other parents sat in the stands, too scared and stunned to move. William Gonzalez didn't hesitate. He ran onto the field, threw the man on the ground and held him in a headlock until the police arrived.

This was the first time Nick had experienced his father's physical fearlessness. Nick stood in the ball field, watching the police handcuff the father and drive him away in the patrol car. Baseball glove still on his hand, Nick recognized his father as the "good soldier," both in and out of the military.

From that day forward, baseball created an even tighter bond between Nick and William, the World War II veteran who had come home to the United States with gratitude that he lived in a country with freedoms not evidenced in other parts of the world. William had fought the oppressive and invasive Nazi and Japanese regimes and instilled in his son a deep patriotic fervor for the United States.

And in the end, Nick's fascination with baseball became an intellectual as well as a physical exercise. He memorized everything he could about the sport, developing a photographic memory. He enhanced his reading and math skills by keeping track of scores and batting averages.

> *I used to study old newspaper clippings, read every book I could about baseball, memorized statistic after statistic, for teams I didn't even care much for, I was obsessed with baseball. My father, in his own subtle way, fed my interests, bringing me home books about baseball, factual, even fictional—there was an extraordinary series of books published in the late 1950s, about a fictional team, that I read with zeal and devotion.*
>
> *In retrospect, baseball wasn't just a "sport" in my life, it was an extraordinary opening in my young boy's mind to adult life, to adult pastimes—to America. Baseball really taught me to read, taught me math—I could figure out quickly not only batting averages, but slugging and pitching percentages in my head. I do remember going to school, remember learning math by rote in the usual pedantic*

dull way of all schools, but I really mastered the art and science of reading, and of math, through baseball. Those hours I spent winter weekends and in mid-summer lazy days studying old records, and current newspapers, and current books taught me how to study, how to learn, even how to think—even how to use the newspaper. We used to have the New York Times delivered daily to our house in Queens, and I would devour the Sports Section, which in those days had complete scorecards and articles for every major league baseball game played the previous day. It was like magic to me, to open the Times and see the lists of players, the times at bat, the hits, and as I read I would in my mind calculate the changes in batting averages based on the latest information, the number of season doubles or home runs hit by Mickey Mantle, or Yogi Berra.

Nick played baseball through high school and into college, his high point the year he had a .500 batting average. Baseball, that quintessential American game, taught Nick the benefits of hard work and good sportsmanship. It taught him the value of competition, how to lose gracefully and more importantly, how to win without gloating. He learned that there were rewards for achievement. He learned to see defeat as only a chance to improve. Baseball became a focal point for his fierce drive, an energy that would carry him through all the steps of his career.

Through baseball, Nick learned how to drag bunt his way through the streets of Queens to graduate with honors from the top Ivy League institutions of the United States. To win with grace, but continue to stay in the game. To slug it out with former mentors and colleagues in academe and with former patients in court. Later in his life, he would approach the study of cancer and other degenerative diseases with the same determination he brought to the batter's box, hoping in his research, to find that treatment or cure, send that homerun, that hit that had always alluded him, sailing into the stands.

Francis Marion Pottenger, Sr. studied medicine with the best researchers in Berlin, Vienna, and Munich, hoping to hit upon treatments for the degenerative diseases of the turn of the early twentieth century. While John Beard was solidifying his research in Edinburgh and Porfirio Díaz had tightened his grip on Mexico, Pottenger, a native of Ohio, returned to the United States to set up practice in a suburb of Cincinnati. He married in 1894, and just six months later, his wife had developed a telltale cough. On the advice of other physicians, the young couple headed to California where the air was dry and the temperature warm, both commonly suggested remedies for recovery from tuberculosis at the turn of the twentieth century.

The Pottengers settled in Monrovia where Francis began another practice, but in 1898, he found himself standing at his young wife's deathbed. There, he vowed that he would dedicate his life to finding a cure for tuberculosis. At the time, physicians knew that tuberculosis was a contagious disease, but little more. They had isolated and identified the bacillus causing tuberculosis in 1882, but the preventative vaccine wasn't developed until 1906. In these pre-antibiotic days, a tuberculosis patient was isolated from the rest of the population in a sanatorium, given bed rest, and lots of exposure to the open air. The physician could do nothing more than cross his fingers that things would turn out for the best.

Pottenger threw himself into long hours of research and became one of the top pulmonary specialists in the country. In 1903, he opened the Pottenger Sanatorium for Diseases of the Lung and Throat in Monrovia. Tucked into the St. Gabriel Valley, the sanatorium stood on the southern slope of the Sierra Madre Mountains on 40 acres of land. The complex was 30 miles from the Pacific Ocean, close enough to have a moderate climate, but far enough away to escape the dampness of the ocean fog. By 1911 the sanatorium, a solid white stucco building with a green roof on beautifully landscaped grounds, accommodated 100 patients, with some living in the administration building and others in outlying bungalows.

Pottenger lived on the premises, believing that patients should have easy access to their doctor. He attended to his patients with care and the sanatorium became one of the most famous in the world, still open for business until 1955 when Pottenger retired at the age of 88. Pottenger maintained a busy practice, but he also conducted research, attempting to figure out why one disease, like TB, caused different symptoms in different patients. His book on neurophysiology—*Symptoms of Visceral Disease: A Study of the Vegetative Nervous System and its Relationship to Clinical Medicine* (1919)—documented his insights into the autonomic nervous system.

With intricate line drawings, the book mapped out the relationships of the body's organs to the visceral nerves and central nervous system. The illustrations showed the autonomic nervous system, a web of nerves that reach into all parts of the body to control the metabolism including the secretion of hormones and enzymes, the secretion of enzymes in the intestinal tract, the function of the liver and kidney, the function of the thyroid and adrenal glands, the digestion of food, the absorption of food, and the circulation of the blood supply.

The autonomic nervous system is divided into two branches: the sympathetic and the parasympathetic systems. The branches both reach into all the tissues, organs, and glands of the body, but work in opposition to each other. For example, when active, the sympathetic nervous system increases the heart rate, raises the blood pressure, and stimulates the secretion of the endocrine glands. Thyroid and adrenal gland production go up. The sympathetic branch is the system that turns on during physical and emotional stress.

In reaction to this "fight or flight" response, the entire digestive system shuts down, the pancreas stops secreting enzymes, the liver function decreases and the digestion of food in the intestines slows. When you're about to be eaten by a tiger, you want your system on alert, your nerves and muscles ready to react with strength and carry you away from danger. You want your left side of your brain activated so that you can think very quickly and make good decisions. You don't want your right brain activated. You don't want to sit in a creative daydream, blissfully digesting your food while you yourself are eaten.

In contrast, the parasympathetic branch is the system of repair and rebuilding. It is especially active at night when the body needs to absorb food, utilize nutrients and regenerate the tissues of the glands and organs. When the parasympathetic system fires, the heart rate decreases, the blood pressure drops, the secretion of hormones and enzymes decreases. The metabolism slows and the right side of the brain, the creative, visionary part, is activated. The two branches of the nervous system work together to keep us balanced in our reactions and responses, depending upon the situations that we encounter.

Pottenger observed that some of his patients came to him with an inherently over-active sympathetic nervous system. These patients had very developed, perhaps too highly active, organs and glands. The heart, thyroid and adrenals, the left brain, and muscles were very efficient. Pottenger noticed that these patients were susceptible to certain diseases and ailments related to their autonomic nervous systems.

Emotionally, these people could be hard-driving and aggressive, anxious and irritable, often angry. But they were also very disciplined and good at routines. They tended to be thin due to their high thyroid and adrenal output. They needed little rest and sleep and were regularly on the go. These patients were usually athletic, had very strong, developed muscles but poor digestion. They often had irritable bowel syndrome, colitis, food intolerances, and chronic indigestion.

Other patients came to Pottenger with over-developed parasympathetic nervous systems, and a correspondingly weak sympathetic system. The glands and tissues of the parasympathetic system were often over-reactive. The muscles, heart, thyroid, and adrenals were more often inefficient and sluggish.

Emotionally, these patients were calm, stable, even-keeled, even happy-go-lucky and slow to anger. They found it difficult to handle stress, and consequently, tended to gain weight easily. They also found it hard to lose weight and tended to drift toward depression. These patients were often the creative types who had disorganized studios but lost track of time while working in them, producing beautiful works of art.

A third group of patients came to the sanatorium with balanced metabolisms. Both branches of their autonomic nervous systems were equally strong, active, and efficient. Their personalities usually fell between the two extremes. They could be organized and focused when needed, but also very creative at the appropriate times. They dealt with stress well, were resilient to what was thrown at them, and were proactive. They were generally the healthiest and happiest of the three groups.

By 1930, Pottenger figured out that the three groups of patients not only had different personalities and reacted to life differently, but that they also had different ways of processing nutrients. In his laboratory at the sanatorium, he spent many hours at his work table, making detailed analysis of his data, trying to determine how these three different types of patients processed fats, proteins, vitamins and minerals. He made the interesting discovery that magnesium tended to block sympathetic activity while calcium stimulated it. In 1936, he found that potassium activated parasympathetic nerves.

After years of seeing patients at the sanatorium, Pottenger learned that he could treat patients with these three nutrients to bring their autonomic systems back into balance. As the patients became more balanced, they began to feel better and become healthier—no matter what their symptoms and disease might be. He gave sympathetic dominant people high doses of magnesium and potassium to return them to health, and he gave the parasympathetics high doses of calcium to relieve their symptoms. Pottenger, then, saw every patient as an individual with unique bio-chemical needs. He did not treat them symptomatically, but systemically.

*   *   *   *   *

Pottenger's son, Francis Marion Pottenger Jr., took up his father's interest in nutrition and his theory that tuberculosis was linked to adrenal deficiency. After receiving his medical license in 1930, Pottenger Jr. joined his father in practice at the sanatorium, but became interested in extending their treatment beyond tuberculosis to other patients with lung and upper respiratory ailments. He bought some of the cottages from the sanatorium and set up his own hospital to treat other lung ailments, especially asthma. Pottenger, Jr. had been impressed with Weston Price's work and he fed his patients a balanced diet of whole foods, including liberal amounts of eggs, cream, butter and liver.

Pottenger Jr. also investigated the nutritional value of raw versus cooked food. He designed a study with cats that has had a wide-spread ripple effect on subsequent generations of nutritional food advocates. Pottenger Jr. used donated cats for his laboratory experiments. On the cats, he tested the potency of adrenal supplements he used for his TB patients and for his allergy sufferers. For his research purposes, he had to remove the adrenal glands of cats. He fed these lab cats a supposedly good diet of raw milk, cod liver oil and cooked meat scraps from the sanatorium.

More donated cats kept coming to his lab door, and these cats bred more cats. Finally, he was running out of food, so he began ordering raw meat scraps from a local meat packing plant, including organs, meat and bone. Then Pottenger Jr. noticed a curious thing. The cats fed the raw meat scraps, survived the adrenal surgeries better than the others. And their kittens grew healthier and more active.

Pottenger, Jr. then designed a controlled experiment involving around 900 cats over a period of ten years. He had anecdotal evidence of the health benefits of a feline raw meat diet, but like any good scientist, he wanted hard data. He wanted answers to the questions that arose from his observations. Why did the raw meat cats survive surgeries better than the cooked meat cats? Why were the raw meat kittens more vigorous? Why did the cooked meat diet fail to nurture the cats nutritionally? Was the cooked food nutritionally deficient? If so, exactly what nutrients wasn't the diet providing?

Pottenger Jr. built large outdoor pens near a stand of eucalyptus trees on a side of a hill near the sanatorium overlooking St. Gabriel Valley. There he isolated two populations of what he called "run-of-the-pen" cats—a normal sampling of animals. One group was fed uncooked, completely raw meat and milk, bones, viscera and a small amount of cod liver oil. The other group was fed the same but with only cooked meat and milk.

The pens were enclosed with hardware cloth and situated to give both adequate sunshine and shade. A trench filled with sand served as a waste depository that was routinely cleaned. Adequate water was provided. Extensive records were kept, with each cat having a clinical chart with daily notes. Charts were created on the kittens with notes on their genetics, diets, state of health and behavior. Pottenger Jr. recorded past medical and dietary histories, and kept daily track of the weight, and general health of the cats.

The study lasted for 10 years. The raw food cats were alert with good coordination and normal sexual interest in the opposite sex. They jumped and climbed in the pen. The cooked food cats were lethargic, displayed a hesitancy in their movements, and some of the cats developed arthritis. They often withdrew or sat quietly in the pen. They also developed tooth decay.

The second and third generations of the cats showed even more significant changes. The second generations of the raw food cats were larger than those of the cooked meat cats. Their fur had a better sheen. Their eyes had a sparkle and their faces were rounded and well-developed, with firmly-developed zygomatic arches, or cheek bones. The calcium content throughout their bodies ranged from 12–17%.

In contrast, the heads of the second-generation cooked meat cats began to flatten, the zygomatic arch incomplete. The calcium content of the bones fell to 10%. The skulls of the third-generation cooked meat cats were considerably smaller, flat with pointed features, a poorly developed zygomatic arch, the bones paper thin, soft and spongey. The calcium content of the bones had fallen to 3%. The third-generation kittens had eye problems, asthma, tooth decay, exhaustion, and impaired coordination. They lacked sexual interests and were not able to reproduce. Those that tried to mate, only produced stillborn litters. On the other hand, the raw food cats produced healthy generation after healthy generation of kittens.

It was difficult to correct the problems that arose from the cooked food cats' diet. It took four generations of raw food before the cats regained their normal facial structure and original good health. But there was one escaped cooked food cat who returned to the wild around the sanatorium, began eating a native diet of mice and small animals—raw food—and slowly began to return to health.

After the experiment was over, came another surprising result. The ground in the raw food cat pen sprung multiple vigorous weeds. In contrast, the cooked food pen contained a few spindly weeds. Later, beans were intentionally planted in the pens, and these vegetables grew in the same pattern as the respective weeds.

The changes in the Pottenger cats were similar to many changes in humans that Weston Price discovered. Cats, like Weston Price's native peoples, developed dental decay and narrowed arches on nutritionally deficient diets. But critics of Pottenger said that a study of cats couldn't be so easily applied to humans.

"I never stated that a one-to-one comparison could be made," Pottenger Jr. said. "But the parallels are so obvious that you can draw your own conclusions."

8

Nick Gonzalez developed a love of cats, dogs, birds, and all of nature as a young boy on family camping trips. Both William and Marie had the summers free from teaching, so they bought a camper, and loaded it up with food, shorts, T-shirts, towels, swimming suits, binoculars, fishing poles and tackle. They hitched the camper to their car with their three children tucked in the back seat and headed out of the city to up-state New York. They camped in various places, but found Lake George their favorite, a vacation spot that was located just about a morning's drive through the Adirondacks from Black Lake, where John Beard had done his research on the long-nosed garpike fish.

Lake George, often called the Queen of American Lakes, is a long, narrow, and deep body of water situated at the southeast base of the Adirondacks Mountains. It drains all the way northward to Lake Champlain and the St. Lawrence River basin. Stretching north to south, the lake is over 32 miles long and one to four miles wide. Originally, Native Americans named the lake *Andia-ta-roc-te* (Lake that shuts itself in.) In his novel *Last of the Mohicans*, James Fenimore Cooper redubbed the lake *Horican,* after a tribe who had lived on its banks.

During the late nineteenth and early twentieth centuries, the rich and famous took up residence on Lake George, building opulent country estates. The Roosevelts, Vanderbilts, Rockefellers, and Whitneys all came to the area for summer vacations and retreats. Their mansions were often built on hundreds of acres of lakeside wilderness. The lake also attracted prominent artists of the day, including Frank Vincent DuMond, Alfred Stieglitz and Georgia O'Keefe.

With the Great Depression and the introduction of income tax, the glitter of the resort began to fade. Many of the mansions were torn down or turned into hotels and restaurants. By the 1950s when the economy boomed back, and the automobile allowed middle-class Americans easier access to travel and vacation spots, Lake George became a popular destination for family camping trips.

By the turn of the twenty-first century, the lake had gotten more polluted and infiltrated by invasive species, but when the Gonzalez family camped there in the 1950s, the lake was still known for its pure water, its abundant trout and pristine habitat. The Gonzalez family's experience of the lake was more spoiled and commercialized than in early settlement times, but it still wasn't too different from Thomas Jefferson's in 1791 when he journeyed there to seek relief from a migraine headache. On May 31 Jefferson wrote in a letter to his daughter, penning what would become a famous quote:

> *Lake George is without comparison, the most beautiful water I ever saw; formed by a contour of mountains into a basin…finely interspersed with islands, its water limpid as crystal, and the mountain sides covered with rich groves of Thuya, silver fir, white pine, Aspen and paper birch down to the water-edge; here and there precipices of rock to checker the scene and save it from monotony.*

In his journal, Jefferson followed up with a description of the lake's fauna:

> *The neighborhood of this lake is healthy but there are few inhabitants on it. It's [sic] waters very clear, except just at the North end, abounding with salmon-trout of 7 lb weight, specked or red trout, Oswego bass of 6 or 7 lb weight, rock bass, yellow perch. There are seagulls in abundance, loons and some wild-ducks. Rattle snakes on it's [sic] borders. Two which we killed were of a sutty dark colour, obscurely checkered. It is infested with swarms of musketoes [sic] and gnats, and 2 kinds of biting fleas.*

The Gonzalez family swatted the mosquitoes and brushed away the gnats. They caught trout, bass and perch, cooking them around a camp fire. They hiked, played games, and slept in the camper. Nick and his siblings enjoyed being away from the city and they liked falling asleep near a lake, breathing deeply into the clean air and darkness. They liked gazing up at the sky, the stars blinking brilliantly without the light pollution of the city.

They listened to the sounds of the frogs and the birds at night and observed their habits and habitats. They listened to the deep resonant call of the bull frog, a species who cannot be raised in captivity as it refuses to eat an artificial diet. And they listened to the *who cooks for you, who cooks for you all* call of the barred owl, a species that lives mainly on the raw carcasses of small mammals. They learned to identify the nocturnal birds' calls at night, and to spot the diurnal activity of the song birds during the sunshine hours.

Nick, with his photographic memory, learned to identify the birds with a quick glance at the guide book. He and his younger brother Bill trekked around the lake bird watching, and they both kept up this hobby well into adulthood. Nick became fascinated with living things, their sizes, shapes and colors, their behaviors, how they developed and grew, how they fit into the larger scope of an ecological system.

Nick and Bill kept birding on a 250-acre property that his parents later bought in northern Vermont on the Canadian border. There, the family engaged in their outdoors activities, spending some of their holidays on the farm, soaking in the natural history of the area. Eventually, Bill did some homesteading there and the usual farm chores of bailing hay, tending bees and raising goats.

Back in the city, Nick breezed through public elementary school, finding it more fun than work. But when he entered junior high school he had to buckle down. He combined the three grades—seventh, eighth and ninth—into two years, essentially skipping a grade. For the first time, he had to begin to really study. He was easily able to access his left-brain analytical capabilities, so he tried to figure out the most efficient way to handle his homework:

> *I was born thinking about solutions to problems. When I arrived in junior high school, I was placed in what was a special track for "smart students," which translated into more work and tougher work. I thought about the situation, and realized unlike elementary school, which seemed like such a breeze and often more fun than drudgery, this was now for real. I thought about the best way to handle the situation efficiently, in a way that would produce maximum results and good grades. I couldn't depend on my teachers—even in this special track, the teachers gave us no advice on studying, how to master what seemed to be an enormous amount of*

material shoveled onto us endlessly with no respite. The classes were big, 37–38 students per class, individualized attention was out of the question and just not going to happen. I and my classmates, I realized in my own analytic way, were on our own.

Even at this young age, Nick had a lot of pride in what he did. He wanted to get good grades to please his teachers and parents, but most of all, he wanted to be proud of himself. He mustered the professional drive of his musical family and the athletic drive of the baseball field to also excel in academics. His teachers and parents outlined no study habits for him. On his own, he decided that there must be a method of studying that would win him high grades and minimize the agony of school, tests, and grades. He was able to make the leap from the observation of the behavior of animals at Lake George and the Vermont farm to human learning:

As I thought about the problem I realized what more sophisticated thinkers and psychologists have long known, that learning, true learning where the information becomes part of the brain, requires one thing—repetition. Repetition is the key to learning in any arena of life, but always for mastering academic subjects. I thought at the time, not knowing any psychology, that I had discovered something so profound, though in respect, the idea is quite obvious. I also began to realize, it didn't matter how smart you were, how high an IQ you might have, what mattered was repetition of the subject matter, whether it might be history, literature, science, or the dreaded math. How simple, I thought, repetition, the key to academic success. Indeed, psychologists will tell you that you really don't learn something, no matter what the subject or the situation, you don't really master it until you have heard or read it at lease 5–6 times. Only at that point of saturation does the information become a part of your brain, as much as your name or your home address. This is true not only for we humans, but for hamsters, cats, dogs, and gorillas—repetition is the key to learning, in life and in school.

At age thirteen, Nick set up strict study habits for himself. He came home from school and dove into his homework, tackling the day's work in English, social studies, math and science. Alone in his room, he piled up his books on his desk, making a checklist of his assignments in a small notebook. When he'd tackled the day's work, he made a small mark beside the entry in the notebook. Check. Done. Resolved. Then with the same focus and knowledge that his ancestors brought to music, he practiced his subjects, knowing how practice makes for perfection. In the same way that his ancestors drew their bows across strings, Nick drew his attention to his homework. After he knocked off the day's assignments, he went back and reviewed all the material:

> *I would really learn the assignment fully. For example, for history reading, I would review it over and over again—usually instinctively 5–6 times—until I could recite it almost by rote. With the math problems, I would redo the math problems repeatedly until I could recite the problems in my mind. I would not only complete the assigned problems, but in addition the other problems relating to the day's subject matter. With the science reading, I would reread and memorize the salient facts, until I could give a lecture on that assignment. While it might seem tedious, I turned it into a game, a game of mastery, to see how well I could learn the material that day.*

The next day, he would begin again, going back and reviewing all the previous assignments before he advanced to the following day's work. Over and over again, he repeated the information to himself until it became part of his very being, until he was as fluent in the subject matter as the teacher. He tapped into his very genome, harnessing the ability to relentlessly practice his score over and over again until he knew his material "by heart."

Later in his life, his patients would be astounded by his recall, the vast amount of knowledge that he had at his fingertips, the quick suggestions and recommendations that he could give for the whole range of their medical complaints.

I had been a patient of Nick's for over twenty years, making the trip twice a year to New York for office visits. I didn't like to bother him with phone calls. I followed the program exactly as it was written on the paper he had given me. But I remember once when I had a severe burn on my hand. I wasn't improving by the instructions given me in the emergency room, so I decided that even though it wasn't his specialty, I would give a quick call to Dr. Gonzalez.

"For burns you need to apply liquid Vitamin E," he told me without pause or hesitancy. His quick recall of his encyclopedic knowledge was no doubt based on his study skills that he taught himself in junior high school.

On lecture tours, his audiences would marvel at his ability to give six hour talks without notes and totally captivate a room packed with listeners.

"I know it's late in the day," he told his listeners, "So if you need to leave, just leave. I'll go on talking." And he did without break or even a PowerPoint to jog his memory.

These abilities all traced back to his astute junior high school observations.

> *Because I was in a special track, I was surrounded by the smartest kids in that big junior high from that middle-upper middle-class area of Queens. But I noticed that some of my mates who clearly were very smart with obviously high IQs were struggling, seemingly lost during class discussions, confused—particularly with science and math—and unable to learn the new material easily. Other students seemed always on top of everything. Young analytic thinker that I was, I realized that some of the blooming "stars" in my class were not necessarily those with the highest IQs but as I learned in conversation with them, students who on their own or from the wisdom of their parents, had learned that repetition was the key to learning and academic success, and like me, would nightly review the previously day's and weeks' work to the point that [they] could recite it...*

Nick aced all his midterm exams. He knew the material cold. He felt no anxiety and didn't even have to study. From an early age, he also began to understand that teachers were overworked, underpaid, and caught up in endless meetings, seminars and the nonsensical demands of the bureaucracy. He recognized that his teachers were looking for shortcuts, and often the math and science teachers drew the test questions from the unassigned problems in the textbook. Nick had already done those problems, repeatedly, reviewing them—in addition to all the other assigned material—over and over again until he had them on automatic recall.

While my approach might appear on the surface to require extra work, in fact, it became quite an efficient way to master school with excellent results. I wasn't lost by the material, confused by the math, desperate before exams. Even at that age, the benefits in psychological peace were incalculable and the rewards in terms of good grades, gratifying.

9

In 1962 Nick Gonzalez was bent over his junior high school math and science books in Queens, working extra problems. Dr. William Donald Kelley, a dentist in Grapevine, Texas, was in the library studying the work of John Beard, Weston Price, and the Francis Pottengers. Kelley was also working a problem, the problem of his own pancreatic cancer. At age thirty-five with four adopted children, a wife who had left him, and no savings in the bank, Kelley, a prominent orthodontist in a small suburb of Dallas, had suddenly become fatigued and exhausted.

An appointment with his doctor resulted in a diagnosis of widespread pancreatic cancer, although no biopsy was ever done. These were the days before CAT scans and today's sophisticated diagnostic techniques. Upon palpation, Kelley's doctor had found a large tumor in his liver, so big that it was protruding from the abdomen. He sent Kelley home to get his affairs in order and plan for the care of his children.

Kelley called his mother. "I'm going to die" he told her. "I'm afraid my kids will be sent back to the orphanage."

"You can't die," Mrs. Kelley told him and immediately packed her bags for Grapevine, Texas, driving there from her farm near Arkansas City, Kansas.

Mrs. Kelley had raised three sons on her own as a widow in the midst of the Depression in a rural area hard hit by the economic crisis. Born in 1925, William Kelley was the oldest child. Always too poor for medical care, Mrs. Kelley had grown up with a folk medicine healing tradition based on nutrition and herbs. She was well-versed in ways to tend to her growing children herself, treating them for the normal childhood diseases. Beyond that, she had read and studied ways to reverse degenerative diseases through food, detoxification and enzymes.

Mrs. Kelley strode into her son's house, threw open his kitchen cupboards and started tossing out all his food. Her son also had an interest in nutrition and saw a direct correlation between the crooked teeth of his patients and their diets. He was proficient in the research of Weston Price. But Kelley did not practice what he preached. He lived on junk food. He worked 12–14 hours a day in his dental clinic, then spent what little free time he had tinkering with antique cars. He gave little thought to what went into his mouth.

Ker-plunk. The candy bars hit the trash can. *Ker-plop, plop, plop.* The frozen pizzas came next.

Mrs. Kelley soaked grains, beans, and seeds in juice and yogurt, and fed it to her son raw, claiming that it would "kill the cancer." She insisted that her son consume most of his food raw, that raw food contained enzymes and other beneficial nutrients that cooked foods did not. She eliminated the red meat from his diet, and filled him with as many vegetables and leafy greens as he could tolerate. She juiced vegetables and made him drink the concoctions every few hours.

"And now you need to do coffee enemas," she told him.

He balked.

"You'll need these to get rid of the toxins."

He ignored her.

He was beginning to feel better. Why would he need to torture himself further? He could effectively test foods and monitor the results of his diet by merely observing his liver tumor. If he ate red meat, his tumor grew, protruding from his abdomen. If he stuck with the vegetarian diet, his tumor decreased slightly. By trial and error, he fine-tuned his diet more specifically and experimented with nutrients in the same way. Some vitamins and supplements made him feel better almost immediately while others zapped his energy. In particular, potassium and magnesium made him feel much better. Calcium, and B vitamins—pantothenic acid, inositol, choline and B12—made him feel much worse. Pill by pill, he worked his way through the supplements, doing empirical research on himself.

Then Kelley began to have serious digestive problems with bloating, gas, pain with meals, indigestion and reflux. The discomfort was so bad that he feared he was going to have to stop eating. Desperate, he went to see a local pharmacist he knew from his country club, who recommended prescription pancreatic enzymes. Kelley bought a case, went home and started to take them with every meal, first two, then four, then eight at a time. The enzymes helped, and his symptoms decreased but didn't vanish completely. He added enzymes between meals. When he took enzymes away from meals, he felt pain in his tumor. He upped the dose and his pain increased. His tumor was inflamed, painful to the touch.

"What's happening?" he asked his mother. "Should I stop the enzymes?"

"No, that's what enzymes are do," she insisted. "They attack the cancer."

So, Kelley began taking the enzymes around the clock, even rising in the middle of the night for doses. Gradually, over the course of a week, he began to feel better and allowed himself hope that he might even live. His appetite returned, and he gained a little weight.

Next, he crashed. His appetite dropped, his sleep worsened, and the pain in his tumor increased.

"That good week was just the calm before the storm," he told his mother. "I'll be dead soon."

His mother wouldn't have it. "You're not dying!" she yelled. "You're just too toxic." She explained that his body was overloaded with toxic waste from the deteriorating tumor. "You need to do those coffee enemas. Now! Or the waste will kill you."

Finally, Kelley gave in, and with a bag his mother bought at the local pharmacy, he performed his first enema. Astonished, he immediately felt better. When his symptoms began to return, his mother brewed more coffee in the percolator, and he was on his feet again—at least for a few hours. In the following days she put him on juice fasts and other routines she claimed would help strengthen his kidneys and liver.

Throughout this ordeal, Kelley had to keep working. He needed the money to support himself and his children. He was barely able to stand, but his mother kept him on a routine that included enzymes, juices, meals, enemas, rest, work, more juices, meals, work and enzymes. It was rough going, but he made it through the first year—which was monumental for a patient with pancreatic cancer with a life expectancy of 6 weeks to 6 months. Then he made it through the second year. And after the third year he considered himself cured. The tumor was gone. His weight and energy had returned, and he was working at a regular pace again. During his ordeal, his hair had turned pure white, never to return to its original color. And the cancer had eaten a permanent hole in his hip that would always leave him with a limp. But these were minor things to this dentist who had once been given up for dead.

A man of faith, in his youth, Kelley had had a vision of himself as a missionary. He imagined that he would go forth in the world, spreading the gospel and helping people in the far-flung corners of the world. But World War II intervened and interrupted his career path, just as it had for William Gonzalez. Kelley enlisted in the Navy and served as an operating technician in the Philippines. Home and discharged after the war, he still clung to his missionary idea until his father-in-law guided him toward a more lucrative career as an orthodontist.

Kelley had majored in biochemistry as an undergraduate at Baylor University, and then he went through Baylor University School of Dentistry in Dallas, at the same time picking up a master's degree in education and beginning his interest in nutrition. Subsequently, Kelley set up a dental clinic and settled down to a life in an affluent Dallas suburb. He had little inkling that he would eventually end up saving people's lives instead of their souls.

After Kelley returned to health, word spread quickly around Grapevine and the greater Dallas area: this dentist knew how to cure cancer. Kelley was a highly esteemed, well-known orthodontist. He fixed the teeth of the children of some of the wealthiest people in Grapevine. But a different kind of patient began to appear in his lobby, adults asking him to treat their breast, prostate, and lung cancers. Patients with brain, colon, and kidney tumors. Kelley was reluctant to take them on as patients.

"I'm just a dentist, after all," he said, shaking his head. His country club physician colleagues began sending him their "hopeless" patients, thinking that, as a last resort, he might offer them some chance of survival. Word spread on the underground alternative health network, and more patients appeared, desperate for help.

So, Kelley began taking cancer patients, trying to teach them to self-administer the same program that his mother had set up for him. Kelley put everyone on a vegetarian diet with lots of raw food, juices, grains and fruits. He required all of them to carry out detoxification routines—the coffee enemas, fasts, and purges. He kept meticulous records of his patients and had some great successes as well as some failures. He began an intense study of the nutritional literature.

His studies were frequently interrupted by the pressure placed upon him from the authorities. At one point he was arrested and put in jail for practicing medicine without a license. Kelley, a tall, lanky, shy man sat on his cot in his empty cell, shaking his head, staring at the toilet in the corner of the room, imagining that all that he had lived for—his family and dental practice, his nice home and antique cars—was going to be flushed away. All because he had been given up for dead, then cured himself of cancer with his mother's old-fashioned remedies? The world seemed to have no logic. In his days of isolation, he became determined to find the scientific basis for his success with his own cancer. A biochemist at heart, he was determined to dig into the medical literature for answers.

His reputation and friends in high places helped bail him out of jail. Yet, his jail stint was just the beginning of a long line of attempts by everyone from the local sheriff to the federal government to force him to cease and desist his forays into alternative medicine. Nevertheless, he went directly from the local jail house to the university medical library, putting his research skills to work. Nestled in a carrel in the stacks, he scoured the medical literature for scientific theories that might explain his program.

Kelley discovered the work of Max Gerson (1881–1959), a German Jewish immigrant physician who had lost most of his family in the Holocaust. Gerson also treated cancer with a vegetarian diet, juices, and detoxification, and thought that tumors developed due to a pancreatic enzyme deficiency. Initially, he developed his program as a treatment for migraines and tuberculosis, then began applying it to people with cancer and other degenerative diseases. Gerson also used coffee enemas, and to Kelley's amazement, he discovered that coffee enemas had a long history in the practice of nursing and were included in the *Merck Manual.* Apparently, even Florence Nightingale had used the detoxification procedure during the Crimean War. No one seemed to know why they worked, but Nightingale found that they helped relieve pain for her wounded soldiers.

Kelley studied the biochemistry of nutrients, trying to determine why his body tolerated some vitamins and seemed to use them effectively in fighting his cancer, while his body rejected others. In the 1960s as today, there was a dearth of scientific information about nutrients, so Kelley learned all he could. He was especially perplexed by the way potassium and magnesium effected his tumors. Like any good scientist, he was a good observer, and he asked the right questions. He had the wits and the skill to watch his own tumor respond to the various substances he ingested. He had the intelligence to then ask why. What was the mechanism at work in the reduction of his tumor? Why did that happen?

Kelley dove into the work of John Beard, his theory of the trophoblast and use of pancreatic enzymes. Suddenly, things clicked for Kelley. At last, he might be able to explain his pancreatic enzymes and how they seemed to shrink his tumors. Kelley read everything he could about the trophoblast, the development of the placenta, the secretion of pancreatic enzymes, and how "primitive" undifferentiated cells, or stem cells, may be the origin of cancer.

Kelley knew that the theory of the trophoblast ran counter to every current idea about cancer, certainly all that he had been taught in dental school. But he had his own and now dozens of other cases that seemed to support Beard's theory. Those cases, though, would just be dismissed as "anecdotal" if they weren't tested in clinical trials. As a trained, conventional scientist, he hoped that the trophoblast theory and his own nutritional program could be subjected to the rigors of a controlled experiment at a major medical school. This became his life goal.

In the meantime, he was flooded with cancer patients knocking on the door of his dental practice, and Kelley began to notice that each of these patients responded a bit differently to his program. Kelley returned to the medical library to study in detail Francis Pottenger Sr.'s work on the autonomic nervous system.

10

Nick Gonzalez learned the basics of the autonomic nervous system in high school biology class. Bent over his book, using his good study habits, he memorized the definition: the autonomic nervous system is a control system, responsible for the unconscious functions of the body, such as breathing, the heartbeat, blood pressure, and the digestive system. Nick pressed the pages open, flat on his desk to the illustration to the two branches of the autonomic nervous system—the sympathetic and the parasympathetic. The diagram of the two nervous systems was similar to Pottenger's illustrations in his book *Symptoms of Visceral Disease.*

Nick traced his fingers over the page of the genderless human, the brain and spinal column finely sketched in detail, the rest of the torso outlined, but left blank. The organs of the body aligned outside of the figure, lined up on the left side of the page, connected to the brain and spinal cord by long lines of nerves. The sympathetic nerves were color coded in yellow, the parasympathetic nerves in green. Each branch of the nervous system connected to all the organs, tissues and glands in the body, but each branch had opposite effects on physical performance.

Now came the fun part. Over and over in his mind, Nick repeated the functions of the two branches of the autonomic nervous system. Sympathetic, sympathetic, sympathetic. Nick ran his hand over the heart, the lungs, and the adrenal glands. The tiger opened its jaws, and your heart raced, your breathing increased, and adrenaline surged throughout your body. Para, para, parasympathetic. You're lying in a hammock near a beach with the sound of the waves lulling you to sleep. Your heart rate and blood pressure lower, your breathing calms, your adrenal glands still. Your eyes close, and your mind drifts and floats beyond your troubles and worries into a deep slumber.

Junior high school required a strict study schedule, but Nick drifted and floated through high school without too much struggle, attaining excellent grades, always using repetition to embed the material in his brain. After school, he finished his biology, math, English, and social studies homework as soon as he could, then turned his attention to the study of ecology, challenging himself to master a new subject, something that he wasn't getting in school, something that wound together the whole natural world.

Nick's high school friend George Powell, who would later became a widely recognized conservation biologist, remembered their high school advanced biology course. They met and became friends in the two hour a day intensive class.

"This class was designed to make us think about biological science in an expansive way, not to just memorize a bunch of stuff."

With the principles of biology well in their minds, Powell invited Nick to his family summer home in the Adirondack Mountains the summer after their senior year of high school. There, the two young men relaxed and observed nature, canoeing, and watching beavers building their dams.

His study of ecology evolved from his love of ornithology and his summer days walking around Lake George with his brother Bill, binoculars in hand. At the family farm in Vermont, he began to connect birds with their habitats, humans with theirs, and how all creatures need food to fuel their bodies. Food couldn't grow in poor soil, without the proper microorganisms—bacteria, actinomycetes, fungi, algae, and protozoa. And humans couldn't grow without the proper nutrients from food grown where it could access the proper nourishment.

From his understanding of ecology came his curiosity about nutrition. He learned that all of life moved through eco-cycles. Botanists and wildlife biologists understood ecological systems as givens. Medical science was slower to grasp the place of human health within an ecological system.

* * * *

Ironically, at this time, Nick's own nutrition was sub-par. He ate more junk food and went through late adolescence trying to sift out his interests, attempting to find a path for himself and his future career. He had two talents, literature and science, almost like the two branches of his central nervous system. The right and left sides of his brain seemed equally developed, and he felt the pull and tug of one way of life and the other. His home life was drenched in music and literature, but his high school teachers could see that he had a flare for science. Yet he hated his science classes and found them dull and plodding.

Nick attended public school, but he hung out with an artsy crowd, many of them attending the New York High School of Performing Arts. The "psychedelic sixties" took hold just at the time Nick was graduating in high school. The Vietnam War was ramping up. In 1964 there were 23,000 United States troops in Vietnam, but after the Gulf of Tonkin incident that year, the troop levels jumped to 184,000. Every year after that more troops were sent, more men drafted to a war that few understood, and few thought we could win. By 1966, even Secretary of Defense Robert McNamara voiced doubts that the U.S. could become victorious.

War protests broke out and the youth of the country, raised on Doctor Spock, grew long hair to defy the clipped and tucked mores and norms of the 1950s culture. A great social awakening swept the nation. The era was filled with civil and women's rights protests, explorations of sexuality, and different interpretations of the American dream. America's youth, who saw their friends and relatives coming home in body bags from the Vietnam War, had become disillusioned with the establishment.

New York City was one of the hotbeds of counterculture in the United States. The city held vast numbers of affluent baby boomers allowed the time and energy to think beyond materialism—a luxury denied their Depression-era and immigrant parents and grandparents.

"We lived in Queens, in New York City," Mia Oberlink, one of Nick's neighbors remembered, "but at that time, it was more suburban. Nick lived directly across the street in a Tudor house, the nicest one on the block."

Mia found Nick very intelligent, funny, and physically attractive. He was always well-kempt, casually dressed in a nice shirt and in comfortable shoes—very collegiate.

"He had big, big ambitions as a writer. Nick looked like James Agee, and he wanted to be James Agee," Mia said. Agee (1909–1955) had been a journalist, poet, screenwriter and film critic. A hard-drinker and chain smoker, Agee's novel *A Death in the Family* had won a posthumous Pulitzer prize, and his reputation had grown after his death from a heart attack in a taxi cab in New York City.

Nick applied and was admitted to many of the Ivy League schools but chose Brown for its lenient requirements and its "artsy" environment. In Providence, he excelled in his literature classes and came back to Queens on his breaks and during the summers.

Nick's struggle with the two equally developed branches of his nervous system continued at Brown. His love of ecology and his knowledge about the magic of the health of the soil pushed his interest in the direction of the study of agronomy. "Nick became restless at Brown," George Powell said. "He didn't think he was getting the kind of attention he should."

Nick dropped out of Brown for a short time and enrolled in the school of agriculture at Cornell, hoping to pursue his study of food and its relationship in the larger scheme of eco-cycling. His program of study at Cornell ultimately disappointed him, though, with its emphasis on industrial agriculture and the use of chemical fertilizers, pesticides and herbicides that had become prominent after World War II.

"Nick wouldn't tolerate any baloney." Powell said.

Nick enrolled in Goddard College for a short time, too, then eventually went back to Brown University.

At Brown, one of his biology professors offered him a position as his research assistant in his laboratory at the Marine Biology Research Center at Woods Hole, Cape Cod. Nick was an English major, but to cover his bases, he had taken just enough science courses to enable him the option to apply to medical school. Woods Hole was a prestigious summer destination for scientists to conduct their research while surrounded by the beach and the pounding of the waves of the Atlantic Ocean.

Nick found himself sequestered in a lab, staring into a microscope, entering figures of data into notebooks, analyzing the biochemistry of crab pigment. Dull, routine work was left to lab assistants. His professor was more often found on the beach or hosting barbeque picnics. Soon, Nick pushed the crabs aside and picked up a copy of Ernest Hemingway's *A Moveable Feast* and dreamed of going off to Paris to live the Bohemian life, writing novels in cafés during the day, partying with other artists at night.

Nick engrossed himself in Lawrence Durrell's *Alexandria Quartets,* a tetralogy of novels set in Egypt before and during World War II. The first three books show a sequence of events through different points of view. The fourth book shows change over time. In a 1959 *Paris Review* interview, Durrell had explained the ideas behind the *Quartets* in terms of the convergence of Eastern and Western metaphysics. He based his concepts on Einstein's overturning of the old view of the material universe, and Freud's challenge to the concept of stable personalities. Durrell aimed for a new concept of reality.

Once again, Nick heard the calling of his parasympathetic/right brain nervous system. After six weeks of working at Woods Hole, he, too, desired a new concept of reality. Nick walked into his professor's office and said, "I quit."

His professor stood there stunned. He shook his head. None of the other pre-meds would ever do such a thing, cognizant of how such a resignation would look on their records and how it would affect their applications to medical school.

"Why?" was all Nick's professor could say.

"Because I'm going to be a famous writer, not a doctor." Nick said and walked out the door.

"I'm afraid you've blown your chances at medical school," William Gonzalez said to his son when he arrived home from Cape Cod.

Nick didn't care. If that was science, he didn't want it.

They worked out an arrangement to have Nick finish off the summer in Mexico City, living with some of his father's relatives. Just the previous year, Mexico City had held the summer Olympics. Restaurants and concerts, festivals, traditional dancing and music filled the streets. Vibrant murals, painted under the direction of Diego Rivera, depicting the characters of the Mexican Revolution—the Maderos, Carranzas, and Villas of the era—all familiar characters of the Gonzalez family past—were splashed across the walls of the buildings.

The stairwell of the National Palace was filled with *The History of Mexico*, a masterful mural by Rivera himself. Even though Rivera was commissioned by the government, he was a rebel who wasn't shy about criticizing authority and foreign domination. The murals captured the richness of the indigenous culture and the colonialism of the Spaniards. The main mural, some 70x9 meters, was filled with conflicts, rebellion, and revolution against oppression.

Nick hung out mostly with his cousin Juan José Calatayud, a famous jazz pianist. A shy, generous man and superb musician, Calatayud took Nick under

his wing, and the two of them walked the streets of Mexico City, sampling the
food, taking in the museums, sitting in the Bosque de Chapultepec, one of
the largest city parks in the Western hemisphere. The musician's adoring fans
often trailed after them, seeking autographs. The freedom and artistic bent of
the summer gave Nick a welcome respite from the crabs of Cape Cod and the
oppressive expectations he felt from a conventional left-brained sympathetic
dominant world.

The highlight of the summer came when Calatayud was a guest soloist with
the National Symphony of Mexico, performing Gershwin's *Rhapsody in Blue* at
the Palacio de Bellas Artes, the large concert hall in the middle of city. A man
often compared to Dave Brubeck in the United States, a pianist who brought
jazz out of the smoky nightclubs and into the concert halls, Calatayud sat at the
piano with the authority of a master, but the humility of one who refused to
believe his own greatness, his hands resting on the keys, his body leaning into the
instrument that held the mystery of the harmonizing of black and white keys, the
tiny hammers hitting the strings drawn tighter, drawn further than his own reach.

> *He played beautifully and flawlessly and received a standing ova-*
> *tion that would not stop. I was so proud of him… He was a little*
> *older than I was, and a cousin, my blood, as well as a successful*
> *artist. He was all I needed to convince me when I returned to*
> *Brown in the fall that I needed to follow my heart and do what I*
> *had long wanted to: go off and be a writer, live in wonderful exotic*
> *places, and write long and passionate novels.*

11

Dr. Kelley simply followed his instincts when working with patients in his office in the less than exotic Grapevine, Texas. For the most part, he did well with cancer patients, treating them all with the exact same routine that had helped him: the vegetarian diet, supplements, and detoxification techniques that he had worked out with his mother. He helped most of his patients return to health, but he also saw his share of failures, and the failures bothered him. Yet, he would have gone on his way treating everyone exactly alike if he hadn't been visited by one very allergic young woman.

When Nick Gonzalez had finished his first year at Brown University and was delving into the study of natural history and ecology, Kelley had an allergic young woman come to him out of desperation. Her condition wasn't a joke. She was so allergic to iodine, for example, that if she came within ten miles of the ocean, she would go into anaphylactic shock.

She walked into Kelley's office with the aid of her mother and with a cartful of medical records from dozens of doctors. "I've tried everything," she said. "Nothing worked, not the desensitization shots, the elimination or rotation diets, not the water fasts, the single food diet, the homeopathy—nothing."

"This will work," Kelley assured her, and put the allergic woman on a vegetarian diet—just as he had done with all the rest of his patients. And she got better for a few months.

A few weeks later, her mother called Kelley. "She's going downhill."

Kelley couldn't believe it.

Just a few days later, the mother called yet again. "My daughter's even worse now," her mother said.

Her allergic daughter had become so weak that she landed in bed, lapsing into a deep depression. Kelley couldn't figure out what was wrong, so by trial and error, he started adjusting her diet. He made the diet stricter.

"Cut the eggs and yogurt," her told her mother. "Increase the raw food and add another glass of vegetable juice a day."

But the woman only worsened.

Kelley then experimented with her nutrients. He upped the doses of magnesium and potassium, the two nutrients that had significantly boosted his system. The allergic woman sank into a deep, deep, three-day depression without the ability to lift her head from her pillow. Kelley gave it a rest for a few days, then asked her to try again. He was unable to believe that what had been so effective for him, wouldn't be for another. The woman took another single dose of the supplements and lapsed into another profound depression.

"She's now semi-conscious," the mother alerted Kelley a few days later, her voice cracking.

"Feed her meat," Kelley said. In desperation, he was trying the only thing he hadn't attempted in the past. "Use raw, organic blenderized meat. And stop all the supplements."

Within a few hours of eating the meat, the woman sat up in bed. Every few hours she ate meat and grew stronger with each feeding.

Next, Kelley began cautiously suggesting she take the very nutrients that had made him ill during his recovery.

"Try calcium, selenium and zinc," Kelley told the mother on the phone.

To their mutual relief, the woman successfully tolerated those supplements. Kelley slowly built a program for her, adding the B vitamins. The woman improved again.

Next, Kelley started experimenting more with the woman's diet. He found that she tolerated root vegetables like carrots and potatoes best. Leafy greens and citrus fruit made her ill. Within a few months, the woman was well, and by this time Kelley had figured out a specific program for her. Soon, he tried the program on some of his other problem patients and was surprised to see them do so well with it. Kelley, who had become an ardent convert to vegetarian diets, had to admit that there were people in the universe who needed meat—sometimes up to three or four servings a day.

Another problem patient blew away one more of Kelley's firm nutritional assumptions. The patient was a young man who today would be diagnosed with chronic fatigue syndrome. Like all his other patients, Kelley put this young man on raw foods. Kelley found support for the use of raw food not only in his mother's suggestions, but in his research of Dr. Edward Howell, an early twentieth century physician who studied the biochemical effects of raw food. Howell, like Francis Pottenger, Jr. found that humans as well as animals, were healthier on raw food—as were their offspring. Raw food contained large quantities of enzymes, proteins that served as catalysts to enable thousands of complicated reactions in cells. High temperatures kill these enzymes. Howell thought that cooked food left humans enzyme deficient and set up for degenerative and infectious diseases.

The chronic fatigue patient was a young graduate student with a brilliant scientific career ahead of him. Severe stress and a romantic break-up left him totally exhausted with fatigue, inability to concentrate, digestive problems, failing memory and depression. His joints were arthritic, his vision blurry. Like the young allergic patients, he had been going from one doctor to another, and in desperation, trying one alterative fad diet or vitamin therapy after another. Nothing helped.

Initially, Kelley put the young graduate student on the raw meat, raw foods diet, and supplements as he had the allergic woman. The program helped the graduate student at first, then made him sicker—a similar pattern to the allergic woman. Kelley then switched him to a mixed diet of raw meat, raw vegetables, sprouted grains and seeds, and sprouted beans. Kelley tested supplements to find the correct combination. Again, the patient improved at first, then went downhill.

Finally, Kelley called the patient with an idea that even he couldn't believe. "Try cooking all your foods."

The young man began eating soups and stews, with meat and vegetables, stopping all the sprouts, juices, salads and grains. He also took a whole array of supplements that had been used with success from both Kelley's vegetarian and meat-eating patients. Within days, the graduate student began to improve and then slowly, over the course of many months, his condition cleared.

Kelley concluded that as enzyme-dense as raw food was, it wasn't easily absorbed by all patients. Some were too depleted to be able to digest it. From then on, Kelley carefully monitored all his patients, adjusting their programs according to their responses. He realized that there was no one diet that would help everyone and that different patients needed different nutrients. As basic as this idea is, it was revolutionary. Most doctors—conventional or alternative, then and today—prescribe the same diet for all their patients, usually the diet either taught in school, or the one that helped them, the physician, return to health. Kelley also learned that he had to check his assumptions at the door. He couldn't cling to one set idea of nutrition. Rather, he realized he had to be open to a range of possibilities, widening his view of the working biochemistry of human physiology.

*   *   *   *   *

Kelley began to sift out his patients into three groups: the vegetarians like him who thrived on raw salads, sprouts and juices, responding to potassium and magnesium supplements; the "carnivores" who did well eating meat several times a day, responding to calcium, selenium and zinc and often needing cooked food; and those in between who needed a more balanced diet and supplementation.

Ever the scholar, Kelley kept searching the medical literature, and became enamored with the work of Francis Pottenger. The workings of the autonomic nervous system became Kelley's fascination. Fifty years before Kelley's first cancer patient showed up at his door, Pottenger had defined three basic types of humans according to the dominant branch of their autonomic nervous system. Pottenger's claim that these three types—the sympathetic, parasympathetic, and balanced—had very different biochemical, neurological and psychological make-ups, echoed all that Kelley had observed in his clinical practice.

Kelley spent long hours going through all his records, noting similarities between his patients and the Pottenger's models. Kelley's vegetarian patients did match up with Pottenger's sympathetic dominants. These patients had strong hearts and body muscles. The left sides of the brains and the endocrine glands were highly developed. Sympathetic dominants rarely had allergies due to their tight cellular membranes. Their body chemistry was usually acidic.

Kelley's carnivore patients, in turn, matched Pottenger's parasympathetic dominants. These patients had sluggish tissues, organs and glands. They were frequently plagued with allergies, and with their weak thyroid glands, they often gained weight easily. Their body chemistry was more frequently alkaline.

Structurally, the sympathetic dominants were good athletes without much training, were thin-framed with thin faces, narrow dental arches and crooked teeth. Sympathetic dominants thrived on fruit, the extra sugar compensating for their inefficient energy metabolism in their cells. They often felt tired and fatigued eating meat and fats.

Like Pottenger before him, Kelley described his vegetarian patients as aggressive, irritable, and prone to angry outbursts. They slept lightly but had great powers of concentration and high energy. They tended to be controlling, act and think quickly and in a linear fashion, all due to the excess levels of adrenaline coursing through their systems. Sympathetic dominants tended to be good at rote learning and routines, but weren't very imaginative or expansive in their vision of the world.

Structurally, the parasympathetic dominants who walked through Kelley's door were more rounded in appearance. They had rounded shoulders and rounded faces with wide dental arches. The parasympathetic dominants had very efficient and even over-active livers, pancreases, intestines, and right brains—all organs stimulated by the parasympathetic nerves. Their weak sympathetic tone left their muscles flabby. No matter how many times they worked out in the gym, they never achieved the tight, sculpted physique of a sympathetic dominant.

Parasympathetic dominants were more even-keeled and could even be passive, shying away from confrontations, and prone to be taken advantage of by aggressive sympathetic dominants. Parasympathetics slept soundly and for long periods of time, often after staying up late at night. Mornings found them slow and sluggish. They were highly creative, taking to the arts or creative sciences. Parasympathetics had little affinity for math. They thrived on meat and fat that broke down slowly in their body, allowing for a slow, steady release of energy at the cellular level.

Somewhere between these two extremes lay the balanced types who presented with well-proportioned body structures and dental arches—neither too thin nor overly rounded. They were fit, their muscles developed, but not over-active. Their glandular functions and personalities were stable. The balanced types could utilize both sides of their brains, accessing one, then the other on demand.

Before he'd read Pottenger, Kelley had already refined his groupings of patients. Ultimately, Kelley delineated 10 "metabolic types," as he called them. He gave numbers to the types from 1–10, the number emerging as he discovered the category. He defined three types of sympathetic dominants, three types of parasympathetic dominants, and four types of balanced humans. He also adjusted the diets and supplements of these patients to match their types.

For example, the sympathetic dominants were divided into extreme sympathetic dominants (Type 1), moderate sympathetics (Types 4), and inefficient sympathetics (Type 6). The extreme sympathetics had all the classic sympathetic dominant traits pushed to the limits. These patients' nervousness, anger, and insomnia were very pronounced. Their muscle tone was superb, but their digestion poor.

In moderate sympathetics (Type 4), these qualities were less extreme. These patients might still be angry, nervous, and awake most of the night, but not with the frequency as Type 1. They were athletic, but their digestive problems might come and go compared to the extreme sympathetic who had chronic, debilitating gastrointestinal diseases.

Inefficient sympathetics (Type 6) showed moderate sympathetic dominance and moderate sympathetic weakness, but neither system was very efficient. In contrast, extreme sympathetics might have a sympathetic system operating at 100 percent, and a parasympathetic system at 20 percent of capacity. A moderate sympathetic might have closer to a 70/30 percent ratio. Inefficient sympathetics might have a 30/10 ratio. These types tended to be very sick and needed a lot of nutritional support on the program.

The parasympathetic types echoed the sympathetics on the other end of the spectrum. The balanced types held the middle ground, with four defined types.

Again, through trial and error, Kelley figured out what foods and supplements best suited which types, illustrated by the chart below that he eventually used to guide his treatment of his patients:

Metabolic Type	Sympathetic Efficiency	Parasympathetic Efficiency	Diet	Supplements
1. Extreme Sympathetic	100	20	80% raw, plant based, fruit, grains, seeds, nuts	Magnesium, potassium, B vitamins, C, D, para-aminobenzoic acid
4. Moderate Sympathetic	70	30	60% raw, unlimited fruit, vegetables, grains, nuts, seeds	Same as 1 but more moderate doses.
6. Inefficient Sympathetic	30–40	20–30	Mostly cooked, plant based, red meat occasionally, grains.	Same as 4, add B5, B12, choline, inositol, calcium, zinc.
2 Extreme Parasympathetic	20	100	Cooked fatty red meat, root vegetables, occasional fruit, no leafy greens.	Moderate vitamin A, niacinamide, B5, B12, choline, inositol, high dose vitamin C, zinc, selenium, chromium, manganese.
5. Moderate Parasympathetic	30	70	Less fatty red meat than 2. Some fruits, root vegetables, no greens. No citrus.	Same as 2 but more moderate doses.
7. Inefficient Parasympathetic	20–30	30–40	Less meat than 2, root vegetables—mostly cooked, some cooked grains. No leafy greens.	Same as 5 but add beta-carotene, thiamine, riboflavin, niacin, pyridoxine, folic acid, magnesium and potassium.
10. Highly Efficient Balanced	100	100	Wide variety (3% of population).	Full range of supplements and minerals.
8. Moderately Efficient Balanced	80	80	Wide variety 50 to 60% raw	Same as 10
9. Moderately Inefficient Balanced	50	50	Wide variety, 20 to 40% raw	Same as 8 and 10 but higher doses.
3. Very Inefficient Balanced	10–20	10–20	Wide variety, mostly cooked.	Same as 8 and 10 but double the doses.

12

Spring. And bright, fresh, stiff blades of grass pushed up out of the soil of the Main Green of Brown University that stretched between the old historical campus buildings. Nick Gonzalez passed the statue of Brown Bear near the Green, its pedestal containing a piece of slate that Roger Williams had stepped on in 1636, claiming the land that would one day become Providence, Rhode Island. Nick headed south past the John Carter Brown Library, a building that housed some of Christopher Columbus' original documents and maps.

His campus had history and Nick was determined to make a story of his own. While Kelley worked to refine his metabolic types in Grapevine, Texas, Nick worked to complete his bachelor's degree at Brown. Nick had followed his heart back to the English Department classrooms, completed courses in the cannon of English Literature, studying Beowulf to Browning to the Beat Poets. He was most interested in following his passion for Hemingway and Durrell, though, and in sharpening his own writing skills to eventually write the great American novel.

Nick put his head down and worked his senior year on his thesis about Hemingway, delving into Carlos Baker's *Ernest Hemingway: A Life Story*, an account of the brilliant creative writer's victories in fiction and his losses in his family relationships and his own mental health. Hemingway, a Nobel Prize for Literature winner and author of seven novels, six short story collections, and two books of non-fiction, had created one adventure after another for himself. He had served as an ambulance driver in World War I, volunteered for a stint in the Spanish Civil War, and gone on safari in Africa where he survived two plane crashes.

Nick was as interested in the workings of Hemingway's mind—what made this genius tick. Hemingway, a great hulk of a man, had become an alcoholic, gone through four marriages, and ended his own life with a shotgun. How could someone so creative become so self-destructive? Was there something inherently dangerous about becoming a famous writer? Or was there some kind of genetic predisposition in a creative person's life toward depression?

At the same time that Nick was pondering these questions, he was covering his own career bases. An English major, he had also made a half-hearted attempt to apply to medical schools. At Brown, he had fulfilled the basic premedical requirements. Now back from Mexico and dedicated to becoming a writer, he still battled the tug-of-war between choosing a career in the arts or sciences. He cherished his memories of the cultural scene in Mexico City, of his cousin Juan José at the piano. Yet, Nick was still conflicted about his career goals throughout undergraduate school.

In November during the fall semester of 1969, Nick found himself in a conference room on another campus. He had an interview at Harvard University Medical School in Boston. Any pre-med student would have been thrilled for the interview. Harvard was the medical school that introduced the smallpox vaccine, that first used anesthesia for pain control during surgery, that first introduced insulin to treat diabetes. To Nick, Harvard was simply the first, the strongest, the smartest—the best. But Nick was skeptical of the life that would unfold for him in a role as a medical doctor. And he dreaded the admissions interview with the famed Dr. Daniel Funkenstein, a psychiatrist investigating the role of the autonomic nervous system in mental illness.

Funkenstein's research topic seemed to have no relevance to Nick when he sat in the conference room. Instead, Nick was anxious about the interview itself. Harvard medical school in general, and Dr. Funkenstein in particular, was notorious for its "stress" interviews, a power play by the professors in charge. Funkenstein was known to nail a window shut, then usher the student into the room and ask, "It's hot in here. Would you mind opening the window?"

Or, Funkenstein would welcome the student, offer him a cigarette, but provide no ashtray or chair. Funkenstein and the other professors liked to watch the interviewees struggle, cope, and squirm, standing throughout their grilling, flicking ashes into their hands.

Funkenstein also had a reputation for quizzing humanities majors about their course of study.

"The future of medicine is in biochemistry," Funkenstein would say. "Why do we need someone like you?"

Most interviewees had no idea that Funkenstein had written an article emphasizing the importance of a liberal arts education for pre-medical students.

With Nick Gonzalez, Funkenstein played no games. Nick sat in a chair provided in the conference room with the famous doctor, a heavy-set balding man of about 5'10" with a wide, open smile seated across from him. Funkenstein's intellect and recall were quick. He was knowledgeable in many fields besides medicine.

Funkenstein spoke to Nick about art, literature, and music. They discussed the Gonzalez family background, his grandfather's musical career, his renowned cousin's jazz career. They discussed Durrell, and of course, Hemingway. They exchanged ideas about philosophy and William James, and talked about some of the great writers who had been physicians—Celine, Keats, Chekhov and William Carlos Williams.

"The admissions committee wants to admit you, but they are concerned you will give up medicine for writing," Funkenstein told Nick. Harvard had just lost the physician Michael Crichton to the writing world and to Hollywood. The medical school thought it had been "burnt," pouring time and money into educating a great scientist, only to have him abandon medicine for writing.

Nick turned to Funkenstein and told him the truth. "I see medicine as a wonderful thing, a noble profession. But frankly, the reality of science seems so oppressive."

No surprise, in the end, Nick decided against going to medical school at the time. He went back to his senior thesis on Hemingway, and to his desire to become a writer.

It was only years later that Nick would connect the dots and realize the irony in his meeting with Funkenstein. The psychiatrist had done major research on the autonomic nervous system. Like, but independent of Pottenger and Kelley, Funkenstein had figured out three groups of humans with three different sets of mental reactions to stress. After twenty years of research, Funkenstein outlined a new model of mental disorders based on abnormalities in the autonomic nervous system. In the end, Nick discovered Funkenstein's research and found it provided a key to the human psyche.

Funkenstein's Group I had strong sympathetic and weak parasympathetic systems. Group II had balanced systems, and Group III had strong parasympathetic
and weak sympathetic systems. Group I subjects were often aggressive, hostile,
angry and blaming of other people, particularly under stress. Group II subjects
seemed to take stress in stride. Group III subjects, even under relaxed conditions,
tended toward melancholia, anxiety, and passivity. Far more subjects with mental
illnesses fell into Groups I and III. Funkenstein concluded that mental illness
was probably caused by an imbalance of the autonomic nervous system. Mental
conditions, he found, from schizophrenia to depression tended to clear up when
the autonomic nervous system was in balance.

"Poets and fiction writers are likely to be parasympathetics," Nick had told
me during one of my office visits—years after his Harvard interview. "Journalists
are more sympathetic. They need to ask questions and be more aggressive. Poets
are the most extreme parasympathics, then fiction writers. They are both creative
and productive, but tend toward melancholia. They often use substances to
self-medicate. Hemingway is a good example. He was very parasympathetic. He
drank and constantly created physical challenges to try to shock his system back
into balance. Finally, he became so alkaline that he sank into a deep depression.
He couldn't even put a paragraph together anymore. That's why he killed himself."

Questions Nick Gonzalez asked himself as a young student, whether medical
or literary, eventually were answered in his adult medical practice.

* * * * *

Spring, 1970, and the Van Wickle gates at Brown University swung open. Nick
Gonzalez stepped through onto the cobblestones and into the world with his
bachelor's degree in English literature in hand, Phi Beta Kappa, magna cum
laude. He had already begun work on a novel, but now he needed to have a day
job. Investigative journalism seemed like a good fit. Hemingway had begun his
career as a cub reporter for the Kansas City Star, the day job keeping a roof over
his head, while he worked on his novels at night.

At first, Hemingway covered fires, crimes, the General Hospital and the
comings and goings at Union Station. He then joined the American Red Cross
during World War I and was sent to the Italian front where he was injured, then
returned to the States. A job with the Toronto Star came next where he was sent

to Paris. Interviews of Mussolini and stories about bobsledding in Switzerland and bull fighting in Spain followed, all eventually material for his fiction.

Nick had the writing skills and the eclectic mind of a good journalist—one who is interested in many subjects, has the intellectual curiosity to chase down the necessary information and background, has an out-going personality, and is unafraid to get out, meet people, and ask probing questions to figure out why people do the things they do.

Nick moved to Manhattan and rented a small apartment on the Upper West Side near Columbia University. He still ran in the same artsy crowd, and Nick started dating the singer-song writer and actor Melissa Manchester, also an alum of the New York High School of the Performing Arts. At the time, Manchester was performing street theatre in the slums of New York.

"Nick was very intense, very handsome, with piercing blue eyes," Manchester said.

Both Nick and Melissa shared a family background in music. Manchester's father was a bassoonist for the New York Metropolitan Opera, so they both understood the life of a performing artist.

Manchester remembered a party Nick had attended where she and others were singing the lyrics of the musical *Hair*. "Nick had masses of bushy hair."

But she remembered Nick as someone who stood apart from the crowd, not fully engaged, more of a scientific observer. "He was sweet, and liked me a lot," she said, "but he also had a sense of intensity and urgency about him." Manchester remembered that they mostly talked about the future. Nick's sympathetic/left brain, parasympathetic/right brain tug-of-war had kicked in again. Just a few years after abandoning himself to his dream of becoming a writer, he told Manchester that his life ambition was to "cure cancer."

Then right away he landed a job with Time, Inc. where he worked for Byron Dobell, one of the most respected editors in New York journalistic history. Dobell himself was an essayist and artist. As an editor, he is credited with nurturing the early careers of the writers Tom Wolfe, David Halberstam, and Mario Puzo.

It was an exciting, active, era in journalism. The Vietnam War was still raging and just as Nick was about to see his name printed on his diploma, the invasion of Cambodia sparked nation-wide protests. Four student demonstrators were killed at Kent State University in Ohio which sparked even more protests. Every day, Americans ate their dinners before their black-and-white

television sets, watching newscasts of the bombings, killings, and the devasta-
tion of war. They opened their *Time* magazines and *New York Times* newspapers
to stories of Buddhist monks setting themselves on fire in protest, and pictures
of children, burned by napalm, pulling off their clothes, and running naked
down the road.

The Pentagon Papers were leaked to the *New York Times* in 1971 by Daniel
Ellsberg who had initially worked on the report, documenting the extent of the
war and the lies that the American people had been told by Democratic and
Republican presidents alike. Richard Nixon then sent burglars to break into
Ellsberg's psychiatrist's office, and the event kicked off the Watergate scandal,
and ironically, a golden age of investigative journalism.

At Time Inc., Nick found the kind of excitement he had longed for after
reading and studying the life of Hemingway:

> *After college, my first job was at Time Inc, in those days considered
> the "Rolls Royce" of publishing with offices around the world, and
> an influential magazine read weekly by millions. Of course, that
> era was pre-Internet, pre-personal computer, pre-email, pre-smart
> phone—you get the picture. These things which some of you take for
> granted weren't even an idea when I started out at Time, pounding
> away at an old non-electric typewriter—which I doubt even exists
> in this day and age. Regardless of the primitive technology, I had
> a blast, with a job giving me access to all sorts of interesting people
> and offering me the opportunity to travel extensively through the
> US and Europe, even into Africa, on stories.*

Byron Dobell took a personal interest in Nick, mentoring him and helping
develop Nick's career in the same way he had done with other young writers who
had eventually made names for themselves in American letters.

> *For whatever reason Byron took me under his wing, and spent two
> years trying to turn an untested youngster into a battle-hardened
> journalist... I still remember with great affection evenings at his
> apartment on East 69ᵗʰ Street in New York, talking late into the
> evening about writing, writers, exotic places and exotic people.*

> *Byron taught me lessons in journalism that have stayed with me and done me well over the years, no matter which direction my life would take. As a start, he was a man of enormous integrity, who looked at journalism as a public service, protecting the weak, exposing the corrupt, lauding the heroic. It was a most honorable profession in those days, and Byron tried hard to get me to understand the responsibilities of a true journalist.*

Dobell was the first in a string of men who would mentor Nick in his career, assuming professional but fatherly roles in the young man's life. Nick seemed to work best in this mode, apprenticing, learning one-on-one at the elbow of an older, practiced man, absorbing all the information and guidance he could from this knowledgeable source. Nick established deep personal and trusting relationships with a series of these mentors, one after another, never quite knowing where the next one might appear.

* * * * *

At age 24 in 1972, Nick had his first big cover story of his career in investigative journalism. Nick's younger brother Bill had gone to Mexico for his first few years of high school, but wanted to return home to New York City to graduate. William and Marie Gonzalez searched for a school that would challenge Bill, a gifted, bilingual, straight A student with a high I.Q. They had known that their son Nick had become bored in public school, so the Gonzalezes found the Sands Point Country Day School-Fetsch Academy located in the midst of the exclusive Sands Point community on the north shore of Long Island. The school had an excellent reputation—with hundreds of newspaper articles to support it—as a "Center for Gifted Children." The Gonzalezes thought it would be just the place for Bill.

In their literature, Sands Point stated that, after extensive screening, they only accepted students of "superior intelligence" who "show promise of high academic achievement." The Gonzalezes arrived at Sands Point for Bill's interview, and at first glance, were impressed with the facility. The school had once been the estate of Edgar F. Luckenbach, a shipping magnate who had invested 40 million dollars in the mansion that was then the main building of the academy. Twenty-five acres of woods and manicured lawns surrounded the buildings, sloping down toward the Long Island Sound. The school was run by the Fetsch family who preached brotherly love, honesty, and manners. The catalogue read: "At Sands Point there is no unrest, no hippies, no long-hairs, no barefoot misfits. We pride ourselves as being an oasis of peace . . "

The Gonzalezes sat down in this oasis with the principal who accepted Bill on the spot. This should have been the Gonzalezes' first clue, but they, as most parents who enrolled their children in the school, found the acceptance flattering. It wasn't until Bill was actually attending classes that the Gonzalezes began to suspect that something was wrong. The principal had promised that Bill, who was already fluent in Spanish, was to be placed in advanced Spanish. Yet upon his enrollment, Bill found himself in a basic Spanish course and was handed a first-year review book.

William Gonzalez, who had a master's degree in Spanish literature, and was a language teacher himself, jumped into gear and complained to the principal. His reply: "All Sands Point classes are advanced." The same routine played out for Bill's other classes. The Gonzalezes then attended a meeting with 70 other concerned parents at one of their homes. One of the teachers at the school also attended and told the parents that the school was a farce. Many of the promised classes and extra curriculum clubs were non-existent. The students who were signed up for calculus were out playing baseball on the field, and the picture of the chess club was staged for publicity purposes. Many of the students, rather than gifted and talented, were troubled underachievers.

The parents requested a meeting with the school, and when they arrived, they found the Fetsches there en masse, lawyered up. Dr. Marie Fetsch threw a temper tantrum, pounded the table, threw papers, and screamed, "You're out to destroy my school."

Dr. Fetsch then told William Gonzalez to withdraw his son from her school. "Why?"

"Because you're a troublemaker," she replied and said she would refund his tuition.

Bill never stepped foot in Sands Point again, and the tuition check never reached the Gonzalez house in Queens.

This scenario was replayed with the other parents and students. Those students who weren't asked to leave, were expelled. Those who weren't expelled, had their bus service terminated. At last, the parents joined together with the Gonzalezes in a lawsuit against the school. Nick Gonzalez investigated the school and its faculty, exposing the fraud and the lack of academic credentials of its faculty and administration. Under the guidance of Byron Dobell, Nick published his piece "Showdown at Sands Point" in *New York Magazine* and helped shut down Sands Point Country Day School-Fetsch Academy.

The publication taught Nick how to research, probe and plumb to the depths of a story, how to truly investigate and see through layers of bluff and obscuration. He became more practiced at his writing skills and at seeing the reality of scams and power structures. The publication opened many doors for him, leading to more articles and interesting assignments. But perhaps most of all, it again gave him a fatherly role model who fearlessly charged into battle to fight injustices.

My father began to investigate, and learned the woman in charge had a mail order Ph.D., and all the administrators had troubled academic histories at previous positions, including accusations of embezzlement and fraud. Most of the other parents, though aware the school was not legitimate, were content to leave well enough alone, get their kids through with a diploma from an esteemed institution. But not my dad. For him it was a question of ethics. He went to the school one day and confronted the founder with the fake Ph.D. and she exploded in a rage, threw my dad off the grounds and immediately expelled my brother. My brother ended up going to Friends Academy in Manhattan, a fine school from which he graduated. My father sued the school and I—working at Time Inc, at the time, and seeing an extraordinary story in a fraudulent school for gifted children, got approval to do a major investigation that would be my first cover story at New York Magazine. I put the school out of business, and that career boost came directly because of my father's fearlessness, and integrity.

13

1970. A 60 year-old female patient from Michigan with colon cancer appeared in Dr. Kelley's office in Grapevine, Texas. The woman, accompanied there by a friend who had read about Kelley, was so weak she could barely walk through the door. Though the patient was skeptical of pursuing any sort of alternative treatment, she agreed to the consultation. Her Michigan doctors had warned that she needed another surgery to prevent an obstruction, but said that even with aggressive chemotherapy, she wouldn't live more than six months.

"I don't want to put myself through anymore suffering with another operation," she had told her doctors. Instead, she reluctantly made the trip to see what to her sounded like a "quack."

By now, Dr. Kelley had a good idea of what made his patients sick. Stress, the usual environmental hazards like toxic chemicals, and bad personal habits like smoking, drinking, and doing drugs were starters. Like Weston Price and the Francis Pottengers, Kelley found that eating nutrient depleted, synthetic and refined foods also caused a patient to weaken. As did eating too many raw or too many cooked foods for the type. And even if a patient were eating all organic foods, eating the wrong foods for one's metabolic type could cause as much havoc or more to their systems.

For example, Kelley knew that heavy meat-eating sympathetic dominant types often pushed their systems into over-drive creating symptoms from chronic indigestion to severe mood swings. Their parasympathetic systems eventually weakened, creating an acid-forming environment, turning off the pancreas and reducing the secretion of pancreatic enzymes that fight cancer. Sympathetic dominant types then tended to develop the hard tumors like those of the breast, colon, and lung.

Vegetarian parasympathetic types pushed their systems in the opposite extreme, fostering an alkaline environment with beginning symptoms of weakness and fatigue. They were prone to viral infections, such as Epstein Barr or herpes virus. As they deteriorated, they could develop poor concentration and memory, allergies, asthma, increased need for sleep, and even suicidal depression. They could become obese due to declining sympathetic and thyroid function and were prone to autoimmune diseases like lupus. Parasympathetics tended to develop the blood cancers like leukemia and lymphomas.

Balanced types generally get cancer with less frequency than the other types, but they could push their systems in either direction with accompanying symptoms. Taking the wrong supplements could also wreak havoc on a patient's system. For example, most women are told to start taking heavy doses of calcium during menopause. While such instructions might work out for a parasympathetic dominant woman, a sympathetic dominant woman taking such doses could find herself developing more symptoms of parasympathetic weakness.

Kelley, like Beard, thought that primitive trophoblastic cells—that we call stem cells—lie dormant in the body, there to repair damaged tissues or defective cells. As Beard had discovered decades earlier, Kelley had agreed that without the proper secretion of pancreatic enzymes, trophoblastic cells could grow uncontrollably and become cancer cells. Decades ago Kelley had predicted that the recommended low-fat, low-animal protein, high grain and leafy green diets would result in an increase in leukemias and lymphomas. And, as it worked out, with a push toward more alkalinizing vegetarian foods, parasympathetic types have begun to develop more cancer to the surprise of orthodox researchers.

Before he even interviewed his patient with colon cancer, Kelley knew that she was probably sympathetic dominant. He drew up a program for her, using care to determine her metabolic type. He added pancreatic enzymes to her daily routine, then worked to find the correct diet and supplements to bring her body back into balance. Kelley, too, was skeptical. Not of his program but of the patient. His program only worked with compliant patients. He thought she was sincere enough to be compliant. He was skeptical that she was a patient at all. In the end, he knew that he would probably never know if she were a plant or not.

In 1969, Dr. Kelley had authored a small book called *One Answer to Cancer*, detailing how cancer could be addressed through diet, nutritional supplements and detoxification. Kelley had hoped that the slim volume would help explain the program to his patients. He charged a minimal $1 per copy. To his surprise, the book was snatched up all over the country by people looking for an alternative to conventional cancer treatment.

The authorities also read the book. It was an age when the link between diet and disease was a complete disconnect in the minds of the medical model world, and in the consciousness of the public at large. Organic food was unheard of, grown and used only by hippies living off the land in communes, or by isolated ultra-conservative religious sects. Who could be bothered growing or searching for organic produce? You certainly wouldn't find it in the grocery stores or even health food stores, for that matter. Why bother with fresh produce in the first place when you could buy frozen vegetables in little plastic bags and boil them on the stove, ready to serve? No washing, chopping, or seasoning. Modern food science had made produce preparation and consumption easier and more efficient than ever.

The Texas State Board of Medical Examiners in conjunction with the Texas Attorney General's office began investigating Kelley, complete with undercover agents posing as patients. The Board concluded that Kelley was practicing medicine outside the scope of his dental license. They obtained a restraining order against Kelley, forbidding him from treating non-dental disease. In addition, the court ordered Kelley to stop selling his book *One Answer to Cancer* or any other publication explaining his approach toward disease. On the basis of the first amendment, Kelley appealed all the way to the United States Supreme Court where the ruling was upheld.

After that, Kelley made his patients sign a form stating that they were not receiving medical treatment but "nutritional counseling." This maneuver helped Kelley legally, but his reputation took another hit when the American Cancer Society put him on their list of controversial cancer therapies. They cited *One Answer to Cancer* and his legal troubles, but no one from the ACS interviewed Kelley personally, or evaluated his theory, treatment methods, or results with patients.

In 1976, on the heels of the Medical Examiners actions, the Texas State Board of Dental Examiners began their own investigation of Kelley. They pronounced him guilty of unprofessional conduct and suspended his dental license for five years. He halted his orthodontist practice but continued his nutritional counseling. In 1981, the Dental Board reversed their decision, giving Kelley the green light once again to practice dentistry in Texas.

Dr. Kelley's real problems didn't begin, however, until 1980 when the actor Steve McQueen called for a consultation. A tough guy anti-hero both in real life and in film, McQueen was a top box-office draw and the highest paid actor in the world in 1974. Born outside of Indianapolis to a stunt pilot in a flying circus and an alcoholic mother, McQueen was batted back and forth among relatives as a child. Finally, he was able to find some stability and refuge from an abusive step-father on a great-uncle's farm. His Uncle Claude gave McQueen a red tricycle on his fourth birthday, a gift that McQueen credited with sparking his life-long interest in racing motorcycles and cars.

Dyslexic and deaf in one ear, McQueen left the farm at age 14 and joined the circus and drifted into a life of petty crime and gang activity. He was arrested for stealing hubcaps, sent to Boys Republic, a school for troubled adolescent boys in Chino Hills, California. There, he mended his ways, became a leader, and eventually joined the Merchant Marines. After that stint, he worked in a brothel, as a carnival barker and in hard manual labor as a roughneck and lumberjack.

For three years (1947–50) he served in the United States Marine Corps, spending his share of days in the brig before he embraced military discipline and heroically pulled five other Marines from a tank before it broke into the sea in the Arctic. Out of the service, he headed to New York and began studying acting. He picked up money by racing motorcycles on the weekends, becoming an excellent racer, going home on Sunday evenings with his jeans pockets stuffed with dollar bills.

McQueen had a succession of bit acting parts, but made his Broadway debut in 1955 with *A Hatful of Rain*, a drama about a young man with a secret morphine addiction. On his way to stardom, McQueen's own addictions included marijuana, smoking, drinking, and racing. Nick Gonzalez, who later in his life ended up in possession of McQueen's medical records, knew the story better than anyone:

> *McQueen started to get sick around 1978–9. He went to his fancy Los Angeles doctors, and they kind of blew it off. No one took it seriously. You live too hard. You have to cut down smoking. Finally, he was so debilitated, he went to his doctors and said, "You've got to do something." Finally, the geniuses get the idea, "Let's do a chest x-ray" He's got tumors in both lungs. They worked him up*

and he's got metastatic mesothelioma. Mesothelioma is associated with asbestos exposure. Well, he was a motorcycle fanatic. In those days the pipes of motorcycles were lined with asbestos and he would work on his own motorcycles. He was a great mechanic. So, he was exposed to a huge amount of asbestos. In those days, and 35 years later today, mesothelioma is completely incurable once it spreads. The only hope is to get it early and do surgery. His doctors had completely missed the diagnosis, so by the time it was diagnosed, it was metastatic.

McQueen's cancer was too wide-spread for a surgical cure, so his doctors tried radiation to his chest without effect. The cancer continued to grow. In the spring of 1980, McQueen read a magazine article about Kelley and landed in his office in Winthrop, Washington, in the Cascade mountains. Kelley had purchased a small organic farm, and had retreated there after his run-ins with the Texas authorities.

McQueen sat in Kelley's Winthrop office, chin jutted forward, his piercing blue eyes meeting Kelley's own blue eyes. The two men held an uncomfortable silence, Kelley knowing that the odds were against both of them. McQueen's personal habits had never changed.

The actor left Winthrop, returning to Los Angeles, thinking Kelley's program too rigorous. Back in California, McQueen's Los Angeles doctors then gave McQueen immunotherapy even though there has never been a study that shows that it is effective with mesothelioma. It failed to help McQueen and he ended up with stage IV advancing cancer. McQueen again called Kelley, this time determined to follow through with the protocol.

Kelley made one fatal mistake with Steve McQueen. He took him on as a patient. He [McQueen] was too advanced and he was a reckless guy, still smoking, still drinking.

McQueen pleaded with Dr. Kelley. "Please take me on as a patient. I will do the program perfectly."

Kelley finally relented, but he didn't feel that McQueen was strong enough to do the therapy himself. So he said, 'I'll treat you, but you're too weak. You can't do this at home the way most of my patients do." He referred McQueen to Plaza Santa Maria Hospital about 50 miles south of San Diego in Mexico.

"Go down to that hospital and I'll direct them."

There the doctors, consulting with Dr. Kelley, were administering a form of the Kelley program. Kelley was not on the staff and had never resided at the hospital. In addition, the Mexican doctors were adding on a number of unconventional therapies that Kelley did not approve nor recommend—like Laetrile.

In July of 1980, McQueen entered the hospital in Mexico, though he never did follow the full nutritional program.

> *He wasn't 100% compliant. He still had the Häagen-Dazs ice cream, kind of smuggled it in from his friends, and cigarettes, but he did enough of it, so he started getting better.*

Kelley had tried hard to keep McQueen's identity and his whereabouts secret, but the *National Inquirer* tracked McQueen down, and broke the story of his unconventional therapy. Suddenly, Dr. Kelley and his program became front page news. Dr. Kelley landed on NBC's *Today Show* with Tom Brokaw with the network physician. The doctor couldn't see any numbers behind the treatment and dismissed it as "sheer quackery."

Brokaw questioned Kelley about the lack of data backing up his methods and Kelley agreed that it was a problem, that he had never had the support to put the program through a thorough clinical trial. Kelley offered to open up his files to the physician for his examination, but the offer was never accepted.

Then matters took a turn for the worse. McQueen flew to Ciudad Juárez, Chihuahua, Mexico for surgery.

> *And then one of his doctors in Mexico got the brilliant idea, let's open him up, because they think the tumor… He had a tumor in his abdomen as well as his chest. Let's take it out, I think it's a dead tumor.*
>
> *They do this surgery and the next day he dies of a pulmonary embolism which is a blood clot in the lungs. He did not die of mesothelioma, and in fact, the tumor was a dead tumor… Kelley used to have it in his office in formaldehyde. It had shrunk down*

from a huge tumor to nothing. It was dead. He didn't die from
mesothelioma. The way the media reports read, which I have, is
like Kelley took a gun and shot McQueen…his crazy quack doctor.
The true story has never been told.

After McQueen's death, the media and the medical establishment alike attacked Dr. Kelley, citing his licensure problems and blaming him for McQueen's death. The attacks focused on the idea that the actor should have had surgery sooner, implying that it was Kelley who created the delay. For example, an article in the *Los Angeles Times* quoted McQueen's surgeon, a heart and kidney specialist in the Santa Rosa Clinic in Juárez. "Somebody should have operated on this man as soon as the tumor had been discovered."

Faced with relentless phone calls, media attention and criticism, Kelley finally got on a train in Washington State, heading to Canada.

II

14

March 27, 1997. The afternoon sun, filmy and gray, filled the court-yard and slanted through the bank of windows behind the desk of Nick Gonzalez, M.D. in his medical practice on East 36th St., in New York City. Dr. Nick, as he was affectionately called, was finished with his patients for the day and he was working on writing up his notes in their charts. He was waiting. And worrying. Trying not to let the wait sideline his day, the intense drive he had to treat his patients and clear them of some of the worst cancers and other degenerative diseases that a human might experience: late stage colon, pancreatic, and metastatic breast cancers, diabetes, lupus, and Lyme.

Nick took up one of the charts and began to write with a long, bold cursive, the letters so oblique that the notes looked more like a musical score than a piece of medical text.

> *She returns here today with a CAT scan report from her local*
> *hospital finding no evidence of cancer cells in her brain.*

Resolved. Done. Another patient treated and cleared. Another tumor shrank down to nothing. Another miracle case. So many miracle patients have come through his office door over the last ten years of his practice, and so many of them have been successes.

Nick took a deep breath and exhaled with a frustration that carried the weight of his medical practice in its vapor. It was hard to believe that after all his successes, another case, the case of a woman with uterine cancer who came to him, then found a tumor on her spine, and returned to the conventional medical model for traditional treatment, was putting the whole Gonzalez program at risk.

The conventional medical model lost cancer patients all the time, Nick knew, and everyone thought it was sad. No premature death was ever embraced, but life went on, and more patients lined up at the door. More radiation was aimed at body parts targeted with black magic marker strokes. More multi-million-dollar research grants were allocated for yet another chemotherapy drug. But if I lose just one patient, Nick acknowledged, just one, I'm sued, taken to court, and vilified as a charlatan. And the most ironic thing about this lawsuit was that the woman was still alive, years later than was typical for a survivor of her kind of aggressive cancer.

And now this waiting was wasting precise time. Nick was trying to stay on task. He straightened himself in his chair, adjusted the Windsor knot in his red tie. He popped up, the usual sparkle in his blue eyes dulling. His 52-year-old face, his skin wrinkleless and so clear it was almost translucent, froze into a stony countenance. His movements matched his stature: quick, powerful and tight. He slid back into his chair. He grabbed another chart, writing, the buttons of his blue shirt cuff scraping against his massive oak desk. But this wasn't working. For the first time in his life he was having trouble concentrating.

Up again, he took off his dark blue suit jacket and laid it on the back of his desk chair. His suits, designed by Peter Raney and purchased ten at a time from a private Hong Kong tailor, were impeccably tailored specifically for him.

"I'm not a normal person," Nick once barked at his tailor, the man bent over on the floor placing pins in his pant leg to mark the cuff. "The cuff will be too long. Shorten it, please. I'm not a normal person."

Nick Gonzalez was not a normal person in height, nor a normal doctor in statue. His pinstriped suits reflected the pedigree of the framed Ivy League diplomas hanging on his office wall. 1970 Magna Cum Laude undergraduate degree in English literature from Brown University, and 1983 Cornell Medical School. His 1984 Vanderbilt University internship and 1984–86 immunological fellowship through Sloan Kettering cap his conventional medical model training.

He whisked into the kitchen and filled the watering can in the sink, heading back into his office to water his plants in the window. Overgrown with fronds that pressed against the glass like wild locks of hair, Nick poured the water into the pot and watched it filter through the soil, trickling into the saucer below. How long does this have to take? Normally, Nick watered his plants every Friday afternoon, a stress release that signaled the end of the week. Normally, he loved to watch and wait for the water to finally pool in the saucer. But not that day. It was not Friday and this water was moving way too slowly. He couldn't stand the wait.

He stared out the window at the courtyard below. One of the draws to this office was the garden that sat between his office and the back of the opposite apartment buildings. The many-floored buildings blocked the wind, and street noise, creating a green refuge in this urban landscape just blocks from the Empire State Building, a quiet and calm space.

In that moment, Nick was anything but calm.

Nick returned to the kitchen and passed his colleague Linda Isaacs, M.D. in the hallway. The two of them, once life partners in marriage, and now colleagues in this medical practice, nod, their lips drawn. Linda, round glasses resting on her round face, her light brown hair cut short, bangs swept across her forehead—all business—usually gave off an air of steady calmness, the yin to Nick's yang. But not at that moment. Nick and Linda did not speak but their eyes met for a fleeting second, a second that acknowledged that they were in a drama that could make or break their medical practices and all the research that they have done together over the last ten years. The phone call could either totally absolve Nick or ruin his livelihood.

Nick slipped back into his office and Linda to hers. Heads down, they tried to go back to work as if this weren't happening, as if they'd overblown the dark possibilities the phone call might bring. Nick took up his pen. Back to the patient notes he was anxious to complete.

> *Patient will continue her program and will be followed in our office and by her local physician.*

Linda stared into her computer screen, her breath slow and trembling. She entered some data, then checked and double checked her entry.

Down the hall, the long passageway connected the reception area and waiting room to the patients' bathroom, the examining rooms, the computer room, the two doctors' offices, and at the very end of the corridor, a kitchen that was a remnant of the apartment that once occupied this space. The kitchen had been an initial attraction for Nick. He had wanted the ability to cook his own meals in the office. He maintained the same, strict dietary measures as his own patients.

The office assistant, the one full-time staff person in the medical practice, stripped the paper off of the examining room table. She picked up the used gown of the last patient and deposited it in the laundry bin. She dropped the paper into the metal waste can and the lid closed with a thud. The sound echoed through the office, the only sound but for the background noise of the honking cars and trucks on Fifth Avenue outside the window where people hustled by on the sidewalk, stepping out onto the intersection in anticipation of the pedestrian green light. Patrons slipped in and out of the Morgan Library across the street on East 36th, then popped in the nearby Starbuck's for a latte. A siren blasted its alternating rhythm of warning.

In the waiting room of the medical office, a sparely but tastefully designed foyer complete with environmentally sensitive furnishings—wooden framed sofa and chairs with 100% cotton cushions—the office assistant straightened the pile of magazines on the coffee table: *National Geographic, Good Housekeeping*, and *Alternative Health*. She ran a dust cloth over the table, then tucked it away in the closet. The phone rang, and she rushed around the counter to answer it, but the call was only from a new patient.

"Please send your complete medical records to our office, then Dr. Gonzalez will review them and let you know if he can help you."

Every potential Gonzalez patient was first screened by Nick to see if they were a good fit for his program. "The Doctor of Last Resort," who saw some of the worst and most advanced cases of cancer and other degenerative diseases, refused children and patients in the last days of their lives. He turned away patients who could no longer eat. The program required swallowing large numbers of supplements each day. He shied away from patients without family support or whose well-meaning families were insistent on a more conventional treatment program. He also had subtle ways of determining a patient's mettle to carry out the demanding program.

"So what makes you think you can do this program?" the receptionist had asked me when I had called to make my first appointment. "Can you fly to New York every six months for a complete re-evaluation?"

Even though I knew the cost of the flights and lodging would strain my budget, I agreed.

"Can you take 100 to 150 supplements a day and stay on a strict diet?"

"I'm already on the diet," I replied.

"What diet? Dr. Gonzalez has 12 different diets with 99 variations. How do you know which diet you'll be on?"

"Aren't all the diets organic? I'm already on a totally organic diet. I grow all my own food so that I can afford to eat organically. I can do any diet that is thrown at me."

I was accepted, had the requested blood work drawn, snipped off a lock of my hair near the nape of my neck and sent it to the office in a small envelope. I didn't have cancer, but I had arrived in New York so weak from damage to my central nervous system from a bad car accident, and hemorrhaging from fibroid tumors, that I could barely stand up. I had to lean into the arm of a friend on the way to the office building. But I mustered the strength to press the buzzer to get through the heavy glass door on the front of the building. Then it took an elevator ride and another buzzer to get into the office itself.

There I embarked on a journey that not only cleared up most of my medical problems but changed my whole view of what a healthy human being could and should be. In an attempt to balance the metabolism of the body and create greater resilience to disease, the program treated disease with diet, supplements and detoxification.

The supplements, taken at each meal, include a battery of vitamins, minerals, and glandulars, all specifically designed for each individual patient and his or her needs. Digestive enzymes and probiotics for digestion, herbs to combat viruses, and essential fatty acids for overall health. Pancreatic enzymes were the chief cancer and inflammation-fighting tool.

"Line up rows of Dixie cups on a table and distribute your pills for the month," Nick had instructed me. "Then pour them into little pouches like this." He held up a 3 x7 plastic bag. He handed me my complete program written on a sheet of paper complete with the phone number and address of the company in California from whom to buy the supplements and the distributor of the herbal company that he used.

I was classified as a moderate carnivore with instructions to eat an 8-ounce portion of fish or poultry and an 8-ounce portion of red meat, either beef or lamb, once a day. My diet was heavy in root vegetables and light in leafy greens. Nuts, seeds, butter and olive oil were allowed, but no processed food, no sugar, white flour, white pasta and noodles, nor alcohol. All the food had to be organic, raised without hormones, antibiotics, pesticides and herbicides. At the time I started the program, in my Midwestern home, organic food couldn't be found in commercial grocery stores. It was even scarce in food co-ops and health food stores.

I was fine with a diet that emphasized protein and fat. I had given up processed food, sugar, caffeine and alcohol years before I began the Gonzalez Protocol. The third leg of the protocol—detoxification—was what gave me pause. Not for the procedures themselves, but for the time involved in administering them.

Other potential patients can't get by the procedures. Local physicians and patient families often disparaged the detoxification part of the program, dismissing it as "gross" or "ridiculous." I was instructed to do two coffee enemas in the morning and one in the afternoon between two and five p.m.

"You do them every day, seven days a week. You do these on the weekends. You do these on your birthday and on Christmas." Nick said. "You don't skip. You don't cheat."

When they discovered this part of the program, many potential patients turned away, never making the initial appointment. Or, some came for the initial office visit which stretched over two days, then they never followed through with the instructions. The Gonzalez Protocol was very different from other medical care. With this treatment you weren't given an I.V. or a drug. You didn't have surgery in a hospital or clinic. In the Gonzalez Protocol, the patient self-administered the treatment in the privacy of his or her own home. The patient had to create and adhere to the schedule without prompting.

"In my program you don't sit in a recliner in a clinic, watch T.V., stick out your arm, get chemotherapy, then have a dish of ice cream on the way out of the hospital." Nick said.

For starters, there was no ice cream allowed on any of the diets in the Gonzalez Protocol. Strict compliance was essential. In addition to the enemas, there was an array of other detoxification techniques required of patients. Liver and colon cleanses, purges, skin brushing, castor oil packs, nasal irrigation, Epsom salt or apple cider vinegar baths all fill in the blank spaces of one's day.

The blank space of this day stretched out before Nick and his staff. The woman with the uterine cancer had eventually gone blind. The patient's husband had blamed Nick and sued, purporting that if she hadn't wasted her time with Nick's program, she could have been cured with chemotherapy. The past few years had been a long, grinding slug through the steps of a lawsuit: the paperwork, the depositions and discovery. Finally, the case had been tried in court where the plaintiff's lawyer painted a picture of Nick as an off-the-wall doctor merely out to rip off dying patients.

On the other hand, Nick felt his own lawyer, supplied by his medical malpractice insurance company, didn't present his case well to the jury. His lawyer hadn't even explained the program, how it worked, the past successes that Nick had had. The lawyer hadn't emphasized the pathologist's report that revealed that, in the end, the growth that had been removed from the woman's spine was necrotic debris, or dead tissue, not a cancerous tumor.

Instead, the plaintiff's lawyer presented Nick on the far edge of the kookiest form of alternative medicine. To the contrary, Nick thought of himself as an Ivy League-trained doctor who was part of the establishment. He steered away from all fads and untried techniques the alternative world had to offer, from crystals to prescribing vegetarian diets for all. He studied every new idea that came along with a deep skepticism. He didn't even think of himself as a practitioner of alternative medicine, but rather, as a physician who offered a new paradigm, a medical treatment with a foundation in exquisitely researched bio-chemistry.

The jury ended up knowing nothing about Nick or the program. They knew nothing about Nick's own disciplined drive and how he had harnessed it to study medicine, dedicating himself to curing cancer. The jury knew nothing of Beard, Pottenger, Price, or Kelley. The jury knew nothing of Nick's determination to carry forward Kelley's work, improve upon it, and perfect the enzyme formulations. They knew nothing of Nick's constant study, the hours he spent keeping up on the latest journal articles and research, the evenings spent returning patient phone calls at no charge.

Nick had set up practice in New York City, in the country that he had loved. He hadn't moved back to Mexico to avoid conflicts with the American medical establishment. His goal had always been straight forward and scientific. He had first presented a selection of his cases to the National Cancer Institute in 1993, and from there with funding from Nestlé Company, he and Dr. Isaacs were running a small pilot study. Nick was anxious to eventually get his data into print. And he was even more anxious to test his theory through a clinical trial run through the conventional medical model.

If he lost the malpractice case, Nick knew it could be for a large amount of money, certainly more money than he had in the bank, perhaps more money than his malpractice insurance would cover. But more than the worry about the money was the thought of the damage to his reputation and what might become of the protocol that he had spent most of his adult life developing. At this point, he had no spouse or children. He had no other passions or responsibilities besides the heavy weight of his practice.

For exercise, Nick walked to work every day from his Manhattan apartment, then saw patients and conducted research, answering calls well into the evening hours. He was back again on the weekends, this time without his suit jacket and tie. He padded around the office in his stocking feet on Saturday and Sunday, writing medical articles and books, and preparing for the week's patient load. At night at home in his apartment, he read the latest medical articles. He had an old T.V. with rabbit ears that pulled in only the local channels. He never went to a movie or on vacation. He lectured throughout the world about his protocol. That was travel enough. When he was away, he couldn't wait to return to New York and get back to work.

And now all he had to do was wait. He eyed his well-worn Bible on his bookshelf. His thoughts turned to theologians that he has read and studied.

> *Pray God to send a few men with what the Americans call "Grit"*
> *in them; men who when they know a thing to be right, will not*
> *turn away, or turn aside, or stop; men who will persevere all the*
> *more because there are difficulties to meet or foes to encounter…*
> *…who, the more they are thrust into the fire, the hotter they*
> *become; who, just like the bow, the farther the string is drawn, the*
> *more powerfully will it send forth its arrows.*

Nick remembered his little lead toy soldiers that he used to collect and keep in their original boxes wrapped in tissue paper. Revolutionary war soldiers, Green Mountain Boys, Civil War rebels, and many more. He'd saved them through the years since he was young, taking them out of their wrappers from time to time, admiring their sturdy demeanors and the fierce fighting spirit they embodied. He imagined fingering the soldiers in his hands, grasping the sheer sturdiness of their bodies. He always admired the way they held themselves—upright, with dignity, their rifles resting upon their shoulders, their bows and arrows drawn.

"The more they are trodden upon, the more mighty will they become in the cause of truth against error," he repeated to himself and he waited, waited for the call from his lawyer with the jury's verdict.

15

1981. Dr. Kelley rode the train through the Canadian Rockies, happy to be able to lean back in the seat and be alone with his thoughts. What a relief. The train ride, with the meditative rhythm of the wheels chugging along on the tracks, was the perfect escape. Here in the observation car, engulfed in its banks of wide windows, he could abandon himself to the landscape. There were no telephones ringing, no mail to answer, no reporters banging at his door. No one threatening to sue him or throw him in jail. He glanced out the window at the craggy limestone and shale rock, the snow-covered mountain peaks, the thick forests, and serene turquoise lakes.

If only his mind could capture this serenity. He had been deeply wounded by all the pushback he had received about his program—from the actions of the Texas State Medical Board, to the negative publicity he'd received about Steve McQueen. He was an orthodontist who found a way to treat his own cancer. He wanted to fix teeth, not patients' terminal tumors, but the patients kept coming and he applied the best of his scientific knowledge to help them heal.

He wasn't out to make millions off of his program. He wasn't happy about his lone wolf status in the medical world and resented being called a quack. He was a scientist and wanted other scientists to investigate his methodology, verify it or prove him wrong. He wanted vigorous testing of his theories and discoveries. Not notoriety. He wanted a clinical trial of his program. Where to go to have that done? He didn't have a famous clinic or a university credential after his name. How would someone like him get funding for a clinical trial?

He knew that his program worked, matching diet with a patient's biochemistry. He knew that every patient had a unique set of variables to address. He believed that his different metabolic types were the end product of an ecologic selection process. Each metabolic type developed biologically suited to the food supply in the native region of their ancestors.

Kelley thought, for example, that sympathetic dominants had a genetic make-up that mirrored cultures that lived closer to the Mediterranean: Italy, Greece, Spain, the Middle East, Northern Africa. The area, known as the Fertile Crescent of the Tigris and Euphrates Rivers, was the seat of agriculture. With its mild climate, it was able to produce an abundance of grains, fruits, vegetables, dairy products from goats, sheep and cattle. Fish and seafood were available in the large rivers and the Mediterranean Sea.

The parasympathetic dominants were genetically more northern people, living in colder climates, depending on meat, fish, and fat for their food. They lived in regions with short or even non-existent growing seasons where vegetables were scarce, and dairy was limited. Some of these peoples, like the Inuit in Alaska, thrived for generations on a nearly complete meat-eating diet without any plant food.

The balanced types, falling somewhere between the sympathetics and parasympathetics, lived in middle latitude regions of the continents with four seasons and a diversity of flora and fauna. These types had a wide range of food to chose from, including meat, fish, grains, nuts, seeds, dairy, and an array of fruits and vegetables.

Whatever the type, Kelley knew that to keep his patients healthy, he had to balance their acid/base or pH. He thought that vegetarian diets were alkalinizing and helped push his sympathetics whose tissues and organs existed in an acid environment, toward a more neutral balance. Kelley thought that a meat diet was acid forming, and that it helped push his parasympathetics, whose tissues and organs existed in an alkaline environment, more toward a neutral balance. Acid/base balance and healing through the adjustment of diet, of course, was beyond the realm of the Western medicine model, yet it had had a long and interesting history in both Eastern and Western civilization.

Before I connected with Dr. Gonzalez, I had spent several years attempting to address my problems with alternative therapies. I had sought treatment with acupuncture and had soon learned that a good acupuncturist is not only skilled at placing needles along well-mapped meridians in the body, but he or she is also a skilled herbalist and dietician. An acupuncturist will determine a patient's deficiencies and excesses, or their "yin" and "yang" imbalances, through a thorough physical exam, a medical history and a "reading of the pulses." I remember my acupuncturist sitting next to me for several minutes in silence, holding my wrist, then pronouncing, "Too yin in the body." To generate more yang in my system, the acupuncturist had prescribed eating more meat, especially in the morning.

For thousands of years Chinese medicine has recognized the yin/yang properties of foods that correspond closely with the acid/alkaline divisions. Detailed lists of "yang," "warm" or "hot" foods, what modern day terminology might call "acid," include: pork, chicken, turkey, lamb, duck, and nuts. Detailed lists of "yin," "cold" and "cool" foods, what modern day terminology might call "alkaline" include: banana, watermelon, Bok Choi, turnips, celery, asparagus, grapefruit, zucchini, snow peas, oranges, cherries and mushrooms.

Yet, the Chinese went beyond merely intuitively balancing pH. Every placement of an acupuncture needle and every prescribed food or herb was based on a complex spiritual foundation. Chinese medicine draws its belief system from Buddhism, Confucianism and Taoism, with the latter the most influential. In Chinese medicine Qi or Chi is the fundamental substance of the universe. Qi, a concept that's hard to describe in the western mindset, can best be defined as "energy," or "life force." Taoism doesn't conjure a complex creation myth like the one found in genesis in the Judeo-Christian tradition. Taoism doesn't conceptualize the beginning of time with setting, characters, and conflict. Rather, Taoism simply states that "From nothing came something." Out of the Void came Qi.

All of the universe, then, is composed of Qi, including human beings. We are all interconnected with each other and with the natural world. The universe is ever-changing but there are natural laws at work that create order and harmony. When we are in harmony with these natural laws of the universe, we are in a true state of health. The universe can be further divided into five elements: water, wood, fire, earth, and metal. The five elements encompass everything from the seasons and weather, to emotions, color, and taste to foods and the organs of the body. For example, the element of water includes: winter, cold, bladder, kidneys, ears, bone, fear, black and salty. In contrast, the element of fire includes: summer, heat, small intestines, heart, tongue, blood vessels, joy/shock, red and bitter.

The first time I had acupuncture, I lay on a table draped with a white sheet. Florescent lights glared overhead, and the smell of a sweet burning herb drifted through the air. My acupuncturist stood over me with needles in his hand and alcohol swabs ready at his side. First, he placed a needle in my hand and told me that we would work on clearing my allergies, then go on to deeper issues. I was perplexed. A needle in my hand would clear my nose? But when I glanced at the acupuncture chart on the wall, I gained a better understanding of the Chinese system.

"Qi flows through the body in channels or meridians," my acupuncturist explained.

There are fourteen main meridians in the body composed of a constellation of acupuncture points. Twelve meridians flow through an organ classified as either yin or yang. For example, the yin, metal lung meridian starts at the tip of the thumb, runs through the palm and wrist, up to the elbow, up the arm to the shoulder. From the shoulder, the channel rises to the throat, then descends through the lungs to the large intestines.

My acupuncturist used diet and herbs to compliment the yin/yang balance he was attempting to achieve through the stimulation of the needles along the meridians. But yin/yang categories of foods seemed so arbitrary to me at first. I spent several dizzying days pouring over lists of Chinese food charts trying to get the drift of the system. The more I studied, the more I realized that dietary healing and food classification weren't unique to the Chinese culture. It was an ancient, wide-spread practice throughout the globe.

*   *   *   *   *

"I have friends who don't have cancer or autoimmune diseases, just pesky symptoms that they want to address," I once had told Dr. Gonzalez during one of my office visits. "They aren't sick enough to see you, but they still need help. Where should they go?"

"They might try Ayurvedic medicine," he said. "At least it understands metabolic typing."

Ayurvedic medicine, practiced in India for the last 4,000 years, is also based on a five-element theory and was influenced not only by the compassionate-wisdom path of Shakyamuni Buddha (550 B.C.E.) and the Medicine Buddha but by the Silk-Road interchange with Indian-Chinese-Tibetn-Sri-Lankan-Burmese-Thai Buddhist monks and itinerant Chinese Taoist priests. In the Ayurvedic system everything in the universe, including human beings, is made up of Space or Akasha, Air or Vayu, Fire or Tejas, Water or Ap, and Earth, or Prithvi. Human beings acquire a soul or spirit which, with everything else in the universe, is an expression of the Creative Principle which is One. Like the Chinese, the Indian system acknowledges an "energy" or "life force" that circulates throughout all creation. The Indians call this energy *"prana."*

In Indian Ayurvedic medicine, three elements, *vata, pitta,* and *kapha,* control the balance of the human body. Although ancient Ayurvedic medicine doesn't discuss pH or hydrogen ions, it has a clear sense of reaching acid/alkaline balance through food selection. Ayurvedic medicine assumes that everyone is born with a particular constitution or *prakruti* that is fixed for life. Your *prakruti* is a specific combination of three *doshas: vata, pitta, and kapha* and their balance influences health and personality. The doshas, in turn, are composed of the five elements. *Vata* contains Space (*Akasha*) and Air (*Vayu*); *pitta* contains Fire (*Tejas*) and Water (*Ap*); and *kapha* contains Water (*Ap)* and Earth (*Prithvi*).

The five elements control the physical structure while the three doshas govern the physiology of the human body. For example, *vata* keeps the body moving physically (its limbs and body parts) and mentally (its thoughts, feelings, and emotions). *Pitta* helps with the digestion of nutrients and the transformation of thoughts, feelings and emotions into understanding, comprehension and perception. *Kapha* helps provide the body with structure, stability and strength—both physically and mentally.

All three doshas are present in humans, but usually one or two dominate. A *vata* person is often slender with prominent features and cool, dry skin with a personality that is unpredictable, energetic, enthusiastic, impulsive. A *pitta* type usually has a medium build with an intelligent, passionate, and articulate personality to match. A *kapha* type is heavier set and is more often loving, compassionate, affectionate, tolerant and forgiving.

If the doshas go out of balance, then disease can set in. Ayurvedic medicine attempts to rebalance your prakruti and bring the doshas back into harmony. Unlike western medicine, Chinese medicine and Indian medicine are not one-size fits all propositions. If a hundred patients present with pain, you don't just give them all the same painkiller. Instead, the Ayurvedic practitioner tries to adjust the body so that it will correct the problem itself. Each patient could have an entirely different source of pain, or an entirely different kind of imbalance.

Vata imbalances can produce hyperactivity, restlessness, anxiety, insecurity, fear, doubt, nervousness, insomnia, dizziness or lack of feeling grounded. Physically, the patient may be plagued with symptoms like constipation, bloating, abdominal distension, gas, dehydration and emaciation. Disturbed *pitta* may manifest as anger, rage, irritability, frustration, impatience, jealousy, violence, and critical and judgmental behaviors. Physical symptoms include diarrhea, nausea, hives, rash, urticaria, profuse perspiration and/or bleeding, inflammation, and infection. Unbalanced *kapha* symptoms include attachment, greed and depression problems as well as congestion, weight gain, shortness of breath, water retention, edema, tumors, fibroids and lumps.

Each patient could also have a different combination of aggravating factors that produce imbalance including interior influences of diet, lifestyle, emotions, exercise and more exterior influences of the change of seasons, weather and trauma. But Ayurvedic medicine looks toward diet both as the main cause of disease and the primary method of treatment. Ayurvedic medicine not only recommends dietary changes to patients, but also uses a pharmacy of thousands of herbs to correct imbalances.

An Ayurveda practitioner sits down with a patient and works out an individual diet and herbal regimen. Ayurvedic medicine classifies foods not as *yin* or *yang,* but with similar qualities of cool or warm, light or heavy, or dry or unctuous. The Indian system also attends to the *rasa,* or taste, of the food—sweet, sour, bitter, salty, pungent and astringent.

For example, the *vata* types need warm, cooked foods like soups with sweet, sour, and salty tastes. In general, balancing foods for *vata* types include: sweet fruits like apricots, bananas, grapes, plums and strawberries; cooked vegetables like asparagus, green beans and potatoes; oats, wheat and rice; almonds, hazelnuts and tofu; occasional beef, and the white meat of turkey and chicken; garlic, ginger, spearmint and turmeric; cow and goat milk, cheese and yogurt.

In contrast, pitta types need to cool down their fiery natures with sweet, bitter and astringent tastes. Balancing foods for pitta types include: sweet, juicy fruits, sweet rice pudding, coconut and coconut juice; vegetables like carrots, asparagus, bitter leafy greens, broccoli and cauliflower. Pitta types should avoid nightshade vegetables like tomatoes, eggplant and peppers as well as hot spices. Grains like Basmati rice, wheat, and oats are recommended.

Like vata types, kapha types need warm foods to balance their sweet, cold qualities. Kapha's should eat foods with pungent, bitter, astringent tastes and veer away from too much salty, sweet or sour food. Kapha types need dry foods in their diets like cereal and rice cakes to counter the watery element of their constitutions and they need to eat light, warming foods including: clear vegetable soups, stews with beans and diced vegetables like carrots, asparagus, okra, bitter leafy greens and broccoli, cauliflower and Brussels sprouts. Recommended grains and spices include: barley, buckwheat, millet and couscous; turmeric, cumin, coriander, cayenne, black pepper and dried ginger.

*   *   *   *   *

Dr. Kelley had worked out similar food regimens for his metabolic types, but was there any history to his dietary program in Western civilization beyond the Pottengers? Did ancient Western civilization connect food and healing? Enter the Greek physician Hippocrates (c. 460–380 B.C.E.), the "father of medicine," a philosopher who wanted to move away from the superstitious healing of the time toward a more rational approach toward medicine. Hippocrates studied in Egypt, a region advanced in the medical arts, having made great strides in such areas as dentistry and pharmacology.

Hippocrates drew on this background to set up more scientific guidelines for the clinical practice of medicine and many of his ideas are still very much in use today. To reach a diagnosis, Hippocrates conducted an extensive interview with the patient, taking a case history. He performed a physical exam and also made his own clinical observations. He kept confidential records.

Hippocates based the treatment of his patients on his theory of the four humors. Humors were body fluids, each attached to an element and a season of the year: black bile (earth, autumn, cold and dry), blood (air, spring, hot and moist), yellow bile (fire, summer, hot and dry), and phlegm (water, winter, cold and moist). Hippocrates' idea of the four elements is linked to Empedocles (c. 490–430 B.C.E.), a philosopher and poet from the Greek colony of Sicily. In addition to postulating the four elements of the cosmos, Empedocles wrote that Love (*philia*) explained the attraction of different forms of matter and that Strife (*neikos*) explained their separation.

In the view of Hippocrates the humors accounted for both physiological and personality types. Black bile types tended to be melancholic. Blood types were sanguine, lively with lots of energy. They enjoyed life and the arts. Yellow bile, or choleric types, often displayed an angry, fiery temperament. Phlegmatic types often were lethargic with dull personalities. Patients usually had a dominant humor, and matching body structure, but all patients were made up of all the elements and an imbalance of any of these could tip the patient toward symptoms. For example, if the patient contained too much earth, she could become severely depressed. If a patient contained too much yellow bile, he could become violent.

"Nature heals; the physician is only nature's assistant," Hippocrates said. When treating a patient, Hippocrates initially prescribed diet, rest, recreation and exercise, fresh air, and a change of climate to balance the humors. He concocted many different soups and broths to cure disease. For instance, he treated tuberculosis with milk. He used a "law of opposites" approach. A high fever was a symptom of an imbalance of the hot, dry yellow bile humor. For this condition, Hippocrates hoped to elicit the opposite humor, phlegm, and prescribed cold baths and cold, moist foods. Hippocrates used herbs as his next line of defense, often inducing vomiting and diarrhea to purge the patient of illness. For Hippocrates, healing took place from within, the body righting itself. He told his students that disease is not only *pathos,* or suffering, but *ponos,* or toil, or the urgency of the body to work to regain its natural state of health.

Hippocrates is hailed as the founder of modern medicine. The theory of the four humours was very similar to the Chinese theory of balancing the two polarities or the Indian theory of balancing the three doshas. Hippocrates moved medicine away from sacrifices, charms and chants. He did not explicitly connect healing with a unifying life force of the universe, but in substance, his theory echoed those of the Chinese and the Indians.

Galen of Peragmon (129–200 A.D.) lived in modern day Turkey, picked up Hippocrates' theories, and helped spread them throughout much of the Western world. He worked as a physician in the gladiator school where he became fascinated with the anatomy revealed by open wounds. He called them "the windows of the body." By 162 A.D. he lived in Rome as a physician to the royal court of Marcus Aurelius. He dissected many animals including the pig, which he considered closest to the human, and made a large contribution to the study of anatomy. Galen also contributed to herbal medicine. He introduced several remedies into Western medicine including willow bark which contains salicin, the phytotherapeutic precursor of aspirin, and laudanum, an opium tincture used as an anesthetic.

Galen wrote of the four humours in his book *On the Elements According to Hippocrates* and based his own theories on these principles. Galen invited spirituality back into the realm of medicine and healing with foods. He postulated that all of life came to being through a purposeful creator. For Galen, the fundamental principle of life was *pneuma,* or "air" or "breath" and *pneuma* was connected to the soul.

Most of Galen's writings were first translated to the Syriac language by Nestorian monks in the University of Gondishapur, Persia. Medieval Islamic medicine then drew on the works of the Greeks and Galen's ideas of the humours. The Muslims carried Galen's ideas into Europe. By the twelfth century Constantius Africanus had translated many classical texts from Arabic to Latin and the Salerno School of medicine in Italy was using the theory of humours.

Salerno became the parent to the other great medical schools in Montpellier, Paris, Bologna, and Padua. John of Gaddesden, Chaucer's model for "doctour of physick" in *The Canterbury Tales* was an English student at Montpellier. His belief in the humours is obvious from these lines:

> Well could he guess the ascending of the star
> Wherein his patient's fortunes settled were.
> He knew the course of every malady,
> Were it of cold or heat or moist or dry.

A good medieval European cook was expected to be schooled in the humours. A cook knew how to balance the ingredients in a dish or a meal to create harmony. A good cook would also know the individual temperaments of food and different cooking techniques. Maino De Mainer, a Milanese writer of the 1330s, set down many of the food practices of his day. Milk was the perfect food and was often fed to invalids. Recipes for the sick often included dishes based on milk, chicken and rice, a clear attempt to balance the humours. Another common balanced dish was sweet and sour rabbit. In this dish, the dry carrots balanced the moist onions, and the sugar balanced the taste of the vinegar.

Cooking techniques reflected the humours. Roasting warmed and moved food toward the fire element while boiling moistened and moved the food toward the air element. Baking fell somewhere in between. Moist meats like pork were roasted while dry meats like beef were boiled. Frying fish helped them to dry out and boiling root vegetables helped to moisten their earthy, dry nature. Wet fruit could be eaten raw but with aged cheese and wine for balance.

Eating lots of meat was warming and led to irritable temperaments that were considered sinful and harmful to the soul by the Medieval Church. So the Church established meatless fast days in Lent and other special occasions designed to improve the morals of the people. During those days, the Church encouraged its followers to eat cooler foods like fish, and so hoped for a populace with more mellow and saintly personalities. In 1256 Ralph of Lenham wrote a treatise on fasting: "We must fast in order to pray to God that he temper that humour that we have within us, that temperament which most closely resembles each season and its temperament."

*   *   *   *   *

Dr. Kelley adjusted his train seat, looked at the majesty surrounding him outside the window, and prayed to God. Kelley was still a religious man and the solitude he found on the train was welcome, opening him to embrace a higher power, the only thing at this point in his life that made sense, the only thing that provided any firm grounding in reality. Kelley prayed that he would have the temperment to follow through with his healing activities, to find someone in the scientific world who would listen to him and put him to the test. He knew he had the history of healing behind him, but who was going to pay attention now to thousands of years of research and practice by the Chinese and Indians? Who cared about Hippocates, Salerno, Galen or any of the rest of it? Kelley decided to keep riding, riding and riding across Canada, then drop down to New York City where surely he could find some support.

16

Nick Gonzalez zigzagged all over New York City to interview top scientists for his assignments for Time, Inc. He rode trains, rented cars, and caught airplane flights to travel throughout the United States to track down stories about medical researchers. His editor was pleased with his articles and kept sending Nick back to do more scientific writing. Gradually, Nick began to see that good, solid scientific research could be as imaginative as the arts. He became enchanted by the scientists he met, the innovative work that they did, and the kind of creative leaps they made in their minds.

In 1976, a lengthy piece that Nick wrote on cancer prevention brought him into contact with eminent researchers like the cardiologist and nutritionist Robert Atkins who would later become known for his low carbohydrate diet. He interviewed Ernst Wynder, the founding editor of *Preventive Medicine*, who was one of the first physicians to establish the connection between smoking and lung cancer. An interview with the Noble Prize winner Linus Pauling, founder of the Linus Pauling Institute, who was considered a father of quantum chemistry and molecular biology, at Stanford University changed Nick's career.

Nick arrived on campus and made his way past the well-groomed tennis courts where, day and night, a ball was hurtling its way over the net. Back and forth, back and forth, the games were played. Love, love, the beginning score. Then the drive, skill, and determination of the players kicked in, a tense volleying played out, until finally there was a winner.

In his office in the Chemistry Department, Pauling swiveled around in his desk chair to greet Nick. Pauling was thin, impeccably dressed in a three-piece suit, with brushy eyebrows accenting his balding head and the fringe of thick, wiry hair sticking out from around his ears. Piles of papers were scattered all over his desk, engulfing his landline phone and its rows of buttons to direct calls hither and yon throughout the university. Books and boxes were piled on top of metal filing cabinets, and a blackboard behind him was filled with drawings and mathematical calculations.

Pauling, who had won the Nobel Peace Prize in 1962 for his protest against the Vietnam War, had stirred up tension in the scientific community for his activism. No stranger to controversy, he again received pressure when he had become interested in the use of vitamins and nutrition. He named the field of orthomolecular medicine, and many in the scientific community thought he had gone off the rails with his interest in the use of vitamins. He had been making headlines for several years with his controversial recommendations for taking large doses of vitamin C to head off the common cold. Even more eyebrows were raised when he advocated the use of vitamin C in the treatment of cancer.

But Nick pulled up an office chair and wanted to hear Pauling's take on preventative medicine. Nick peppered Pauling with deep, probing questions that impressed the renowned scientist who couldn't believe that Nick had not had more formal scientific training. They talked in depth about vitamins, nutrition, and the state of human health. They explored larger questions of the food system, ecology, the workings of the universe.

"You don't have a science degree?" Pauling asked.

"No, I have a degree in English literature."

"You haven't been to medical school?"

"I thought about it once, but decided to become a writer."

"Well, you need to go to medical school."

"Really?"

"You're asking some of the best questions I've ever been asked, more sophisticated than some of my Nobel Prize winning colleagues. You need to become a doctor and fully use your talents and intellect."

Nick thought Pauling's suggestion a joke. Nick had turned that corner once, and he was now firmly established in his journalism career. He was making good progress on his novel, too. Why would he throw that all away to go to medical school to join the nerds? But when he left Pauling's office, retracing his steps and walking back across campus near the tennis courts, his old career confusion resurrected itself. The incessant whack and bounce of the tennis ball echoed his thoughts. Keep going in journalism, a job that he so enjoyed? Go to medical school and challenge himself further? Love, love.

He adored his artsy, creative life. He was having a blast writing, interviewing, and traveling. But these researchers that he had met were doing the most exciting work he'd ever imagined. He thought his ideal challenge would be a medical research career. He could take his investigative journalism skills and apply them to scientific research. Maybe he could, after all, find the cure for cancer.

Nick kept in touch with Pauling, and Atkins, and many of his other interviewees, and soon there was a whole chorus of voices urging him on toward medical school. Nick ran the idea over and over in his mind, then discussed it with his father who was supportive of this career change. At last, Nick decided that he would go to medical school. He would take his study methods, all the drive and aggression that he had developed on the baseball field and throw himself into medicine.

He only had one problem. He needed more pre-med courses in the sciences. Luckily, he found a pre-med program at Columbia University that was geared toward students just like him, offering a science intensive. Nick hadn't saved any money during his journalism days, so William and Marie offered to help pay his tuition.

"And while you're in school, you can move back home and live here," Marie said.

In 1976, after a seven-year career in journalism, Nick closed down his Manhattan apartment, left his writing desk, novel, and Hemingway and Durrell behind, never reading another word of fiction. He moved back to his parents' Tudor-style house on 45th St. in Flushing, setting up his desk just where it had been in high school, and enrolled in Columbia University. His friends in the arts and journalism worlds thought that he had lost his mind. They couldn't believe that he was throwing away such a young, bright journalist career. He was a rising star.

The rising star didn't listen. Instead, he caught one subway every morning in Flushing, and headed on under the East River into Times Square in Manhattan where he caught another subway, transporting him on up to Columbia University. Over an hour commute each way, he used the time to study his organic chemistry, anatomy and physiology, and microbiology—the courses that most pre-med students dreaded. Nick's friends thought that he would hate his classes and eventually drop out. Instead, he found the classes fun and engrossing. With his study habits in gear—going over and over the material until he had it down cold—he aced all his courses.

Two years at Columbia, zipping back and forth on the subway, and studying in his old boyhood room, and then it was time to apply to medical school. Nick sent out applications and was accepted to all the best places including Columbia, Harvard, Stanford, Yale, and Johns Hopkins. But when he opened the acceptance letter from Cornell, it didn't take him but five minutes to decide that that was where he wanted to go. Cornell was the home of Sloan Kettering, the premier cancer research institute in the country. Nick had his heart set on doing cancer research with the director, Dr. Robert Good.

Dr. Robert Good, known as "The Father of Immunology" was one of the best known and most widely published physicians and scientists in the United States. Raised and educated in Minnesota, he received both his M.D and Ph.D. at the age of twenty-five at the University of Minnesota. A pediatrician, micro-biologist, and pathologist, he was one of the early pioneers of the bone marrow transplant. He documented the importance of the thymus gland and the role of tonsils, doing much to halt their automatic removal during childhood. He also had an interest in nutrition and had studied the effects of nutrition on cancer.

Dr. Good was an impressive figure at the Cornell-Sloan Kettering medical complex. He was a tall man, I would guess at least 6'3", and built like a football player. He walked with braces on both legs, as a result of an attack of Guillain-Barre syndrome he had suffered during medical school in the early 1940's. Guillain-Barre is a virus illness that like polio attacks the motor nerves that control muscle function. However, Dr. Good was famous for never letting his damaged legs and braces slow him down. He used to tear down the corridors of Cornell and Memorial Sloan Kettering, with the inevitable group of fellows and residents in white coats scurrying to keep up with him, their books and pens flying as Good crashed through swinging doors. He walked always with great determination and purpose, whether going to visit some six-year-old with a brain tumor, or a member of the Rockefeller family to discuss Sloan Kettering finances.

Good had been the chair of the department of pathology at the University of Minnesota for years before coming to Cornell University in 1973 where he became chief scientist, president and director of the Sloan Kettering Institute for Cancer Research in New York City.

This position allowed him to continue his study into the body's defenses against the invasion of foreign organisms, including cancer.

Good trained thousands of students and they worked together on his research. In March of 1973 his head shot graced the cover of *Time Magazine* with the headline: *Toward Control of Cancer, Immunologist Robert Good.* Radio and TV appearances followed. If a physician could be a popular celebrity, Dr. Robert A. Good took on the role. Yet his fame didn't go to his head. A driven but caring and charismatic man, his students and colleagues flocked to him.

Then shortly after Dr. Good's *Time Magazine* cover story, he became the center of a well-known scandal, perhaps the most sensational medical scandal of the twentieth century, which tarnished his reputation for the rest of his life. Good had been nominated three times for the Nobel Prize, and the scandal killed his chances of ever winning the award.

In 1974 Good had supported a young physician researcher named Dr. William T. Summerlin who claimed to have shown success in transplantation immunology. He said he had uncovered a method to allow transplantation of tissues and organs between genetically unrelated animals. Right in Dr. Good's office, Summerlin announced his discovery to the public, showing a white mouse with a black patch of skin. Summerlin claimed that the patch had been transplanted from a mouse with black skin without rejection.

The halls of medical research centers buzzed with the news. Great strides had been made in the relatively new field of transplantation, but the problem of rejection had never been solved. Now, here was a solution. Or maybe not. The technician working with Summerlin became suspicious when he wiped the black magic marker color off the white mouse's skin with an alcohol swab. It was a hoax! Summerlin had created fraud right under Dr. Good's nose.

In the preceding months, Dr. Good had been talking up Summerlin's discovery among his colleagues, and now he looked sadly foolish in the eyes of the medical world. Even though Dr. Good had not been involved in Summerlin's fraud, he still fell for it, and that was enough for many of his colleagues to lose faith in the great scientist. A later inquiry at Sloan Kettering absolved Dr. Good of any blame, but did reprimand him for not supervising Summerlin more closely. Dr. Good was allowed to continue on as president of Sloan Kettering, and he maintained his role as remarkable researcher and mentor, but the damage had been done.

In 1979 Nick entered Cornell Medical School expressly to study with Dr. Good. Even while Nick was still a young, first-year student, Dr. Good recognized the medical student's potential. Dr. Good took a quick liking to Nick, taking him under his wing, inviting him into his lab, and into his home where he wined and dined students and other celebrity scientists alike. Nick studied hard, excelled in his courses, and relished the attention of his famous new mentor. They met regularly to talk about Nick's interest in cancer research.

Then in July 1981, after Nick's second year of medical school, he received a phone call from an old friend from his journalism days, an accomplished writer, who was always on the hunt for the next best seller.

"Nick," his friend said. "I've been in touch with Dr. Kelley, the dentist who treated Steve McQueen. Do you know anything about that case?"

"I followed it a bit." Nick had not been too interested in the case but found the attacks against Kelley peculiar. After all, McQueen had an incurable cancer that the conventional medical model could not treat.

"Kelley is now in New York. I think there's a real story here. I'd like you to meet him."

"No, thanks. Look, I'm in medical school and don't have time to meet with some weird dentist who thinks he can cure cancer."

"You're right, he is eccentric. But I can't figure out if he's crazy, or brilliant. Or crazy and brilliant. I want you to come and talk to him and tell me if there's a book here that's worth writing."

Nick protested that he was just a second-year medical student and wasn't really qualified to evaluate this man. And he didn't want to waste his time on some quack.

But his friend persisted. She said that Nick was just the right person to meet with Kelley. Nick had both a journalistic and medical background.

"Look," Nick's friend said. "Kelley is in New York now and spouting all sorts of biochemistry. It's way over my head. I could arrange a meeting for you. Just listen to the guy and tell me if he's for real. Give it a half hour."

Nick was working in the lab of Dr. Walter F. Riker, Jr., another accomplished mentor, that summer. Riker had been the chair of pharmacology for years at

Cornell University and had a lot to teach Nick. But again, just as his lab experience at Woods Hole had proven tedious, Riker's lab had become laborious to Nick. He was anxious for an adventure.

Finally, Nick agreed to the meeting with Kelley, and a few days later, he was on his way to a chiropractor's office in Forest Hills, Queens. Nick was skeptical about Kelley, but his journalism mentor Byron Dobell had trained him to be open-minded. Dobell had told Nick that if you go into a story with preconceived ideas, with biases and prejudices, you will most likely miss the real story. Nick had gone to medical school with this same attitude. He didn't so much reject the science taught to him, he simply questioned everything. So, Nick met Kelley with the approach of an investigative journalist.

Kelley stood when Nick entered the office, a shy awkward, bumbling man who was so soft-spoken Nick could barely hear him. Kelley's six-foot three-inch frame did little to command a presence, and he was not what Nick had expected from someone who had been cast as a money-grubbing snake oil salesman. Kelley's long, thin face was haggard, and he had a head of unruly thick grey hair. Kelley had a noticeable limp, and was dressed in a frumpy conservative grey suit and blue tie. The two men exchanged pleasantries, but Nick had a difficult time getting the conversation going. They talked about Kelley's train trip across Canada and Steve McQueen's death.

It wasn't until Kelley began to explain the details of his program that the energy in the room came alive.

"The two branches of the autonomic nervous system, the sympathetic and parasympathetic, are the key to human health," Kelley said.

Quickly, the two men were engaged in an elaborate discussion of pancreatic enzymes, and the origins of cancer, of organic, raw food, vegetarian, balanced and carnivore types, of nutritional supplements and detoxification. Much of Kelley's information on the intricacies of the autonomic nervous system were more advanced than Nick had learned in medical school, but he swiftly grasped the gist of the program—that the road to health meant bringing the body back into balance. The readings that Nick had done in sustainable agriculture, ecology, and Weston Price suddenly became resonant. Kelley's theories and his clinical experience lifted Nick up out of the tedium of the laboratory and into an exciting discourse on biochemistry.

"I knew in twenty minutes that Kelley was a very smart man," Nick once told me. "Kelley may have been wearing a frumpy suit, but I learned that day that frumpy suits don't matter. The man inside can still be smart."

Nick asked Kelley his goal.

"Do you want a book written about you and your program?"

Kelley didn't really care about a book. He wanted his program put to the test by a clinical trial run by a reputable medical school. If his program was proven to be of value, then conventional medicine should administer it for people who wanted a nutritional approach to cancer.

"If my program turns out to be a bust, then I'll go fishing," Kelley said.

Nick was surprised Kelley brought up a clinical trial. He had been taught that most alternative medicine practitioners never wanted this kind of challenge. Nick mentioned that he could go back to Cornell and ask Dr. Good about how to proceed in an evaluation of Kelley's program.

"Dr. Good?" Kelley asked. "Dr. Robert A. Good?"

Dr. Robert A. Good had been Kelley's hero, the one conventionally trained physician Kelley thought might be open-minded enough to grasp the principles of his program. Kelley wanted Nick to begin an evaluation at once in his Dallas office. Kelley was returning there to begin his practice again after his sojourn in Washington State and Canada.

"I'm leaving for Dallas in the morning," Kelley said. "You come with me and begin an investigation of my work."

Whoa, Nick thought. He tried to explain to Kelley that Dr. Good might not even be interested in his work. And Nick wasn't sure he could leave Dr. Riker's lab. After talking for several hours, Nick finally agreed to go back to Cornell and approach Good.

In Manhattan, Nick pressed the elevator button for the top floor of Sloan Kettering and stepped into the waiting room of Dr. Good's office, a nicely furnished suite looking out over all of New York City. Dr. Good was on the phone discussing a medical conference when Nick arrived without an appointment. Nick wasn't sure the famous director would even have time to see him.

"I would like to see Dr. Good. Even for five minutes," Nick told the secretary.

She buzzed Dr. Good and he said, "Send him in. Always happy to see Nick."

Dr. Good gave Nick a broad smile, his lips parting to reveal his straight white teeth set in a face that seemed to have the furrows of the plowed prairie forming across his high forehead, his hairline receding, his temples greying. Nick and Dr. Good talked for an hour, with Nick explaining his encounter with Dr. Kelley. He discussed the controversy with Steve McQueen. Despite the negative media Kelley had received, Nick thought him serious about his work.

"Perhaps he's even onto something," Nick said.

Dr. Good listened attentively, interjecting questions, keeping a measured distance from displaying any emotion over Kelley, but approaching the topic with interest.

Nick related how he'd been invited to Dallas the next morning to investigate Kelley's methods. As expected, Dr. Good was open to the idea.

"Even if Dr. Kelley turns out to be a complete charlatan, you'll learn a lot of medicine by going down to Dallas. A student learns best through projects of his own devising."

Nick was hesitant to leave Dr. Riker's lab, but Dr. Good dismissed his concerns.

"Dr. Riker will understand," Dr. Good said. "As a scientist you have to always look beyond the tried and true for the next big advance."

Dr. Good offered some advice on Nick's preliminary review of Kelley. He asked Nick to try to locate charts of patients who had been appropriately diagnosed with poor-prognosis cancer, and by standards of conventional medicine, were alive years beyond expectations. Good seemed especially interested in patients with pancreatic cancer.

"If you can find even one patient on this program with pancreatic cancer who lived for five years, I will be impressed," Good said. "To my knowledge no one else in the history of medicine has had such a case."

Good said that one case wouldn't prove Kelley's program valid, but it would go a long way in gaining the attention of a fair-minded researcher in the conventional medical world.

The next morning Nick Gonzalez was on the first flight to Dallas.

17

At that time in 1981, Dr. Kelley's main office was in Arlington, Texas, just outside of Dallas, an area carved out of range and grassland. The one-story building was brand new, modern, very white, and low-slung. Kelley's workplace was large and spacious with a frenzy of ringing phones and fifteen different employees bustling around tending to patients and paperwork. A large desk commanded Kelley's office itself, with framed pictures of his four children on the wall behind it. On another wall were his diplomas and certificates, a patent for a dental appliance from the 1950s, and photographs of Dr. Kelley in his cap and gown receiving his postgraduate certification in orthodontia.

Nick immediately started going through Dr. Kelley's records. Kelley had kept meticulous, computerized charts, his patients' cases well-documented with copious progress notes. Nick pulled up chart after chart, surprised to observe one cancer patient after another who had done well on the Kelley program. Some had gone into significant periods of remission; others had survived for years. Nick found one patient who had had properly diagnosed pancreatic cancer and was still alive seven years later. Nick found another patient properly diagnosed with myeloid leukemia—as deadly as pancreatic cancer—that chemotherapy had failed. She had gone into remission within months of starting the Kelley treatment.

Nick pulled out a yellow legal pad and filled up the sheets with notes on the patients. He was engaged in the perfect blend of investigative journalism—the search and discovery that had always excited him about his old profession—and his new-found knowledge of medicine. Nick worked with his usual abilities of intense concentration, arriving in the conference room when the office opened in the morning, ordering in food for lunch, then working late into the evening without a break, locking the door behind him when he left to return to Dr. Kelley's small, one-bedroom apartment.

During this time in Dallas, I stayed in Kelley's small one-bedroom apartment, with him sleeping on the couch. Each morning, he would get up at five or six, and for half an hour read his Bible. He would make me breakfast, the 14-grain cereal I would learn to appreciate, and fresh carrot juice. I was amazed at how simply and unpretentiously he lived.

I spent hours a day, poring through Kelley's files, and hours a day, and at night—neither of us slept very much—talking about the basics of his program. I heard the names John Beard and Francis Pottenger for the first time. I also began to appreciate Kelley's long struggle to keep his therapy going.

At the end of two weeks, Nick gathered up his notes and several of the patient charts and flew back to New York. He spread his patient case reports on Dr. Good's desk. Over the course of the next couple of weeks, the doctor and medical student met many times, hovering over the stacks of paper, carefully going through each chart one by one.

"I have to caution you not to get too excited," Dr. Good said. "This is still a very preliminary investigation and a million things could throw off this data. But, I have to say that at this point, I'm impressed."

Slowly, Dr. Good and Nick devised a plan to continue to evaluate Kelley's work. To their knowledge, no conventional academic researchers had ever seriously examined the work of an alternative medicine practitioner. They had no models, no examples to follow, and as they proceeded, Dr. Good was still ever careful and guarded.

"This kind of retrospective investigation can't be used to prove or disprove the efficacy of Kelley's treatment," Dr. Good warned. "Only a controlled clinical trial could do that."

But Dr. Good did think that they could derive value from the study. He thought carefully documented case studies could teach much about the potential of a new approach.

"Great advances in medicine," he told Nick, "often begin with observations of even a single patient. We need to pay attention, watch, and see. A patient may take an unusual turn while taking a new treatment."

Dr. Good advised Nick to become familiar with Kelley's theoretical framework, to do an in-depth survey of background readings about the nutritional treatment. Secondly, he recommended that Nick put together a series of case studies of 50 Kelley patients who had done well on the program. These patients would need to be appropriately diagnosed, and they would need to include a variety of poor-prognosis cancers. Dr. Good asked Nick to write up each case at some length and include the medical records with his report.

"If you can find 50 patients like that from Kelley's files—or any practitioner's files for that matter—I will want to seriously investigate this program."

Thirdly, Dr. Good requested that Nick track down every patient with pancreatic cancer who had seen Kelley during a specific period of time and to write up those case studies as well. As he had told Nick many times before, survivors of pancreatic cancers were the most impressive to the academic research world.

Nick plunged into this research work during the fall of his third year in medical school, a momentous period of time in his life in many ways. The demands on a third-year medical student are intense. In any small windows of free time he had, Nick worked through the charts of Kelley's patients, interviewing them on the phone, talking to their referring doctors, and tracking down extra bits of information. He even visited some of them in their homes. Nick called Kelley on the phone almost every night, discussing the theory behind his program. From these conversations, Nick began to relearn and appreciate biochemistry, physiology and neuroanatomy in a way that he hadn't in his first two years of medical school.

Nick met with Dr. Good frequently who had agreed to supervise an independent study the following year. The fourth year of medical school is largely elective, and the two worked out a plan for Nick to conduct a more formal study of Kelley. Nick was thrilled to be involved with this work, and his research and studies were both going along well that autumn. Then he got a call from his father.

"I'm having terrible hiccups and difficulty swallowing," he told his son.

Nick immediately arranged a consultation with a gastroenterologist at Memorial Sloan Kettering. William Gonzalez was seen right away and diagnosed with one of the deadliest esophageal cancers.

This probably resulted from his two pack a day cigarette habit
he picked up in the Army—the Army used to give free cigarettes

to all soldiers to help with "stress." In addition, as a teenager he
had received radiation to the chest, believe it or not, for acne, a
common treatment approach in the 1920s. So he was a set up for
esophageal cancer.

William Gonzalez underwent surgery, but the disease had already metastasized, and he went downhill very fast. Nick visited him every day and supported
him as his father faced death.

He confronted his disease and death remarkably, as he has faced
every other challenge in his life—with great courage, never com-
plaining, never regretting the things he hadn't accomplished, just
grateful to have me nearby, to help in whatever way I could.

William Gonzalez died in the Intensive Care unit with Nick at his side. His
son was already well into his cancer research and wished, beyond wishing, that
he could save his father. But the disease was already too advanced.

All Nick could do was stand beside his father's death bed and say, "Someday
I'm going to find a cure for cancer."

I never got over the loss, and certainly his disease only firmed my
resolve to devote my life to the battle against cancer. I am saddened
that he never saw my career take off, as it has, but on the other
hand, I know the controversies of my therapy and the scorn at times
of my colleagues would have troubled him. But his lessons of cour-
age and quiet dignity have given me the tools to survive whatever
my critics may throw at me. After all, he's the guy that would throw
batting practice with me for hours without a complaint, and he's
the guy that effortlessly wrestled a psychotic bully to the ground
without a second thought.

Nick grieved the loss of his father, but pushed himself to finish that semester of medical school with high marks. He had plans to spend winter break at
Kelley's organic farm in Washington State. To Nick, a period of intense study
with Kelley was the kind of relaxation he relished. After Christmas, he caught a

flight to Washington and settled into Kelley's home on 160 acres in the Methow River Valley, in the foothills of the high Cascade Mountains.

Kelley had seen patients in an office on his farm from 1976–1981. Kelley kept the hard copies of all his patient records dating back to 1970 in that office, and the papers were a treasure trove of information and data for Nick. Kelley's home was on a bluff, overlooking the river valley, the green conifers clinging to the mountain sides, and the snow-tipped peaks in the distance. Nick felt like he was truly in Shangri-La. The pair worked steadily for two weeks straight, and Nick returned to New York holding an even stronger hunch that the dentist had made a significant discovery.

> *Life couldn't have been better, I thought when I returned home. My apartment in a Cornell building on 70th Street faced south, directly opposite the large Memorial Sloan Kettering complex, and I remember looking out my window, in a typical New York January twilight, facing Sloan Kettering and thinking my life was opening up before me. I would continue my research as a student under Dr. Good, join his group when I graduated, and hopefully at Sloan Kettering have the resources to test and develop Kelley's work appropriately.*

Then one day in early spring Nick dropped by to see Dr. Good. When he reached Good's office, he was greeted by a strange, new secretary.

"Is Dr. Good in?" Nick asked.

"Dr. Good is no longer at this office."

"The president's office has moved?"

"Dr. Good is no longer president of Sloan Kettering. You can find him in his lab at the Sloan Kettering Research Building."

Nick raced to Dr. Good's lab and spotted him there in a small cubical where his fellows did their work. Books and papers were piled everywhere. Dr. Good sat at his small desk with his head in his hands, barely able to meet Nick's eyes.

"A new president is in. From Columbia, a molecular geneticist."

Good himself had been demoted to Vice President.

"It's a meaningless title," Good said. "I've been told to find another position as soon as I can. I hope to be out of New York in several weeks."

But Good made it clear to Nick that he would continue to work with him and support his research in any way that he could.

> *The Sloan Kettering dream came to a crashing halt. It was days before I could tell Kelley what had happened, because I didn't know how he would respond to the bad news. But Kelley, after a long silence said simply, "God closes one door and opens two others." I think I was more depressed than he was, because I knew of no one at the Cornell complex that would support an unconventional research study such as the one Kelley and I envisioned.*
>
> *Within weeks, Dr. Good was gone to the University of Oklahoma where he was to set up a cancer research and bone marrow transplantation program. To me, Oklahoma seemed a strange place for him to go, since he was so at home at the medical centers of the Northeast. But I also heard through the rumor mill that colleagues felt his career was finished, he was too controversial, his reputation was still tarnished by what had happened nearly ten years ago.*

Coups d'état are not confined to the Mexican Revolution. The very structure of academe fosters ruthless competitiveness and jealousy. A famous man in leg braces who is good at everything he touches inevitably has a target on his back. Good's involvement with the Summerlin hoax was an added issue. And I imagine to many of his colleagues, Good's support of Nick's research looked like another set-up for fraud. So, off Dr. Good went to a public university far removed geographically and philosophically from the Ivy Leagues, a move that looked like a humiliating step-down in the elite medical world. Off Dr. Good went, leaving Nick to finish up his fourth year of medical school without the access and influence of his mentor.

Dr. Good did continue to encourage Nick long distance. Supervised by Dr. Good in Oklahoma, Nick was scheduled to spend a semester of his fourth year in medical school in Washington State, reviewing Kelley's files. But even this plan ran into trouble as did Nick's plans for his internship in the year following medical school.

Nick learned that medical students planned their fourth years like a military campaign. The most prestigious internship could open the right doors and have a huge impact on one's future career. The right elective here in the fourth year might lead to the right letter of recommendation from the right professor at Cornell who might write to the right professor at another Ivy League school which might lead to a letter of acceptance at the top program.

> *I met with my advisor, who to my surprise, had already begun to plan my fourth-year elective rotations. He wanted me to spend a month in a hematology rotation he had already arranged at Johns Hopkins, with a friend of his from medical school now on the Hopkins faculty. This would help my chances of acceptance into the Hopkins residency program. Then, I would spend October with the Chairman of Pharmacology at Cornell, a very well-respected scientist, who had taken a liking to me and had already offered me a job in his department at Cornell after I finished my training. A reference from this professor would help my chances anywhere I applied, and certainly, several months working in his lab would guarantee a position at Cornell.*

Nick grew depressed listening to his advisor's plan, and interrupted him. "I've already made plans for an independent project with Dr. Good."

His advisor, who had always been friendly to Nick in the past, became enraged. "A project with Dr. Good is the worst thing you could do! Don't you understand that Robert Good was forced out of Sloan Kettering? His career is over. No one takes him seriously anymore. Do you think that Good ended up in Oklahoma for fun? Do you think he wants to be in a place like that?"

Nick tried to remain calm and explain his investigation of Kelley's work, the progress that he had already made, and the promise it was showing.

"I don't want to hear this," his advisor growled. "You have enormous opportunities to work with top scientists. It is beyond my comprehension that you would throw away your career to chase day dreams with Dr. Good."

Nick listened for awhile longer to his advisor's rant then said, "I have to leave."

Nick never met with his advisor again. Instead, Nick focused on his Kelley project. In late August, he finished up his internal medicine rotation with an honors grade, a prerequisite for an internship in a major institution. Then Nick applied for his internships on his own, without anyone's help.

18

In early August, Nick left New York City and flew to Seattle where Kelley met him at the airport.

"Time to get to work," Kelley said, picking up Nick's bag and tossing it into the trunk of his car. Kelley was in a great mood. He had been waiting twenty years to have his methods evaluated, and he was thrilled that Nick could spend several months with him concentrating on the study. Nick was anxious to not only dive deeper into Kelley's records, but to observe him in action. Dr. Good had told Nick that Kelley's program was worthless unless it was transferable. Other doctors needed to be able to replicate his method and results.

The pair drove north out of Seattle, then east through the North Cascade National Park toward Winthrop. Back and forth, up and around the conifers, glaciers and lakes, the road ran through the mountains that harbored grizzly bears, and gray wolves. Nick breathed in the fresh, cool air, his lungs feeling vibrant for the first time in months.

He felt liberated from the predators of his own medical world in New York, and open to the continuing adventure of investigating new territory. North Cascade National Park was a refuge to 200 species of birds, including everything from bald eagles to hummingbirds. Nick, the amateur ornithologist, felt an ascending force overcome him in this serene landscape, a natural setting that provided the same kind of comfort he'd found as a child in the beauty of Lake George.

Nick was welcomed into Kelley's home in Winthrop by Mrs. Kelley who had arrived to take charge of the cooking and household, allowing time for the two men to do their work. Mrs. Kelley was perhaps more excited than her son to finally have a professional study done on his treatment plan. After his long trip, Nick sat down to a beautifully prepared organic dinner, then exhausted, he fell into bed, dreaming of the possibilities that were unfolding before him for a bright future in cancer research.

The next morning Nick and Kelley got right down to their job. Nick had worked in Kelley's basement briefly that previous winter, but this time he fully registered with the enormity of his task. He walked down the basement steps and realized that Kelley had at least 10,000 charts of past patients, dating back to 1970. Earlier charts had been lost in a fire when Kelley had first moved into the house. Nick surveyed row after row of mental filing cabinets. He knew that there would be enough material here that, even if he didn't have complete records, he could make some sort of statement with the information that he garnered. Yet, making sense of the mass of records before him was going to be arduous.

Each morning for the next four months, Nick and Kelley rose very early with the sun breaking over the mountains. The album opens to a picture of Nick and Kelley in 1982 standing on the wooden porch steps, Kelley a good foot taller and wider than his younger colleague. Nick stands barefoot with his hands in the pockets of his tan slacks. He's dressed in a blue polo shirt and wears his wired-rimmed aviator's glasses. Kelley, in his stocking feet, is dressed in tan slacks and white shirt, the sleeves rolled up to his elbows as if he's ready to get to work. His head is tilted slightly to the right, a broad smile on his face. I imagine them having had breakfast on the deck, now ready to start their day.

The two men carted the charts out of the basement and worked in a study on the ground floor of Kelley's home, with large picture windows opening to a view that stretched miles to the Cascades. With the stunning scenery bolstering his spirits, Nick began trying to put the masses of data into some coherent order.

Systematically, Nick went through all the charts in the house, starting with group A and ending with Z. First, he had to sift out the cancer and non-cancer patients. Kelley had treated many people with autoimmune disease and other disorders besides cancer. Next, he had to eliminate many of the patients who had had cancer but may have been cured by other, orthodox treatments that they had received before coming to Kelley. Still other patients didn't appear to have been appropriately diagnosed. Fortunately, Kelley's files were filled with the kind of patients that Dr. Good had requested: appropriately diagnosed terminally ill patients with a poor prognosis who had done well for years on the Kelley program.

Nick made calls to the patients, interviewing them repeatedly, taking notes, assessing their cases.

Slowly over the months, with Dr. Good's guidance, I felt I began to make progress. We worked seven days a week, 12–14 hours a day, through the end of summer and into autumn, as the leaves of the cottonwoods and birches and aspens along the Methow River winding through Kelley's farm below us turned brilliant yellows and reds and oranges.

After Kelley had retired to bed around 9:00 P.M., Nick began a rigorous reading program. Well into the late evening hours, he began earnestly schooling himself in physiology, neurophysiology, nutrition and cancer medicine. He felt he needed to master all of these subjects to make his study work. Nick and Kelley kept to a tight schedule, beginning early in the morning, breaking for lunch, working through the afternoon, then breaking for dinner. Throughout the whole day, much to the annoyance of Mrs. Kelley, Nick peppered Kelley with questions about his past, his work, about nutrition, biochemistry, and physiology.

"When did you first learn about John Beard's work? How long did it take for the enzymes to begin shrinking your own tumors? How did the autonomic nervous system evolve in humans? Is it different in different mammals?"

Kelley had clear answers to all Nick's questions. He seemed to know more about medicine than any of Nick's professors at Cornell. And he could put the human body into a framework that, bit by bit, was beginning to make exquisite sense to Nick.

I had never worked so hard, willingly and gladly, in my life.

The autumn began to turn toward winter and Nick knew that he needed more time to finish his study. He asked for another semester devoted solely to the Kelley project and Dr. Good supported the idea. In November, Nick wrote to the Dean of the Medical School at Cornell, asking to extend his study for another four months. The Dean called him from New York.

"Nicholas," he said rather sternly. "You may not have additional time. You are to return to New York in January and finish more appropriate course work here."

Eventually, the Dean explained that Nick's advisor, to whom Nick hadn't spoken for many months, had been causing trouble. His advisor had even suggested that Nick not be given credit for his semester-long independent study with Kelley, characterizing the whole project as "typical Robert Good bizarre." Nick needed the course credit to graduate from medical school. Dr. Good jumped in and defended the project strongly. Nick ended up with credit for the semester, but he knew that his very intense and productive time in the Cascades was coming to an end.

Thanksgiving went by in a blur with little time devoted to a large, fancy turkey dinner. Instead Nick and Kelley were now working 15–16-hour days, hoping to at least finish the basics of the study. Nick knew that by the end of the project he would have had to review 10,000 charts, send a questionnaire to 1,300 people, interview nearly 450 patients on the phone, hoping to eventually chose 50 for his written report. By this point, Nick realized he had taken on a several year project. Nick discussed with Kelley and with Dr. Good the possibility of postponing his internship. He didn't want to be a clinician anyway. He wanted a research career.

"No, you need to do your internship. There will be no postponement."

Dr. Good instructed Nick to bring the project to some sort of completion, then pick it up after his residency.

But Nick knew a residency was three years. He thought Kelley shouldn't have to wait that long.

> *Winter came to the mountains in early December, with a heavy snowstorm that left the farm and the distant mountains pristine white. I have never seen such white, nor, when the storm passed, such a blue sky. It was crystal aquamarine, unlike any sky color I had ever seen. Kelley chose this spot, this particular bluff, because he felt it was one of the most serene and beautiful places on earth. I knew he was right.*

But the serenity wasn't to last. Nick spent Christmas on the farm with Kelley, then flew back to New York City to the grind of rote learning, lectures and rotations. His return to medical school in Manhattan felt like imprisonment compared to the freedom of working independently in the mountains. Nick fulfilled his requirements in classes at Cornell, but he kept the Kelley project going on the weekends and in the evenings. He wrote up 20 cases in fulfillment of his independent study and Dr. Good was impressed by the quality of the work, his original skepticism about Kelley's strange nutritional treatment beginning to soften.

Suddenly, it was March and Nick received word that he would be going to Vanderbilt University in Nashville, Tennessee, for his internship. Vanderbilt, an excellent school, is ranked in the top 15 residency programs in the United States, but it falls down the list below Johns Hopkins, Massachusetts General, and Brigham and Women's Hospital on the east coast—all the more typical matches for someone from Nick's background and ability, all the more typical matches that his advisor had pushed.

By this point, Nick was happy to be leaving New York. He packed up and headed south to Tennessee.

Nick entered into a demanding internship in internal medicine at Vanderbilt University Medical Center, attending to his patients with a clipped efficiency. He wrote his notes in their charts, then was one of the first interns out the door at the end of the day, his work always done, his patients loving him. Home in his small apartment, he continued to work on his Kelley project. In the evenings, he made a few more phone calls to interview past Kelley patients. He wrote a few more letters to track down more medical records and histories, gathering data for his case reports.

Back in the hospital the next day, he was on a team with a bright young medical student named Linda Isaacs who had graduated with a Bachelor of Science degree in biochemistry with high distinction from the University of Kentucky, Phi Beta Kappa. She then enrolled at Vanderbilt University School of Medicine.

"He was always late and came rushing in at the last minute, his hair wet and slicked back from his shower. Then over the course of the morning, his hair dried into a beautiful bushy crown," Isaacs told me.

Years later in an article for *The Townsend Letter,* Isaacs described her first impression of Nick as "striking: a fast-walking, fast-talking New Yorker, brilliant and witty."

In contrast, Isaacs, with straight light brown hair, existed more in the realm of the shy, polite Southerner. Both of her parents were from the South—West Virginia and Kentucky—and both had been in technical fields. Her mother had received her degree in medical technology from the University of Kentucky. Her father had degrees in industrial chemistry, industrial management and law. He had a career in the military, serving in both World War II and Vietnam and rising to the rank of General before retiring to begin his own business in Alexandria, VA.

For six weeks, the intern and medical student worked side by side, then on the last day of her rotation, Nick asked Linda out on a date. They met for lunch and Nick spoke about his Kelley project. Isaacs was intrigued by this new approach to cancer, impressed by the case histories that Nick related. Isaacs' mother had studied and was interested in nutrition, so her daughter was open to an approach based on diet and supplements. Nick and Linda continued to date, seeing each other in the brief moments they had when they weren't working.

Nick talked more about the Kelley case studies and Linda listened. In particular, she remembered a patient that he'd discussed with metastatic prostate cancer, who after doing the Kelley program, was alive and well and playing in a ragtime band. Another patient with uterine cancer metastatic to the lung followed the Kelley program for several years. Repeat chest x-rays showed no evidence of disease. Case by case, Isaacs began to understand why Nick had risked so much of his professional career to study Kelley's approach.

Nick kept in touch with Dr. Kelley as best he could, but Kelley was getting more and more perturbed at the slowness of the research project. He was staying on the farm with his girlfriend who was there with him intermittently, but he seemed to be lapsing into a depression. Kelley was no longer seeing patients. He had tried to train a group of doctors and lay counselors to administer his program, but that experiment wasn't going well. Patients weren't responding as well as they had under his care, and to make matters worse, his pancreatic enzymes didn't seem as effective as they had once been.

In November Nick received a phone call from Dr. Good. "Would you like to come here and spend Christmas with my family?"

Nick quickly agreed, and even though he only had three days off in late December, he hopped on a plane in Nashville and flew to Oklahoma City. The invitation seemed to cheer up Kelley. At least Dr. Good was still interested in the project. Dr. Good was a gourmet cook and Christmas dinner was a real treat to an intern exhausted with his demanding routines in the hospital and the pressure he placed on himself to finish his Kelley project.

Dr. Good and his wife hosted a beautiful dinner with all their adult children—three sons and two daughters—and their spouses and children sitting around a long table complete with linen tablecloth and the good china. The Good extended family had flown in from all over the country. The dinner unfolded like a well orchestrated symphony, Dr. Good an accomplished conductor, Nick humming some Beethoven to himself, feeling that he, like his grandfather, had an essential part to play in a fine assemble.

On the second day of Nick's visit, Dr. Good began talking to him about his plans for his future.

"I'm getting through my internship," Nick said. "That's all going fine. But I really want to complete my Kelley project. Kelley is anxious to have it completed and so am I."

"Nicholas," Good said. "I'd like you to join me here in Oklahoma at the end of your internship year. You would be a full research fellow. You would have some clinical responsibilities, but you would have a salary and some funding to continue your Kelley research."

Nick immediately accepted the invitation. To him, this was a remarkable opportunity. Physicians usually receive fellowships after they have finished their full residencies—not after just one year of internship. Oklahoma was not Nick's pick of an ideal location, but at that point, he would have gone anywhere to finish his project under Dr. Good.

Back in Nashville after the holidays, Nick called Kelley to tell him the good news. Kelley sounded very strange on the phone, almost incoherent. His girlfriend got on the line.

"Several days ago, Dr. Kelley suffered a grand mal seizure. I called the ambulance and they took him to the hospital 30 miles away."

Tests showed nothing but atrial fibrillation, a condition he had had off and on since his cancer 20 years earlier. He was now home, on medication and doing better. But Kelley kept having seizures over the course of the next few months. Multiple neurologists performing multiple tests in Seattle couldn't find the cause. Kelley began to suspect that he had arsenic poisoning. He thought it would have been easy enough for someone to have poisoned his well at his farm. He had made plenty of enemies with his cancer treatment, and he had had plenty of threats on his life. He began taking homeopathic remedies for arsenic poisoning, and he began to feel better.

19

Nick left Linda Isaacs behind to finish medical school at Vanderbilt, keeping in touch on the phone. He found himself in Oklahoma City in July 1984 working for Dr. Good, helping to staff his immunology and bone marrow transplant unit. Nick fulfilled his professional duties, but had more time than he had had in Nashville to work on his Kelley study. Again, in any free moments he could squeeze in around his work days, he tried to complete his project. Nights, weekends, early mornings, 15 to 20-minute intervals between patients were all devoted to writing up his study. This frenetic work pattern had now become habit and would remain with him the rest of his life. Practicing an instrument, practicing baseball, practicing math problems, writing a novel like Hemingway, writing about preventive medicine or writing about the Kelley Program, all became one history, one continuum.

Nick did have the time to visit Kelley frequently. He made quick trips to Dallas where Kelley had once again taken up practice. And Nick and Dr. Good even saw one of Kelley's patients at their clinic in Oklahoma City. It was around this time that Nick was also introduced to the work of Roy Sweat, D.C. Several of Kelley's patients who had been stuck in their programs—making little progress against their diseases despite complete compliance with their protocols—had received atlas orthogonal adjustments from Dr. Sweat at his clinic in Atlanta. They credited Sweat for bringing their bodies back into proper alignment to facilitate healing. Kelley had dismissed the idea that chiropractic adjustments could have any bearing on his program or the treatment of cancer, but his patients swore by the method. Kelley was open to investigating.

The Atlas Orthogonal procedure is a chiropractic adjustment of the atlas, or the first vertebra in the neck. Theoretically, when the atlas is out of position due to trauma—from car accidents to improper lifting—the whole spine can go out of alignment in an attempt to try to compensate. Roy Sweat, a graduate of the Palmer School of Chiropractic in Davenport, Iowa, with the aid of engineers at Georgia Tech, developed a computerized instrument to adjust the atlas with minimal force. Patients from all over the world travelled to his clinic in Atlanta seeking his treatment.

Both Kelley and Nick flew to Atlanta to see Sweat in action. They observed patient after patient x-rayed with a special low-dose radiation machine that Dr. Sweat had also invented. A patient lay on the adjustment table, Dr. Sweat positioning their heads in his instrument with great precision, a stylus aimed at their skull, just behind their ear. *Bang.* Dr. Sweat's foot hit a pedal activating the stylus with a pressure that feels like the tap of a pencil. And the atlas slipped back into place.

Roy Sweat, a tall man with a wide grin, has relieved the pain of thousands of patients with his adjustments.

"Nicholas showed up here when he was just a young man. He asked a lot of questions." Dr. Sweat told me. After successive visits, they became life-long friends.

"Roy Sweat is one of the smartest men I've ever met," Nick told me years later. "To design that atlas instrument is a real feat. And his years of helping patients is remarkable."

At the end of his year in Oklahoma City, Nick, the man known to ask a million questions, asked one big question of Linda Isaacs: *Will you marry me?*

Isaacs accepted, and they hastily arranged a wedding, squeezing it in at the end of Linda's fourth year of medical school and the end of Nick's first year of his fellowship with Dr. Good. Nick was following his mentor to All-Children's Hospital in St. Petersburg. Good had become Physician-in-Chief at All-Children's affiliated with nearby University of South Florida. There, Dr. Good had also become Chairman of Pediatrics. Nick and Linda had one day for the wedding in Alexandria, Virginia before they had to move to Tampa, Florida. A week after Linda graduated from medical school, they were married on May 18, 1985, in St. Lawrence Catholic Church with Reverend John J. Munley officiating.

"I don't even remember where we were married," Linda Isaacs told me. "Everything was so rushed. We had to be in Florida the next day."

She did remember wearing Nick's grandmother's veil and the fact that Dr. Good was the best man and Dr. Kelley was in attendance. The album opens to a picture of Linda dressed in a traditional white gown with puffed short sleeves, a bouquet of white roses in her hands. Nick wore a grey morning coat accented with a boutonniere and a grey and white striped tie.

St. Lawrence was a 1970s, Modernist style church, known for its simplicity and abstract forms. Track lighting shone down from the open beams of the ceiling above the altar. A large crucifix hung on the wall flanked by the pipes from the organ, with statues of the Virgin Mary on one side and St. Joseph on the other. A few friends and relatives were gathered in the dark oak pews. A Mass was celebrated, and Nick and Linda approached the altar rail, exchanging their vows. The organ blasted a recessional hymn, the young couple walking out arm-in-arm. They then rode away from the church in a limousine.

And then it was back to work. No time for a honeymoon, they flew to Florida that evening. Isaacs immediately began her internship at the University of South Florida, and Nick became Dr. Good's fellow at nearby All-Children's Hospital in St. Petersburg where he buried himself again in his Kelley project. They scarcely had time to even take in the campus or surrounding area. University of South Florida, a relatively new school, had opened in 1960. The first independent state university conceived and planned during the twentieth century, USF was built on the site of an old World War II airstrip. Before the war, the site had been part of a 5,000-acre temple orange grove.

When Nick and Linda arrived in the spring of 1985, palm trees had taken the place of the orange trees. The palms towered over the sleek, concrete and glass university buildings. USF had experienced swift, rapid growth. The medical school had opened in the 1970s, and the university emerged as a major research institution in the 1980s just when the young couple had taken up their positions.

> *I followed him [Good] there, and in a frenzy of work, finished my fellowship, and my Kelley study, among the palm trees and endless summer of Tampa Bay.*

Nick kept in touch with Kelley on the phone, working through the book page by page. He read whole chapters to Kelley, seeking his approval or suggestions for revisions. The two of them were pleased to see the manuscript taking shape. Sometimes they were almost giddy with excitement. They were both convinced that they were involved in a significant advancement in cancer research, something that ultimately would be a great benefit to humankind.

"I just talked to Dr. Good for about two and a half hours," Nick told Kelley one night. "He's raring to go!"

"Did you show him the manuscript?"

"No, not yet. I want to wait until it's all finished."

"You're writing a big, gigantic H-bomb. You have it all together there in one package. Now you just have to explode it. And then that will separate the catfish from the cows."

Kelley wasn't naïve about the consequences of releasing a book about his program. He'd been harassed for his ideas and fought significant battles. And he was measured and humble about his own successes with patients. He never bragged about his own discoveries, but credited divine guidance with helping him establish his protocol.

Nick was quick to see the rightness of the intricacy of the program, how all the prongs of the method fit together. He emphasized that the program shouldn't be altered or adjusted at the whim of the practitioner.

"When we get this book out, every doctor in the world is going to make suggestions. I don't think normal human suggestions are really that valid. That's not where your program comes from, and that's what I'm beginning to under-stand... ...I think that even if you would incorporate suggestions that I would make, they probably wouldn't be very valid."

Nick recounted how when he had gone on the program himself, he had had severe reactions. His colleagues and friends told him to either go off the program, or address his symptoms through conventional medicine, or quit the enemas.

"I had faith in you and trust in the program," Nick told Kelley, "I think the program as it comes from you is pure and right and accurate... No one can believe that you have to do the enemas. But I did it." So Nick soldiered through, doing everything as he was instructed. In the end, he felt considerably better.

"How could I ever ask a patient to do the program if I hadn't had the balls to go on it myself?" Nick asked.

Kelley wanted to make long-term plans as he feared his work would be lost. He knew that if he should die, Nick was the only one who had complete knowledge of his program.

"You're it," he told Nick.

Kelley also knew that it might take many attempts to get the program accepted into conventional medical practice. "Most of the major contributions to civilization took three, four, five attempts. Local people and their egos and the suppression that ensues blocked the way. That and getting off the track by tinkering with the program."

Nick stayed on track with his work on his manuscript until it reached completion.

> *I barely remember anything but days in the library, and days at my computer. The final manuscript was 500 pages long, and followed the outline Dr. Good had suggested years earlier, when I was planning my project as a fourth-year medical student.*

By the end of May of 1986, Nick had completed his hefty monograph detailing his results from his Kelley study. During the last week of the month, he fact checked everything in the book, making endless tiny adjustments, proof reading every sentence and every word on every page. Finally, he copied the whole book, bundled up the manuscript in a box, and personally delivered it to Dr. Good's office. Then he nervously awaited Dr. Good's response.

The report was organized into sections reflecting the outline originally suggested by Dr. Good. Part I discussed Kelley's theory—his concept of balancing the autonomic nervous system, and the use of pancreatic enzymes. Part II took a detailed look at 50 Kelley patients originally diagnosed with poor prognosis cancers. All survived beyond expectations, either returning to full health or going into remission for significant periods of time. These patients represented a range of 26 different kinds of cancers, from bile duct carcinoma to uterine cancer.

> *For each patient, I wrote up a lengthy, detailed case history that usually ran around five typed pages. I also included along with the case summary copies of pertinent medical records for each of these patients, such as copies of biopsy reports, doctor's notes, X-ray and CT scan reports. The copies of the doctor's notes, and CT scan reports documenting tumor regression, made for very convincing reading.*

In the last section of the book, Nick focused on the cases of all the 22 patients who had come to Kelley between 1976 and 1982 with inoperable pancreatic cancer. He obtained complete medical records for these patients, including death certificates for the deceased. Nick interviewed the surviving patients repeatedly and at length. He interviewed the family members as well as the original attending physicians of those who had died.

Ten of the pancreatic cancer patients had visited Kelley but had never followed the program. They had been discouraged from carrying out Kelley's treatment by their families and attending physicians who thought Kelley an outright fraud. These patients all died quickly with a median survival rate of 60 days. They served as a handy control group.

A second group of pancreatic patients had followed the program incompletely for various periods of time, ranging from one to 12 months. Nick put together a complete report for each of these patients including death certificates and a record of their supplement orders from the recommended supplement manufacturer. Interviews revealed that most of the patients had given up the program, bowing to pressure from their families and physicians. One patient had simply run out of money. These patients all died, too, with a median survival rate of 300 days, far beyond the usual expectation.

A third group had followed the program religiously, some for 10 years with an average survival rate of 8.3 years. The group was small but had eye-popping results. Every single patient who had followed the program fully had survived.

Nick acknowledged that his retrospective study had its drawbacks. A controlled clinical trial would have followed these patients from the very first day of treatment, carefully charting their progress. In his study, Nick reviewed patients who had been treated in the past, under uncontrolled circumstances. And Nick included a couple of patients in the third group of pancreatic patients who did not strictly fit the criteria.

> *One of these patients did have islet cell carcinoma of the pancreas, cancer of the endocrine portion rather than the enzyme producing cells of the pancreas. Islet cell cancer, although usually fatal, does have a slower course than adenocarcinoma. However, with Dr. Good's approval, I included this particular patient in the pancreatic evaluation because he had a particularly aggressive form of islet cell, and when diagnosed, he had failed experimental chemotherapy and the disease was widely spread throughout his liver. Under Kelley's care, the tumors in the liver had regressed, and at*

the time I completed the project, he had been on the Kelley program
for nearly six years.

Another patient in the third group of pancreatic patients had experienced jaundice and weight loss. In exploratory surgery, his surgeon found a large pancreatic tumor that had engulfed adjacent blood vessels and invaded the liver. The surgeon thought the diagnosis so obvious and the prognosis so dire, he didn't want to risk a biopsy. He sewed the patient back up and told him to get his affairs in order. Instead, the patient sought out treatment from Kelley. Technically, the patient did not have an appropriately diagnosed biopsy-confirmed case of pancreatic cancer, but in consultation with Dr. Good, Nick included him in the study. The detailed operative note clearly documented his pancreatic tumor.

The other three survivors of the pancreatic cancer survivor group had adenocarcinoma of the pancreas and Dr. Good helped Nick review their slides to confirm their diagnoses.

One of these patients ran a gas station with her husband in Wisconsin. After developing signs of obstruction of the gallbladder ducts—a very common presenting problem with patients suffering pancreatic cancer—she went for exploratory surgery at her local hospital. Her surgeon discovered a pancreatic tumor, and metastases to the liver. A biopsy of a liver tumor revealed adenocarcinoma. She subsequently went to the Mayo Clinic in Rochester, where the doctors confirmed the diagnosis. Since the disease was so advanced, they recommended neither chemotherapy nor radiation. The patient then learned of Kelley, began the therapy and at the time I completed my study, she had been alive nearly five years.

A couple of weeks later, Nick was summoned to Dr. Good's office. Nick sat on the other side of his desk and Good thumbed through the notes he'd taken on the manuscript on one of his famous yellow legal pads. He pushed his chair away from his desk.

"Well, Nicholas," Dr. Good began. "I know I've been in on this project from the very beginning…" he paused.

Nick glanced at his mentor, unsure where he was going to go with his response. He'd worked furiously for five years on this project, sacrificing all other aspects of his life.

"These results…" Good said at last.

"Really good, no?" Nick said.

"Too good."

"I've documented everything. Interviewed everyone who is still alive repeatedly. The medical records are all there."

"But these patients with pancreatic cancer…To live five years with the disease? This woman in Wisconsin is still alive?"

"I've spoken with her over and over again. Would you like me to visit her personally? Go to Wisconsin?"

"Go to Wisconsin? No, no… What I don't know is where to go with these results. A retrospective study like this… based on diet and pancreatic enzymes, coffee enemas and liver flushes."

"We need to publish the results and get funding for a clinical trial."

"That would be ideal. The medical world certainly needs to know about this study. It doesn't prove anything, as you know. But these results, if you let yourself believe them, are astonishing."

Dr. Good turned his face toward the window. Good's forehead was beginning to show his age from the years of toil in a field that he loved but that had ultimately disappointed him. He was frustrated that he himself had never cracked the riddle of cancer. He had poured his heart and soul into medical research but had never won that allusive Nobel Prize. He still carried the stigma of the Sloan Kettering scandal from previous decades. He had once been the most highly respected and published physician in the world, the best teacher who had nurtured a whole generation of top scientists, and he had ended up at a small new medical school in Florida, well away from the Ivy League power base. Once he could have arranged for publication of Nick's manuscript with a few phone calls. But now he knew that he didn't have the resources or influence to properly test a nutritional program like Kelley's.

Yet, that afternoon, the two researchers made a plan to try to publish the monograph, first as isolated articles in medical journals, then as a whole book. They made a list of established and well-respected editors and journals, all people and publications Good had known in his previous life in New York. Just the talk of a plan for publication lifted both their spirits. At the same time, they were realistic. They recognized the forces that were working against them.

Nick knew from the start that Good's energy was fading, his influence waning, that publication was going to be tough going. In a subsequent meeting, Nick told Dr. Good that he was determined to publish his manuscript, that only then would they be able to get funding for a clinical trial. But when they began submitting parts of the manuscript in hopes of getting articles placed in medical journals, the reception was anything but positive.

Journal editors began turning down the manuscript, even those who had been good personal friends of Dr. Good's. They sent their rejection letters straight to Good, warning him away from another fraudulent case that would further damage his reputation. Dr. Good seemed shaken by these letters, and Nick knew that Dr. Good's support for the Kelley project was diminishing. He had hoped that Dr. Good would co-author an article on the Kelley program with him, but for Dr. Good, co-authorship was out of the question. He couldn't risk another case of fraud. And emotionally, he couldn't deal with Nick's research. Dr. Good was one of the most widely published scientists in the history of medicine.

"You know, people come from all over the world for my expertise. I don't have the slightest idea what Kelley is doing, yet I've seen successful cases that I can't explain. And you're telling me that I don't know anything about cancer. I can't live with that."

Nick made a final appointment to see his mentor.

"I've decided that Linda and I should return to New York to try to generate interest in my Kelley project," Nick said.

Dr. Good's face relaxed. Relieved, he wished Nick well, and the two shook hands.

Nick left Dr. Good's office, never to see his mentor again. Nick stepped into the intense Florida sun, the light filtering down through the palm trees. He walked toward his apartment to start packing, crossing the campus that had once been an airstrip, launching fighter planes into the clear sky.

20

Nick opened the door to Kelley's Dallas office and knew that everything had changed. What in 1981 had been a bustling, humming business, by 1986 had deteriorated into a hollowed-out shell. Gone were the secretaries and assistants. Gone were the patients. Gone was the furniture, the waiting room chairs, the conference room table, and even Kelley's desk. What was left were just a folding table, a few chairs and the waiting room couch where Kelley slept. Cardboard boxes were piled everywhere containing office records and mementos of past years.

Nick had wanted to make this last visit to Kelley's office before he and Linda headed to New York where they hoped to get Nick's manuscript published. Linda, under the stress of her first year of her residency, had developed chronic fatigue syndrome. She managed to complete her residency and passed her licensure examinations but experienced extreme exhaustion and lack of concentration. She had worked in a biochemistry lab as an undergraduate and had been exposed to a dangerous chemical—beta-Mercaptoethanol, most commonly used in DNA extraction. She traced her illness back to toxic exposures to this chemical.

Plagued with these difficult symptoms that made it impossible for her to function as a physician, she dropped out of her South Florida residency to place herself in Nick's hands. She hoped to regain her health through the Kelley program. But first, Nick and Linda wanted to visit Dr. Kelley in Dallas. Nick was excited to show Kelley his finished manuscript and was optimistic that the thought of publication would cheer his mentor.

From their frequent phone calls, Nick knew that Kelley was doing better physically. The arsenic homeopathic remedies had stopped the seizures, but one look at the office convinced Nick that Kelley's mental health was fragile. Kelley showed flashes of his old self—the scientific genius and genial host—but he could no longer focus with the precision nor converse about biochemistry with fluidity. Kelley knew that his program wasn't working as effectively as it once had, and from his research, Nick had verified that after 1982, the program hadn't produced the miracles of the past.

Kelley had set up a network of counselors to treat patients throughout the country. Kelley didn't think the counselors were the problem. They had been managing patients effectively before 1982. Something else seemed to have changed. But after 1982, without the success rate they'd once had, the counselors began to get discouraged. Even patients whom Kelley had successfully treated in past years began to dissuade other patients from pursuing the program.

At last, Kelly concluded that the pancreatic enzymes themselves were the problem. He experimented with different enzymes from various manufacturers, but none of them became effective against cancer. The counselor network collapsed. Kelley stopped taking new patients, and in frustration and despair, he closed his Dallas office.

Nick and Kelley sat in the folding chairs, Nick trying to be upbeat about his manuscript. Kelley was genuinely pleased when Nick showed him the finished monograph.

"Oh, thank you. This is what I've been waiting for all these years."

But ultimately, Nick's optimism about his research didn't penetrate Kelley's dark mood. Kelley could barely look Nick in the eye and could only nod when Nick read him the list of editors and publications to whom he intended to send his book and journal articles.

The phone rang and Kelley got up to answer it himself. "No, this is the janitor...No, no, I have no idea where Dr. Kelley is." He hung up quickly.

Nick realized that Kelley had probably been talking to a bill collector.

Nick and Linda left for New York City. Kelley left for Pennsylvania and moved in with Carol Morrison, his physician girl friend who supported him.

*   *   *   *   *

Before he had departed Florida, Nick began sending his manuscript to agents in New York. He secured a top notch literary agent who thought the book would have an explosive effect on the scientific community. But more rejection letters came flooding back from the medical editors. They called Nick an outright fraud who was trying to perpetuate a hoax. Others wouldn't read beyond the first section of the manuscript:

> *Dear Dr. Gonzalez:*
>
> *Your manuscript arrived in my office promptly and I have read it. More accurately, I have read the first 75 pages (eight chapters) and scanned the rest. To be blunt, I find absolutely no merit to it.*
>
> *On the contrary, I feel that the whole text, is a seriatim building from one nonscientific or unproved premise to another with the product most kindly describable as gobbledygook, but possibly more accurately as pure charlatanism...*
>
> *I very much hope that this book is never published. In my opinion, it could only serve to promote a dangerous illusion, to eliminate any possibility that you might have to contribute to medicine and science, and to do Dr. Good immeasurable harm because of his association with it.*

Nick and Linda spent long stretches of 1986–87 with Dr. Kelley in Pennsylvania. Linda worked through the Kelley program to attempt to regain her health, while Kelley's mental state deteriorated even further. He was in despair at the reception of Nick's monograph. He thought that Dr. Good should be the director of the National Cancer Institute. He began to think that his work would never be properly tested, that it never would receive the attention it deserved.

A flicker of hope arose in early 1987. A representative from the Office of Technology Assessment, a Federal agency charged with investigating controversial scientific issues at the behest of Congress, asked for Nick's Kelley monograph. She explained that she had heard of his work through the grapevine through Dr. Good. Nick sent off the manuscript, but didn't hear anything for months. Finally, he called the OTA himself, but simply received a vague, noncommittal response. Nick was beginning to realize that the medical world would never publish his monograph, but he had hoped that the OTA report would give

Kelley the recognition that he deserved. As the months dragged on, Kelley just became more despondent.

As difficult as it was to live with Kelley, Nick stuck with it for the chance to observe patients like Sonia Nemethy. Kelley still saw occasional patients that had been with him for long periods of time. In 1970, Nemethy had been diagnosed with breast cancer with a radical mastectomy of the right breast. In 1973, a reoccurrence of the disease necessitated a radical mastectomy of the left breast. In the summer of 1975, the cancer metastasized to the spine, shoulder blade and skull. Nemethy then had a bilateral oophorectomy (removal of both ovaries), a procedure intended to slow the cancer growth and ease her bone pain by reducing her estrogen levels. Despite the surgery, Nemethy was told she probably wouldn't live out the year.

A few days later at the check-out counter at the grocery store, she happened to pick up a copy of the *National Inquirer* with an article about a man who had cured himself of cancer. He was now teaching other patients his methods from a home office in Washington State. Nemethy bought the magazine and drove home, rushing into the house and leaving her groceries in the car. She and her husband were on a plane to Seattle the next morning where they rented a car and drove to Kelley's home in the Cascades.

Within six months her pain and depression completely resolved. A bone scan at the end of 1975 showed some improvement, and another scan in mid-1976 showed complete regression of the skeletal lesions. The radiation technician thought that she had mixed up Nemethy's x-rays with another patient's.

"Can you come back, and we'll re-take those pictures?" the doctor had asked Nemethy.

The next set of x-rays were just the same.

Nemethy met Nick for the first time in Pennsylvania. "He was a young handsome man, then," she said. "Very nice."

By this time, Nemethy had been alive 16 years since her diagnosis. She was the kind of patient that made Nick commit to researching the Kelley program, even when he knew he was putting his future career on the line.

Dr. Kelley was then living in a small house on the Delaware River with his girl friend. He had gone off his own program and become increasingly paranoid, making comments about conspiracies. Kelley became suspicious that the CIA and the medical world were trying to block Nick's book from publication. Kelley reached the point where he thought that Nick was part of the CIA conspiracy, trying to block his own book publication. Kelley's conversations became more and more irrational.

Meanwhile, editors at trade publishing houses began rejecting Nick's manuscript. They thought the book wasn't written for a popular audience, and they had doubts that they could get it through their medical divisions. Nick kept at it, urging his agent to keep submitting the book. The book made the rounds, but Nick was dissatisfied with the agent's submissions and the targeted publishing houses. He broke with his agent in April of 1987, again plunging Kelley even deeper into depression.

In June of 1987, the two researchers, Kelley and Nick, mentor and mentee who had spent six years working closely together, parted.

> *When, after a year, I was unable to publish my manuscript as a book, or even selected case histories in any journal, he [Kelley] became convinced his enemies were engineering the destruction of his therapy. When the atmosphere became intolerable, in June of 1987, I decided I had to return to New York. I wasn't sure what I was going to do, but I knew, as I had known a year earlier with Dr. Good, that it was time to move on. I said good-bye to Kelley on the porch of the old house, surrounded by tall, leafy trees, and with the Delaware River in the background, only 50 feet from the house. Kelley seemed suddenly very old, very worn, very tired. We shook hands, and I left.*

Then in August of that year, having returned to New York City, Nick learned that Kelley had again been slandering him. In a profound twist of irony, Kelley had been interfering with the publication of Nick's book. Nick wrote Kelley a letter, completely severing all ties:

> *Let me advise you as I have so many times in the past that I do not work for you, that you are not in charge of this study, and you are totally out of line to try to affect this study.*
>
> *As a result of your behavior, I am writing to inform you that I am dissociating myself completely from you, your present and future plans, schemes and organizations.*

Nick and Linda moved back to Nick's family home to live with his wid-owed mother in New York City with just $200 in their pockets. Nick had an unpublished manuscript in his briefcase that he had spent five years of his life researching. He no longer had a literary agent. He had left his mentor, Dr. Good, in Florida, and he had become estranged from his mentor, Dr. Kelley, in Penn-sylvania. Nick was a researcher who had always intended to spend his life in a lab at Sloan Kettering. It had never entered his mind to actually practice medicine. Yet when a physician he'd known from his journalism days offered him a small, cramped room in the back of his office suite to see patients, Nick took it.

"Why don't you start your own practice and collect data?" his friend suggested.

Nick was still committed to the value of the Kelley program, but he wasn't even sure it was transferable to another physician. He knew that the life of an alternative physician wasn't going to be pretty, that the bias in the medical world and in society at large was largely against him.

> *At the time I first thought of seeing patients during the summer of 1987, I already knew that the state medical boards in general had long waged war against any physician practicing any form of nutritional and alternative medicine. So strong was the prejudice and bias against nutritional approaches to disease, especially can-cer, that the mere fact that a physician used nutritional therapy was in itself proof of fraud, insidious motivation, and profiteering off of vulnerable patients. Kelley had been through it all, over and over again; he had been jailed, his dental license had been revoked, and he had been hounded out of Texas by legal harassment. His first house in Washington State had been burned down, perhaps intentionally. During my research study of Dr. Kelley, I had inves-tigated the ongoing deliberate harassment of practitioners who used nutritional medicine. I had also been warned when I first set up my own practice that the fact I treated cancer patients and operated outside the academic mainstream would make me a likely, and very vulnerable, candidate for regulatory attack.*

Nick also knew that if his practice was going to be successful, he would have to have the proper pancreatic enzymes. What had gone wrong with the enzymes? Why had they become less effective after 1981? Nick was determined to solve the riddle.

The processing of pancreatic enzymes had always been tricky. In his work at the end of the nineteenth century, John Beard used injectable enzymes in his research. He adapted the general medical thought of the day that believed that enzymes would be destroyed in stomach acid, and only injectables that by-passed the digestive tract were viable for cancer treatment. Scientists thought that oral preparations would be useless in treating systemic problems. Beard himself went to the slaughterhouse and supervised the processing of his enzymes.

An injectable preparation needed a concentrated solution of pure trypsin, a powerful proteolytic enzyme. But extracting enzymes from the pancreas wasn't a simple procedure. Trypsin had to be activated, then extracted at the slaughter-house in a precise, controlled way. The pancreatic glands, a complex blend of the vacuoles containing the trypsin in its inactive form and fibrous tissue, arteries, veins, and stored fat, were minced into a slurry and allowed to sit for a number of hours at close to freezing temperatures. There, the precursor trypsinogen molecules would very slowly convert to trypsin.

Processors waited for maximum activation to occur. Scientists found that the tissue mush needed to sit at 30 degrees Centigrade for exactly twenty-four hours. Then the mixture would be soaked in solutions of water and alcohol where the pancreatic enzymes would separate out into another solution from the sur-rounding tissue and fat. But this separation only solved one problem. A bigger headache involved stopping the continued enzyme action in the solution.

Scientists knew that if the mush were allowed to sit longer than twenty-four hours, the enzyme potency would rapidly deteriorate, the activated enzymes furiously digesting each other. The biochemist Ezra Levin, working out of Champaign, Illinois in the 1940s, discovered that certain low-molecular solvents containing a halogen molecule—chlorine, bromine, or iodine—could stop enzymatic activity without damaging the enzymes themselves. Levin discovered that ethylene dichloride worked the best as a solvent to put the enzymes into a type of suspended animation.

In 1969, the FDA outlawed the use of injectable enzymes. Kelley, of course, had discovered the use of oral pancreatic enzymes while suffering probable pancreatic cancer. Kelley's pharmacist recommended the enzymes formulated by Levin, thinking that they were the most active. He had hoped that they would improve Kelley's digestive problems. Kelley, knowing nothing of Beard's work at the time, found only serendipitously that the oral pancreatic enzymes worked to reduce his tumors.

Nick's back was up against the wall. Injectable pancreatic enzymes were outlawed, and the oral enzymes were no longer effective. Kelley was convinced that their solvent was the problem. In 1981, the U.S. Food and Drug Administration had banned the use of ethylene dichloride. Animal studies indicated that the solvent, used in high doses for prolonged period of time, might be carcinogenic. Kelley had tried scores of other brands of pancreatic enzymes. None of them worked well.

What was Nick going to do?

21

Nick and Linda rolled up their sleeves, washed and dried the dinner dishes in the sink in the family house in Queens, replacing the silverware in the drawer—knives in the knife, spoons in the spoon, and forks in the fork compartments. They set up a rack of test tubes on the kitchen counter. With Linda's background in biochemistry, and Nick's dogged determination and research into the working of pancreatic enzymes, they worked round the clock to find the perfect formulation. Nick had given himself two weeks to figure out the enzyme problem. In a fortnight, he would be out of money—dead broke. He'd have to quit, abandon his plans to go into practice, and find something else to do to make a living.

Nick studied Ezra Levin's patent from 1950 for hours at a time, analyzing each stage in the production of his enzymes. Levin had theorized that the ideal pancreatic product should contain the entire enzyme component, not just select enzymes such as trypsin. Levin, of course, was making his enzymes to improve digestion. Nick suspected that they had worked so well—even helping Kelley treat cancer—because they contained the full protein complement of the pancreas, all the known enzymes, perhaps some that hadn't even yet been identified.

Nick also speculated that a whole array of enzymes working together might be more effective than a single isolated enzyme. The array of enzymes might contain peptides and smaller proteins that could activate, stabilize and protect the major enzymes. The unidentified enzymes could even have an anti-cancer effect.

Nick's argument for using the whole array of enzymes was based on research on vitamins and herbal remedies that were found to work best as complexes found in nature. For example, B vitamins were sifted and sorted out in the 1940s. In experiments, scientists fed larger doses of single vitamins like thiamin

155

to lab animals and to humans. Quickly, the scientists discovered that both the lab animals and humans developed deficiencies in other B vitamins. Today, we know that B vitamins work better together as a complex.

Hypericum perforatum, or St. John's Wort, an herb commonly used to treat mild depression, has a similar story. For decades the whole herb was used in Europe with positive results. Scientists eventually isolated the herb's active ingredient hypericum and attempted to treat with just that component. Success rates plummeted. The herb worked much better as a whole plant complex.

Nick and Linda kept experimenting with the enzymes in their test tubes on the kitchen counter. Now that they had determined that they wanted to use an array of enzymes, they turned their attention to activation. Both Kelley and Levin assumed that a fully activated product was best. To make a maximally potent product, Levin thought that all the pancreatic precursors needed to be in the activated state. Kelley always clung to the belief that this kind of product was most efficient against cancer.

But here's where Nick's skeptical, probing journalistic training entered into play. He asked question after question until the facts were exhausted. Was this activation theory true? Nick asked. These two remarkable scientists, Levin and Kelley, had thought so, but Nick had also been trained by Dr. Good to know that true scientific discoveries often came from oblique angles.

"What if it were possible to use a partially active product?" Nick sat up in bed one night, awakening Linda from a deep sleep.

Linda glanced at the clock. 2:00 A.M. She rolled over and groaned. It was going to be a fight to get back to sleep.

"Do you think that's possible?"

"Perhaps. There're a lot of variables. But it's a hypothesis worth testing. Let me think about it when I'm awake."

Nick didn't need much sleep and he couldn't wait. He hopped out of bed and descended into his kitchen laboratory to think over and tinker with the test tubes. A fully active formula needed the ethylene dichloride to prevent the enzymes from destroying each other. A partially active formula wouldn't need a solvent. That would be a big plus.

The body had a system for precursor activation in the small intestine that worked quickly. Nick knew that Beard had required an active product. Beard injected the enzymes and there was presumably no way to activate the precursors in the bloodstream. But Nick reasoned that oral enzymes in the precursor form should be able to be activated. Even if most of the oral enzymes were in the precursor form, they should be activated rapidly in the small intestine.

The partially active product should be stable through the processing and find an ideal environment in the digestive tract. The precursors should be even more stable in the acid in the stomach than the fully active enzymes. And the partially active enzymes, unlike the active enzymes, wouldn't be colliding with each other. Instead, the partially active enzymes such as trypsin, would be as likely to collide with, and activate another precursor, creating an activation cascade. So, Nick thought he'd give a partially activated product a try.

"But what about the fats in the product?" Nick circled around Linda as she tried to eat breakfast. He paced back and forth in the kitchen.

Again, Levin and Kelley had never doubted that the product needed to be fat or lipid-free. But the investigative journalist questioned this premise, too. Nick and Linda plunged into a review of the biochemistry of fats in the human body, from essential fatty acids to prostaglandins to leukotrienes—all substances affecting a range of metabolic processes including inflammation, the immune response, circulation, and respiration as well as salt and water balance.

Next came an in-depth study of triglycerides, phospholipids and cholesterol. These substances often have a bad rap, but in effect, they have a dramatically positive role to play in human physiology. Among other functions, triglycerides store calories which can eventually be broken down into energy. Phospholipids are the foundation of all membranes of all cells of living organism. Without them, life could not exist.

Cholesterol is transformed into bile salts which aid in fat digestion and the absorption of the soluble vitamins such as A, D, E, and K. Cholesterol is also the starting point for the manufacture of all steroid hormones in the body, including various hormones produced by the adrenal cortex. These hormones provide the energy stream in the body, protect against inflammation, and help regulate the fluid balance in the body, and in turn, blood pressure.

Cholesterol is also the basis for the manufacture of sex hormones including estrogen and progesterone produced in the ovaries of the female, and testosterone produced in the testicles of the male. Cholesterol is also vital to the cellular structure and fluidity of the body. Without cholesterol, the cell membrane would literally fall apart.

Finally, cholesterol provides skin protection. It prevents evaporation of water from the skin that can be life threatening. Burn victims, for example, whose skin barriers are damaged, can become severely dehydrated. Cholesterol also prevents the absorption of many toxic water-soluble chemicals through the skin including salts, acids and bases that would otherwise dissolve away the surface of the human body.

"I understand Levin's aim to dehydrate the enzymes," Nick told Linda, plunging his hands into the sink full of suds and dirty dishes. In a watery environment, the active enzymes would soon set off a chain reaction cascade, one with another, and result in total destruction. "But why strip out the fat?"

At last, Nick decided that the best anti-cancer pancreatic enzymes would be dehydrated, only partially activated, retain all their fat cells, and be derived from pork. But where was he going to find a supply of enzymes to meet those specifications? He was a young, beginning doctor doing his research out of his mother's kitchen. What manufacturer would come to his aid? His only hope was to find an enzyme on the market that came close to what he wanted.

First, Nick checked the known and recognized supplies of pancreatic enzymes that were on the market. Nick sat down at his mother's kitchen table, picked up the receiver of her punch-button phone, the hard plastic receiver to his ear, and made call after call to the major pharmaceutical manufacturers. All of their enzymes were solvent extracted, containing fully activated enzymes stripped of fat, and derived from beef from the cattle lots of Omaha. A dead-end.

Next, Nick strolled into Willner Chemists, at 39th and Lexington. Willner's had once been an old-fashioned drug store complete with a soda fountain and aisles of over-the-counter tablets and remedies. Then in the 1970s, owner Irving Willner worked with leading orthomolecular and holistic physicians of the day to develop a line of nutritional supplements that would meet their stringent and exact requirements for purity and potency. By the mid-1980s, Willner's had evolved into a full-line health store, carrying its own brand of supplements.

On a hot August day, a blast of cool air hit Nick's skin upon entering Willner's store. Nick asked to see Irving Willner, the owner and pharmacist. To Nick's astonishment, Willner came out from behind the pharmacy window and sat down and discussed Nick's quest.

"I would suggest you try the pancreatic enzymes made by the Allergy Research Group," Willner said.

Nick knew that many alternative physicians used ARG products and that the company made a whole line of glandular products, including liver, thymus, and adrenal.

"All the animal products, including the enzymes are minimally processed," Willner said, explaining that Stephen Levine Ph.D., a microbiologist and the owner of the company, believed that processing destroyed too many active ingredients in supplements. His products were all in capsule form, not tablets. He felt that the compression of the enzymes into tablets would damage their effectiveness.

Nick pulled several bottles of the enzymes from the shelf. Wow, Nick thought, they're pork enzymes from New Zealand, the country with the highest and purest standards for animal husbandry. Nick couldn't believe his good fortune.

Nick bought a dozen bottles of the enzymes and took them back to his mother's home. He sat at the kitchen table, pulled apart the capsules and dumped the contents of several enzymes on his tongue. From his years of work with Kelley, Nick knew the taste of a good enzyme. His tongue felt tingly—a good sign, a sign that the enzymatic action was active and working. His tongue also detected a slightly meaty and greasy feel—an indication that the enzymes contained some fat.

Then Nick gulped down a number of the capsules and waited. He knew that good enzymes should not cause any digestive distress. Toward the end of his career before Kelley closed his office, his patients had complained of digestive problems when taking their enzymes. Whatever enzymes Kelley tried, his patients had the same complaints, all while the effectiveness of the supplements diminished. The ARG enzymes caused Nick no distress. They passed another test.

At last, Nick had to determine the actual potency of the enzymes. Nick and Linda had no funding to put the enzymes through an expensive laboratory assay, so Nick set up his own cheap but efficient test. Nick used his test tubes to compare the amount of Knox gelatin—a pure protein—digested over time by the ARG enzymes compared with the amount digested by the Viobin enzymes. The ARG product had approximately two to three times the strength of the Viobin enzymes. Nick figured this result indicated that the ARG enzymes were partially, not completely activated—just what he was hoping for.

Nick picked up the phone and called Dr. Stephen Levine in California and began asking questions.

"Yes, the enzymes are minimally processed and do contain some fat," Levine told Nick. "The water is extracted through freeze-drying. No, I don't believe any chemical solvents are used at any point in the manufacturing."

Nick told Levine about his interested in the enzymes. Levine didn't blink when Nick told him he was just beginning to start his practice.

"I can guarantee a steady supply of the enzymes," Levine reassured him.

Relief spread through every cell of Nick's body. At last, he had the enzymes he needed to begin his practice.

He just needed an office that he could afford.

And patients.

22

Dr. Robert Atkins leaned into the microphone at the WOR radio studios in New York City. "We're here today, folks, with *Health Revelations* on the *Design for Living* show to talk about an alternative treatment for cancer."

Across the table from Atkins sat Nick, a set of headphones squashed down over his ears, flattening his curly dark hair.

"With me today is Dr. Nicholas Gonzalez, a young medical doctor who treats cancer with diet, nutritional supplements, pancreatic enzymes, and detoxification. Dr. Gonzalez, can you tell us about your method for cancer treatment and how you developed it?"

Dr. Atkins, who had worked in radio and had thoughts of being an entertainer and comedian in his youth, engaged thousands of listeners every week with news of alternative health treatments. He had already become famous for his low carbohydrate diet, had his own radio show, and had a thriving alternative health practice on E. 56th St. in New York City. Nick had interviewed him during his journalism career, and in turn, Dr. Atkins had followed Nick's progress through medical school with interest.

When Nick and Linda had returned to New York, Atkins invited them to dinner and asked Nick to bring along his Kelley manuscript. Over dessert, Nick told of his quest to find a steady supply of the proper pancreatic enzymes. A few days later, Atkins called Nick to tell him not only had he read the manuscript, but he wanted Nick to come by his office and talk.

"I'd like you to come and work with me," Atkins said. He offered Nick a job with a generous salary, a support staff, and a steady supply of patients.

But after a few days of shadowing Atkins, Nick decided he wanted to be his own boss and administer his program out of his own office. Atkins accepted his decision and offered to help Nick by hosting him on his radio program.

On Atkins' talk show, Nick explained the "Gonzalez Protocol" as he now called it and answered questions from curious call-in participants, some who would find their way to his office where his name had gone up on the door. Situated on Park Avenue and 71st Street on the East Side of Manhattan, the address was one of the priciest locations in the city. Nick and Linda had moved out of his mother's house and into an apartment on East 51st Street, and Nick would often walk to his small rented office up York Avenue, past Rockefeller University where scores of eminent scientists worked, past Memorial Hospital and Sloan Kettering Institute where he had studied under Dr. Good, regularly meeting with him in his elegant penthouse with its view of all Manhattan.

But those days were all behind him. Squeezed into a tiny back room of his physician friends' office suite, Nick was open for business with his supplements and enzymes set to be purchased and distributed by the Allergy Research Group. A number of other alternative cancer resource agencies such as the Cancer Control Society had also tried to spread the word about Nick's treatment. On weekends and evenings, when the suite was cleared of the hub-bub of his friends' busy medical practice, Nick began to see patients.

One-by-one, they came to his office door, all very ill, most having tried conventional cancer therapy without success. Nick's first patient was a 55-year-old woman from Long Island with metastatic pancreatic cancer, her disease so advanced that tumors were growing in her liver and lungs. Her conventional doctors had already given up hope, so she and her husband were grateful to try an alternative method. Nick went right to work and designed a full program for her including round-the-clock doses of pancreatic enzymes.

The patient tolerated the program well for the first couple of days, then she began to respond as Kelley's patients had. She lost her appetite, became fatigued, and developed severe pain in her abdomen at the site of the pancreas, the discomfort worsening about a half hour after she ingested the enzymes. She also suffered widespread aches and pains and a low-grade fever. Nick knew from his years of working with Kelley that when patients complained of pain in a particular area, the enzymes were working, attacking the tumor at that location.

From Kelley, Nick knew that as tumors died off, their waste is released in the blood stream. The debris is processed by the liver, then excreted by the intestinal tract. More and more die-off can overwhelm the liver and cause the toxic debris to build up in the system producing a flu-like illness, muscular aches and pains, and a low-grade fever in the patient. Nick and Linda knew that while the patient felt ill, it was really a good sign.

After about a month on the program, the patient passed a large egg-like mass with tentacles that looked like an octopus. The patient's husband preserved the specimen in alcohol and brought it to Nick. He and his M.D. colleagues were convinced that the patient had thrown off one of the tumors that had invaded her duodenum, a cause for celebration. Unfortunately, this cancer patient also had a history of heart disease. Several weeks later she died of a pulmonary embolus, a blood clot to the lung.

Nick had other losses and failures, but he also had more and more successes, some of them still alive at the writing of this book. Alternative health magazines began to interview him and gradually, he began known as the "Doctor of Last Resort." More and more patients began to seek out his expertise, some even choosing Nick's program as their first course of treatment, not their last resort. His volume of patients became too heavy for evenings and weekends and he began seeing patients during regular work hours.

Raphaela Savino remembered arriving in Nick's office in 1989. At that time, she was a 56-year-old registered nurse who had been diagnosed with Stage IV ovarian cancer with a poor prognosis. A short time before her visit to Nick, Savino had had surgery. One or two days post-op, still lying in her hospital bed, her oncologist appeared to explain the chemotherapy regimen that she would soon begin.

"Being a nurse," Savino said. "I knew what this meant. "I had taken care of many people who had died of cancer. I had buried a good friend who had graduated from nursing school with me in 1965."

Then two other friends visited her with a copy of Dr. Kelley's book. They had researched alternative therapies and thought that Nick might offer more hope than conventional treatment. Savino was discharged on a Friday. She went home to her apartment in Brooklyn, read through the whole book, and called Nick that afternoon for an appointment on Monday.

Supported by a rich network of supportive female friends determined to see her through the Gonzalez program, Savino arrived at Nick's office ready to do whatever it took.

"The program is demanding and intense," Nick told her. "You'll have to stop working for a while."

Savino was single, her sole financial support. She couldn't stop working, but she promised to follow the program religiously.

"I had once been a nun," Savino said. "I had learned to be very disciplined. And I understood torture," she joked.

In contrast, when she didn't keep her chemotherapy appointment, her oncologist was furious. "Don't do that program," he insisted. "You'll die."

Her medical colleagues and her family echoed her oncologist's sentiments, thinking that Savino had lost her mind.

But she said good-bye to her oncologist, turned a deaf ear to her colleagues and family, and followed the Gonzalez program.

"He was all business at first," Savino said. "Rather cold. But I knew that he didn't want to waste time and emotional energy on someone who was not going to do the program. I imagined that there were plenty of people who came to his office for their first appointments, then found out all that was required, and turned around and said, 'Forget it.' And beyond that, there were people all too ready to sue him.'"

But Savino set up her routine and jumped right into it, and when Nick began to see her dedication to the program, he became softer and gentler. Savino got a glimpse of his humane and caring side shining through.

"I did the whole program and I worked eight-hours a day," Savino said. "I had a stressful job as a supervisor. I had to go against all of my co-workers, bringing my own lunch to work and downing all my pills right in front of their disapproving faces."

Eventually, her family came around, but their attitude didn't make the routine any easier.

"I worked all day, then came home at night and cooked, did the enemas, readied the pills, slept, cooked, worked, cooked and did the enemas. There wasn't any organic food in Brooklyn at that time, so I had to drive into Manhattan once a week and load up the car. It was exhausting and time consuming."

"Finally, after three months, I just collapsed. I had to take a leave of absence from work. I was self-supporting, and the program was expensive. I didn't know what I was going to do. I lay on the floor and cried to my best friend. "I will just have to put my faith in God.'"

Then Savino's mother died and left her an $8,000 inheritance.

"It was enough to carry me through the rest of that year. Dr. Gonzalez had recommended that I take the rest of the year off from work to rebuild. My scores came down that year and I have been stable since then. In 2015, I celebrated 25 years since my diagnosis and I brought Dr. Gonzalez a bottle of Martinelli sparkling apple juice. And after that year I was able to cut down on the enzymes. And I transitioned to a less stressful job as a health care consultant with a financial firm. I kept working then and didn't retire until I was 70 years old."

* * * * *

Meanwhile, with the help of the better-quality enzymes that they were using, Linda had regained her health on the program under Nick's supervision. During the time of her healing and recovery, the toxic chemical beta-mecaptoethanol that has a very strong odor, seemed to be seeping right out of her skin. She realized, and everyone around her also noticed that she smelled like rotten eggs. Then she began to feel better, and the experience convinced her of the Kelley program's validity. In better health, she resumed her residency in June of 1989, this time at the Department of Veteran's Affairs at New York University Medical School.

During this period, Linda read the work of Norman Vincent Peale, and she began attending the Church of Christ in Manhattan. Eventually, she brought Nick to these services with her, and ever the curious scholar, he became interested in the Bible. Raised a nominal Catholic, Nick had never before been engrossed in sacred texts, but now he sought out the help of Sherwin Mackintosh, one of the lay ministers in the Church of Christ.

Mackintosh realized that Nick was highly intelligent, and that his nutritional program was effective. Several members of their church had gone to Nick for treatment and had long outlived their prognoses. One patient had brain cancer and was given but a few months to live. He did Nick's program and lived another 15 to 17 years.

At one point, Michael Landon had come to Nick for an appointment. In church, the congregation prayed that Nick would be able to help Landon, but when he arrived in Nick's office and discussed the program, Landon decided against it. He wanted something quicker and easier, so he didn't follow through with the treatment.

Nick became more interested in a Christian way of life and worked with the homeless, bringing one shivering HIV positive man a blanket to keep him from freezing to death. During this era of his life, Nick took a call from a friend whose father lay on the floor unable to move with severe back pain.

Nick rented a car, driving all the way out to the New York City suburb, helping the man up, and almost carrying him to the door. Nick put the man in the car and took him to an atlas orthogonal chiropractor in New Jersey. The man received an adjustment and was relieved of his pain.

"Nick Gonzalez was a maverick with a direct line to the Divine," Nick's friend later told me.

Nick opened his door and his heart to others, especially congregants in his church with cancer and other diseases. Whether they had lymphoma or migraines, he urged them to call him when needed. Day or night.

"I always sleep with the phone next to my bed," he told them.

Most were hesitant to bother him. Many didn't have insurance that would cover his treatment. Some paid what they could. Some couldn't pay at all and Nick saw them for free. He tried to help them and wasn't interested in money or power. But he was upset when people wouldn't listen to him and follow his directions.

Nick still retained remnants of Catholicism, his heritage faith, carrying some of the structures and beliefs he'd learned through his family and culture. He believed in God but not a personal relationship with Jesus Christ. Nick joined a Bible study group through the Church of Christ, then he met with Mackintosh individually, trekking down to the Village for their appointments. They read the Bible together. At the beginning of their studies, Mackintosh told Nick to read one chapter and to come back the following week. Nick returned, having read the whole New Testament in one sitting.

Nick poured his energy and attention into his Biblical studies the way he'd done with his medical studies, reviewing chapters and verses over and over again, quickly assimilating long passages of sacred text with his photographic memory. Overtime, he examined both the Old and New Testaments from all angles, studying and examining the Bible as if it were a patient presenting with mysterious problems difficult to solve. With his quick, scientific mind, he asked probing, incisive questions of the text, quizzing the minister just as he had quizzed Kelley about his treatment for cancer.

Finally, Nick decided that he would officially join the Church of Christ and become baptized into the fold. He had been baptized a Catholic in infancy, but now he was entering into adult Christian commitment of his own free will. The service was held in the baptistery, a large walk-in pool half-filled with water. An intimate gathering of family and fellow congregants gathered around the baptistery, the minister standing up to his waist in water. He waited to hear Nick's profession of faith, waited to submerge Nick's whole body into the water. Nick had skipped the usual pomp and circumstance of ritual and robes, and inched toward the baptistery in his bare feet, dressed in shorts and T-shirt.

The minister, standing in the water, beckoned to Nick. "Are you ready to dedicate yourself to your savior Jesus Christ?"

"Yes, I am," Nick responded, and he waded into the water.

23

The waters of Nick's life ebbed and flowed, rocked and waved, lifting him up and crashing down around him as he plunged from one decade into the next.

By 1988, just a year after Nick had set up his practice, the Office of Professional Medical Conduct of the Department of Health in New York began requesting the files of several of his patients. Nick contacted these patients to see if they had lodged complaints against him. The patients all protested that they had not and were startled to hear that their records were being read by the Department of Health.

Nick suspected that some of the complaints were coming from New York physicians determined to put alternative medicine doctors out of business. Several of these doctors had joined together, and working with the medical boards and insurance companies, attacked physicians stepping outside of "the medical standard of care." Several of Nick's patients had also told him that their orthodox physicians had cautioned them against the "Gonzalez Protocol," and suggested that they contact these "quackbusters" to get the low-down on his fraudulent practice.

Starting in 1988, the OPMC had initiated a series of meetings with Nick to discuss his practice. These were not hearings, but were framed as dialogues about his work. Nick stepped into the conference room and was seated at the long table across from the physicians, but when he tried to explain his research, Nick was chagrined when the investigators showed no interest and refused to listen or even try to understand his methodology. They seemed to have made up their minds and held firm in their belief that Nick was a fraud, preying on the vulnerability of very ill patients.

"We going to send an investigator to your office to thoroughly examine 25 of your patient files for comprehensive review," the investigators finally told Nick, and Nick knew that such a "review" inevitably led to charges.

169

In 1988, Dr. Good began writing Nick a series of letters asking him to cease and desist in associating his name with Nick's program. Good did not want to be associated with another student issuing what he feared might be false claims. In addition, on March 14, Good wrote a notarized statement "To Whom It May Concern" distancing himself from Nick and his treatment:

> *When Dr. Gonzales (sic) was a student of medicine at Cornell, he asked me if I would act as a faculty advisor for an elective project which he wished to pursue as a senior student at Cornell. He wanted to study a particular unproved remedy involving a very complex nutritional regimen that was based upon an unfounded theoretical framework. Although I would have much preferred to have this apparently highly intelligent, highly motivated student do an elective using conventional reasoning and established techniques of evaluation of anti-cancer activity, (e.g., in experimental systems), I considered that there might be heuristic value in the project Mr. Gonzales (sic) proposed, and that at the very least, Gonzales (sic) might learn important facts about the natural history of cancer.*
>
> *Gonzales (sic) thus spent several months while a student and later, much of his spare time while he worked as an Immunology Fellow in my laboratory, evaluating cases which he selected from a large population of nutritionally treated patients allegedly suffering from advanced cancer. At no time did I personally investigate these patients directly as I would have were I carrying out such a study myself. I did observe under the microscope tissues allegedly derived from the diagnostic biopsies of the cancer in the patients, and I carefully perused the medical records, generally from leading cancer centers throughout the country, which ostensibly defined some of the patients Gonzales (sic) was showing me as very advanced or terminal cancers. Indeed, the collection of cases Gonzales (sic) showed me were generally representative of the kinds of cancer I recognize as being forms of cancer most refractory to any forms of cancer treatment. These patients were then identified to me as patients who had experienced extremely long survivals and were often described as being patients in vigorous good health. Gonzales*

(sic) said he had interviewed some of these patients and their family members in some detail.

Gonzales (sic) appeared to be convinced that the nutritional therapy being used to treat these patients was responsible for the apparent success of their treatment. I could not in any way vouch for the authenticity of the records and biopsies, or the relationship of either of these to the patients who allegedly showed the long-term survival, but if one accepted the apparent observations presented by Gonzales (sic) at face value, the experience with the 50 cases that Dr. Gonzales (sic) showed me were far outside general experience with any medical treatment of cancer I have experienced, read about or heard about in more than 40 years of medical practice, much of which has been focused on cancer in its many forms.

Dr. Gonzales (sic) generously asked me to author or coauthor a scientific article or a book about these patients, and I refused...

It is incorrect to infer that I advocate the approach Gonzales (sic) discussed in his testimony for treatment of any form of cancer at this juncture. To my knowledge, I have never used this approach in treating any of my cancer patients. I have never referred any of my patients to anyone for such therapy. I do not accept this approach or any nutritional approach as being an alternative to full chemotherapy with induction, consolidation and maintenance phases for treatment of any of the forms of acute leukemia of childhood.

This having been stated, I wish to add that I respect Dr. Gonzales (sic) as a person. He is a well-informed, reasonably trained clinical scientist who should be able to carry out investigations of his working hypothesis and try to do appropriate testing of that approach in a properly randomized, controlled clinical trial in patients who suffer from currently incurable forms of advanced cancer...

Nick had been prepared for the visit by the State Medical Board. He had even anticipated Dr. Good's disclaimers. His mentor, who had served as his best man at his wedding, had suffered a major blow to his reputation by the Summerlin case. Good didn't need another fraudulent student, and he had always been skeptical about outlier, untested treatments. But Nick was caught off guard in 1990 when he received a copy of a letter from Dr. Kelley's girlfriend—a physician who eventually lost her own medical license—sent to the New York Department of Health. Dr. Kelley and his girlfriend had filed a complaint against Nick, claiming that he was endangering the lives of his patients.

Soon after, Kelley actually sued Nick and Dr. Good. By this time Kelley had become convinced that Nick was a CIA agent set-up to spy on him and steal his program. Nick knew that the whole case was a result of Kelley's mental deterioration. It saddened him to see his previous mentor, such a brilliant man, in such shape, but the case was time consuming and did not endear him further to Dr. Good.

Finally, the case was abruptly resolved, thrown out in court, when Kelley threatened the judge.

Later in 1991, Good wrote letters to several of the well-known "quackbusters" of the era disavowing his relationship to Nick and his alternative treatment of cancer. A call from, and articles written by insurance representatives, were referenced. In his letters, Good insisted that he did not approve of the Kelley program and had advised Nick that its protocol needed to be subjected to clinical trials before he could even entertain its validity:

> *What seems to be presented for Dr. Gonzales (sic) in the article written by the insurance representative, as far as it goes, reflects, although incompletely, the advice I gave Dr. Gonzales (sic) in this heuristic context. What is said is factually correct as far as it goes. What the insurance representative does not state is that I advised Dr. Gonzales (sic) repeatedly, and also the insurance representative who called me, that it would be wrong to promulgate any nutritional approach to the treatment of cancer, without establishing the validity of that treatment in an appropriately monitored, controlled clinical trial. When he left my laboratories and clinics six year ago, Dr. Gonzales (sic) said he was going to do such a study. He said his work in New York would be monitored by two disinterested but concerned practitioners of internal medicine with whom he would be sharing offices in New York.*

Despite these troubles, Nick's practice began to grow during 1990–91, the word spreading through the alternative medicine underground. He and Linda continued to work on getting the supplements perfected, even manufacturing their own enzymes to be used in their program. This project would consume them for the next 5 years. In addition to their own research, Nick now had a difficult practice with very ill patients.

Nick plunged into a life of work, work. And more work. He saw more and more patients, seeing those who lived near New York City every couple of months. For those who were travelling distances, he required them to return at least every six months when he did a complete re-evaluation of their programs and a thorough physical examination.

He constantly reviewed the charts of patients seeking his help. He accepted those he thought he could help, and turned down those whom he thought would have more success with conventional therapy, or those who were too close to death, or those who couldn't eat or swallow properly, or those whose families were unsupportive and adamantly against his program. At the end of his day, after seeing as many as five or six patients for an hour each, he ate a snack, then sat down at his desk to return phone calls from patients. He never charged patients for these calls, and problems could range from how to pack a coffee percolator for travel, to emergencies with patients in life-and-death situations.

Nick had known that his practice was going to be stressful, but it took all the strength that he could muster to ride through the ups and downs of his patients' responses. He found solace in his Christian faith and even incorporated it into his program with his patients for several years until non-Christians objected.

He was a member of the Republican Party, another organizing belief system that brought stability to his life. He had been a great supporter of Ronald Reagan and a believer in free markets. He gave money to the party, and was actively engaged with current affairs, writing letters to his representatives on major issues of the day.

He was a patriot, clinging to his belief in the constitution of the United States and the principles of its founding fathers. Patriotism brought comfort to Nick and underlined his belief in a secure society and culture. And patriotism brought thoughts of his own patriarchal line—all that his father had taught him and the closeness they had experienced while playing baseball and watching WW II documentaries on television.

And finally, he clung to his belief in science. He loved being a doctor and hated being an outcast from the institutions of conventional medicine. He cringed when he was called a quack or charlatan. He had gone to all Ivy League schools and felt that he was part of the team.

Yet, he had studied medical and scientific history, how major discoveries were often made outside the normal channels of prestige and influence. He realized that revolutionary scientific ideas were often discounted and dismissed, and lone individuals often had to persevere until recognition came years later.

Look at Ignaz Semmelweiss, the early pioneer of antiseptic procedures. Nick knew Semmelweiss had been mocked for washing his hands before delivering babies. In the end, that simple procedure had dramatically reduced infant and maternal mortalities during deliveries. Look at Joseph Lister who sterilized surgical instruments and wounds with carbonic acid. In 1865, surgeons operated in very unsanitary conditions, wearing blood stains on their unwashed hospital gowns like badges of honor. Lister's research significantly reduced infections.

Nick clung to these stories and knew that finally, he had to have an absolute belief in himself. He only hoped that in the end, the medical world would reinstate him on the squad.

Nick referred many of his patients to the chiropractor Roy Sweat, D.C. in Atlanta for structural work, and Nick and Roy frequently spoke on the phone. At one point, Nick had accidently walked into a glass door, and twisted the vertebrae in his neck, so he himself became Roy's patient. Nick flew to Atlanta when needed and after his treatment, he often had dinner with Roy's family. Old enough to be Nick's father, Roy counseled Nick about the difficulties in his practice, and filled in the gap Nick had felt with the loss of his mentors Kelley and Good.

> *There were moments of severe discouragement. Some patients just didn't survive; some were just too sick, some had been subjected to too much prior chemotherapy and radiation, some just didn't have the will to live, some just didn't do the program properly. But always, when the work seemed to be going nowhere, and discouragement would become oppressive, a patient with terribly advanced cancer would turn around and start improving, and get well. Tumors would stabilize, or regress; a patient with chronic*

fatigue would get better. A patient with depression would send a letter of appreciation, thanking me for giving them their life back.

There were enough successes to keep Nick going and make him more determined than ever to gain recognition for the program from the conventional medical world. But recognition, let alone an ebbing of the hostilities, wasn't possible without a real test of the program, the test that Dr. Good had called for, the test that Nick thought he would have the funding for by this time—a clinical trial.

Then his personal life became a trial. Linda completed her residency and passed her boards in 1991, joining Nick in his office. But the stress of her residency was a real test of her marriage. Nick was functioning as both her husband and her doctor, and in an article that Linda wrote for the *Townsend Newsletter*, she explained that they had one too many 2:00 A.M. discussions about pancreatic enzymes. In addition, Linda and Nick came from very different parts of the country with ethnic and cultural backgrounds that they eventually found incompatible in a marriage.

Yet like divorced parents who maintain a relationship for the sake of the children, Nick and Linda remained together as scientific colleagues. The divorce brought great sadness to Nick. He had told several members of his church how much he had admired Linda, how smart he thought she was. Nick and Linda worked to weather the divorce and find compatibility in the office. Eventually, Linda remarried a man from her church whose work was outside the medical field. Nick left the Church of Christ and continued to study the Bible on his own. He developed a life-long habit of reading the Bible on every morning in his apartment.

To add an additional level of stress, in 1991, a physician from the New York Department of Health buzzed Nick's office door. She entered with a team of investigators.

"We will be going through all your files today," she announced, perching herself in front of his file cabinet where he stored his patient charts. Very systematically, she remained in her chair all day, reading through the charts, sorting and stacking them, taking copious notes. By five o'clock p.m., the physician and her investigators left Nick's office with 25 charts, all of the patients deceased. They exited the suite, the charts tucked under their arms, and without saying a word, let the door slam shut.

24

But Nick knew that another door had already opened. In 1989, a slight, dark-haired woman named Sandy Miller had buzzed his office. A patient with chronic fatigue syndrome who had been to conventional and non-conventional doctors alike without success, Sandy had researched alternative medicine and had taken a deep interest in the Gonzalez program and Nick's association with Kelley. With Nick's treatment, Sandy began to feel better within months, her energy and stamina improving, and as a result, she became an enthusiastic supporter of Nick's program.

Then one day Sandy called Nick. "Can you come to dinner this weekend with me and Ernst?"

Ernst Wynder was her longtime partner, a physician famous for his research into the cancerous-causing properties of tobacco.

"Ernst wants to meet the young doctor who helped me. He also wants you to bring a copy of your Kelley study. Ernst is very skeptical of your approach. Doesn't put much stock in coffee enemas, you know. But he sincerely wants to meet you."

Without hesitation, Nick agreed to come to dinner. He had actually met Wynder years before. During his journalism days, Nick had interviewed Wynder for a long article that he had done on cancer prevention. Nick knew Wynder's whole back story and how he had gone from an outcast to a hero in the medical community.

A Jewish refugee from Nazi Germany, Wynder immigrated to the United States at age 18, learned English quickly, then was drafted into the army and sent back to Germany working in intelligence. At the end of the war, he visited his hometown of Hereford, only to find it completely destroyed by Allied bombs.

During the summer after his third year of medical school at Washington University, Wynder had a job working in the pathology laboratory at Bellevue

Hospital in New York City. He started reading case reports of autopsies performed on patients dead from lung cancer. He began to notice that there was a correlation between these lung cancer patients and their heavy use of tobacco, and he suspected that there was a link between the disease and smoking.

Back at Washington University, his discovery was met with skepticism, but while he was still a fourth-year medical student, he wrote up his research and published an article in JAMA, the *Journal of the American Medical Association*, linking cancer and smoking. These were the days when cigarette smoke filled most doctor's offices, homes, restaurants and public spaces. Students and professors smoked in lecture halls. Airplanes, buses, and taxis were blue with smoke. Most doctors thought smoking was perfectly safe, and even recommended it to their patients as an antidote to stress. Cancer was viewed as a random accident, completely unrelated to dietary habits or environmental exposures. The medical research establishment reacted to Wynder's publication with dismissal and scorn.

Despite the push-back, Wynder did manage to make a name for himself, and after his residency, Sloan Kettering set him up with full funding and a laboratory to study the tie between cancer and smoking—an extraordinary opportunity. Wynder eventually headed his own research department that studied not only the toxicity of tobacco but the damaging effects of other environmental hazards such as asbestos.

Wynder's group pumped out scores of articles on the carcinogenicity of tobacco and other toxins, which did not endear him to the powerful tobacco industry. Wynder also became interested in the role of nutrition in cancer, and he did some of the first research linking vitamin B2, or riboflavin deficiency, to Plummer-Vinson syndrome, a disease associated with esophageal cancer that had a particularly high prevalence in Scandinavia.

Finally, in 1964, the Surgeon General officially linked smoking to cancer and Wynder was at least partially vindicated. But the battle continued. In 1969, the tobacco industry offered funding to Sloan Kettering in hopes of silencing Wynder. "There are more carcinogens in a tomato than a packet of cigarettes," the chain-smoking director of the Sloan Kettering Institute told Philip Morris, showing up at their headquarters to solicit a donation. Beginning in 1962, Philip Morris made a three-year $25,000 annual contribution to Sloan Kettering, and soon other cigarette manufacturers ponied up similar sums.

By this time Wynder was an internationally renown medical researcher. He refused to resign. Instead, he appealed to his many colleague friends for help, but for fear of losing their own jobs, they declined to help him. At last, Wynder caved. He resigned at 47 years old with no future job in sight, little money in the bank, and no funding resources. But it didn't take him long to regroup and decide to set up his own research institute.

In a rented storage room in the basement of his old East End Avenue apartment building in Manhattan, Wynder created the American Health Foundation, an institute to study preventative medicine. He hoped it would be a safe haven, protected from the forces of industry and medical orthodoxy, for scientists who were working against the mainstream to do their research.

Nick first met Wynder just seven years after he had founded his institute. By that time, Wynder's foundation had gained international fame for the study of cancer linked to dietary and environmental factors. Wynder had finally been accepted, even lauded by the medical community and he was heavily funded by both government and industry. He had backing from real estate developer William Levitt, philanthropist Naylor Dana and the Charles Dana Foundation, and David Mahoney, founding chairman of the Dana Alliance for Brain Initiatives. He was wined and dined by presidents, heads of state, and Hollywood actors.

A few weeks after Sandy Miller's call, Nick showed up at Wynder's apartment in the UN Plaza Building off of 48th Street. The door opened, Wynder greeted him warmly, and Nick handed him a copy of his Kelley study which he began reading immediately. Wynder was a ruggedly handsome man, a shock of dark hair framing his high forehead and square jaw. His eyebrows, thick, dark and prominent on his supraorbital ridge, almost knit together, accenting his large, penetrating brown eyes with a glare of brilliance that could cut to the core of a problem like a laser beam. Nick waited while Wynder read through his monograph, taking in the surroundings. Nick was wowed by the view:

> *His apartment faced south, with the East River clearly visible to the left, the park-like UN Grounds in front, and the large, rectangular shaped UN building looming off the River, its many offices brightly lit in the twilight. Beyond the UN stretched the buildings of midtown Manhattan. And although I had heard that the apartments in that building tended to look like hotel rooms, Wynder had completely redone his own space in the style of a 19th century English club. He had knocked out one of the bedrooms, and*

created an intimate study with built- in shelves, and dark mahog-
any paneling. The large dining room, also with an exquisite view
southward, was, like the study, darkly paneled. Wynder had filled
the apartment with unusual antiques, which he had accumulated
over the years during his many trips to Europe. The dining room
table and chairs dated from 17th century Germany; a sideboard had
the signature of the craftsman who created it, and the date—1639.

Nick and Wynder talked in the living room surrounded by Wynder's enlarged and framed photographs that graced the walls, capturing his travels to Tiananmen Square in China, to the canals of Venice, and to medieval towns in Eastern Europe.

The two physicians talked for awhile before moving into the dining room. Then when the UN building lit up in the late autumn darkness and dinner was served, Wynder turned to Nick.

"Tell me of your research under Dr. Robert Good?" Wynder began. He probed Nick about his background, his years at Columbia, and his experiences with Dr. Kelley.

Nick dove into his story, how he had met Kelley quite by accident, studied with him, and documented his many properly-diagnosed patient success stories in his monograph. He told Wynder of the opposition he had already faced from the orthodox medical world, and Wynder shared his own battles with getting funding and recognition. The two men bonded over their shared experiences and Wynder invited Nick to lunch at the American Health Foundation.

A couple of weeks later, Nick arrived at Wynder's executive offices on the fourth floor of the Ford Foundation on 43rd St. By this time, the American Health Foundation had close to 300 employees and around 90 senior level scientists. Wynder's office took up most of the floor, more of his photographs covering the walls with shots of people and places from around the world. Additional photos captured him with senators, heads of state, and Nobel Laureates.

The two doctors had lunch in the Foundation dining room overlooking a lush atrium filled with flowers and potted bushes and trees. Wynder had studied Nick's monograph in depth and Wynder grilled him about the methodology, about John Beard, the enzymes, the coffee enemas and the metabolic types. Wynder questioned Nick about some of the case studies in the monograph, then asked him to present some unusual cases from his own practice.

"So what do you want for the future?" Wynder finally asked Nick.

"I know that there is something very useful in this therapy, but I want it tested. I want to prove its worth in a properly run clinical trial." Nick said.

Soon Nick was on a train up to visit Wynder in his home in Westport, Connecticut where Sandy had invited him to spend the day. Several other scientists were spending the weekend. Nick had been working so hard that he hadn't been out of the city in months, and barely noticed that autumn had arrived. The day was clear, brisk and windy. He took a deep breath, staring out the window, fully enjoying the blur of brilliant orange and red changing leaves on the trees.

> *Wynder's house in Westport was again, uniquely Wynder. It wasn't an exceptionally big house, but had considerable character, like an old Connecticut farm house. The house was on two acres, through which flowed a large, wide stream, complete with ducks. His house, with an outside terrace, abutted the stream. Inside, he had completely redone the house with his trademark wood paneling. There was a huge fireplace in the living room, a book lined study with a large window overlooking the stream outside. His large bedroom was downstairs, and upstairs were two guest bedrooms.*

The other guests that Saturday included a cancer researcher from Harvard and a molecular biologist from Germany. Nick thought that they were a bit surprised to hear about Nick's own research—complete with coffee enemas—but they accepted him as another guest of their host. After lunch when the group moved to the outside terrace, Wynder asked Nick to present some of his cases. All gathered listened attentively, and Nick relished the feeling of being in the company of a group of fellow scientists—a camaraderie that he had missed since he'd left Dr. Good's group.

After that luncheon, Nick became a frequent guest at both Wynder's Westport house and his apartment in New York City. He met with some of the scientists at Wynder's foundation. Gradually, Nick realized that Wynder hosted scientific salons at his properties, making introductions among researchers, and listening intently when his guests presented their research.

"I learned much from my brilliant and creative guests," Wynder later told Nick.

As much as Nick enjoyed the salons and the connections that he was making through Wynder, he grew impatient. Ever hard-driving and ambitious, Nick knew that Wynder was such a renowned and powerful scientist that he could merely pick up the phone, make the right calls, and put Nick's program on the map.

"You have to be patient," Wynder told Nick over and over while they were at dinner at his apartment or overlooking the stream in Westport.

"Let's get this treatment out to the world," Nick shook his head. "We could be saving so many more lives."

"For now, you have to continue doing what you're doing, seeing patients, refining the treatment, collecting data, writing up unusual cases."

And again and again, Wynder reminded Nick that it had taken him 20 years before his own tobacco research was accepted by the most extraordinary oppositional forces of the industrial and medical world.

"But I need funding for my research."

"Be patient. It will happen when the time is right."

Nick grew more frustrated. He stood in Wynder's shadow, the older man receiving more and more awards, more and more funding. At the time, Wynder's research had turned to children's health, a safe topic, applauded by both the Democratic and Republican political parties. The foundation had initiated a *Know Your Body Campaign* that provided schoolchildren from K-6 with information about health, nutrition, and exercise. Actress and comedian Whoopi Goldberg served as the spokesperson for the campaign featuring two puppet characters—Nurse Whoopi and Doctor Aaah who bore a striking resemblance to Dr. Wynder.

Meanwhile, Nick was running himself ragged, seeing more and more patients in an attempt to keep his own research afloat. Just one phone call, Nick thought to himself, that's all it would take, one phone call from this man the whole world now embraced, and he could have his treatment tested. All Wynder had to do was pull one string.

25

On September 7, 1992, Nick sat at a dinner table full of internationally recognized scientists in Tel Aviv, Israel, but he wasn't thinking about pulling any strings. He was thinking about enzymes and his lecture the following morning. He accepted this lecture because it meant a trip to the Holy Land, a place of particular importance to him as he had become more and more of a Biblical scholar. He always hoped to connect with other pre-eminent scientists and gain support for his program. Networking was necessary, and he was honored to have been asked to give a talk at this conference, but in general he hated travelling such distances. No matter what the circumstances, he disliked being away from his work—even in Israel. He was happiest at his desk doing his research. He didn't have time to waste on chit-chat.

So, at the dinner table, he didn't engage in conversation with any of the other guests. Instead, he rehearsed his presentation again and again in his own mind. He thought about pancreatic enzymes. He always thought about pancreatic enzymes. In his lectures, he never used a note card, chart, or graph. He could talk for hours at top speed with conviction, wit, and charisma, with perfect recall with all the information drawn from his own memory. Mostly, the other guests barely noticed that Nick was in the room, but he caught the attention of Dr. Hans Moolenburgh, a preeminent cancer researcher from the Netherlands, who was seated next to his wife at another table.

"Look at that man over there. People have told me he's Dr. Gonzalez from New York and will be lecturing in the morning," Moolenburgh said to his wife. "He seems to be totally self-absorbed. What in the world is the matter with him?"

Suddenly, Nick stood up and walked away toward the bathroom.

"Got it. Timothy!" Moolenburgh said, referring to the son of an English friend.

"Whatever are you talking about?" Moolenburgh's wife said.

"That Dr. Gonzalez. Look at him! He's top heavy, just like Timothy. He's super intelligent. We may expect fireworks tomorrow morning."

And fireworks there were. Nick stood before a packed room, in his pinstriped suit, blue shirt and matching blue tie immaculately pressed and fitted to his compact, muscular body. At a fast clip, he began his soft-spoken narrative about Kelley and how the dentist had treated himself for his own pancreatic cancer, about Beard and his work with enzymes, about Pottenger and Price, and back to Kelley with his 12 metabolic types. Nick spoke about his apprenticeship with Kelley and how he had eventually set up his own practice in New York City.

He detailed some of his "miracle cases" as he liked to call them, patients who had returned to health against all odds. There were breast cancer patients, one whose cancer had even spread to her brain and metastasized to her bones, who were now in total remission. There were lung, colon, and kidney cancer patients who had had good results. There was Raphaela Savino who beat stage IV ovarian cancer. And there was Mort Schneider who came to Nick in 1991 with metastatic pancreatic cancer to the liver. A bookkeeper from Florida, he had been told he only had weeks to live, but his wife had found an article about Nick in a health food store, and off Mort went to New York. A year later, Mort was still alive and "feeling great."

After his talk, the packed room burst into applause, with attendees rising to their feet with a long-lasting standing ovation. People rushed the podium to ask Nick questions. During his forty years of practicing medicine, Dr. Moolenburgh had never heard such good results from any alternative cancer treatment.

"Your results are hardly to be believed!" Moolenburgh told Nick, standing before him at the lectern. "I've never heard anything like this before."

Nick's eyes shot open and he bristled. "Sir, I am a Christian and I do not lie."

"Sir, I am a Christian, too, I do not lie either," Moolenburgh echoed Nick. "I will come to New York and see for myself."

"But I never do that."

"Then I will be the first!" Moolenburgh said.

Nick's temper subsided, and he and Hans quickly became friends, spending the rest of their free time at the conference together, discussing the Bible and Nick's trip to the Church of the Holy Sepulchre. Nick had arrived in Israel a day early and had visited Jerusalem, finding the city center to visit the holy sites.

"It was a disaster," Nick told Hans. "I had a nasty hangover for the rest of the day."

Hans agreed that the site was horrible with every Christian denomination claiming its own little piece of ground. "Serene holiness is the last thing you can find there." Then Hans explained that on his last trip to Israel he had been told by his inn keeper that the grave in the city was "just poppycock," that Mosaic law forbade burial within the city walls, and the real grave was in another entirely different location outside the ancient walls. The inn keeper connected Hans to another Dutchman, the guardian of the site, and Hans visited at sunrise when the place was empty and free of tourists.

Hans and Nick agreed to stay an additional day together in Israel after the conference. Early in the morning, Hans took Nick out of the inner city through one of the big gates in the wall. After a short walk they came to a sheltered garden where they felt a deep serenity. A sense of astonishment enveloped Nick's face. Suddenly, the garden opened up to a high rock wall, rounded at the top with deep holes pushed into its surface. It looked exactly like a skull. At the foot of the rock, a hole had been hacked into the stone with a three-foot wide stone bench on the right side, a bench large enough to hold a corpse.

"There is Golgotha!" Hans said, telling Nick about his first visit to the grave when he had stood there at sunrise for some time, remembering Mary Magdalene who had come to the tomb and found it empty.

"Yes, yes, yes! Here it is!" Nick went into the grave, getting more and more excited. The two men stood in awe together in the sacred site.

The next day they took a boat tour of the Sea of Galilee. Hans and Nick sat on the deck staring out into the cool, calm blue water, the verdant stretches of grasses dotted with palm trees near the shore and the brown, dry mountains in the distance. Hans leaned back in his chair and reveled in all the famous Bible stories that took place on this body of water, from Jesus calling his disciples in their fishing boats, to Jesus walking on water, to the Sermon on the Mount. *Blessed are the poor in spirit, for theirs is the kingdom of heaven. Blessed are those who mourn, for they shall be comforted. Blessed are the meek, for they will inherit the earth.*

Suddenly, Nick turned to Hans and said, "I have a patient I would like to discuss with you."

"Nick, another time," Hans said. "You are welcome to discuss patients with me, but now I am on the Sea of Galilee and would like to experience it."

Nick was miffed by the response. At all times, even in the Holy Land, Nick's mind was on his practice and research.

Nick's mind was very much on medicine when several months later, Hans flew across the Atlantic to New York from the Netherlands to observe Nick in action in his practice for a week. Hans arrived in Nick's tiny office on Park Avenue and sat uncomfortably in a simple straight wooden chair. Nick sat at a plain desk, surrounded by file cabinets, the written records of his patients neatly alphabetized inside. Nick's examination room was even smaller in size.

The day began at 10:00 A.M. sharp. Hans folded his tall frame into the wooden chair beside Nick, his attention completely focused on Nick's patients until 1:00 P.M. Nick opened all his files to Hans, showed him complete sets of records, with x-ray films, laboratory tests, and scores. Hans asked Nick's patients questions and attended their physical examinations. They took a short break for lunch at a health food store, then it was back to work seeing patients steadily until 5:30 P.M. when Nick began returning patient phone calls for an hour. By then Hans' back was aching so badly that he yearned to get up and stretch, but he was impressed by how Nick kept up with patients all over the United States.

The two men walked to a health food restaurant for a quick dinner, then back to Nick's apartment where they sat in front of his computer discussing patients. Hans saw what meticulous records Nick kept, registering everything into the patient charts. At 1:30 A.M. in the morning, Hans finally got back to his hotel, and in the early morning hours before he grabbed a few hours of sleep, he made notes on all that he had observed. Then it was up and back to Nick's office again by 10:00 A.M.

And what observations did Hans record in his notebook? Hans realized that Nick hadn't exaggerated his case studies in his presentation in Tel Aviv. To the contrary, Hans felt that Nick had been humble about his successes. Hans observed patient after patient coming into Nick's office with late stage cancers who had been seemingly without hope, now in good health, their cancers under control or completely vanished. Hans studied their charts, from their original diagnoses through their treatments from the conventional medical model world, to their experiences with Nick. He found it all above board. He felt that he had at last found a master of alternative cancer therapy.

In years past, Hans had followed Dr. Kelley's work and had referred patients to him and had seen good results. But because Hans could not get the proper enzymes in the Netherlands, he did not pursue Kelley's methodology. Now here was another, younger man, an impeccable physician who had very scientifically perfected and expanded on Kelley's work. Hans was especially impressed with Nick's methods of detoxification. Upon returning to the Netherlands, Hans incorporated some of these techniques into his own practice with considerable success.

Hans also zeroed in on Nick's use of hair analysis as a diagnostic tool. Again, Hans couldn't figure out how Nick was getting such specific and detailed information from the small strands of hair that Nick's patients sent to be analyzed several weeks before their appointments. Then Hans realized that Nick was using an electronic apparatus invented by a San Francisco medical doctor named Albert Abrams, and perfected by an Oxford, England engineer named George de la Warr. Both inventors were attacked as quacks practicing pseudoscience, ridiculed for their research, and driven into bankruptcy. Hans himself had worked with the apparatus and was able to sort out many mysterious patient complaints. But he, like Nick, did not openly discuss the use of the apparatus, always mindful of the reaction they might receive from the traditional medical establishment.

Once Hans had returned to the Netherlands, he turned around and invited Nick to come to Holland and lecture to his colleagues. Nick accepted the invitation and brought his intellect, his great recall of facts, and his ability to relate his groundbreaking research to his audience. He astonished the alternative medical world of the Netherlands who were wowed by his abilities. His lectures cemented his relationship to Dr. Hans Moolenburgh who would serve as a mentor and sounding board for Nick the rest of his life. Hans supported Nick spiritually and emotionally, through the roller coaster of his life.

When they had met in Israel, Hans had asked Nick if he had ever been persecuted for what he was doing.

"Why should I be?" Nick said. "What I do is perfectly above board. Why should I be attacked? I am not some quack without a medical degree!"

Hans, Nick's senior by several decades, knew that a medical degree would not protect Nick from professional jealousy and attacks on his out-of-the-box research that veered away from the conventional medical model. Hans just shook his head and held his breath for what was to come.

26

One day several weeks before Thanksgiving in 1992, the phone rang.

"My name is Dr. Pierre Guesry, the medical director from Nestlé in Switzerland. I will be in town in a couple of weeks and want to schedule a dinner with Dr. Nicholas Gonzalez."

Nick's office assistant took the message and, later in the day, handed the slip of paper to her boss.

"I don't know anyone named Guesry," Nick shrugged. He discussed the call with Linda and the rest of the staff. No one had a clue. "And why would a doctor from a food corporation in charge of employee health be calling me?" Nick wondered. "If he calls back, tell him I'm too busy to see him."

Dr. Guesry called back the next day, and when Nick's assistant relayed regrets, the doctor became insistent.

"Okay, Nick said. "Since he's so adamant, go ahead and accept the invitation."

Two weeks later on a dark, cold, rainy late November evening, Nick sat across from Dr. Guesry in Le Bernardin, an elite French restaurant on West 51th St. in Midtown Manhattan. Over hors d'oeuvres of Hamachi tartar with caviar resting on gold-plated white china, and champagne in a crystal flute, with the white linen tablecloth brushing his knees, Nick asked Guesry why he had asked him to dinner.

"You don't know who I am, do you?" Guesry asked.

"No, I'm sorry I don't."

"I am a pediatric immunologist—a friend of Dr. Good's. I'm in charge of the scientific research division of Nestlé."

The light bulb went on. Nick was sitting across from Pierre Guesry, the man who in his early forties had been chosen by the President of France to be

189

Medical Director of the Pasteur Institute, one of the most prestigious research institutes in the world. Guesry laughed at Nick's naïveté, then explained that he had been lured from the Pasteur Institute to Nestlé to set up a division in nutritional research in a variety of areas.

Several years before, Nestlé had quietly entered into an agreement with Hoffman La Roche in Switzerland to start evaluating promising alternative treatments from around the world. Several million dollars have been allocated to the project, sending researchers everywhere looking for herbal and nutritional treatments. But to date, they hadn't come up with anything good.

"I kept hearing about your work and your great progress with advanced stages of cancer. I've heard about the study you did under Dr. Good."

"Yes, I haven't been able to get it published."

The two doctors moved into their main courses of pan roasted lobster for Dr. Guesry, and crispy duck breast with snow peas for Nick.

"Can you show me some evidence of what I've heard about your research?" Guesry asked. "Present some cases?"

"Of course," Nick replied.

"Good. Because then Nestlé might be able to fund a research study to help get your work accepted."

Guesry spent the next day in Nick's office, going through his files. He situated himself next to the file cabinet, pulling out one chart after another. Nick showed him several dozen cases of patients with advanced stages of cancer who had gone into remission. He showed him charts of patients with large tumors that had drastically decreased in size. Nick gave Guesry a copy of his Kelley study.

"I've seen enough now," Guesry said at last. "I'm convinced that your work needs to be funded. You'll hear from me in a couple of months."

*   *   *   *   *

Several weeks later Nick opened a letter from Michael Friedman, the Associate Director for Cancer Therapy and Evaluation of the National Cancer Institute, inviting him to submit a series of cases as part of a new program to evaluate alternative cancer treatments. Nick thought the letter signaled a change in attitude at NCI. For so long it had been indifferent or even openly hostile to alternative and nutritional treatments.

> *The Associate Director suggested I write up a series of at least five reports, describing patients I had treated with appropriately diagnosed cancer, with an obviously poor prognosis, who had undergone documented regression of tumors while on my therapy. After the NCI reviewed these cases, if the cases seemed acceptable, I would be invited to present in person at a formal NCI session. I discussed the letter with Dr. Wynder, and to this day I do not know what role he played in arranging that first meeting. But I know he wasn't surprised by the invitation.*

During the early months of 1993, Nick regularly corresponded with Dr. Guesry in Switzerland. Guesry had read Nick's monograph, and he and his colleagues at Nestlé had agreed to fund a clinical trial. Guesry suggested the trial focus on advanced melanoma because there was no orthodox protocol for that disease. Nick told Guesry that the NCI was also interested in his work and had invited him to present cases. Unsurprised by this news, Guesry suggested there might be a way to coordinate the interest of the two institutions. Guesry thought Nick might come to Switzerland after his presentation at NCI. He invited Nick to Lausanne on Lake Geneva to present cases to the senior scientific staff at the Nestlé headquarters.

In March of 1993, Dr. Wynder called Nick. "I want to drop over this afternoon. I have something important to discuss with you."

From his tone of voice, Nick figured that Wynder had a health issue. Wynder arrived in Nick's office looking very somber and pale. He had just had a physical and his rectal exam revealed a very enlarged prostate. His PSA score, a marker for cancer, was elevated at 28 when normal is 4 or below. Wynder's doctor suspected cancer and had ordered a biopsy, bone scans, and other tests.

Wynder had refused.

"I want to go on your program," he told Nick.

Nick was astounded, but reluctant to accept Wynder as a patient. Wynder knew all that the program involved, and Nick was worried that his constant world travel and 14-hour days wouldn't leave enough time for his treatment.

"Could you comply with the program?" Nick asked Wynder.

"Of course, I can," Wynder said sternly. "I intend to do your program as best as I can. I want no standard therapy whatsoever. I will do no standard therapy. "

But Wynder refused to curtail his schedule and 14-hour days. If he couldn't do the things that he loved, he saw no reason for living. He promised to do the best he could and asked the same of Nick. When Nick asked about blood tests and biopsies, Wynder again refused.

"I will do none of it. I am only going to do your program anyway, no matter what the tests show, so let's get started."

So, without a biopsy and tests, Dr. Wynder began Nick's program about a week later, in April of 1993.

* * * * *

The three-hour session at the National Cancer Institute was scheduled for July 7, 1993. Tirelessly, for two straight months, Nick and Linda worked to assemble 25 case studies for his talk. They combed over charts, decided on which cases provided a diversity of cancers, symptoms, and positive responses. Then they wrote up the cases in fluid prose with absolute detail and accuracy, going over each sentence, comma and period. They produce a 150-page manuscript including original medical records.

"This is one of the first sessions that NCI has initiated to evaluate an alternative cancer therapy," Dr. Wynder told Nick, informing him that he would go down to Washington to be present for the presentation. "And I don't have to tell you, you need to make a good impression. It could lead to NCI support for your research."

Head down, Nick reviewed his manuscript, using his repetition technique that had served him so well throughout his career, going over and over each case, committing them to memory. Everyone—Nick, Linda, the assistants—all knew how much was riding on the presentation. Nick knew he had to do a superior job, and that any little slip-up could be disastrous to his future research. Oh, how those who opposed alternative therapies would love to find something, even the smallest inaccuracy, to criticize. Here, at last, was his chance to get his research examined and tested in a traditional medical setting.

Nick told his business manager to hold all calls—nothing short of a 911 emergency. He closed his door, stood at his desk as if it were the lectern at NCI, and rehearsed his talk, sketching in each patient, the diagnosis, the kinds of prior treatments, the date they went on Nick's program, the outcome, and the final survival rate. The patients' stories all came back to him, became a part of him, until he no longer needed to glance down at their records. He had his write-up of the 25 cases and their medical records printed and bound in a monograph, with enough copies for all the scientists at the NCI meeting.

On July 6, Nick stopped at his office to check-in and pick up a few items before he hailed a cab to LaGuardia airport. He dabbed sweat from his forehead with a handkerchief and his heart was racing. His tie was askew, and his assistant prompted him to look in the mirror and fix it.

When he returned from the restroom with a much more together appearance, his assistant sent him off with a pep talk.

"You have brilliant oratory skills," she said. "You're going to make a fine presentation."

Nick shrugged off the compliment.

"Be true to your mission. Don't water down the program and protocols. Think of all the patients that you've saved."

Nick left the office and hustled to LaGuardia, wheeling a large suitcase stuffed full of his patient files, their x-rays, MRIs and other scans and tests. In D.C., he checked into his hotel room and began rehearsing his presentation one last time before the big event. He changed some very minor points in his talk, writing in the edits in longhand. Everything needed to be perfect. Then he went through the whole speech again, integrating the changes, until he was satisfied that no further edits could be made, collapsing into bed. He slept fitfully, getting even less sleep than usual. He was up early, in the shower, his hair slicked back, downstairs to breakfast, and toting his huge suitcase. Then it was off to the main campus and building of the NCI in Bethesda, M.D.

Through the glass doors of the entryway of the NCI building and up on the elevator, Nick again reviewed his lecture notes through memory, each page a screen shot in his photographic memory. Wynder greeted him at the door of the conference room, the older man's eyes meeting his with reassurance. Dr. Michael Friedman, the Associate Director of NCI, was also there waiting in the room.

Then other scientists began to fill the chairs—first Dr. Wayne Jonas then at the Department of Defense but rumored to be in line to head the new Office of Alternative Medicine, the National Institute of Health's division designed to evaluate non-traditional therapies. Next came Dr. John Spencer, also from the office of Alternative Medicine, who would later co-author the popular *Complementary and Alternative Medicine: An Evidence-Based Approach.*

Dr. Wynder began the session with an introduction of Nick's program and its methodology. Wynder talked about how he had met Nick, and he outlined the program. He said that he thought that Nick was onto something and urged all the assembled scientists to listen carefully and take the information very seriously.

Then Nick rose to the podium and without an "um" or "ah," without even a pause for a drink of water, presented about half of the 25 cases, including patients he designated #1 and #3.

The first patient whom I will call Patient #1, was at the time a 68-year woman with a history of metastatic breast cancer. In July, 1987, she underwent a modified radical mastectomy at a California hospital for what was thought to be localized breast cancer. After the surgery, she was started on tamoxifen and did well until September 1988 when a routine CT scan showed multiple new tumors in the liver, consistent with metastatic disease. A bone scan and a chest X-ray were both negative for metastatic disease.

In November, 1988, Patient #1 began aggressive chemotherapy with the drugs Cytoxan, methotrexate and 5-FU. After six cycles of chemotherapy, a repeat CT scan showed no improvement, and her oncologist added vincristine, a very powerful chemotherapy drug, to her protocol. However, she suffered such severe side effects that she decided, with her oncologist's support, to discontinue chemotherapy. She was told that her survival would most likely be measured in months.

After Patient #1 heard about my therapy, she came to see me for the first time on June 26, 1989. After Patient #1 returned to California to begin her protocol, her local oncologist sent her for a baseline abdominal CT scan which revealed that the liver tumors had only progressed despite chemotherapy.

Patient #1 initially suffered ups and downs on her nutritional protocol, but she remained compliant and determined. Her local oncologist in California continued to follow her progress, and after she had completed nearly a year on her protocol, a CT scan of the abdomen on April 3, 1990 revealed significant improvement as documented in the written report: the left lobe tumor measured 2 cm in diameter as compared to 3 cm on the previous examination. The tumor in the anterior segment of the right lobe measured 2 cm as compared to the previous measurement of 2.5 cm in diameter. No new lesions were identified. A year later, on April 15, 1991, nearly two years after beginning her program, she went for another CT scan which again revealed significant improvement: the tumors had reduced to less than 0.5 cm in diameter, one fifth to one sixth their prior size. In July of 1993, she had been on her nutritional program for over four years, and appeared to be in excellent health.

Patient #3, at the time was a 68-year-old white male with a history of metastatic renal cell (kidney) carcinoma, a deadly disease, with survival usually measured in months. In October 1990, during a routine medical exam, Patient #3 was noted to have a large abdominal mass: MRI and CT scan studies both revealed a huge 14 cm. tumor in the left kidney, with no evidence of metastases. Subsequently, on October 26, 1990, he went for exploratory surgery and removal of the left kidney. The pathology report indicates renal cell carcinoma, which unfortunately had spread to an adjacent lymph node, a very poor sign.

In December of 1990, Patient #3 began an experimental protocol with alpha-interferon, an immune modulator, administered at New York University Medical Center. The regimen ended in August of 1991, after eight months of treatment. Thereafter, Patient #3 did well until late November of 1991, when he noticed a lump in his left back skull area, behind his ear, which rapidly increased in size over a period of days. On December 5, 1991, a needle biopsy confirmed that the lump, already the size of a lemon, was metastatic cancer from the kidney. A CT of the head on 12/9/91 documented the large lesion invading the lower left parietal bone. The tumor appeared to be invading through the skull into the surface of the brain. CT of the abdomen and chest were negative, except for several questionable pulmonary nodules that were thought to represent artifact. Bone scan was consistent with metastasis to the skull.

Patient #3 then began a one-month course of radiation to the skull mass, in an attempt to prevent the tumor from invading into the brain. The radiation was completed on January 23, 1992. Unfortunately, kidney cancer is notoriously resistant to radiation, and the mass did not regress during the therapy.

Patient #3 then learned of my work and since he had been given a terminal prognosis, he decided to pursue my protocol. I first saw him in my office on January 30, 1992 and at that time, he reported about a 20-pound weight loss over a period of six weeks. In addition, his orange-sized left parietal area tumor was immediately obvious.

Patient #3 began his nutritional protocol in February of 1992. Within weeks, he noted an improvement in his energy and well being, and began gaining weight. In addition, within three months on his protocol, the previously noted large skull mass had completely resolved. At the time of the presentation, Patient #3 was completely compliant with his treatment, in excellent health and disease-free.

After Nick worked his way through 13 cases, for more than three hours, the scientists in the room began interrupting and firing questions at him, arguing among themselves, asking him for more information or clarification.

"Would you be willing to conduct a pilot study with patients with advanced pancreatic cancer?" Dr. Friedman finally asked.

Pilot studies, or Phase II small clinical trials, are usually the first step in evaluating new treatments. These studies involve a small number of patients suffering from a malady resistance to conventional therapy, in this case pancreatic cancer patients who had failed to respond to chemo or radiation. Unlike Phase III studies where a new treatment is compared to the best standard treatment, the smaller Phase II studies have only a single arm, lacking comparison data. Pancreatic cancer patients were chosen because they have the worst prognosis of any cancer, rarely responding to chemo and radiation.

"If you can show some results with pancreatic cancer," Dr. Friedman said, "your work will be taken more seriously. Positive results in a pilot study could lead to more definite Phase III clinical trials."

Nick readily agreed to the pilot study, then asked, "What would you consider significant results?"

"If you get three patients with inoperable adenocarcinoma out of ten to live one year, I would consider those significant results."

Nick took up the challenge and Dr. Wynder agreed to supervise the study. "It needs to be done," Wynder said.

On the way to the airport in a shared cab, Wynder thought the session had gone very well. Nick confessed that he was disappointed that Friedman hadn't moved immediately into a Phase III clinical trial.

Wynder was irked. "Be patient. One step at a time. The fact that you had this presentation today is a victory. The fact that Dr. Friedman suggests a pilot study is a victory. It took me fifteen years before the world took me seriously, and what I did was far more obvious and straightforward than what you are talking about."

27

Two weeks later, Nick stood on the balcony of an elegant old hotel room overlooking Lake Geneva in Lausanne, Switzerland, again rehearsing his presentation—this time for Guesry and his colleagues at the Nestlé Corporation headquarters. Fresh flowers filled his room. The lake, a tranquil aquamarine, seemed to open with opportunities stretching out before him, and the Alps—massive, imposing and jagged—rising above the water in the distance, challenged him to take his research to new heights.

The next morning at the Nestlé headquarters Nick was at it again with new enthusiasm, explaining his program, its history, its theory, all the advancement he'd made with the pancreatic enzymes, and a review of his presentation of the case studies he'd made at the National Cancer Institute. After his talk, the twenty gathered scientists were full of questions and curiosity, wanting even more information and detail.

After an hour of discussion, Guesry called an end to the session and walked Nick back to his office. A message lay on Guesry's desk:

> URGENT: Dr. Gonzalez needs to call his office in the States immediately.

Nick excused himself and placed the call.

"We have an emergency," his assistant replied with a detectable quiver in her voice. "The New York State Attorney General's office called this morning. The Department of Health has brought a series of charges against you and they are trying to close your office."

Nick tried to calm his assistant, then tried to calm himself. He returned to Guesry's office as if nothing significant had happened, attempting to carry on a light conversation as Guesry toured Nick throughout the facility. Guesry would never know the content of the phone call.

Back in his hotel room, Nick called his assistant again who had already faxed copies of the charges to his lawyer.

"Your lawyer said that the charges are very serious, and the medical board was going to try to take away your license."

The whole situation seemed ludicrous to Nick. There he was presenting his research to the former head of the Pasteur Institute and his colleagues at the Nestlé Corporation. The National Cancer Institute asked him to design a pilot study of his treatment plan, and the New York Department of Health was accusing him of gross negligence and incompetence!

When he returned to New York, he went through another brief period of chaos. In August of 1993, he and Linda moved their offices to East 36th Street, directly opposite the Morgan Library, a white marble building, originally designed to house J.P. Morgan's personal library in 1906, and now designated a National Landmark. Moving file cabinet after file cabinet of patient records and research materials took effort and organization, but at last it also brought a feeling of peace and respite to Nick. His new office suite faced a garden in the back with squirrels scampering up and down a tree and mourning doves cooing. In the middle of the busy and crowded city, Nick could enter his office and recapture a snatch of the natural world that had meant so much to him in his youth.

His new office had ample space for a waiting room that Nick and Linda furnished with environmentally correct sofas and chairs, all made from natural woods in a small factory in Vermont without any synthetic chemicals. Even the office paint was non-toxic and natural without bothersome "new paint" fumes. A long corridor connected the waiting room to Nick's office whose windows overlooked the garden. He saw patients there, stationed behind a large oak desk. The corridor was lined with additional doors opening to Linda's office, to exam and bathrooms, to storage and research rooms, and finally to a kitchen and a shower. Nick was particularly delighted to have a kitchen where he fixed himself a hamburger and steamed vegetables every day for lunch and stored cheese and other snacks in the refrigerator for a late afternoon break.

In total, the new office provided an escape from the storm surrounding Nick and his staff. He awaited word from both the NCI and from the Department of

Health. On September 27, 1993, he received a letter from NCI reiterating that they didn't think that a full-blown clinical trial was called for at this time. Instead, they wanted Nick to begin with a pilot study of ten patients with appropriately diagnosed adenocarcinoma of the pancreas. The NCI would offer its expertise in design, and Dr. Wynder, they suggested, could oversee the study.

Nick immediately called Wynder.

"You must begin work on a formal protocol at once," Wynder said. "This is going to be an exemplary study. We're going to do it right."

From his office in Switzerland, Guesry was also supportive. "I will contact Dr. Friedman at NCI myself and let him know that Nestlé is willing to fund the study in its entirety."

Just at this same time, Nick received a call from his lawyer. "Get ready. Your medical board hearings will begin soon."

The late fall of 1993 and early winter of 1994 began with snow, snow that kept falling over the tall buildings of Manhattan down onto the streets and sidewalks, snow that turned to slush under the feet of the pedestrians who walked from home to subway, from subway to bus, from bus to office building. Seventeen snow storms in all tangled traffic and cancelled flights coming into LaGuardia and JFK airports. Nick had never seen so much snow in his usually temperate New York City.

The medical board hearings stretched through the whole snowy season. The first day that Nick entered the hearing room, he knew that he was doomed. The hearings were held before an administrative judge who was the arbitrator for the proceedings, and two physicians and a lay member of the Department of Health. Nick thought it strange that judges from the Department of Health would be trying him on charges brought by the Department of Health.

The atmosphere in the room seemed clear. The Department of Health thought they had an open and shut case of quackery. The board had selected six cases from Nick's files, all with advanced terminal cancers, all patients who had consulted other physicians and failed other treatments before they had seen him. All had died. Most had not been compliant with his program. Some were simply too sick and advanced to do the program, and a couple had lied and said that they were doing the program when they weren't. And Nick, young and naive early on in his practice, had believed them.

Patient #1 was a forty-year-old woman who in the spring of 1989, developed a breast mass that her gynecologist suspected was only an infection, which he treated with antibiotics. The patient was also referred to a surgeon, who also suspected only an infection, and no biopsy was done. Eventually, in July of 1989, the patient finally underwent a biopsy that proved to be malignant. A metastatic work-up, including a bone scan, was negative, and in mid-July, the patient underwent a lumpectomy. There was no spread of axillary or armpit lymph nodes, but there was evidence of cancer right to the margins of the surgical specimen. After leaving the hospital, the patient consulted with an oncologist who recommended aggressive chemotherapy with the protocol known as CMF, which consists of the drugs Cytoxan, methotrexate, and 5-fluorouacil. The patient refused chemotherapy and began treatment with a well-known alternative practitioner in New York (not me). The patient was then referred to a second alternative practitioner in Virginia who detected a recurrent tumor in the chest wall. The patient again refused chemotherapy, and instead began treatment with a vaccine made out of her own urine.

In September, 1989, the patient was seen by her original surgeon, who immediately referred her to a radiation oncologist. The tumor, clearly very aggressive, was already 6 X 7 centimeters in diameter. She was told her alternative treatments had not worked, and in October, she finally consented to begin chemotherapy with CMF. After two sessions of chemotherapy, the tumor did regress, and subsequently, she received aggressive radiation to the chest wall, for a total of 7100 rads—about as much as can be given. After the radiation, the patient refused to continue with chemotherapy, though additional therapy had been recommended.

Subsequently, she continued only her nutritional treatments, before learning about me and consulting with me in early February of 1990. Thereafter, she initially tried to do my program, but had great difficulty because of TMJ problems that interfered with swallowing. She eventually developed fluid in her lung, and when it became apparent that she could not do my program, in July of 1990, only five months after I first met her, I referred her to an oncologist who did innovative work in Toronto. Eventually, she died. She had been treated by a number of orthodox and alternative doctors with a variety of treatments including surgery, chemotherapy and radiation before she ever consulted me; she had a very aggressive cancer that broke through all prior treatment; she had great difficulty doing my program, and I referred her to another doctor when I realized she could not do my therapy. But I was charged with negligence.

Patient #2 was a very, very sad case. She was a lovely woman who when I met her was only 38 years old, with a very complicated and long medical history. At age 15, she had developed a type of bone cancer that led to amputation of a leg. She subsequently, while still a teenager, developed recurrent cancer in her lungs, that required four major lung surgeries at Memorial Hospital. She then underwent an experimental vaccine treatment, and miraculously, seemed to be cured. She did well for the next 23 years, marrying, and having two children. However, in March of 1988, she noticed a breast mass. When mammography showed nothing, the patient was told not to worry. However, over the next three months, the mass continued to grow, and Patient #2 was referred to a surgeon. Unfortunately, the tumor was so big surgery was not feasible, and instead, she began an aggressive chemotherapy regimen with Adriamycin, 5-fluorouacil, and methotrexate. The tumor shrunk only slightly, but enough to allow surgery. But 17 axillary lymph nodes were involved with the tumor—a sure sign of an aggressive cancer, and a dismal prognosis.

After surgery, Patient #2 had more chemotherapy, followed by aggressive radiation to the tumor site. After completing radiation, she then resumed chemotherapy with the same aggressive protocol before on her own accord discontinuing chemotherapy in April, 1989 after three months because she felt the drugs were "destroying" her body. Patient #2 then traveled to Switzerland, to begin treatment with the mistletoe extract, Iscador. While in Switzerland, she developed multiple tumor nodules in her chest wall. She returned to the U.S. and underwent surgery again for removal of the nodules, all of which proved to be cancerous.

Patient #2 then went to the Nieper Clinic in Germany, run by the well-known innovative physician (now deceased) Hans Nieper. There, in June, 1989 a chest X-ray showed evidence of metastatic disease in the lung. In Germany, Patient #2 received a variety of experimental immune enhancers, as well as Laetrile and other nutritional substances. When she returned to the U.S., she started treatment at the Atkins Center in Manhattan. Her orthodox oncologists suggested additional chemotherapy, which the patient adamantly refused. Unfortunately, shortly after returning to the US, she developed a new nodule on her chest wall.

When I first met her in mid-July, 1989, she seemed somewhat overwhelmed by her situation, and unsure what her next step should be. Because she didn't seem committed to following my program at that time, I actively discouraged her from starting with me. However, two weeks later, she called my office requesting that I treat her. Her chest tumors were growing rapidly, and she felt she had no other option, having failed repeated surgery, aggressive radiation, and multiple courses of intensive chemotherapy as well as at least three major alternative treatments.

I had no illusions about her, but because she and her husband were such wonderful people, and she was so young to have been through so much, I agreed to see her again, and become her physician. But it was just too late, and her previous treatments had done significant damage. While under my care, her chest wall literally broke down, I believe to this day because of the aggressive radiation that had been given. She had constant flu like symptoms, and at times was so sick, she couldn't stay on the program. Eventually she died in June of 1990. Her husband had nothing but gratitude for my attempts to help her, and he has over the years stayed in touch with me. I will never forget her, and only wish she had heard about me sooner.

None of that mattered. As far as the Department of Health was concerned, I was grossly incompetent and negligent in her treatment. When I read the charges, it was as if I was single-handedly responsible for her cancer. Apparently, to the OPMC, it was all my fault that she had been sick and died.

The State centered their case on the belief that Nick was totally incompetent and knew nothing about the natural history of cancer. His therapy with 150 pills a day, carrot juice and coffee enemas was a joke. No mention was made of the fact that all six of the cases in the charges were terminal patients who had failed conventional treatment. Nick, the State alleged, was a danger to patients.

Nick sat in his chair dumbfounded while the State's lawyer continued to shame and blame him.

To make matters worse, Nick's lawyer was unprepared. He had arrived in Nick's office the day before the first hearing ill-equipped to go into battle. Nick suspected he hadn't even read through the files of the six cases. Instead of preparing Nick, Nick had to prepare his lawyer. A few days into the hearings, Nick became furious and fired this lawyer. Eventually Nick would have him disbarred for incompetence. In the meantime, Nick hired another lawyer. The second one worked harder, but was at a disadvantage because he had entered the case mid-stream. Fortunately, snow delays gave him extra time to catch up on the complicated case.

The State called only one witness, an oncologist in private practice in upstate New York who explained the standard of care for cancer patients.

Next, it was Nick's turn.

Nick raised his right hand and swore to tell the truth on top of a Bible, a book that he knew almost by heart, line by line, a book that was now the basis for his whole vision, outlook, and conduct in life. Faced by the threat of losing the medical license that he had worked so hard to win, he mustered up his warrior spirit, a spirit passed down from his grandfather riding with Pancho Villa, to his World War II hero father.

Nick, of course, had a complete command of the theory and implementation of his program and articulated it with detail and ease. He explained the application of his therapy and emphasized his role as "physician of last resort" in the treatment of the six scrutinized cases.

Nick's lawyer thought that he was an excellent witness and clearly made an impression on the three judges.

At the end of the day, even the State's lawyer approached Nick's lawyer and said, "He wasn't what I had expected."

Nick's lawyer called two witnesses, one a surgeon, professor, and internationally acclaimed researcher from Boston. He made a very aggressive and impressive defense of Nick's treatment of the six patients.

Nick's second witness, a well-established New York oncologist, was less impressive. His court appearance had been cancelled repeatedly due to snow, so when he did take the stand, his memory blurred and he appeared unprepared.

Nick had discussed the charges with Guesry in Switzerland who was astonished by the news. Guesry offered to do anything he could to help, but Nick's lawyer didn't call him as a witness. Nick regretted that he didn't push harder to fly Guesry in for the hearings and put him on the stand.

The State's lawyer claimed that the charges were solely against Nick for incompetence, not because he practiced alternative medicine. But Nick and his lawyer had a hard time believing that.

The snow let up in early spring and the hearings finally ended. Then the wait for the decision began.

28

All through the snowy winter of the medical board hearings, Nick and Linda worked on the protocol for the pilot study. Conventional pilot studies are usually funded by national institutes and run out of academic centers with all the infrastructure, support, data bases and scientists in place. Funded by Nestlé, Nick and Linda were swimming on their own and were left to their own devices to accrue patients and design the study. They set up air-tight criteria for a patient's admission into the trial, and slowly, the patients began to trickle into the office, sitting across from Nick behind his large oak desk, awaiting their instructions to begin the program.

> Before entering any patients into the trial, the written protocol had been reviewed by Dr. Friedman and others at the NCI, as well as by Dr. Wynder and Dr. Guesry. The protocol outlined in detail the criteria for acceptance into the study. We required each patient be diagnosed with adenocarcinoma of the pancreas by doctors other than Dr. Isaacs or me. Each patient must have actual biopsy confirmation of the disease, evaluated by a pathologist. Patients must have evidence of existing disease at the time of entering the study, and have had no prior chemotherapy or radiation for their pancreatic cancer. Initially, since the disease is so aggressive and the average survival measured only in months, we required that potential subjects be diagnosed within eight weeks of entering the trial. However, since at that time we did not have access to the usual academic referral sources, after consultation with Dr. Wynder we discounted this last criterion.

When the winter turned to spring in 1994, Wynder slipped on the icy streets in New York, landing face down, and smashing his ribs on the curb. Nick insisted that he have an x-ray. No ribs were fractured, but the radiologist found a tumor in the left lung with perhaps several satellite lesions. The radiologist suggested a CT scan which Wynder didn't want to do, but upon Nick's insistence, scans were performed on the abdomen and pelvis. The scans showed a tumor on the right kidney in the area of the right adrenal gland, the kidney itself atrophied. Wynder clearly had advanced disease. He continued his program as well as he could, but he would not curtail his constant travelling and lecturing. And he would not have a biopsy.

That spring also brought a sea change in attitudes toward alternative medicine. The state medical boards kept up their aggressive attacks on alternative practitioners, but the national agencies began to at least entertain the idea that alternative therapies had some value. The Office of Alternative Medicine, part of the NIH in Bethesda, MD, was established in 1991 through the urging of Senator Tom Harkin of Iowa and others. It was later renamed the National Center for Complementary and Alternative Medicine, and it began to push for the testing of alternative treatments. The OAM office had survived accusations of "quackery," and at the same time, the American public had shown an ever-increasing interest in and use of alternative medical practices.

On June 6, Nick stood before another group of scientific researchers at an NIH workshop in Rockville, MD. He had been invited to give a lecture about his methodology in his Kelley study at an all-day seminar titled "Workshop on the Collection of Clinical Data Relevant to Alternative Medicine and Cancer." This workshop was one of the first government-sponsored meetings on research methodology to study alternative medicine. The organizers of the conference, NIH and NCI, thought that Nick could provide insight into the problem. He had been one of the first alternative medicine physicians to present at NCI, and he had a pilot study in process.

Nick brought his usual flare to the podium, speaking for an hour, feeling once again respected by his peers. He detailed the approach that Dr. Good had designed for him while studying Kelley. He displayed his documentation of all 50 cases in his still unpublished monograph. He discussed his NCI presentation and his presentation in Switzerland to Dr. Guesry and his colleagues. He explained the design of his pilot study. Several of the other presenters at the conference, including Dr. Wayne Jonas of the Department of Defense, also alluded to Nick's Kelley study. What affirmation! All the while, in the back of his mind, Nick worried about the medical board's ruling.

Shortly after the workshop, the ruling arrived in a large envelope in the mail. Nick took a deep breath and ripped open the envelope with a letter opener, his hands sweating, grasping the document. After hundreds of thousands of dollars in attorney's fees, he hoped that he wasn't going to have to close his practice and lose his livelihood. He hoped that he wasn't going to have to abandon his patients and the research that he loved, that he had dedicated his life to.

Whew. The medical board had not taken away his license.

But they had found him "negligent" for not recognizing the signs of disease progression. The judges admitted that no harm had been done to his patients, but regardless, they put him on probation for two years and sent him for a four day "evaluation" to the SUNY Upstate University in Syracuse, New York, where the Department of Health had set up a special program to deal with problem physicians. Nick was also required to undergo some kind of retraining and super-vision, and 200 hours of community service in a hospice program. And, much to the relief of his assistant, he was to start using a dictation machine because they found his handwriting illegible.

This is not the best news, Nick thought, but at least I get to continue my work.

Nick appealed the decision, petitioning for a new hearing on the grounds that an alternative medicine physician should have been on the review board. The judge rejected this idea. Nick requested that the board's decision should be annulled on the grounds of bias against alternative medicine. The judge found Nick's arguments without merit. Nick contended that the Administrative Officer excluded Nick's Kelley monograph as evidence. The judge found this assertion "unavailing." Lastly, Nick asserted that the community service, and the educa-tional training courses in the field of oncology were "harassing and a wasteful interference in his practice." But the judge ruled that the penalty would only serve to improve the "petitioner's capability to diagnose and perhaps distinguish between true metastasis and the disguised effects of his unconventional therapy."

Filled with dread, Nick finally took the almost 6-hour train trip from Penn Station to Syracuse the first week of April, 1995. Upstate Medical University is part of a large university hospital complex. More practicing physicians in cen-tral New York received their training there than any other school. A plaque in

Weisskotten Hall, College of Medicine, reads: *Dedicated to all those of scientific mind and investigative spirit who purpose to serve humanity.*

The evaluation program was run by Dr. William Grant who had a doctorate in education—not medicine. Grant sat before Nick at his desk in street clothes, a dark suit with a gold lapel pin, his glasses fixed firmly on his rounded face, and spoke candidly with Nick.

"Why are you here? How did you end up in this program?" Grant asked.

"Political harassment," Nick said.

The Evaluation Program was intense. Nick was busy eight hours a day for four straight days. He went through a battery of neuropsychological tests, assessment tests of medical knowledge, evaluation of his ability to read articles, do physicals, take histories, and read charts. The Syracuse group went through a random selection of 10 of his charts to monitor his record keeping.

At the end of the four days, Dr. Grant, looking visibly upset, called Nick into his office.

"In all the years of running this program evaluating physicians, I have never seen a physician so lacking in deficiencies." Dr. Grant said that Nick had tested superior in most tests, and that the physicians who had reviewed his records—contrary to the medical board—found no problem whatsoever. "The result of my testing shows that you are a very qualified and dedicated physician."

Grant shrugged and said he couldn't understand why Nick was there. He shook Nick's hand and said the evaluation was formally over.

Nick felt some small victory. An enemy had been won over to his side.

In November of 1995, Dr. Grant sent Nick a copy of his final evaluation to the State, reiterating what he had told Nick six months earlier. Grant found no deficiencies, no problems in any areas including record keeping, medical knowledge, assessment of patients—all areas attacked in the final OPMC decision. "This is an exceptionally bright individual," Grant wrote, "who wishes to make a contribution to the medical field. He does not seem to be pursuing this field purely for financial gain."

Nick had hoped that Grant's report would push the OPMC to reconsider its mandate that he undergo retraining. But he was wrong, the requirements would stand. Nick braced himself for more harassment. Instead, he was surprised to find Julian Hyman, a retired oncologist he'd met through one of his witnesses in the hearing, willing to work with the State Medical Board on Nick's "retraining." Dr. Hyman was to come to Nick's office three days a week to observe his practice, and Nick was to spend one afternoon a week with one of Dr. Hyman's oncologist colleagues.

These visits back and forth from office to office lasted a full year. Hyman was far from a harasser. Instead, he became totally intrigued by Nick's program, asked many questions, and was impressed by Nick's patient outcomes. Eventually, Nick and Hyman became friends. Over the years, Hyman, whose son Steve became the director of the National Institute of Mental Health in Washington D.C., became one of Nick's staunchest supporters and most loved mentors.

Nick completed all the requirements for the State and the probation ended, but the damage to his reputation remained. Throughout the ordeal with the New York State Medical Board, publicity in the media was negative and it was hard for Nick to shake the original accusations and conventional public mindset that he was a quack or charlatan, acting only out of greed.

* * * * *

Throughout all of this "retraining," Nick and Linda's pilot study pushed forward. Some patients came referred by other physicians, colleagues of Nick's, and some came from patient referrals. Yet even though pancreatic cancer had a dismal prognosis and no successful conventional treatment, most patients themselves were hesitant to step away from the medical model and engage in a treatment that was going to take so much work—even though the cost was free. Other potential patients had family pressure against using alternative medicine. Eventually, enough patients did wrap their minds around Nick's treatment plan and enter the study, hoping that Nick's alternative program might give them more time than the conventional treatments.

One patient, an employee of Proctor and Gamble, came to the attention of the vice president for health care. Fascinated by the patient's progress, the vice president called Nick's office to investigate the program. After some discussion, Proctor and Gamble entered into a research agreement with Nick, providing funding and welcome scientific input. During this time, Nick and Linda went back to work, perfecting their enzymes.

Nick made frequent calls to colleagues and friends like Dr. Roy Sweat, when he needed support or guidance.

During this time, Nick was fretting about the purity of the hogs and sheep providing the enzymes. He didn't think that the enzymes were working as they should.

"Where are they raised?" Sweat asked.

"New Zealand."

"That's supposed to be the cleanest country in the world."

"But I feel like there is still some impurity in the livestock there."

"Why don't you fly down there and figure out if anything has changed in the processing," Sweat advised.

Nick also put in calls to Dr. Hans Moolenburgh in the Netherlands who also used the enzymes in his practice. Nick wondered if Moolenburgh, too, had noticed that the enzymes had lost some of their efficacy. Yes, Moolenburgh had noticed.

"I want to know what happens to the pigs in New Zealand," Moolenburgh said. "Everything. Starting from birth and ending when the pancreas, after the slaughter, is deep frozen for the capsules. Every food, the way the animals live, the slaughtering process—everything."

Nick donned his investigator's hat and eventually figured out the problem, calling Moolenburgh with excitement. A new firm had taken over the production of the capsules and had changed the process. Formerly, a pig was slaughtered, and the pancreas was taken out and set aside for 20 minutes. Then it was pulverized, deep frozen, and capsulized. The new firm pulverized and deep froze the pancreas straight away.

"Why would that make a difference?" Moolenburgh asked.

Nick explained that when the pancreas is taken out, it begins to digest itself with an activated co-enzyme in play. The same process occurs in the body. The enzymes leave the pancreas on their way to the duodenum and the co-enzymes awaken. The pancreatic enzymes are then turned on full-force when they hit the stomach, ready to digest food. The new firm had rendered the co-enzymes inactive and the pancreatic enzymes were only able to do a poor second-hand job.

And so, adjustments were made.

Moolenburgh not only served as a medical advisor, but as a spiritual director for Nick. By now, Nick had abandoned organized religion—too many trappings, too many control issues, and too open to corruption—but he still pursued his Biblical studies.

Moolenburgh suggested that Nick read E.W. Bullinger's *The Companion Bible* and Nick found the text enlightening. Bullinger (1837–1913), an Anglican theologian and scholar, was the author of many books with his editorship of *The Companion Bible* among his most well-known works. In print for over 100 years, the book is a Bible study tool filled with exhaustive and detailed commentary, etymology, definitions, historical context and appendices that help interpret the sacred text. Nick and Moolenburgh often spoke on the phone at night, after putting in long days at their practices, of the nuances and revelations in the Bullinger text.

At one point, Nick feared that *The Companion Bible* would go out of print, so he started buying up copies, stacking them in his apartment, and giving them away to friends he thought might enjoy them. The national political journalist and medical writer Peter Barry Chowka, who had become well-known for his documentation of alternative medicine practices and cancer therapies, had profiled Nick and his program many times. With a shared interest in journalism and alternative medicine, Nick and Chowka eventually became good friends. In one conversation Peter mentioned that he had begun probing his belief in Christianity. Nick was delighted and offered to help facilitate his quest.

"Nick was a true Biblical scholar," Chowka said. "All of a sudden all of these books began arriving in the mail."

Bullinger's work and Moolenburgh's guidance gave Nick the intellectual grounding he needed in his scholarship. But his Bible study also helped him develop the spiritual and emotional fortitude necessary to do battle with the forces attacking him and his program. And he would need all the strength he could muster to face what was coming next.

29

In April of 1997, Nick sat in another New York courtroom in front of a judge and a jury, defending himself against Julianne Charell, a patient who had sued him. Dressed in his blue suit and tie, Nick cringed, listening to the expert witness for the plaintiff characterize his diagnostics as "bogus," his program as a complete deviation from the standard of care, and his failure to obtain proper informed consent as a lack of good judgment.

Julianne Charell first came to see Nick in March of 1991. Charell had had a long interest in alternative medicine, and when she had a six-month bout of vaginal bleeding, she by-passed her conventional physicians and went straight for the Gonzalez program. Nick refused to see her, sending her back for a gynecological examination. A month later, she phoned again, asking for an appointment, and again, Nick referred her to a gynecologist. Five months later in September, she called again. She'd finally seen the gynecologist who, upon an endometrial biopsy, diagnosed her with carcinoma.

Nick took her call. "It isn't wise for me to see you now. I want you to have surgery. At this point it could be curative."

She went ahead with the surgery at Mt. Sinai Medical Center in New York and had a complete hysterectomy and oophorectomy, removing both her uterus and ovaries. At first, her doctors thought that the cancer was confined to the uterus, but unfortunately, the pathologist found three different types of aggressive endometrial cancer capable of invading surrounding tissue. All three types of cancer were notoriously resistant to chemotherapy and radiation. Yet patients like Charell usually receive radiation to the pelvis, despite any data suggesting that the treatment has any effect on survival rates.

Nick knew that at this time, there had been only one controlled clinical trial on the use of radiation with conditions like Charell's. The results of the trial were published in *Obstetrics and Gynecology*, October 4, 1980. In the study administered by Dr. Jan Aalders, patients were randomized into two groups: 1) those who were treated with surgery only, and 2) those treated with surgery followed by radiation. Aalders found no difference in survival rates between the two groups, and no benefit for those who had had radiation.

There was a significant decrease in pelvic recurrence in the radiation group, but there was also an increase in metastases in more distant sites. Aalders also found that the subset of patients with Charell's particular diagnosis showed an even higher rate of distant metastases than the others. Overall, the actual death rate was higher with the patients receiving radiation. Yet external beam radiation remained the postoperative standard of care for endometrial cancer.

Charell's Mt. Sinai doctor, an oncological gynecologist, offered Charell an experimental aggressive course of chemotherapy and radiation. He acknowledged that the traditional therapies for her endometrial cancer didn't work. In his protocol document, the oncologist rationalized his experimental treatment:

> *Although the long-term prognosis for patients with Stage I, Grade I lesions is excellent, those with Stage I, Grade 3 (similar to Mrs. Charell's situation), papillary serous histology and advanced stage do poorly with traditional postoperative treatment. Standard adjuvant treatment consists of postoperative radiation therapy which clearly decreases the incidence of local and regional recurrence but has no effect on five-year survival in patients with Grade 3 tumors or the papillary serous histology...*

Charell decided to pass on the Mt. Sinai experimental treatment, and pressed Nick to take her on as a patient. He knew that she didn't have a chance of survival with conventional therapies, so he finally agreed to see her. Years later, he learned that, indeed, every patient in the Mt. Sinai experimental trial had died.

Charell arrived in Nick's office on October 11, 1991. Years later, sitting in the courtroom, Nick deeply regretted not having had Charell sign a statement of informed consent. On the advice of his lawyer, for much of a year during 1991–92, Nick did not have patients sign a statement of informed consent. His lawyer had argued that such a statement was an admission of offering a non-standard treatment. Nick trusted his lawyer's advice, and later realized it was a serious mistake. Prior to and after 1991–2, he had always had patients sign the statement.

Charell immediately began his program. She did well for about 8 months, seeing a positive leap in her overall health. Then on June 10, 1992, she called with an exacerbation of back pain, pain that she had carried for years before she'd seen Nick.

"I've had back pain for years," she said.

"But if it persists, we'll need to get some x-rays, and get some tests."

Nick recommended a chiropractor and she also went to one that she knew. She got only temporary relief. An erratic period of three weeks followed where her pain improved, then worsened. Charell consulted an orthopedist she's known from her previous episodes of back pain. X-rays showed a tumor in her spine and Charell underwent surgery at Mt. Sinai to remove this growth. The Mt. Sinai doctors gave her 18–24 months to live.

Nick never saw her again until the lawsuit. When he received her Mt. Sinai records, he found that she had had two tumors removed, one from the spine, and one from the adjacent area. One tumor was completely dead. The second tumor only contained a few cancerous cells. Unfortunately, her Mt. Sinai doctors had never done CT scans on her back in their initial work-up. Nick surmised that she had had these tumors when she walked into his office, and his program had killed them. He found it hard to believe that these two large tumors could have grown then died in the short time she was under his care.

Charell's Mt. Sinai doctors then gave her a course of radiation to her back, despite the fact that the tumors were dead, and that endometrial cancer doesn't respond to radiation. She was also given a week of 5-FU chemotherapy. After Charell developed a low white count and a number of side effects, she was put on intravenous Cipro, a very potent antibiotic, to prevent infection. Unfortunately, while Cipro kills infectious organisms, it also kills the normal bacterial flora in the large intestine, and can cause a syndrome called pseudomembranous colitis, a life-threatening infection itself. And Cipro can also cause retinal damage.

To make matters worse, Charell did develop a case of pseudomembranous colitis that was treated with Flagyl, another broad-spectrum antibiotic that can cause neurological side effects including damage to the facial nerve, and less frequently to the retina.

Toward the end of 1992, Charell began to have visual problems, which in retrospect, Nick thought were related to the antibiotics she had been given. Her Mt. Sinai doctors saw it differently and diagnosed her with "carcinoma associated retinopathy," a rare type of retinal damage that occurs when, usually in the early stages of the disease with active cancer present, the patient's immune system becomes hyperactive. Eventually, Charell went blind, many months after Nick had last seen her. She was treated with a high dose of steroids that did not improve her sight. Instead, the drugs caused avascular necrosis in her left hip that required extensive surgery.

Charell's Mt. Sinai doctors, and consequently her lawyers, blamed her blindness on Nick. They claimed that she had wasted precious time fooling around with Nick's program when she should have had radiation therapy immediately.

> *One Mt. Sinai physician, we have learned, encouraged her to sue me and even helped her find a lawyer, telling her incorrectly that I was at fault for all her problems because I discouraged her from receiving radiation after her surgery. According to Mrs. Charell's own testimony, her Mr. Sinai doctors never told her the back tumors were dead, and never told her that she had no evidence of cancer anywhere after her surgery.*

Yet Charell also testified that Nick had dissuaded her from having radiation and chemotherapy. A tape of the conversation records Nick telling Charell not "to mess" with those modalities. He had experienced a 75% success rate with patients in her condition. He also told her that cancer cells, undetected by her Mt. Sinai doctors, but picked up by hair analysis, remained in her body. She said that she was not informed that Nick was not an oncologist and that his program was experimental. Charell had attended one of Nick's lectures and had listened to his tapes. She had followed his protocol religiously. After some months, he had noted a reduction in the cancer cells in her body, but he had advised her to remain on his program.

Nick's lawyer, provided by his insurance company, didn't launch a vigorous defense. He didn't mention the outcome of the studies of endometrial cancer treated by radiation and chemotherapy. He didn't explain the theory behind Nick's protocol. There was no mention of John Beard and pancreatic enzymes or Dr. Kelley and metabolic types. He didn't fill in Nick's background, his presentation to the NCI, his pilot study, his work with Dr. Pierre Guesry or funding from Nestlé.

Charell's lawyers stood in front of the jury in their closing argument, hammering home the fact that Nick had not obtained proper informed consent and that he had strayed from the proper standard of care. They claimed that Nick was "negligent" and legally liable for Charell's blindness, even though it hadn't occurred under his watch.

"This man is a fraud," Charell's lawyers said.

* * * * *

March 27, 1997, and Nick returned to his office prepared for the worst. He and Linda waited for the dreaded jury verdict. He went back to work and saw patients, then began working on writing up their charts. And he waited, waited for that call from his lawyer with the jury's verdict.

Then the phone rang.

"I have some bad news," his lawyer said.

The jury had found Nick guilty of negligence, his protocol a departure from good and accepted medical practice. They found that his program was responsible for Charell's injuries. The jury said that Nick did not inform the patient of the risks of his treatment and the alternative available. They determined that Nick was 51% liable for Charell's injuries. On the other hand, the jury said that Charell should have known that there was a risk involved in Nick's treatment and determined that she was 49% liable for her own blindness.

The jury awarded Charell $2,500,000 for pain and suffering, $125,000 for past loss of earnings, and $75,000 for future loss of earnings. And, the jury said that Charell was entitled to punitive damages, ultimately awarding her an additional $150,000.

Nick put down the phone and walked into Linda's office to tell her the bad news. Her eyes filled with tears.

"The whole thing was so unfair," Linda said.

She just couldn't face the reality of the verdict, nor the reality of the office a moment longer. She picked up her briefcase and left, tears spilling down her cheeks.

Nick slumped down in his office chair, holding his head in his hands. He had no idea what he was going to do. The jury award was way over his insurance coverage. Nick was responsible for the excess award: $1,300,000.

Eventually, Nick filed for bankruptcy. Charell responded with a motion of intervention, and the two parties settled for $330,000. But the ramifications of the lawsuit continued. Nick had to sell his apartment that he loved. The practice struggled financially and took a hit to its reputation. Nick was barraged by an endless mound of paperwork from attorneys and calls for interviews from reporters, and both positive and negative articles in the press. Nick filed appeals without much luck, then finally in 2004 won a lawsuit against his own lawyer for incompetence.

Though none of her Mt. Sinai doctors thought that Julianne Charell would survive beyond 1994, she lived another 20 years after her original diagnosis, passing away in 2010, 19 years after her first visit to Nick.

III

30

September, 2013. On her show *A Healthy You & Carol Alt* on Fox News, Carol Alt told her national viewing audience about her first visit to Dr. Gonzalez. Legs crossed, Alt sat on a high stool in the television studio in a sleeveless white dress with a lavaliere mic clipped to the neckline, her long shiny hair flowing to her shoulders, a vase of cheery Soraya sunflowers behind her.

She proclaimed that Nick had saved her life. When faced with a cancer diagnosis, she had been forced to choose between standard treatment with devastating side effects, or an alternative with a better quality of life. "It can mean the difference between quality of life and suffering. At least that's what I felt." She chose the better quality of life.

She introduced Nick, flashing to a photograph of the cover of his new book *What Went Wrong: The Truth behind the Clinical Trial of the Enzyme Treatment of Cancer.*

"I was supported by my family and friends," she said, "but when I came to you, one of the things that I had to get over was the fear of following an alternate therapy."

"When patients choose an alternative therapy, they are often going against their family, certainly their doctors who think that alternative therapy is a waste of time—at best," Nick said, seated across from Alt in her studio with its floor-length glass windows looking out on the busy streets of New York, cars and pedestrians streaming by. "You know when you go to Sloan Kettering to be treated for cancer, you're going to Mecca. Everyone's on board—the friends, family, the neighbors, the postman, the health food store owner. All of them are happy, you're going to Sloan Kettering. When you chose an alternative therapy, everyone starts to get nervous. *Are you sure this is the right thing?*"

Nick explained the three prongs of the program, and its grounding in the research of Dr. Kelley and Dr. Beard and his book *The Enzyme Treatment of Cancer and its Scientific Basis.*

"Dr. Beard wrote a wonderful book in 1911 that should have changed the course of medicine, but unfortunately it did not. It should have changed cancer research, showing that pancreatic enzymes have an anti-cancer effect," Nick said. "Kelley had rediscovered Dr. Beard's work in the 1960s when he himself was confronted with cancer. He got well. He had been an orthodontist, but his practice quickly changed when all the local doctors started sending their cancer patients to this dentist. Back in the 1960s there weren't a lot of treatments for cancer."

Alt showed the viewers her boxes of pills and the ways she sorted them to organize her days, strictly adhering to the program.

"I don't think about the program anymore," she said. "I just do it. When I eat, I boldly hold up my pills to show everyone what saved my life."

Nick agreed. You just do it. He said he was on his own program. "I credit the program with being able to work 12–14-hour days, 7 days a week. I feel healthy 99 percent of the time. Without the program, I can guarantee you that I would have been dead fifteen years ago.

* * * * *

Soon after, Nick and Jonathan Landsman from Natural Health 365 sat in Nick's office, the walls lined with book-filled shelves, the plant with its twisted fronds in the window. Landsman, a tall thin host of a weekly radio news show, towered over Nick, introducing a show about the history of chemotherapy. He told the audience that he is not there to bash chemotherapy, but to give the viewers the information that they needed to make an informed decision.

Nick stared straight ahead into the camera, Landsman turning to him. "Dr. Gonzalez, what do you tell patients when your ideas and protocol don't really fit what they want to do? They say that they would be more comfortable doing chemotherapy."

Nick replied:

> *They should absolutely do chemotherapy. A primary rule in our office is we never talk people into doing our treatment. The single most important determinant in how a patient does, no matter what ther-*

apy they choose—moon dust, my treatment, or Sloan Kettering—is their belief system. If they don't fundamentally believe in what I do or what alternative practitioners do, whether I think they should or not, it doesn't matter. They should do it. If they think Sloan Kettering has the answer, M.D. Anderson has the answer, Massachusetts General Hospital has the answer, that's where they should be.

Next, Landsman asked Nick to trace the development of chemotherapy, and Nick explained that the drug therapy arose out of World War II when the government had stockpiles of nerve gas which were left over from World War I. The Germans first used mustard gas on the Allies in the first World War with devastating results. Neither side was using it in World War II.

Someone at the Department of Defense had this brilliant idea to try and convert these nerve gases into useful modalities. And serendipitously at the same time, some American soldiers were inadvertently exposed to some nerve gas at an experimental research center.

And what they noticed at autopsies—because they had all died—that their white counts had all gone down because their bone marrow had all been suppressed. So one of the Department of Defense doctors got this brilliant idea—that was about 1945—that perhaps you could use nerve gas, in this case it was nitrogen mustard—to treat leukemia and lymphoma and knock out the bone marrow. Leukemias and lymphomas are diseases of the white cell line.

The nerve gas seemed to wipe out the bone marrow, so the Department of Defense contacted Dr. Alfred Gilman at Yale University where he and his colleague Dr. Louis Goodman, both professors of pharmacology and toxicology, tested nitrogen mustard compounds on lymphomas in mice. They found that the nerve gas killed the tumors—although they grew back—but it extended the life of the rodent. And it was very impressive as it was the first time that anyone had seen cancer addressed through a drug treatment. There had literally been little treatment for any kind of cancer up to this point.

Soon, a Polish immigrant with lymphomas in the cervical spinal regions would be the first recipient of chemotherapy. His tumors receded, although he did not survive the treatment.

But low and behold it was an impressive event. It was the first time in history that doctors had witnessed the regression of tumors in a patient with advanced disease. So they started to tweak it and developed a variety of drugs, beginning at Yale, but then it went to other medical centers where they were using these toxic chemicals, ironically from nerve gas. Very few people today realize that a whole array of drugs—and there are over 100 of them—were originally derived from poisonous nerve gas used for warfare. It didn't begin with anything good. Its origins are pretty unpleasant. The Department of Defense contracting medical schools to use their chemical warfare reserves.

Why did conventional medicine get excited about this treatment? They were enthralled because for the first time they'd discovered a pharmaceutical drug that could kill tumors. This was the era of the discovery of antibiotics when suddenly they had a drug that could reverse terrible infections like pneumonia that previously had no treatment. Antibiotics had saved the lives of thousands of World War II combatants. And here was chemotherapy that looked like another magic bullet. It was an amazing event in the history of medicine. They thought that this nitrogen mustard derivative was the next penicillin for cancer… There were natural treatments for cancer at the time that had real potential, but the medical community had become enthralled by the drug approach.

Experimenting throughout the next two decades, researchers found that chemotherapy did shrink tumors in patients with leukemias and Hodgkin's lymphomas—two cancers of the bone marrow. Chemotherapy destroyed the bone marrow, so the treatment was often effective. The problem rested in generalization. Researchers jumped from the idea that chemotherapy shrank tumors in blood cancers, to chemotherapy shrinking tumors in all cancers. But the great majority of cancers are not blood cancers. Rather, tumors of the lung, of the breast, brain, colon, pancreas, prostate, stomach and so on usually do not respond to chemotherapy. All you do in those cases is kill the bone marrow. And the survival rates of metastatic solid tumor cancers haven't changed much in the last 30 years when cancer was treated primarily by surgery.

*I don't know how you consider the war on cancer is being won
when 600,000 people die in the U.S. from cancer each year.*

* * * * *

A *Nicholas Gonzalez M.D.*, Wikipedia page—an entry that anyone in the public
could write, edit, and post—appeared online. The page provided Nick's background, including his degrees from Ivy League schools and his Phi Beta Kappa
and magna cum laude status from Brown. The page sketched in his career in journalism that led to his interest in medical research, and his training as a physician.
Nick's degree from Cornell, work at Sloan Kettering under Dr. Good, internship
at Vanderbilt University, and fellowships at the University of Oklahoma and All
Children's Hospital are all mentioned on the page.

But as a whole, the page emphasized the rejection of his methods by the medical establishment. It stressed how the "quackbusters" labelled him a "fraud" and
"quack," and how he was reprimanded in 1994 and placed on two years' probation
by the New York State Medical Board for "departing from medical practice."

The page detailed Nick's malpractice lawsuits, explaining that a 1997 New
York court found him "negligent" for his cancer treatment. He was forced to
pay $2.5 million to a patient he wrongly claimed he'd cured of cancer using his
unproven methods of dietary supplements and frequent coffee enemas.

The American Cancer Society noted there is "no convincing scientific evidence that [the Gonzalez treatment] is effective in treating cancer" and that some
portions of the treatment may be harmful. The page cited an article from the
Journal of Clinical Gastroenterology that noted that the efficacy of coffee enemas
has not been proven and the therapy is associated with adverse effects previously
described in a few case reports.

At her computer in her office, Linda discovered the page. She showed it to
Nick and they both rolled their eyes. A few hours later, Linda figured out how
to get into the Wikipedia site, updating the article to provide more background
and understanding about the program. She reoriented the page toward Nick's
research, the efficacy of the pancreatic enzymes, and the kinds of success he has
had. She clicked "save" and posted her revisions to the page.

The next day, the Wikipedia page was changed back to its original profile of Nick.

* * * * *

October, 2013, late morning. Nick's office manager took a phone call. A woman's voice came on the line.

"I've called to warn Dr. Gonzalez," she said.

"Who is calling, please?"

"There are people who are going to poison Dr. Gonzalez."

"Wait, who is calling?

"I don't know exactly how it's going to be done."

"Where did you get this information?"

There was silence on the other end of the line.

"What is your name and where are you calling from?"

"These are head guys at cancer research centers. They are planning a slow kill approach so that nobody will know he's being poisoned."

"Poison?"

"Again, I don't know exactly how or when it will happen, but it could be through his water or food."

"Can you give me any additional information?"

"No," the woman said, and she hung up.

The office manager headed down the hall with tears in her eyes. She stood before Nick and informed him of the threat. His eyes widened. Nick told her to write down everything she could about the call and see if she could trace the number. Nick would contact his lawyer.

The call could be traced only to a fax machine.

Nick's lawyer advised him that it was useless to call the police. They were too busy to track down every crank call in Manhattan. A death threat should always be taken seriously, but the call was probably just a disgruntled patient or someone Nick had turned down for treatment. His lawyer was sure that this call was from a "nut" who might even believe she was helping Nick.

Nick sent his office manager home early.

At the end of his work day, Nick walked home on his usual path, putting the incident out of his mind. He never mentioned it again to anyone.

31

After the Charell case, Nick thought his life had changed, but one day in 1998 he received another large envelope in the mail. He sliced it open to find he had been sued a second time. Once again, he was charged with deviating from the medical standard of care, failure to obtain proper informed consent and failing to disclose the risks and benefits of his therapy, and for recommending that the patient not undergo a bone marrow transplant.

This time the plaintiff was Jack Gray, the husband of a patient named Hollace Schafer who had died in 1995. Ms. Schafer was a professor of musicology at Holy Cross University in Worchester, Massachusetts. She was just 24 years old when in 1977, she was diagnosed with stage 4 Hodgkin's Disease, the most advanced stage. She was treated with the gold standard aggressive chemotherapy agent, and she went into remission.

Then, seeking an alternative medicine solution, she went to the Nieper Clinic in Germany that used Laetrile, among other treatments. She followed the Nieper regime, including a strict diet, for about two years at home, and remained in remission until December of 1989 when a routine chest x-ray showed a right lung mass. She underwent lung surgery at Massachusetts General Hospital with a diagnosis of recurrent Hodgkin's Disease of the lung. Her doctors urged her to have a bone marrow transplant which she refused, opting instead for a "watch and wait" approach.

In 1990, Schafer had a second recurrence diagnosed at the Dana Farber Cancer Center in Boston. Her doctors there also recommended a bone marrow transplant, but Schafer again refused the procedure. Instead, she began a very aggressive experimental chemotherapy protocol. This therapy was known as a "salvage" regimen, a treatment that is given when the cancer is not responding to other chemotherapies.

After a year in remission, Schafer had a third recurrence. At Harvard she was urged again by her doctors to have a bone marrow transplant. A college professor proficient in research techniques, she hit the stacks of the medical library, and finally decided against further chemotherapy. Instead, she flew to Mexico and became a patient at the Gerson Clinic, embarking on an intense nutritional program for 5–6 months. Unfortunately, her disease only spread.

In 1992, she landed in Nick's office and her health improved for about 18 months before it dipped into a downward spiral when she had trouble sticking to the program. She died in 1995, two years and nine months after starting with Nick. The autopsy showed extensive fibrosis in the lymph nodes, but very little cancer.

Nevertheless, Schafer's husband brought suit against Nick. Gray focused on the bone marrow transplant. Nick claimed that he and Schafer had never discussed the procedure, and that Schafer had turned down the treatment three times before she had ever stepped a foot into his office.

And furthermore, Nick thought Schafer a poor candidate for a transplant. She had had three recurrences of cancer, the last after an aggressive experimental round of chemotherapy. Hodgkin's patients who have recurrences within a year of this kind of chemotherapy suggest they harbor a very aggressive cancer with a dire prognosis. Experimental chemotherapy and bone marrow transplants were generally recommended, but by 1993 there had not been a single controlled clinical trial on patients with Schafer's condition undergoing a bone marrow transplant.

In 1993, *The Lancet* published such a study, but the results were inconclusive. Initially, the statisticians attached to the trial concluded that a minimum 66 patients were to be enrolled to draw any sound conclusions. After much struggle, only 40 were enrolled, throwing the validity of the study in question. And, in the end, the researchers documented that there was no greater survival rate with the bone marrow transplant than with the "salvage" chemotherapy treatments.

In the early autumn of 1998, after he had filed his lawsuit and before the trial, Gray was interviewed by ABC News. The reporter sketched in Nick's treatment involving coffee enemas, pancreatic enzymes, and organic food. He mentioned that the NCI wanted to study his treatment. He told the audience that many patients swear by the Gonzalez program, but others thought that Nick was a quack. Then the reporter spoke to Schafer's husband about his wife's death.

"This guy killed her. He lied to her," the husband said. "All of this hope that he was pumping her full of was just slime."

In December Nick filed a complaint against Schafer's husband seeking damages arising from defamation. The judge ruled against Nick stating that a "reasonable viewer would understand that Gray's statements are not statements of fact, but represent the opinion of a distraught widower who recently lost his wife to a terrible illness."

Nick was back in court for the trial of the malpractice suit in 2000. This time he had hired an experienced trial lawyer to work with his own lawyer. Nick sat beside them behind a table in the courtroom when the plaintiff's lawyers made their opening statement.

"Nick Gonzalez's treatment is snake oil," the lawyers said again and again. Even the judge used the term "snake oil" when referring to Nick's program.

The plaintiff ran a video of Dr. George P. Canellos, their expert witness whose testimony had been taped before the trial. Canellos was highly credentialed, a professor of oncology at the Harvard Medical School, Chief of Oncology at the Dana Farber Cancer Institute in Boston, and Editor-in-Chief of *The Journal of Clinical Oncology*. He began by giving his opinion of Nick's treatment:

> *I think it's outrageous. I think it's outrageous using such remedies of totally undemonstrated scientific value to treat a patient who still had a potentially curable disease with already understand-able but acceptable treatment by all people who ever deal with Hodgkin's Disease. In my view none of those things were ever shown by anybody to be useful for cancer, and most of it I think is based on myth.*

Canellos then announced on video that the British study of the Hodgkin's Disease patients had 60 patients, not the actual 40, and the ethics committee stopped the trial prematurely because the results were so good for the bone marrow transplant.

Nick exhaled a deep breath and shook his head. This time he was prepared to mount a vigorous defense. His lawyers had a big job. First, they had to establish that Nick and Schafer had never discussed a bone marrow transplant. Then they had to address the issue of bone marrow transplants for Hodgkin's Disease patients. Next, they had to educate the jury about a very unfamiliar alternative cancer program, attempting to dispel the biases that had already been brought into the courtroom. And finally, they had to demonstrate Nick's competence as a physician and his ability to administer his program.

Dr. Julian Hyman, the physician from the Department of Health who had observed Nick during his "retraining" took the stand, to testify to Nick's competence and professional treatment of patients. Dr. Jonathan Wright, a Harvard and University of Michigan graduate, founder of the Tahoma Clinic in Washington State, and a well-known physician of biochemical treatments, raised his right hand to explain how Nick's program fit into the wider field of alternative medicine. Dr. Pierre Guesry, former director of the Pasteur Institute, flew in from the Nestlé headquarters in Switzerland. Dr. Hans Moolenburgh, a world-renowned cancer specialist flew in from the Netherlands. Both physicians attested to Nick's international reputation and the efficacy of the program.

Dr. Moolenburgh did not relish his time on the stand:

> *They called me and there I sat with the jury on my left and the judge on my right. Quite a novel experience because we have no juries in the Netherlands. There came the questions and I had the impression that matters took a disastrous course. The attorney for the defense asked about the diet, and up popped the attorney for the prosecution who said, "Objection. No relevance."*
>
> *"Sustained," the judge said. "Next question."*
>
> *And so it went. One after the other. All my preparations blown out the window. But then (and my heart made a terrific jump) up came the questions about the hair tests, and this time the attorney for the prosecution held his tongue and I had the impression that I could hear him purring like a content tom cat who had just licked up cream. Well, I tried my utmost to explain how the rest worked, feeling all the time as if I was putting a rope around Nick's neck.*

After his testimony, Dr. Moolenburgh returned to the corridor where he sat down next to Dr. Guesry who was holding his head in his hands.

"C'était un désastre complet," Guesry said. "Une catastrophe!"

The two physicians sank into an angry depression, feeling that they had come all the way from Europe for nothing.

The jury filed out to begin their deliberations, Nick waiting next to his lawyers and agonizing again over the verdict. There were eight issues in the case.

The judge had thrown out two of them in Nick's favor before they had even stepped into the courtroom.

When the jury finally returned, the foreperson read out the verdict: Four of the six remaining issues were decided for Nick. Most importantly, Nick was found not negligent in offering his therapy. Of the two issues not found in Nick's favor, he was found to carry 49% of the blame and Schafer 51%.

Nick's lawyers stepped out into the hall and shook the hands of Guesry and Moolenburgh. "Brilliant, brilliant, we have won!" he said

Guesry and Moolenburgh were flabbergasted. How is this possible? They both wanted to know.

They all had a celebratory lunch and Nick's lawyer thanked them all over again for taking the stand and vouching for Nick's treatment methods and reputation.

The Schafer case, though, wasn't a total victory. The two issues that went against Nick were enough to satisfy those set against his protocol. Nick was instructed to pay Jack Gray $282,000. Again, Nick's reputation took a hit as it did after the Charell lawsuit. Negative articles circulated on the internet attacking Nick's honesty and competency. Nick could only console himself with the overall history of his practice.

> *I have treated hundreds and hundreds of very advanced patients over the years, most of whom, like Hollace Schafer, have failed repeatedly orthodox treatments. Of course, not all are going to do well; some don't comply, some can't comply, some live with such stress, no therapy is going to work. Sometimes it's just too late. The majority of these patients and their families have always been very grateful for our efforts, the risk we take to offer the therapy, and our determination to have our work properly tested under the most rigorous academic standards.*

Dr. Roy Sweat counseled Nick to abandon his role as "doctor of last resort," and to take patients who wanted the Gonzalez Protocol as their first choice. The toxic effects of chemotherapy and radiation all accumulate in the system, particularly the liver, and Sweat thought patients would fare better when their bodies weren't so compromised when they started Nick's therapy.

"You just can't cure everybody," Sweat said.

Dr. Hans Moolenburgh echoed these sentiments. He had known how hard Nick took each of his failures, and was concerned that the stress would take a toll on Nick's own health. Nick had often called Moolenburgh when one of his patients who had been doing well took a turn for the worse, or even died. Nick felt personally responsible for these events, and he constantly worried about what could have gone wrong and what he had overlooked.

Moolenburgh counseled Nick that physicians, even the best of them, should not overestimate what they could do. Moolenburgh emphasized that there is a strong doctor/patient bond when patients are fighting for their lives. A patient's death is likely to send a physician into a period of mourning just as it would a family member. Moolenburgh shared these thoughts with Nick:

> *The only thing you have to do is to lead your patient through this illness as best you know how. The abstract attitude toward the sick person, as if the patient is just a thing among things, that was taught us in medical school, in my view was well meant but completely wrong. I think that we should love our patients, realizing that we are ourselves part of the healing process.*

32

Nick would come to deeply mourn a very important patient—Ernst Wynder. In his mid-seventies, Wynder still wouldn't curtail his schedule. He kept up with his lecturing and tried to stay on Nick's program, doing it "his way." His health began to slide downhill, but he continued to be dedicated to helping supervise Nick and Linda's pilot study. In the spring of 1998, at the same time that Nick was battling the Gray lawsuit, his study was beginning to produce some interesting results.

The written protocol for the pilot study had been reviewed by Dr. Friedman and others at NCI. Dr. Wynder himself and Dr. Julian Hyman reviewed all the patients' records before they were entered into the study. Both Wynder and Hyman agreed that all 11 patients in the study had been properly-diagnosed, inoperable adenocarcinoma of the pancreas. Eight of the 11 patients in the study had stage IV disease, the most advanced form, with metastases to the kidney and liver. The other three patients had stage II pancreatic cancer, one with extensive disease effecting the whole pancreas. The remaining two patients had large inoperable tumors.

All of the patients were quite ill when diagnosed, appearing in their doctors' office with pain, jaundice, and weight loss. Five of the patients had signs that they had had their cancers for some time before entering the trial and starting the Gonzalez program. Pancreatic cancer patients often have serious, complex problems with blocked bile ducts that drain both the liver and the gallbladder. A severe blockage can result in jaundice and liver failure, a result of toxins circulating through the bloodstream.

By-pass surgeries and stents are used to address the blockages, intended only for temporary relief of the symptoms. Stents can be inserted by endoscopy but the procedure only lasts eight to twelve weeks before it is dislodged, or infection sets in. But by then, unfortunately, the patient is usually dead.

In the pilot study, nine of the eleven patients had bile blockages with six of them receiving palliative by-pass surgery, and the remaining three stent placement. Only one of the patients lived in the New York area, so Nick and Linda had to rely on local doctors for the management of surgeries and stents. Not all of the local doctors were cooperative.

One doctor refused to speak to Nick.

"Gonzalez is a fraud," the doctor told his patients. "There is no pilot study. This guy is just preying on vulnerable patients, putting money in his own pocket."

The patient protested that the study paid for everything, including the supplements, but the local doctor merely became hostile in reply. The patient finally died after three years and seven months on the program—of a stent infection.

No orthodox researcher would have to face such obstacles, Nick thought. And he slid into moments of despair over cases like these. He couldn't believe how such medical bias could endanger patient's lives.

"I just can't do it anymore. I'm going to close my practice," Nick confessed to Dr. Moolenburgh in one of their phone conversations. He sat on the sofa in his apartment, surrounded by books, hardcover medical texts filling his bookshelves, paperbacks on all aspects of the functioning of the human body stacked in tall piles on the floor around him, copies of medical journals filling the coffee table in front of him with notes on yellow Post-Its sticking out of the pages. His kitchen was filled with pots and pans hanging on the walls. He cooked for himself, keeping himself on his own program of organic foods. His apartment had two bedrooms. He slept in one, and the second one was empty. He didn't have time to decorate. He disliked socializing and dinner dates, all things that took up too much time when he wanted to work.

"This is just what your attackers want," Moolenburgh replied. He pleaded with Nick to continue.

Interiorly, Nick was tough on himself and took a very Old Testament view of his difficulties and his patient losses. What had he done wrong? Why was God punishing him?

Moolenburgh had to pull every countering Biblical verse he could muster out of his head to try to bring Nick to his senses. He reminded Nick that innovative research outside of the medical model is often viciously attacked. And in the wider society, good acts, and the people who engage in them, aren't always well received. Finally, Moolenburgh convinced Nick to keep his practice open and continue his important research.

And Nick battled on. Often calling Moolenburgh months later in the same despair. Moolenbugh always helped rally Nick again. And Nick slogged on and on, never backing down from a fight, whether in court, in print, or in person.

Exteriorly, Nick was tough with others. In an interview with Frank Lampe and Suzanne Snyder in *Alternative Therapies*, Nick spoke about his response to his critics:

> *Well, coming from a journalism background, I never had an over-whelming belief in the goodness of man. I always had a belief in the goodness of truth, and I think the truth can be a revelation. The truth can change people, and that's what we aim for.*
>
> *I heard that some of my enemies were really annoyed when I said in an interview years ago that I treat critics like they are mosquitoes buzzing around my head—like a minor annoyance. I just slap them away, and don't pay attention to them.*
>
> *We concentrate on the work, the research, and the patients, and on helping people. If people lose sleep over me and what I'm doing, that's their problem. They need to get a life. It doesn't matter to me if I have no friends in the world or two friends or a thousand friends. It doesn't make any difference.*
>
> *Nothing would change if I were given 75 Nobel Prizes or sustained 75 attacks. I will continue to see patients and do the work because I focus on the truth…I pay as little attention to my critics as possible and address them only when I'm forced to.*

By late 1997, Nick's mood began to lift. The results of the pilot study had already surpassed anything that he and Linda could find in the medical literature relating to inoperable pancreatic cancer. By 1997, nine of the eleven patients had lived a year, five patients had lived longer than two years, and four had already passed three years. Normally, no more than 10% of conventionally treated pancreatic cancer patients survive two years, and virtually none survive three years.

By early spring of 1998, even Wynder, who was usually very cautious about Nick's results, agreed that the data was very significant.

"It's time to write up the data and quickly get an article published," Wynder said.

Nick and Linda first submitted the article to *JAMA*, the *Journal of the American Medical Association,* who promptly rejected it. The article had been submitted to the standard process of peer review. The first reviewer was positive about the article. Though the reviewers were not identified by name, Nick immediately recognized the second reviewer as one of the "quackbusters" who had been attacking his work for years. The second reviewer did not discuss the data. Instead, he sang the common tune of Nick, the fraud, the money-hungry huckster.

"This review is unbelievable," Wynder said, recalling many of the negative responses he had seen to his own work. "I've never seen anything this bad."

Wynder picked up the phone and called his friend Gio Gori, editor of the well-respected research journal *Nutrition and Cancer.*

"I'm happy to personally review the article and find unbiased reviewers," Gori told Wynder.

Unfortunately, Wynder's health was deteriorating. He had developed a tumor on his thyroid, had it removed, only to have it grow back again. He started to sound weak and worn, and had been hospitalized for low blood pressure, a slow pulse, and fainting spells. He had had a pacemaker placed in his heart, but the slow pulse, low blood pressure and fainting spells continued. Nick suspected that the tumor on his one good kidney had destroyed his adrenal gland which normalizes blood pressure. Nick put Wynder on a high salt diet and gave him adrenal supplements, and his blood pressure and pulse normalized. And through all of this, he kept in daily touch with Nick about the pilot study.

Later in the spring, Nick received a call from the office of Republican Congressman Dan Burton of Indiana who had had a long interest in alternative treatments. Burton had worked with other Washington legislators to increase government funding for the evaluation of alternative treatments.

On a hot and humid early July day Nick found himself in a meeting in Burton's Washington D.C. office with 12 other participants including Dr. Richard Klauser, director of NCI, Dr. Wayne Jonas, then Director of the Office of Alternative Medicine, and Ralph Moss, a journalist with a specialty in alternative medicine and a former science writer for Sloan Kettering under the directorship of Dr. Robert Good. The two-hour meeting was focused and productive.

At its conclusion, Dr. Klauser turned to Nick and said, "The preliminary results of your pilot study look interesting. The NCI will support a large-scale clinical trial of your program."

Nick almost skipped out of the meeting. This is what he had been working on for 17 years. The weight of the New York Medical Board investigation, the lawsuits, and all the other attacks by his critics began to dim. His warrior spirit, his persistence, and all his hard work throughout his whole life—from his repetition drills to his investigative journalism skills—were finally paying off. Thank you, God. All of his family role models and mentors, each in their own distinct ways, ways that they themselves couldn't have imagined, were blending together to create this result: a clinical trial of an alternative treatment for cancer that had the potential to save so many lives. Thank you to his grandfather Guillermo José Gonzalez, to his father William. Thank you to John Beard, Weston Price, Francis Pottenger, Bryon Dobell, William Kelley, Robert Good, Roy Sweat, Hans Moolenburgh, Pierre Guesry and Ernst Wynder.

Nick returned to New York and immediately called Wynder with the good news.

"This," Wynder said, the strength returning to his voice, "is a major development."

"The study will have to be run out of a major academic institution," Nick said.

"I'll call my friend Karen Antman at Columbia."

Dr. Karen Antman was the Chair of Oncology at Columbia, and the past president of the American Society of Clinical Oncology, one of the most esteemed oncologists in the country. During the next couple of weeks, Nick, Linda and Wynder met with Antman several times. On the basis of the preliminary results of the pilot study, Wynder's support, and the NCI funding, Antman finally offered Columbia as the academic site of the long-term clinical trial.

By January of 1999, Gori had agreed to publish Nick and Linda's article about the pilot study. They were finally going to get their article in print as the lead piece in a top journal, and Wynder was to write an editorial to introduce their research. But during that first week of January, Wynder collapsed at a conference in Florida. He was rushed to a hospital with pneumonia and aggressive cancers in his lungs and spine. After several days on antibiotics, he was flown back to Memorial Hospital in New York by private plane.

On a dreary Sunday, Nick went to see Wynder the day he was admitted to Memorial Hospital. Nick's shoes clicked through the halls, haunting passageways he had not revisited since his medical school days and the death of his own father. Wynder had lost a lot of weight. He was on oxygen and had a feeding tube in his nose. His eyes were sunken into his sallow face. Nick stepped over, sat on the bed, and held Wynder's hand.

Wynder looked up at Nick. "The docs are giving me a week or two to live."

Nick kissed him on the cheek and said, "Nonsense."

Wynder took a deep breath and relaxed into his pillow. "What do we do?"

"This is God's way of telling you that you have to give up your crazy pace and concentrate on my protocol." Nick joked.

Nick told Wynder that first they would need to clear up his pneumonia, then he would need to fully implement the nutritional supplements, diet and detoxification of his therapy. Wynder's wife Sandy went into full gear, setting up the program for her husband right there in the hospital room.

With Sandy by his side, day by day, Wynder gained strength. He asked for Nick who visited him every night in the hospital. Exhausted from a long day's work, Nick often didn't arrive until 9:00 P.M., but then the three of them sat and talked about their lives and medical successes. Wynder's fever went down and his cough cleared.

Two weeks later Wynder was able to go home where Sandy watched over him and kept him on the program. He rallied, then regressed, then rallied again. Nick visited him a couple of times a week and on the weekends. Despite his illness, Wynder was never too tired to discuss the pilot study and its pending publication in June, 1999.

Nick and Linda had rewritten the article since its first submission to JAMA six months earlier. They updated the survival statistics. Nick and Wynder spent hours together on the weekends, going over and over data and reviewing the galleys when they arrived in early spring. Wynder wrote his editorial and read it to Nick from bed, a plea for the medical establishment to take Nick's work seriously. The editorial would be the last of several hundred articles that he wrote in his life.

> *Eventually, our article came out as the lead article, with Dr. Wyn-der's editorial, in the June 1999 issue (Volume 33, Number 2) of Nutrition and Cancer. At the time of publication, nine of 11 patients (81%) had lived one year, 5 of 11 had lived two years (45%), 4 of 11 had three years (36%) and two past four years. To put this data in perspective, in the article I compared our results with the data from a recently published article detailing the results for the latest chemotherapy drug, gemcitabine, approved for the treatment of pancreatic cancer. Of 126 patients with pancreatic cancer treated with the gemcitabine in the study, only 18% lived 12 months, and not a single patient lived longer than 19 months. In our little study of 11, we had five live two years!*

The day the first printed copies of the article arrived, Nick rushed over to show Wynder. Frail and withdrawn in bed, Wynder immediately sat up and beamed at Nick.

"This looks great!" Wynder said. "Given all the obstacles we've faced, the results are extraordinary."

The two doctors beamed at each other.

"I told you to just be patient…"

* * * * *

On a Sunday in mid-July, Wynder again deteriorated and was rushed to Memorial Hospital unable to eat and with another case of pneumonia. He was placed on oxygen. Nick was working in his office as he often did on Sundays, preparing his patient programs for the week. He picked up the call from Sandy, finished the programs, then rushed to the hospital two hours later.

"What took you so long?" Wynder asked.

Nick explained that he came as soon as he could.

Nick and Wynder talked for a while, Nick attempting to cheer him up. Several hours later, before he left, Nick hugged Wynder.

"This is the last time you'll see me," Wynder said.

He was right. At age 77, he had struggled with cancer for seven years. That night on July 14, 1999 in his bed at Memorial Hospital, Wynder died quietly.

33

Throughout the early part of 1999, Nick's hopes for a properly run clinical trial were very much alive. Repeatedly, Nick and Linda hailed cabs to the Upper West Side where they pushed open the heavy glass doors to Columbia University Medical School to meet with Dr. Antman's group. Dr. John A. Chabot, an expert in the surgical treatment of pancreatic cancer at Columbia, joined the study as a co-investigator.

Chabot told *The Boston Globe*, "Frankly, when I first read [about the pilot study] I said, 'That can't possibly work.' Then I had to come to grips with it myself. I have no idea how or why it might work, but the data is compelling enough that I can't ignore it. It doesn't matter what the underlying theory is about why it works. That's something for us to investigate once we demonstrate that it works."

With Nick and Linda's input, the Columbia team came up with a protocol for the clinical trial which quickly gained approval from all the federal agencies involved: the National Cancer Institute, the National Institutes of Health through the National Center for Complementary and Alternative Medicine, and the U.S. Food and Drug Administration.

The clinical trial, like the pilot study, was set up under the National Cancer Institute. The pilot study had been a Phase II trial. The study focused on a small number of patients with an untreatable disease. They were treated with a therapy without comparison to a control group receiving a placebo or another medication. The clinical trial was designed as a Phase III, including two groups of patients with the same illness. The two arms of the study would receive different treatments, with one group receiving the new treatment (Nick's) and the second group receiving the best available conventional therapy (chemotherapy).

The NCI suggested that they again test Nick's program on patients with inoperable pancreatic cancer. The NCI also demanded that the study be randomized.

The patients were required to sign up for the trial without knowing which arm they would be assigned. They could be assigned to receive either chemotherapy or the Gonzalez Protocol. Randomized studies are the gold standard of clinical trials. Researchers believe that they eliminate bias in the selection of the patients.

"I want the study to be as rigorous as possible," Nick told Antman and Chabot, "but I worry about randomization. The two therapies are so different. This isn't like comparing two drugs."

Nick and Linda tried to explain how different and unconventional their program was compared to traditional drug treatment. In chemotherapy the patient is a passive participant. The patient is administered a drug in a clinic. At the end of the session, the patient returns home. In the Gonzalez program, a patient literally administers the treatment to him or herself, taking around 150 supplements a day, radically changing his or her diet and lifestyle, and performing various detoxification techniques.

"I can't imagine a patient interested in the study not caring where they were assigned," Linda said.

But Antman urged Nick and Linda to try randomization. "This study is so unconventional and controversial that it will be scrutinized by the medical community from every angle. You want it to be set up as tightly as possible. You don't want to open its very methodology to criticism."

Nick and Linda were reluctant to agree, but at the same time, they were so grateful to have their work tested by top-notch scientists like Antman and Chabot that they finally acquiesced.

Next, they had to find a way to publicize the clinical trial to attract patients. In more conventional trials, scientists often go to the media to get the word out about a new treatment. But again, this trial was so unusual that they were leery about going straight to the media who wouldn't fully understand the intricacies of the program. In further meetings at Columbia, Nick, Linda, Antman and Chabot agreed to cautiously approach the media. On July 7, just a few weeks after the publication of the article on the pilot study, Reuters sent out a very positive story about the clinical trial.

The Reuters article discussed the pilot study, Beard, pancreatic enzymes, and the coffee enemas. Then a cascade of interest poured in from other media outlets. A Scottish journalist called from Edinburgh intrigued with what he had learned about Beard from the Reuters piece. *The Boston Globe* wrote a positive article that was syndicated around the world. *Natural Health Magazine* also published a positive piece.

Several professional publications including *Oncology News International, Medical Tribune,* and *Primary Care and Cancer* wrote serious pieces about Nick's research and the pilot study. Even the American Cancer Society's newsletter carried an objective article discussing the results of the pilot study. In December of 1999, CNN ran a story featuring one of Linda's patients from the pilot study, a woman who was still alive four years after her stage IV pancreatic cancer diagnosis. The segment was syndicated and broadcast on local stations throughout the U.S. and around the world. ABC-TV news ran two reports within one week during June of 2000, one negative, the other fairly positive.

Yet despite the generally good publicity, the clinical trial was having trouble attracting patients—but not for lack of interest. Between December 1999 and March 2000, Columbia had received 200 queries from perspective patients. 197 of them refused to enter the trial once they found out that they had a 50/50 chance that they could receive chemotherapy—rather than the Gonzalez program. Two of these three patients quit the study when they were assigned the chemotherapy arm. The other patient was assigned to Nick and Linda—the nutritional arm—but in the end, wasn't able to follow through with the program.

Later, Dr. Chabot reported to a White House Commission on Complementary and Alternative Medicine Policy:

> *The initial year of the trial, we had a huge interest. There was a fair bit of publicity about this, none of it solicited by us, but with a lot of press involvement in these sort of trials. We were on TV and in the newspapers. We had huge numbers of patients call with interest. Many, many, many of the patients did not fit the eligibility criteria we had set, which are really very narrow. Those patients who did fit the eligibility criteria, there were almost none of them who were willing to enroll in a randomized trial.*
>
> *In the first year, we randomized three patients into the trial, despite a huge interest, enough patients to easily fit into the pattern where we would expect to be able to complete the trial. It became very clear that we would never collect adequate numbers of patients to come to a conclusion.*

And Nick concurred:

> *After another 60 prospective patients had contacted Columbia but refused to enter the study when they learned of the randomized design—for a total of 260—we decided we had to change the study design so that patients could choose their treatment. No one could say we didn't try—we had tried fervently for a year. Eventually, after much discussion with the National Cancer Institute and the National Center for Complementary and Alternative Medicine, everyone involved agreed to modify the trial to what is called a case control study. In such a clinical trial, patients can choose the treatment arm, in this situation, either chemotherapy or the Gonzalez-Isaacs treatment approach. We would try to match patients evenly, so that the groups would be fairly equivalent in terms of extent of disease, age, and other medical problems. Once the decision had been made to restructure the trial as a case control study, the protocol had to be rewritten and resubmitted to the various regulatory agencies for approval. We received final approval from the last agency as of July, 2000—and the first patients were entered several weeks later.*

Yet Chabot voiced his reservations about the randomized trial and the kinds of patients it was drawing to the nutritional arms of the study. He thought that the randomized design helped to eliminate biases. Among the people screened for the clinical trial to date, the bias toward alternative therapy had been strong. The vast majority of the people who called Columbia were only interested in the nutritional arm of the study. And the patients who met the criteria were clearly healthier than the general population of advanced pancreatic cancer patients.

> *One has to be very careful coming to any conclusions comparing these patients with the general population of pancreatic cancer patients.*

Chabot also brought up the issue of giving the patients support and hope, and how it would affect the outcome of the study.

The effects of psychosocial support and delivering hope to these patients is not insignificant. In the absence of a blinded, randomized trial, separating these effects from the physiologic and pharmacologic effects will be a major challenge in trial design.

Regardless of the potential problems with the study, Nick himself was hopeful. The Gray lawsuit was over, and the clinical trial was up and running. Nick was ready to move into 2001 with new optimism, riding on the attention that his work was receiving. In his editorial accompanying the publication of the pilot study, Wynder had written:

> *Gonzalez and Isaacs are to be commended for agreeing to participate in a randomized clinical trial to compare their approach with the treatment of patients with gemcitabine (Gemzar), a trial funded by the National Cancer Institute under the direction of Drs. Karen Antman and John Chabot at Columbia University.*

Nick clung to these words, that he and Linda were to be commended for having agreed to a randomized clinical trial. They hadn't resisted a trial, as so many alternative medicine practitioners were accused of doing. Instead, they had sought out the proper medical model testing of their research. Nick and Linda embraced a clinical trial and thought that finally they had the green light to progress through the proper channels. If the clinical trial was a success, they would continue their research with new vigor. If the trial was a failure, they would close up shop. It was that simple, but just the initiation of the clinical trial gave them a legitimacy that they had never before had in the eyes of the medical world.

Still Nick weathered attacks from critics, but he tried to keep his eyes on the future. The published pilot study data had generated a lot of criticism. The study had been supervised by Wynder and the protocol carefully conceived and reviewed by NCI and researchers from other institutions, but that didn't prevent condemnations from other scientists. They never spoke with Nick but questioned his methodology in press interviews.

And they criticized his results. They pointed to his disciplining before the New York Medical Board. They pointed to his departure from his Vanderbilt residency, claiming that he wasn't properly trained in oncology. They thought the hair test ludicrous, and the supplements, diet, and enemas a way to defraud and burden patients. They pointed to his lost lawsuits. They pointed to the fact that Dr. Victor Herbert, "quackbuster" and professor of medicine at the Mount

Sinai School of Medicine, testified for Charell at the trial. In a *Washington Post* article in 2000, Herbert had said "People want to believe in magic. He's selling magic." Herbert said he considered federal funding for a study of the Gonzalez program "a terrible waste of money."

In the same *Washington Post* article, a physician from Harvard had also gone on the record claiming that a number of patients in the study did not have pancreatic cancer, even though all the participants had been screened and approved by the supervising physicians. "It's not clear that all 11 patients had pancreatic cancer," said Dr. Robert Mayer, director of the center for gastrointestinal oncology at Boston's Dana Farber Cancer Institute, former president of the American Society for Clinical Oncology, and an associate editor of *The New England Journal of Medicine*.

Furthermore, Mayer claimed that the patients in the study were much healthier than normal pancreatic patients. The study patients had traveled great distances to see Nick and Linda, after all. And Mayer, too, questioned the pilot study results. The study had not counted the patients who had dropped out after just a few weeks on the program. Mayer claimed this skewed the results and violated accepted research practice. Nick countered that he was certain that all his patients had properly diagnosed pancreatic cancer, and that pilot studies routinely have a lead-in period to eliminate people who decide not to follow through.

Others were more excited about his pilot study. After the publication of Nick and Linda's article, Dr. Guesry at Nestlé provided funding to test the enzyme treatment on animals, hoping to provide supportive data as the human clinical trial moved forward. The Eppley Institute at the University of Nebraska Medical Center set up the experiment under the supervision of Dr. Parviz Pour. The Eppley Institute was well-known for its pioneering work decoding the molecular mechanisms of pancreatic cancer. Dr. Pour was celebrated for developing mouse models useful in testing new treatments for the disease.

Pour worked with furless, in-bred mice lacking a functional immune system. The mice were injected with a virulent strain of human pancreatic cancer. In these compromised mice, tumors grew rapidly and could kill quickly. In the first experiment, Pour divided the mice into two groups, one that received Nick's specially-formulated pancreatic enzymes, and the other that received no treatment. The animals receiving the enzymes lived much longer than the control group and appeared happy and healthy. The untreated mice went downhill immediately, seemed listless, inactive, and bloated as the cancer spread.

In a second experiment, the mice were again divided into two groups. Again, one group received enzymes and the other no treatment. This time, selected mice were periodically sacrificed and examined for cancer. The treated group showed a small and localized growth of cancer where the untreated group showed an aggressive spread of cancerous tumors that eventually killed the mice. The enzymes clearly slowed the growth of the tumors.

The mice protocol had three factors that didn't correlate with the human patients' protocol used in Nick and Linda's practice. First, no previous animal experiments studying the effects of porcine pancreatic enzymes on pancreatic cancer had ever been conducted, so Nick and Linda had had to guess at the doses that were appropriate for the mice. Second, the chow that the mice were fed contained a fair amount of soy, a Bowman-Birk inhibitor, which dramatically neutralizes the trypsin in the enzymes, reducing their efficacy. Third, the mice were not given the same vitamins, minerals, trace elements, nutritious food and purified water that the humans received on the Gonzalez program. Yet, even with these challenges, the enzymes in the animal study were still effective.

Dr. Pour and his colleagues would publish an article on the mice experiment in May 2004 in the peer reviewed journal *Pancreas* with Dr. Guesry and Nick listed as co-authors. In the discussion section of the article, Dr. Pour wrote:

> In summary, PPE [Porcine Pancreatic Extracts] is the first experi-
> mentally and clinically proven agent for the effective treatment of
> PC [Pancreatic Cancer]. The significant advantages of PPE over
> any other currently available therapeutic modalities include its
> effects on physical condition, nutrition, and lack of toxicity.

In late 2000, Nick was interview by Michael Specter for a cover article in *The New Yorker,* one of the most established and elite weekly magazines in the United States. Nick was beginning to believe that his luck was truly changing. The past decade had been so stressful that Nick didn't want to bring another mate into his sphere. He didn't want a wife to be subjected to the kind of pain and ridicule that had been directed toward him. He thought that he didn't have the time to be a good husband, and certainly not a good father. His own father had spent so much time with him, watching movies, going to the ball park, and coaching him in baseball, that Nick couldn't comprehend how he could have a family life. He remained single and dedicated to his work, solely focused on fending off his enemies, advancing his research, and seeing patients. He didn't go out to bars or other gatherings, or give much thought to a social life.

Until one day when he found a beautiful young woman standing in his waiting room.

34

In December of 2000, Mary Beth Pryor, an attractive, dark-haired 34-year old woman with sparkling eyes, high cheek bones and a wide smile, stood in Nick's waiting room, unannounced. Nick's assistant hadn't buzzed her in the outside door, nor had she buzzed her into the door to the office suite. The security system was tight in the building. Nick only took on patients he thought he could help. Rejected patients had been known to somehow gain entrance to the building, then camp out in the hallway, trying to plead their cases to Nick in person. Mary Beth was on a mission to meet the famous Dr. Nicholas Gonzalez, and she knew that he wouldn't see her. She wasn't another doctor nor a patient. So she slipped into the office when another patient pushed open the door to leave.

Mary Beth, a marketing executive living in New York City, had a family member dying of cancer—her brother's mother-in-law. Mary Beth was a fixer and a researcher. She was close to her brother and wanted to fix his mother-in-law and the heartache that her whole family was experiencing. She researched the very best cancer treatments available in New York City. Nick's name came up over and over again. She had called his office and was told that she was to send her mother-in-law's records and Dr. Gonzalez would review them, deciding if he could help her or not. Mary Beth thought that would take too long—her brother's mother-in-law was dying—so she decided to deliver the records herself to Nick's office.

Nick was saying good-bye to another patient when he found Mary Beth standing at his reception counter. He was immediately drawn to her and curious about her identity. She looked into the handsome face of Dr. Gonzalez standing before her in his Brooks Brothers suit with his crown of thick, dark hair.

"Who are you and how did you get into my office?" Nick asked.

Mary Beth stood there in her heavy winter coat, blurting out her story, begging him to see her family member.

"I'll review her file and see if I can help," he said. He asked a few questions, then said he was busy with another patient and they could continue the conversation over dinner. "Please leave your contact information with my assistant." He shook her hand, turned and walked back down the hall toward his office. Nick called her later that afternoon and scheduled a dinner for the following evening.

But the next day Mary Beth came down with a cold, and called and rescheduled the appointment. Nick called her back, offering to come to her apartment with some natural cold remedies. Mary Beth was taken aback. She wasn't used to doctors making house calls.

The next day, she wasn't feeling much better. She was still running a fever but didn't want to delay her brother's mother-in-law's possible treatment any longer, so she met Nick at the Judson Grill that evening.

"You're still not feeling well, are you?" Nick said, sitting next to her in the restaurant. He took her hand. "Let me see if I can help." He closed his eyes and squeezed her hand in his.

Mary Beth immediately began to feel better! And suddenly realized, this is not a medical meeting, this is a date! She had been asked out on a date by this dashing young doctor.

Soon the son of one of Nick's patients walked by and stopped.

"Doctor Gonzalez?"

"Yes."

"I just want to thank you for all that you've done for my mother," the son said and walked away.

Nick turned to Mary Beth. "I didn't pay him to say that, I promise."

Mary Beth was falling for Nick. They arranged to meet again. Mary Beth went home that night and called her boyfriend who was living in California. She broke off their relationship.

A whirlwind courtship began with Nick and Mary Beth meeting for dinner whenever he could slip away from his practice. He put in his full days in his office, doing research, seeing patients, and returning phone calls in the early evening. Then he disappeared into his office bathroom, showered, shaved, and slipped out the door, arriving at Mary Beth's door soon afterwards. On weekends, Nick also arrived in suit and tie, just as he had done when coming directly from the office.

"Can't you go casual on the weekends?" Mary Beth asked, and Nick got a hurt look on his face. Mary Beth soon learned that Nick was a man of habits, that he felt best in a suit and tie, that he never wore shorts (Mickey Mantle didn't wear shorts, he claimed.). For years, Nick had had a personal shopper who bought his clothes and the same tailor who altered them. Nick always ordered his stationery from the same shop and had his meat and vegetables delivered to his office by the same organic distributor. He cooked himself the same thing for lunch every day—an organic cheeseburger with a whole wheat bun, and steamed organic vegetables, always broccoli, cauliflower, and carrots. He had so much unpredictability at work that he liked predictability in his personal routine.

Nick and Mary Beth frequented the same restaurants: The Judson Grill, Josie's, the Artisanal Fromagerie Bistro, and Bouley at Home. While New York City has few organic restaurants, Nick knew all the owners and wait staff at these establishments where they could at least buy meals with fresh vegetables and high-quality ingredients.

By the beginning of February of 2001, Nick and Mary Beth were beginning to discuss marriage and Mary Beth's parents came in from Bedford, New York, to meet Nick over dinner.

"I liked him right away," Judith Pryor, Mary Beth's mother, said. "And we were behind his work and research one hundred percent. I immediately knew just by talking to him that Nick was brilliant and that his cancer research had to be brilliant, too."

The Pryor's support was a huge boost to Nick. His own nuclear family had always been perplexed by his alternative medical protocol.

On February 5, 2001, *The New Yorker* published a 16-page article on Nick by Michael Specter called *The Outlaw Doctor*. The periodical fell open to Nick's full-page portrait, his hands crossed, a wry smile on his face, flanked by a handful of his patient success cases, all looking toward him with awe and gratitude.

The Specter piece created a detailed summary of Nick's family background, Nick's credentials and his program, from how he stumbled upon the work of Dr. Kelley, to the use of the supplements and enemas, to background information on John Beard and his research on pancreatic enzymes. Specter detailed Nick's work with Dr. Good at Sloan Kettering, his monograph, his study with Kelley, marriage to, and divorce from Linda, and eventual medical practice. The article discussed the pilot study and the $1.4 million NIH grant to conduct a full-blown clinical trial. The piece touched on the help that Nick had received from Proctor and Gamble, Dr. Ernst Wynder, the Nestlé corporation, and Dan Burton. The article didn't shy away from Nick's trouble with the New York Medical Board, and his critics. It quoted Dr. Antman at Columbia stating:

> *I worry very much that the fact that we are doing this trial will*
> *put a university imprimatur on the Gonzalez regime, and that*
> *patients will assume that means Columbia supports this treatment.*
> *We do not.*

The article concluded with Nick expressing his chagrin in finding himself on the fringes of medicine, and that he still dreamed that his exile would end.

> *I'm really not much of a revolutionary. I wear only blue and grey*
> *pinstripes. The greatest sadness of my life—other than my marriage,*
> *to Linda, which didn't work—is that I have been forced to work*
> *outside the academic mainstream.*

Once the article hit the newsstands, word of his treatment immediately buzzed through the alternative medicine underground as well as through circles of the curious but cautious in the conventional medical world. In his office, his phone rang off the hook with calls from prospective patients.

Nick didn't want to read the article. He didn't like to read about himself and was fearful that the article would be negative. Mary Beth persuaded him that he needed to read the piece.

"You have to read what's been written about you in *The New Yorker* magazine," she said. "How many people get profiled in *The New Yorker*?"

Back in his office the next day, Nick opened the magazine and right away he saw a reference to his graduation from Brown University in 1970. He immediately picked up the phone and called Mary Beth.

"Don't read the article," Nick said.

"Why? What's wrong?"

"Just don't read the article until I come over. I need to talk to you."

Mary Beth couldn't figure out the problem, but suddenly after work, Nick was at her door, breathless.

"We need to talk," he said.

Mary Beth let him into her apartment, bracing herself for anything.

"You see," Nick said. "We've never discussed my age."

"Your age?" she asked. She couldn't imagine that this was an issue. She had assumed that he was her age—34. He didn't have a grey hair on his head, and not a single wrinkle around his eyes. He was fit, trim, and lively.

"I'm 53," Nick said.

"53? How could you be 53? You look 35."

"I'm on my own protocol."

"53?" Mary Beth was crushed. She had had dreams of finding a mate her age to marry and start a family. She thought she had found one. Then she became furious. Why hadn't he told her he was 53? Nick was 19 years older than Mary Beth. How in the world was that going to work?

"I don't want you to end this because you think I'm too old to be a father."

She asked him to leave and broke up with him.

They didn't speak for three days. Mary Beth's sister-in-law called her and told her she'd never seen Mary Beth so in love. Did she think that she was going to find someone this good again?

So Mary Beth and Nick talked.

"I love you so much that I want to have children with you," Nick said. At the same time, he voiced his hesitancy to become a father. He didn't feel like he had enough time.

Mary Beth began to wonder if his busy schedule would even allow enough time for her.

"Okay," she said. "If we were to get married, what would be your priorities?"

"You would be my second priority," Nick said.

Again, Mary Beth was not happy to hear that she would be playing second fiddle to his work. "And your first priority is work?"

"No, that's my third priority. My first priority is to God. You would be my second priority, and work is my third."

They were engaged before Valentine's Day. The wedding was set for October 20, 2001.

Then they were off to find a ring.

Mary Beth explained that they could find a ring style they liked at a fancy jewelry store, then have a dealer in the diamond district make it for them at half the price. One Saturday morning they planned to meet at Cartier on 5th Ave at 10:00 a.m. when the store opened. Then they planned to visit all the jewelers in that area: Tiffany's, Van Cleef & Arpels, and Fortunoff.

Mary Beth ran into Cartier's in the pouring rain. "I'm meeting my fiancé here," she told the clerk. But by 10:45 a.m. there was no Nick. She was beginning to think she was getting jilted at the jewelry store. Nick didn't own or carry a cell phone, so she had no idea where he was and had no way to reach him.

Around 11:00 a.m. Nick came charging into the store as if he were that short stop headed for home plate, sweating and soaking wet from the rain, and out of breath from running down the street.

"A patient called with an emergency and I had to pick up the call," Nick blurted out. "I thought it would be quicker to run to the store than try to find the store number and call you."

The two shopped all morning, not finding what they wanted at Cartier's. Or at Tiffany's. Or Van Cleef & Arpels. Or Fortunoff. The rain was coming down in droves, sideways. Mary Beth was beginning to get frustrated and distraught. She wondered if this was a sign that they were rushing their engagement.

"Let's stop and give it a rest," Mary Beth said.

"Okay, let's grab a burger at the Plaza bar. We'll regroup there," Nick suggested. "After we eat, you can decide if you want to call it a day."

They dried off in the Plaza and had a relaxing lunch. Mary Beth had a glass of champagne and calmed down.

"Let's try just one more jewelry store," Nick said, and Mary Beth agreed.

They walked the two blocks to Harry Winston's, Nick pulling open the doors to the lobby where a receptionist and a security guard greeted them.

To Mary Beth's surprise the receptionist said, "Good afternoon, Dr. Gonzalez." She ushered them into the vault room. Mary Beth wondered how many other women Nick had taken here. How else would they know him by name?

They were then ushered to a private desk with a jeweler. "Good afternoon, Mary Beth," the jeweler said. Now how did the jeweler know her name? Mary Beth wondered.

"Did you find anything you liked at the other stores?" the jeweler asked.

Mary Beth, now dazed, still couldn't figure out how the jeweler knew her name, and why they were in this particular store.

Harry Winston's has no display case. All the jewelry is in the vault. The jeweler pulled out a small blue velvet tray with one ring on it. An absolutely perfect ring.

Nick picked up the ring and put it on Mary Beth's finger. Mary Beth burst into tears. It was the perfect ring! They kissed.

Mary Beth began to imagine how she would describe this ring to the man in the diamond district who would make a cheaper version.

But Nick blurted out, "We'll take it!"

Mary Beth kicked him under the table.

"This isn't the plan," she whispered in his ear. "We can't afford that ring."

"No, Mary Beth," Nick smiled, his blue eyes dancing from her face to the ring. "This is the plan."

35

The plan for the progression of the clinical trial was not going as sweetly. Nick and Linda never expected to be embraced by the medical community, and shortly after the trial was on its feet, the attacks began. The most blatant hit came from the "quackbusters" who reared up again and tried to have the whole trial shut down. They filed a complaint with the Department of Health and Human Services (DHHS) in Washington in an effort to stop the project.

Other opposition came in subtler forms. Universally, oncologists failed to refer their pancreatic cancer patients to the trial, despite its backing from NCI and its home in Columbia University. Over the course of the eight years that the trial was in progress, all of the patients in the nutritional arm were self-referred. They found out about the trial through word-of-mouth through other Gonzalez patients, through the media, or through alternative medicine underground channels. Not one patient came to the trial through an oncologist.

Unfortunately, the early randomized trial format put a damper on the ability to attract patients through word-of-mouth. Even though the randomization had been dropped, the impression lingered that a patient could be assigned chemotherapy. Most of the patients who would have sought treatment in the nutritional-only arm of the study, still shied away. Nick and Linda urged the NCI to become more proactive. At one point the NCI agreed to place ads about the trial in leading medical journals—a standard for major clinical trials. But the ads were never placed.

Oncologists not only passively failed to mention the trial, but they actively advised against it. A numbered of suitable candidates had learned of the trial on their own and asked their oncologists to refer them, only to be met with the by now familiar refrain of "fraud" and "huckster" accusations directed at Nick.

Some patients who had actually entered the trial were then urged by their oncologists to abandon the study. Unfortunately, the protocol required that each patient needed to be followed by a physician once a month for follow-up blood work and exam. Chemotherapy trials often have this same requirement with monthly visits to patient doctors to monitor toxic side effects of the drug and immune suppression.

Patients who lived in New York City could be easily followed by Nick and Linda, but most of the trial patients lived great distances from New York. Only three of the patients finally admitted into the trial lived in New York City. So most of the nutritional-arm patients were followed by their local oncologists who had no knowledge of the program and were openly hostile toward it. Patients reported that when they went to their monthly visits, their local oncologists often forcefully urged them to stop the Gonzalez program and take up standard chemotherapy—even though conventional chemotherapy had proven ineffective for pancreatic cancer. Even patients who were clearly responding to the Gonzalez program were told to quit the trial by their oncologists.

"It's such a shame," their oncologists told these patients, "that you have chosen such a restricted diet and lifestyle. It's quality of life that we emphasize. You should be able to enjoy the pleasures of ice cream and pizza in the last days of your life."

Indeed, the Gonzalez program requires a radical change in lifestyle. Even though it seems like organic is prevalent today, obtaining it can often mean hours of searching and driving. It is rarely sold in commercial grocery stores, and health food stores aren't a guaranteed supplier. A rigid schedule of meals and enzymes must be maintained, the enzymes needing to be taken at least an hour clear of eating food. Then all the detoxification routines need to be factored into the day.

Gonzalez trial patients needed support, not criticism. Other clinical trials requiring a change in diet—like the Diabetes Control and Complications Trial conducted in the 1980s—required that patients on restricted diets receive frequent encouragement and positive reinforcement. In that major, multi-year study, all potential patients also received 40 hours of screening, including multiple assessments by a psychologist, before admission into the trial.

Eventually, at least five patients dropped out of the Gonzalez clinical trial due to the monthly discouragement they received from their local doctors. Convinced of the fraudulent nature of the Gonzalez program, Nick's critics supported the local doctors. The critics thought all patients should be warned against the program. Repeatedly, Nick and Linda requested that the NCI send out a letter to the local doctors asking for their cooperation for the sake of science. Initially, the NCI staff agreed to draft such a letter, but it was never sent.

Some patients washed out of the trial before they even met with their local oncologists. In the pilot study, at Dr. Wynder's suggestion, Nick and Linda included an eight-week preliminary lead-in from biopsy. During these 14 days, a perspective study patient would be evaluated for compliance. Those who could not or would not comply were eliminated from the study. Those who followed through with the program were then officially entered. Those who died during the pilot study—although none did—were to be counted as a failure. Dr. Wynder insisted on the lead-in period to help insure that the admitted patients were willing and capable of adhering to the prescribed nutritional program.

Many clinical trials in oncology do not include a lead-in period. Tests of chemotherapy require nothing more from the patient than to show up at a doctor's office or hospital and receive an I.V. Issues of motivation and compliance are minimal compared to a patient who is administering a complicated program to him or herself at home. But sometimes clinical trials of chemotherapy drugs do indeed include a lead-in period. For example, in 1998, the FDA approved the chemotherapy drug Gemzar, or gemcitabine, for the treatment of pancreatic cancer based on a clinical trial with a one-week lead-in observation period. During this time, the administrators eliminated any patient whose pain could not be controlled.

With the resources that they had, Nick, Linda and Wynder knew that extensive pre-screening might not be possible, but a one-to-two-week lead-in period would have helped sift out the patients who could not or would not follow the program. Nick and Linda knew that without such a safeguard, the whole study could be undermined. There are patients, for instance, who just can't swallow 150 pills a day due to physical problems—no matter how motivated. The chief administrators of the clinical trial refused to initiate a lead-in period.

In addition, Dr. Antman had initially agreed that Nick and Linda should participate in the selection of the study subjects. But in July of 2000, after the trial had been running for 20 months and only four patients had been admitted for treatment in the nutritional arm, Nick and Linda were removed from the patient selection process, ostensibly to eliminate selection bias. They were required to refer all patient queries to the administrators of the trial at Columbia University and not converse in any way with potential patients.

Dr. Chabot was left to be the sole administrator selecting patients for the clinical trial. Chabot had a busy schedule himself, and he had no previous experience with trials entailing radical lifestyle changes. He had no knowledge of the intricacies of the Gonzalez program, and he had no familiarity with screening patients for the program. There was considerable lag-time between the day the potential patients called Columbia and the day they were told of their qualification for the trial. Sometimes the patients would wait weeks or even a month. Often in desperation, these patients, running out of time with their dire prognoses, called Nick's office. If they were referred to Nick and Linda at long last, the patients were often very, very ill—at least one even appearing in the office for the first time in a wheelchair—and had a difficult time complying with the program.

Unfortunately, those whom Chabot selected to enter the nutritional arm of the trial began to fail to comply with the program. In the end, if even a one-week lead-in period had been established, Nick and Linda could have eliminated 11 of the 39 total patients referred to them for the trial. In total, Nick and Linda calculated that 30 of the 39 patients entered into the trial were non-compliant for a number of reasons including physical disability, psychiatric instability, lack of social support, poor motivation and physician harassment.

In contrast, the case of Sarah Ann Cooper showed just what compliance could do. Cooper was a clinical trial wash-out who became a Gonzalez Protocol success story. In late 2000, Cooper, a 59-year-old business woman, had been diagnosed with pancreatic cancer. Her diagnosis had been confirmed from Kaiser then the Mayo Clinic. Her doctors all wanted to perform a Whipple operation, a complex surgery to remove the head of the pancreas, the first part of the small intestine, the gallbladder and the bile duct. Cooper had scheduled the surgery twice but cancelled each time. When she researched the procedure, she questioned the common sense of having the operation. Without the surgery, her prognosis was three to six months, but with the surgery and chemotherapy, her prognosis only extended to 15 to 18 months.

Cooper started praying. She went to her pastor and he said, "Ann, God doesn't come down and visit you and say, "'Now you are healed.' It doesn't work that way. Rather, healing takes a slow investigation on your part."

Cooper was tormented by her diagnosis. She wanted to see her grandchildren grow up. She wanted to live a full, diversified life. She thought we had been placed on earth to enjoy life, not ask, "Why me?" She discarded the idea that illness was God's will. Bunk. No, she thought, God wants us to live to 120 years old!

Cooper, who didn't even know what her pancreas was, started her investigation. She went to the medical library and delved into the medical journals, reading everything she could on cancer, its conventional treatment and the available alternative treatments. She got on the internet and wrote for information from the AMA and the NCI. She combed through medical books at bookstores. She read close to 100 books on cancer. She wanted to live, to be present at her children's weddings, and to love her grandchildren. She wanted better odds than her doctors were giving her.

On her own, Cooper found Dr. Kelley's work and tracked him down. She spoke to him twice on the phone, then found the Gonzalez-Isaacs clinical trial. She called Nick and Linda's assistant who referred her to Chabot's office at Columbia. Chabot's nurse sent her papers to fill out and Cooper quickly returned them with her medical records. She waited a month until she heard back that she had qualified for the trial. She knew what she was in for with the Gonzalez program and realized that she would have to make huge lifestyle adjustments, but she was ready. She marshalled her financial resources together and her sister gave her a ticket to New York City.

In early spring of 2001, Cooper made hotel reservations and flew across the country by herself, stepped off the plane and into her first experience of New York City. Quickly, she found an accommodating taxi driver who took her from place to place. First, she met with Linda in her office to go over the protocol, making certain that Cooper understood its commitment and complexity.

"Are you sure this is what you want to do?" Linda asked.

Cooper agreed. Then her taxi driver zipped her up to Columbia-Presbyterian. Cooper felt well and looked healthy and happy walking into Chabot's office unattended.

Chabot's nurse went over Cooper's records and paperwork, then said that she would be given the final approval by Dr. Chabot. Everything was falling into place until the nurse asked, "You could have surgery. Why haven't you had surgery?"

"I can have surgery, but I've chosen not to. I turned down surgery. Twice. I want to try the protocol."

The nurse quickly ended the interview and said she would have to consult with Dr. Chabot.

Chabot entered the room and said he could not approve her for the trial since she could have surgery.

"I will not have surgery, chemotherapy, or radiation, now or ever," Cooper said, tears welling up in her eyes. "I should be able to have the treatment I feel is best for me."

Cooper explained that she had flown to New York on her own expense and wanted to start the protocol. She knew what she was doing as she had watched family members die of cancer. She met all the criteria, had been waiting a month, and wanted to immediately start the treatment. But Chabot had made his decision.

Her taxi cab driver ferried her back to her hotel and she collapsed on the bed in tears. She knew she wouldn't do the Whipple operation, but she feared she didn't have enough time to investigate other alternatives. She knew that without treatment she would go downhill really fast.

Just then the phone rang. Linda was on the other end. Chabot's office had just called her and informed her of their decision. Linda was concerned for Cooper and told her she would like to see her.

"Do you want to be on the protocol?" Linda asked. "Would you want to be on the protocol if you paid your own expenses?"

Linda offered to treat Cooper outside of the clinical trial. Cooper could hear Nick in the background saying it would cost $800–1000/month for the supplements, but that they would adjust their fees.

Cooper zipped over to Nick and Linda's office first thing the next morning and began the protocol that very day. Cooper became Linda's patient, meeting with her for two hours, going over the protocol, giving her instructions on how to get the supplements, how to find the food, how to install a reverse osmosis water filtering system, even what cookware to use. Periodically Nick poked his head in and out of the room, making certain that everything was on track.

Cooper's local physician was cooperative. Her cancer cleared, and she didn't see Nick and Linda again for two years. Her protocol has changed slightly over the years, but as of this writing she is still alive from her original 2000 diagnosis of pancreatic cancer. Nick and Linda never charged Cooper for her office visits. She has lived long enough to enjoy her own grandchildren and to celebrate her own 50th wedding anniversary.

36

On September 11, 2001, Nick had taken a rare day off of work with an even rarer head cold. Mary Beth also called in sick to take care of her fiancée. They were sitting on the couch together, holding hands in Nick's apartment on the upper east side of New York City when an alert flashed across the screen: *Plane crashed into the north tower of the World Trade Center.* Nick grabbed the remote control, turning up the volume of the T.V., trying to figure out what was happening. Then together, Nick and Mary Beth watched the second plane fly into the south tower.

For Nick and Mary Beth, like most people in New York City, September 11 was a day of terror and trauma, disbelief and deep mourning. Patients began calling the office to check on Nick and Linda, hoping that they were okay. The office assistant was overwhelmed by the volume of calls that only built throughout the day, and finally all the circuits were jammed. Lower Manhattan was evacuated, traffic snarled, all flights at the airport shut down. Nick's home phone, which rarely rang in the middle of the day, began to ring and ring, with friends and relatives checking on him.

In the wake of the disaster, patients—old and new—were hesitant to fly to New York City. National and international patients alike cancelled appointments. Potential patients throughout the world decided to try treatments closer to home. Nick and Linda's practice took a financial hit, and it would be years before they made a recovery.

In his personal life, Nick and Mary Beth were going through their own modifications. Mary Beth quickly learned that she hadn't become engaged to a conventional physician. Over the course of the summer, she learned to adapt to the lifestyle of the Gonzalez Protocol. First step: an organic diet. Testing showed that Mary Beth, like Nick, was a balanced metabolic type, so together they could eat a wide range of foods from both the vegetarian and the carnivore sides of the scale. But Mary Beth's first food shopping trip was full of blunders. She had gone to a conventional grocery store and returned to the apartment with things like Heinz ketchup.

"No, see that has sugar in it," Nick said. He took Mary Beth on a $20 cab ride to a health food store and introduced her to organic fresh fruits and vegetables and products made from organic ingredients without additives and preservatives.

Next, he taught Mary Beth how to cook very simple, nutritious foods.

"I wasn't a great cook in the first place," Mary Beth said. "So, the cooking lessons were helpful."

They might fix a piece of fish, steamed vegetables, and a grain. Or a piece of meat, a small potato and a salad. Nothing elaborate, all meals that could be made in a short time with a limited number of ingredients, and all satisfying. Easy enough.

There were more difficult days, of course. Like the afternoon Mary Beth's phone rang and Nick, who was out of town at a conference, was on the other end.

"I'm sorry, I won't be home tonight."

"Bad weather?" Mary Beth asked.

"No, on my last flight, a suitcase fell out of the overhead compartment and reinjured my neck. Now I need to fly to Atlanta to see Dr. Sweat and get an adjustment."

An old neck injury was Nick's chronic complaint throughout his life. Dr. Sweat, with his atlas orthogonal technique, was the one person who Nick knew could help. Mary Beth, of course, was unfamiliar with this whole backstory.

"Can't you see someone in New York?"

"I need to see Sweat."

"Sweat?"

"That's the chiropractor's name."

"A chiropractor? You're going to see a chiropractor?"

"Yes, he's agreed to see me on an emergency basis. My plane won't be there until late tonight."

They hung up and Mary Beth, concerned, called her mother. Judy told her daughter that she should fly to Atlanta to meet Nick to give him support. "You're engaged now. That's what a fiancée does."

Mary Beth called Nick back and told him she had made plane reservations and would meet him in Atlanta.

Later that evening, Nick and Mary Beth met in the Hartsfield-Atlanta air-port. Six-feet tall, 75-year-old Roy Sweat, his white hair combed back away from his face, was there waiting to pick them up in his red pick-up truck.

"We can all squeeze into the front seat," Roy said, the soft inflections of his Georgia accent blending in with the muggy heat of the Southern evening.

Mary Beth sat between Roy and Nick, maneuvering her legs around the gear shift. She looked down at a big hole in the floor of the truck where the freeway concrete whizzed by beneath her.

They arrived in Sweat's clinic in the pitch dark, a small office with paint peeling off the walls and with several well-worn hard-backed chairs in the tiny waiting room. Dr. Matt Sweat, Roy's son, was in the clinic warming up the x-ray machine where he immediately shot images of Nick's neck. Once the x-rays were developed, Roy and Matt analyzed Nick's cervical injury, then lay him down on the long treatment table. They checked his leg length. A short leg can be indic-ative of poor alignment of the pelvis and the cervical vertebrae. They palpated his neck for trigger points, then set up the adjusting instrument to the precise angle with its stylus contacting Nick's skull just behind his right ear.

In the corner, Mary Beth watched with fear and fascination when Roy stomped on the foot pedal of the instrument and *bang*, the stylus touched Nick's skull with a light tap. Nick immediately felt better. Roy checked his legs again which had evened-out, then checked the muscle tension in his cervical points, and declared the treatment a success.

"While we're here, we should check Mary Beth, too," Nick said.

Mary Beth had also had a past injury—hers from a car accident—so Roy took a complete history and work-up, then sent her to the x-ray room.

She returned to the exam room and she could hear Roy, Matt and Nick scurrying around developing, then going over the x-rays.

"Oh, no."

"Whoa."

"Oh, my God!"

"I can't believe she's still alive."

Now Mary Beth's eyes widened. Roy returned to the room and found that one of her legs was much shorter than the other and her neck muscles were extremely tight. He adjusted her with his instrument, and she, too, felt better right away. She hadn't realized she felt badly, but once she was adjusted here on what looked to her like a set from the *Twilight Zone*, she noticed a huge difference.

"I only trust and send my patients to one kind of chiropractic treatment—atlas orthogonal—and only one chiropractor—Roy Sweat. The only other chiropractor I trust is Roy's son Matt." Nick said.

Meanwhile, Dr. Roy Sweat took Mary Beth aside and into his office. "Now, if you are going to marry Nicholas, you have to understand, he won't be taking you to a Walt Disney movie every week."

Mary Beth took a deep breath, beginning to understand that not only had she become engaged to an unconventional physician, she had become engaged to an extraordinary, but most unconventional human being.

The summer progressing toward autumn, Mary Beth and Nick moved through the routine wedding preparations. Mary Beth threw herself into planning the wedding of her dreams with all the traditional decisions of invitations, music and ministers, attendants and receptions. Nick had little concept of the social etiquette of any of these rituals.

"What's a rehearsal dinner?" he asked Mary Beth.

Mary Beth had to make a list and explain the different parts of their wedding. Nick ticked down the list, but stopped at the wedding dance.

"I can't dance," he said.

"Me neither," Mary Beth said.

The stared at each other, *What to do*? Then they decided there had to be a remedy.

They hired a dance instructor.

"That's it, now step, step glide," she coached.

Nick tried. Mary Beth tried.

The instructor showed them again. "Like this," she said, demonstrating with a pantomime partner.

Nick and Mary Beth held each other awkwardly and stepped on each other's toes.

Nick fired the instructor.

"Can't we just have fun?" Nick asked Mary Beth.

She hoped for the best, sending out the invitations and finalizing everything else that was under her control.

Then the Twin Towers collapsed, and Mary Beth feared the wedding she had fantasized her whole life would go up in smoke. She and Nick discussed postponing the wedding, but the invitations had been sent, and it became too difficult to try to reschedule and reserve the various venues. They didn't want terrorists to stop their wedding, and they thought they were showing their American Resilience by having the wedding on 10/20/2001. So, they went ahead and were married in St. Matthew's Episcopal Church in Bedford, NY on October 20, 2001. The reception was held at the Westchester Country Club.

St. Matthew's is on a historic site that dates back to the era of the Puritans, with the brick edifice built in 1810. That October the trees that lined the road to the church with its columned entryway and simple steepled bell tower were still turning their vibrant yellows and oranges. The church, surrounded by 65 acres of land including a parish house, a graveyard, an outdoor chapel and a trail leading over a small bridge to the Ketchum Preserve, invited the guests to participate with an air of dignity and tradition.

Inside, the pews filled with relatives and friends. A large wedding party processed in with many attendants including Nick's best man Harry Flynn who had been Michael Landon's publicist, and J.P. Jones, Vice President of Research for Proctor & Gamble, the man who supported Nick's experiments with pancreatic enzymes. Mary Beth's girlfriends were her bride's maids, many of them flying in from all over the country. Mary Beth came down the aisle on the arm of her father, and then the minister conducted a traditional Episcopalian service with exchanged vows and blessings.

The Reverend Terry Elsberry asked Mary Beth, "Do you take this man Nicholas Gonzalez to be your wedded husband?"

Mary Beth knew exactly what it meant to marry such a man as Nick. She shouted, "I DO!"

The whole congregation laughed.

The service concluded with the whole congregation singing *God Bless America* in response to the 9/11 attacks.

Outside the church, the bride and groom posed for their wedding picture, Mary Beth in a strapless, Vera Wang flowing white gown and veil, a strand of pearls around her neck loaned from Harry Winston, and a bouquet of flowers in hand. Nick, with his arm around Mary Beth, beamed out at the camera, his dark hair neatly tamed and brushed away from his forehead, the black tie of his tuxedo winging out at his chin, a boutonnière in his lapel, and his gold wedding band on his finger.

Then it was off to the reception at the Westchester Country Club in Rye, New York, an elegant private club. In the Westchester Room, the round tables were set for the guests with flowered centerpieces, china, silver and crystal champagne glasses waiting to toast the bride and groom. The draperies to the tall, arched windows, were tied back to reveal a view of the manicured golf course. Peter Duchin's small band played throughout the dinner, and Mary Beth and Nick became increasingly anxious about their wedding dance. Every part of the day had been perfect so far. They didn't want to blow it now. But they knew that they had flunked out of dancing lessons…

So, they both took a deep breath and Nick took Mary Beth's hand, leading her toward the musicians. When the band saw the bride and groom making their way toward the dance floor, the strains of *The Way You Look Tonight* filled the room, the melody and the chords playing off each other, the drummer's lateral brush strokes underscoring the rhythm, their syncopation echoing out across the tables of guests chatting and finishing their desserts, taking a few last sips of wine with the wait staff making the rounds with coffee and tea. The entire room full of guests stopped talking, turning their attention toward the striking couple about to translate their love into movement.

Nick took his bride in his arms, his sweaty hand meeting hers.

"Let's just wing it," he whispered in her ear.

Nick took a moment to listen to the band, absorbing every note, allowing the music to fill all the pores of his body. Suddenly, he was back in his childhood listening to his grandparents playing classical music in the living room, the cello and the harp blending their harmonies, building a sense of closeness in their family. He was at his father's knee listening to him play the French horn, his lips pursed on the mouthpiece. He was back in Mexico with his cousin Juan José Calatayud at the piano playing *Rhapsody in Blue* with the Symphony of Mexico at the Palacio de Bellas Artes.

Nick took one step forward and Mary Beth followed. They stopped. Then his legs caught the rhythm of the music, hers matching his, their bodies in perfect sync, their feet tapping across the floor to the notes of the piano, the beat of the bass, and the brush of the drums. Nick was creating his own dance steps, creative, commanding, and graceful but completely unorthodox, and Mary Beth supported his every move. They were a duo, a bride and groom, partners in an even larger dance. They were whirling through the darkened room, the candles on the tables flicking, emitting heat, the guests radiating that same warmth back toward the bride and groom.

Nick twirled Mary Beth around and bent over her, righting themselves again. His eyes locked into hers, they whirred past the band and the tables full of guests. They smiled and laughed and spun around some more. They looked as if they had been dancing together for years, learning the same choreography, practicing the same steps, their legs anticipating each other's moves by shear muscle memory. They were Fred Astaire and Ginger Rogers. They were Gene Kelley and Rita Hayworth. Fixated on this handsome couple, the crowd burst into applause. Holding hands, they both bowed to the crowd to more applause.

Nick and Mary Beth had reserved a suite at the country club, but when they came to the end of the day, exhilarated and exhausted, they just wanted to go back to their own home. Nick called a car that drove them back to Manhattan. They took the elevator up to their apartment and Nick stopped before the door, turning to Mary Beth.

"I would carry you over the threshold," he said. "But I'm afraid I would throw out my atlas adjustment and then we'd have to go back to Atlanta to see Dr. Sweat."

"Thanks, I'll just walk," Mary Beth replied.

37

B ack at work, Nick settled into a rhythm of alternating exhilaration and
exhaustion. The clinical trial was a constant source of stress. He and Linda
discovered that in addition to a growing list of protocol issues, the administrators
had dropped the ball on some of the basics. In the past, Nick had learned his
lesson about obtaining informed consent from patients, so he wanted to make
certain that he had a signed form from everyone admitted to the trial. Yet, Nick
and Linda discovered that three of their patients in the trial had not signed the
proper paper work.

All clinical trials run through the NIH and NCI in the United States require
that patients sign an informed consent before entering the study. The consent
form outlines the nature and intent of the study, the possible positive benefits
and the possible dangers and side effects of the tested treatment. The patient
is obliged to physically sign the form, acknowledging an understanding of the
complexity of the study and their readiness to be a willing participant.

The administrators at Columbia University devised a lengthy consent form
detailing the trial. Patients admitted to the study were to sign the form, administrators making two copies, giving one to the patient, and keeping the other
in an appropriate file in their office—not in the patient charts. Nick and Linda
were told that no patient would be admitted to the trial or sent to them for the
nutritional enzyme arm of the study, without a signed consent.

Nick and Linda glided along through the early years of the trial assuming that
their patients' consent forms were properly filed in the offices at Columbia. Then
in July of 2002, Columbia sent Nick and Linda a patient whom they assumed
had been vetted and approved for the trial. Linda became her physician, but
shortly after the initial work-up, the patient had a series of strokes, discontinued
the program, and died. After her death, Columbia called Nick and Linda saying

that Dr. Chabot had disqualified the patient from the trial because she had never signed the consent form. The patient had asked to take the form home "to think about it," but had never signed the required paperwork.

At the time, Nick and Linda thought the incident strange, but did not make much of it. Then in the summer of 2003, they received word that they would need to have a signed copy of the consent form in the trial patients' charts. Nick wasn't on the Columbia University staff, so the administrators decided that he would have to sign a sub-contractor's agreement with the school at the beginning of each fiscal year defining his responsibilities with the clinical trial. Nick and Linda read the agreement and realized that they would now be required to have a copy of the consent forms filed in their trial patients' charts in addition to the original held at Columbia.

Linda immediately called Dr. Chabot's office requesting the forms. Columbia did not send them. After waiting a few months, Linda embarked on a paper chase. She took a cab up to Columbia and arranged to copy the forms herself. At this time, she discovered that in addition to the disqualified patient, two other patients (designated #9 and #16) were missing their consent forms. Both of these patients had been non-compliant and had discontinued the program, yet had been counted as fully vetted failures in the trial.

A bureaucratic game of dodge ball ensued for over two years, with Nick and Linda pressing for the forms, and Dr. Chabot and his staff admitting that the forms were missing, then stating that they were searching for them here and there. At one point, Dr. Chabot emailed Nick and said that his staff had loaded them into the system, but no such forms ever appeared. Finally, Dr. Chabot admitted that no forms existed for the two patients in question, that the patients had "walked off" with the forms. Chabot added that the charts of patients #9 and #16 contained written verification that the patients had consented. Yet Nick and Linda had never been informed of this fact. Nick kept emphasizing that he and Linda were required by their sub-contract agreement to have the consent form in their patient charts. And above all, informed consent was vitally important in any study.

> *Proper informed consent has become a major issue in academic circles, to the point that even the United Nations' World Health Organization has weighed in on the matter. The National Cancer Institute requires that all candidates sign an informed consent doc-*

*ument before admission to any clinical trial under its jurisdiction,
and that the original be kept in the patients' charts. This rule is not
optional nor can it be ignored or disregarded at the whim of the
any IRB (Institutional Review Board).*

The paper chase took a particularly odd turn later in the study. In 2006,
Nick was sent a list of all the patients who had qualified and had been approved
for both arms of the study. To Nick's surprise, neither patient #9 nor patient #16
appeared as approved trial subjects.

* * * * *

Meanwhile, off-trial, Nick's practice started to rebound from the hit it had taken
after 9/11. He certainly had his own failures and still didn't cure as many patients
as he hoped. He mourned his patients who died, and their passing upset him
so much that his assistants hated giving him the news. He tried to figure out
what had gone wrong. He developed ways to discover if a patient had followed
the program and knew that there was no way to control compliance. He also
became frustrated when a patient was not responding, and he worked hard to
figure out why. He readily adapted the program to move a patient off a plateau
or prevent a downward spiral.

Nick had one leukemia patient who just wasn't responding the way he had
hoped, and he began quizzing her about her living situation. Any stress? Any
abuse? Any toxins in the home? They worked down the list until he discovered
that a cell phone tower had gone up near her home.

> *Kelley always said,—Your success will kind of make you feel self-sat-
> isfied, but your failures will keep you up at night. And that's true.
> This was a woman in her late thirties when she started with me.
> She did well, but she didn't die, which was good. But she wasn't
> getting better either. She lived in a metropolitan area, near a major
> airport or one of the major radar centers in the country. She could
> look at her window and see a cellphone tower.*
>
> *I insisted to have someone go to her house, and she was like
> living on a toaster oven that's so electromagnetically active. We*

tried to do things to neutralize it. Finally, I had to tell her to sell the house and move out, and she moved. That was one of the most extraordinary experiences I've had—her life didn't normalize until she left that house. We had it checked by an expert. As soon as she moved, the kids started sleeping better, and her husband felt better. The whole family did better. Electromagnetic field pollution is becoming the next great nightmare we have to deal with.

"Cell phone towers emit EMFs—electric and magnetic frequencies," Nick told her. "There hasn't been enough research on their effects, but you'll notice I don't even carry a cell phone."

Nick filed this patient away in his mind as one of his "miracle patients," patients who had been given death sentences by other doctors, patients who didn't respond to conventional medicine, or patients who were left without a treatment plan by the medical model.

David Yoffie was another one of Nick's miracle patients during this time who was treated in Nick's private practice. In 2002, Yoffie, a businessman in St. Louis with major real estate investments, was diagnosed with stage IV liver cancer at the age of 46. He underwent a couple of rounds of chemotherapy without much success. Then his conventional oncologist told Yoffie that at this point chemotherapy wouldn't be much help.

"I went home to die," Yoffie said. "I sold 17 of my buildings and made out my will."

But Yoffie's mother wouldn't hear of it. She was determined that there had to be something that could help her son. She researched various treatment centers and went online looking for information. She weighed the possibilities and decided that David had the best chances with the Gonzalez program.

"I decided to give it a shot," Yoffie said. "I called and made an appointment."

Yoffie flew to New York City to see Nick, then back home where he immediately jumped into the routine of 150 pills a day, coffee enemas, skin brushing, Epsom salt baths, and various other detoxification routines. He retired from his work to eliminate stress and began to eat the prescribed diet.

"This is going to work!" his mother insisted, taking over the cooking and making certain that David did everything exactly the way it was described on his protocol sheet.

"My mother was really supportive," David said.

After three months, a CAT scan showed that his cancer was beginning to shrink. After six months, all traces of the disease were gone.

David stayed on the program and returned to his oncologist for a follow up appointment. His local doctor was astonished to see him so healthy.

"You're really lucky," he told Yoffie.

But Yoffie knew he'd had more going for him than luck. He and his family were determined that he would stay on the protocol.

"It makes a huge difference if you're committed to the program," he said, speculating that some of the patients in the trial didn't have the support that he did."

Eventually, Yoffie was able to trim down his program and the number of supplements he took. His trips to New York City became less frequent, but he continued to stay on his diet, and he resumed a normal life.

As odd as it may sound, Nick thought treating cancer was a slam-dunk compared to the autoimmune and other diseases like Lyme, Multiple Sclerosis, and diabetes. These conditions were less straight forward and were less well-researched. They often produced physical pain with accompanying psychological symptoms that could be trying for both patient and physician. Patients with these kinds of chronic conditions began coming to Nick when they heard about his success with cancer.

Most of these immune-related diseases were viewed with skepticism by conventional medicine, and probably always will be until there is some breakthrough in research. For example, MS was considered "all in your head" until the early 1970s when researchers discovered it was a disease of the central nervous system that caused deterioration of the myelin sheath around the nerves. Patients with these immune conditions generally get only symptomatic treatment from conventional medicine. They are often left to their own devices to bat around in search of a cure in the world of alternative medicine.

Nick established a good track record with Lyme disease. Whole families who were living in wooded areas of New England began making their way to his office, often suffering severely with neurological symptoms from tick bites. A parent might find relief for his or her issues, then slowly begin to bring in a spouse or child, and eventually the rest of the family. Many of these people had been active and healthy, only to suddenly find themselves exhausted, with memory loss, or with stiff necks, rashes, or joint pains—a wide array of symptoms that often stumped their physicians and gained the patients the label "crazy."

"It's a hopeless situation," one Lyme patient said. "It feels like a whirlpool sucking you down. And nobody is able to help you."

The patient remembered that once she herself was feeling better, she brought her young son, a boy who loved baseball, to see Nick. The son had Lyme disease and had been bullied in school for his illness. Nick was very protective and fatherly toward the boy, talking to him about baseball and things that the boy enjoyed. Nick adapted the program for the boy to make it less onerous. Almost miraculously, gradually, the boy began to respond and heal.

Word travelled through word of mouth, with one patient with Lyme or MS, or Crohn's, or lupus telling another, and most patients often bringing in a sibling, son or daughter. One day a big white van pulled up in front of Nick's office building and a whole family of Amish trooped up the stairs.

Nick treated all types of patients, but down the line, he was perhaps proudest of his work with diabetes. In an article for *Alternative Therapies in Health and Medicine*, Nick wrote up a case study of a 44-year old athletic male whose health had suddenly deteriorated after a serious hockey injury where he twisted his spine. The injury landed him in bed and off of work for a month. When his situation did not improve, he returned to his primary care physician who did extensive testing, but the results were within normal limits.

A year after his accident, the patient's health went dramatically downhill again. He returned to his primary care physician who did more testing to find that the patient was slightly hypothyroid, medicating him for that condition. Yet a month later, the patient found himself falling asleep during the day and developing a severe case of insomnia at night. He walked around in a fog with terrible fatigue and his muscle weakness worsening.

The patient then sought the help of an internist at Hahnemann Medical College in Philadelphia, famous for solving "difficult cases." The internist put the patient through more tests, finally finding one abnormality indicating a possibility of myasthenia gravis. The patient dutifully took a medication for that condition for three weeks, discontinuing the drug when he saw no improvement.

Next, the patient checked himself into the Myasthenia Gravis Specialty Center at the Sidney Kimmel Medical College, Jefferson University Hospital in Philadelphia, where they did yet more testing to determine that the patient did not have myasthenia gravis. Frustrated, they took the default position that the patient's problem was "all in his head," referring him for a psychological evaluation. Ready to try anything at this point, the patient saw a psychiatrist who prescribed one anti-depressive medication after another, all to no avail, and some even making him feel worse.

Then the patient consulted a local neurologist who diagnosed him with Lyme disease and put him on a 6-week course of antibiotics. Which only made the patient feel worse. Next the patient tried a well-known alternative physician in New Jersey who once again raised the issue of myasthenia gravis and Lyme, treating him with an intensive supplement program and placing him in the hospital for a three-day course of antibiotics. Despite the treatment, the patient saw no improvement.

He only got worse with eyelid twitching and bags under his eyes. His hands began to shake and he developed severe bilateral pain in his feet. He rapidly lost all the hair on his arms, legs and chest. Even his eyebrows began to thin. He developed acute onset periodontal disease and potency issues.

The patient tried yet another alternative physician who prescribed intravenous vitamin C and testosterone shots. The doctor put the patient through intensive allergy testing but came up with nothing. And the patient felt no improvement yet again. The patient tried another physician specializing in "difficult cases" who found that the patient was diabetic. He was hospitalized for two days in an attempt to stabilize his blood sugars and educate him about his therapy. Upon discharge, his blood sugars remained unstable, his symptoms intensified, and he ended up passing out and landing in the local hospital with diabetic ketoacidosis with respiratory failure, acute renal failure and acute pancreatitis. In addition, he was diagnosed with mastoiditis and uncorrected hypothyroidism. He began an emergency course of dialysis treatment for his renal failure.

After a two-week hospitalization, the patient continued on out-patient dialysis and worked with the endocrinologist assigned to his case to regulate his blood sugars and help him become more compliant with his diet. The endocrinologist taught the patient foot care which he practiced three to four times daily.

The patient finally found his way to Nick who suspected that despite a family history of diabetes, this patient's condition was most likely related to his hockey injury. Nick thought that the injury had significantly injured the patient's pancreas, resulting in his subsequent rapid decline. Nick determined that the patient was a balanced metabolic type with a tendency to be closer to the sympathetic side of the scale.

Nick put the patient on the program including all the supplements and diet to match his type. Nick included glandulars in the program and six pancreatic enzymes with each meal. The pancreatic enzymes contain digestive enzymes but also homeopathic doses of insulin which seem to be absorbed active in the blood stream. In contrast, purified insulin preparations denature in the stomach when taken orally.

Nick recommended three to four servings of vegetables per day, both raw and cooked, many of them drawn from the cruciferous family, and the inclusion of dark leafy greens. The patient was allowed non-GMO whole grains, preferably sprouted. He could eat nuts, seeds and beans. Even though he leaned toward the sympathetic dominant side of the scale, Nick allowed the patient a fair amount of animal protein including two organic eggs a day, and raw milk, yogurt and butter. The patient was also allowed two to three servings of seafood and of poultry, and two to four servings of grass-fed meat per week.

Nick met with the patient for two sessions in consecutive days, explaining his program in detail, then asked to see him again in three months. A year later the patient returned, smiling, with the glow of good health. When asked about his disappearance, the patient explained that money was tight as he had been out of work. Now he felt significantly better, was working again, "felt great," and that the program had changed his life. He had been totally compliant and had gone ahead and done what he was told without needing coaching or support from Nick. With his new-found energy and vigor, he had taken a job that he enjoyed and was working long hours. He was exercising regularly, going to the gym, and once again lifting weights.

His kidney function had returned to normal, he was off of dialysis, and the nephrologist had discharged him. He had regrown his hair and had no more periodontal disease. His thyroid was functioning well. He became a "low mainte-nance" patient, continued to improve, and conscientiously stayed on his program, sticking to his diet that interestingly enough, contained a fair number of whole, complex carbohydrates, in contrast to the common practice of carbohydrate restriction for diabetic patients. Finally, although he stayed on his insulin, after a couple of years, the patient was able to adjust the dosage downward.

After each visit, Nick sat at his desk writing up his notes into the patient's chart, thrilled with his progress.

38

Nick and Mary Beth had a lot of adjustments to make in their first few years of marriage. After 9/11, life was chaotic in New York City, in Nick's practice, and in their own household. Extra security searches were set in place in New York airports and throughout the country, with members of the National Guard roaming through hallways with rifles slung over their backs. A week after the 9/11 attacks, letters containing anthrax were mailed to media news offices in New York and Florida, and to senators Tom Daschle and Patrick Leahy in Washington, D.C. A journalist in Florida died, a postal worker in Virginia contracted inhalational anthrax, and reporters at ABC and CBS became infected with the deadly bacterium.

The patients who did travel to New York to Nick's office were on edge. Nick's worries about the state of the world only compounded his worries about the state of the clinical trial. While many Americans sought refuge in their religious faiths, others abandoned them. They could not reconcile a "Just God" with the horrors they had witnessed. Many also could not reconcile their bank accounts. The attacks on the World Trade Center had set the United States markets into a tail spin, and the whole world went into a financial slump.

Mary Beth and Nick entered their own personal tailspin. Mary Beth had never been married before, and Nick had been a bachelor living alone and progressively set in his ways since his divorce to Linda. Mary Beth moved into Nick's apartment. When they met, Nick hadn't been looking for a girlfriend. Nick had thought that he would never get married again until he met Mary Beth. She was ready to be married but had never lived with a man. She wanted to have children right away, but Nick was hesitant. But, they were both committed to working out their problems.

Nick practiced the lifestyle that he demanded of his patients. He not only ate organic food, took supplements, and did the detox procedures, but he used only non-toxic cleaning supplies. He prepared his food in non-toxic cookware and furnished his living quarters in furniture made of natural fibers. He wore only cotton, silk, and wool. Mary Beth had to adapt and change all the things that she thought she knew about keeping a good home. Out went the Lysol and in came the baking soda and vinegar. Out went the Pledge, and in came the damp cloth.

Mary Beth loved to decorate, so right after their wedding, she embarked upon a campaign to make their apartment homey and comfortable. But when she moved any of Nick's things to a different location, he protested.

"Don't touch that!" he barked.

A creature of habit, Nick liked things to be predictable, always in the same place, always at the same time, always in the same process. So Mary Beth worked out a system where she would move an item just an inch a day until, perhaps a few weeks later, it was where she wanted it.

"This lamp is so much better here," Nick said, oblivious to the slow, creeping movement of items throughout the apartment.

Next, Mary Beth wanted a fresh start and set out to transform the bedroom furnishings. She talked Nick into dismantling his old bed and hiring movers to transport and place it in storage at her parents' house. Mary Beth researched, then found an organically-made bed with an organic cotton mattress. She showed it to Nick.

"Yes, that looks fine," he said, with some reservations that the piece of furniture would take too much of his time to assemble.

"Don't worry about a thing, Babies," Mary Beth said. "I'll put it together. You won't have to lift a finger."

The bed arrived in the mail on a Saturday in about 20 different boxes. As soon as Mary Beth saw the delivery, she knew she'd made a huge mistake. Nick came home from the office, eyeing the boxes.

"I'll take care of everything. It'll be a cinch," Mary Beth said. "You just sit there in the living room and work."

Nick sat in the living room, reading medical journals in his black pinhole glasses that he had used to improve his vision. With his pinholes, he shed his normal lenses, and as he had aged, he had never needed reading glasses. He also had a bandana tied around his forehead, catching the drips from a lotion he was testing on himself in a hair-growth experiment. He was determined to find a way to cure male baldness. He cleared up so many of his male patients from cancer to find that what bothered them the most was their male-pattern baldness.

Mary Beth shoved all the boxes into the bedroom and slumped down on the floor with boxes of nuts, bolts, screws. She turned the directions this way and that, but couldn't make any sense of them. She gathered up screw drivers and wrenches, laid out the large wooden bed pieces, but nothing seemed to fit together intuitively. She struggled and worked, and worked and struggled, then tears filled her eyes.

Finally, Nick called through the door. "How's it going in there?"

"It's all good, Honey," she said, choking back her tears.

A few more hours passed. Mary Beth wasn't going to give up. She wasn't going to be defeated. She had to make this work. The old bed was gone, and they needed something to sleep on that very night. Finally, Nick walked into the room to find Mary Beth in tears.

"Let's just call and have those movers deliver our old bed back here," Nick said.

A few days and $1,000 later in moving costs, their old bed was re-established in their bedroom.

Their next impasse came at holiday time. Nick was used to working through the holidays. He declined to venture out for holiday meals and celebrations, preferring to cook his hamburgers and steamed vegetables by himself in his office kitchen.

"We didn't see him much," his niece said. "But he was very generous at holiday time. Once when my mother had been in the hospital, he had a whole organic turkey dinner with all the trimmings delivered to our house."

Nick loved having his office to himself during these breaks. No phones were ringing, few patients were demanding his time and immediate attention. He enjoyed the quiet in the courtyard outside his window, and when he watered his plant, he paused to watch birds float by to alight on the trees below. Standing in front of the glass, he was a naturalist again, rediscovering the ways the ecology of the world fit together. His courtyard made sense of all that he was doing, trying to restore the ecology of his patients' metabolisms.

One of the reasons I like my office so much is because of this garden,
which sits between the building that houses my office and the back

*of the apartment house opposite. The many-floored structures block
any street sound, so even though I am three or so blocks from the
Empire State Building in the center of Manhattan, it is very quiet,
as well as very green. Birds routinely make the garden their home,
some of them quite distinctive, and the place becomes particularly
active during the migratory seasons of spring and fall.*

During the stressful year of 1995 when Nick was fighting the New York
Medical Board, a 12-inch owl had landed and perched on a tree outside the
window—just two feet away from his office manager's desk. The owl visited for
two days, sleeping all day, its head tucked under its wing. Occasionally, it would
awaken, and peer in the window at Nick and his staff.

*At night, it would disappear, presumably to hunt—perhaps in
Bryant Park, where mice live, perhaps further north in Central
Park, certainly a suitable forage site. In the morning, it would be
back by the time the office opened. It seemed unperturbed by the
activity inside, as if it felt completely safe, despite its proximity to
us. The owl had stopped on its journey south for the winter, an
unexpected gift in the midst of Manhattan. After two days, it was
gone. It never returned.*

But as the years progressed, Nick returned to that window, and just the
thought of the owl was enough to induce relaxation.

*Today, years later, as I approach the window of my workroom I
start thinking about the owl, with its searching eyes and tilted
head. I immediately feel a sense of relaxation in my gut and, as if
by magic, all concerns about the day, all thoughts about cancer,
editors, agents, and uncompleted books in need of finishing, all
that goes away. I begin smiling, feeling a sense of pleasure, not of
urgency. I become a little saddened thinking of the owl and how
it helped me forget, at least for a moment or two, my legal battle
for survival.*

> *...I look out the window and gaze at the leaves of the trees, all very quiet in the still late afternoon light. The noise from the world—the questions from my staff, the extraordinary and under-standable and sometimes desperate needs of very sick patients, the sound of the phone, clinical trials, all that is hushed.*

Mary Beth, on the other hand, was used to big family celebrations at holiday times, with her relatives all gathered in one place eating elaborate dishes of food, making lots of noise and merriment. Nick tried to blend into this scene, but could only handle it for about an hour before he wanted to return to the refuge of his office, his work, the quiet of the courtyard, and his memory of the owl.

Nick had no interest in going on vacation at other times of the year, either. Trips to Europe or cruises in the Caribbean had no allure. Events with a lot of social interaction and chit-chat were Nick's idea of a complete waste of time. So, Mary Beth talked him into taking some short trips—just the two of them—to nearby locations where they could get out in nature. Mohonk Mountain House in New Paltz, New York, just 80 miles north of Manhattan was a favorite get-a-way with its views of the river, the mountains and expanses of gardens.

Eventually, Mary Beth bought a condo on Sanibel island off the coast of Florida near her parents' retirement home. Nick did enjoy going to Sanibel for a few days during the holidays where he could observe egrets, herons, pelicans and roseate spoonbills in the Ding Darling National Wildlife Refuge, recapturing some of peace he felt with his owl at his office window. Then he and Mary Beth would stroll along the beach picking up crabs and shells, returning to the condo where he could resume his research and writing in front of the plate glass window.

"Mary Beth often came down earlier, before Nick," Judy Pryor, Mary Beth's mother explained. "Nick would work until the last minute, then fly down for Christmas."

Christmas Eve at the Pryor home was festive with lots of presents under the tree and lots of pots cooking on the stove.

"Nick loved my cooking," Judy said. "He would walk around the kitchen and lift the lids on the dishes and savor their aromas. He loved cheese, so he would dig into any dish I made with cheese. He didn't drink, so he passed on the wine, but indulged himself in his favorite dishes. At the end of the meal, he would roll up his sleeves, push his tie away, and do the dishes. I thought that totally unnecessary, but Mary Beth said, 'Oh, he wants to do that, so let him.'"

On Christmas morning, the Pryors all gathered for a big breakfast, a major celebration, with grapefruit and orange juice, egg casserole with bread, cream, grated cheese, mushrooms and sausage. John Pryor, Mary Beth's father was originally from Milwaukee, Wisconsin, and he enjoyed stollen, a German fruit bread with nuts and spices, and had it shipped in from Chicago every year.

It took all morning to open the presents, with one relative playing the elf and handing out packages one by one. Then the family took naps, walked on the beach, or swam in the pool. And then it was back again for a dinner of roast beef, mashed potatoes, vegetables, salad, and Yorkshire pudding. Later everyone went home stuffed and exhausted.

Judy Pryor wasn't just the Christmas chef in Nick's life. Just 10 years his senior, Nick bonded with Judy and he asked her to help him edit some of his writings. A professional with a long career as a learning specialist, Judy remained fascinated by Nick's work. She asked him probing questions. They discussed science together. They laughed and joked together.

"Our family has always gotten along well together," Judy said. "And Nick fit right in. We've never had someone drunk in the corner of the living room picking a fight."

Back in New York, the handmade Christmas wreaths and hors d'oeuvres left behind, Nick continued to flip his burger and steam his vegetables in his office kitchen, and while he cooked, he fought over and over with himself in his mind about the clinical trial protocol. He blamed himself for the problems of the trial and continually attempted to figure out what had gone wrong with the protocol. Had he not designed it correctly? What could he have done differently? How could he trouble shoot the trial now? Most of the patients in the nutritional arm hadn't even ordered the supplements. Nick knew that money wasn't the problem as the trial covered the costs. The patients were just too sick to follow through.

He put on a brave face for his patients, his staff, and for Mary Beth, but underneath, he was fearful that his dreams, his future, and his years of work were unraveling.

At home, Mary Beth tried to find a way to lift Nick's spirits, so she began to greet him at the door with what became known to the two of them as "the Babies dance."

"Baby, Baby, Baby," she cried when he walked in the door, dancing up and down, embracing him, the two of them falling into each other's arms, a wide grin spreading across his face.

Nick had never watched T.V., but Mary Beth slowly inched a set into the living room, suggesting that they watch a movie together from time to time to relax. Nick agreed to that but would only tolerate action movies, preferably about World War II, reminiscent of the films that he and his father had watched together when he was a child. If Nick found that they had selected something different, he stood up and walked out of the room, stating, "Too much dialogue."

Over time, Mary Beth began pre-screening their movies, targeting action-filled war films with little dialogue. Then she and Nick were able to sit on the couch together, enjoying the movie. In this way, they began to become more comfortable with each other, and connect as a married couple. Gradually, Nick allowed himself to feel the love and support that Mary Beth gave him—all that had been missing in his life. Gradually, his calls to Hans Moolenburgh and Roy Sweat began to diminish. But when the action ended, and the credits rolled across the screen at the end of the movie, Nick was up and back to work.

He had to get the clinical trial back on track.

39

"This study must be ended at once," Dr. Jack Killen said, seated in the conference room at Dr. Chabot's office at Columbia University on December 13, 2004. He was surrounded by various Columbia, NCCAM, and NCI personnel assigned to the project. "We'll send out a press release as quickly as possible to counter the positive data of the pilot study."

Nick and Linda's brows wrinkled and their eyes met. This was the first time they had been introduced to Dr. Killen, a career NIH oncologist. He had been recently transferred to NCCAM and now served as the lead investigator on their clinical trial.

Dr. Chabot had just presented a graph depicting the status of the two arms of the clinical trial. It was at this moment that Nick and Linda grasped in more profound detail than ever before the pronounced disparity in the study between the number of subjects entered into each group and their staging distribution. Chabot's graph clearly showed a disappointing median and mean survival in the range of 7 and 9 months for the nutrition arm, far less than what Nick and Linda had observed in their pilot study. Given the lack of compliance he'd experienced with these patients, Nick wasn't surprised by their survival rate,

Dr. Chabot's review of the chemotherapy arm, though, showed an unusual longevity for the group with a median and mean survival in excess of a year. These results not only outdid the nutritional arm of the trial, but they surpassed survival statistics of any drug regimen used in the treatment of patients with inoperable pancreatic cancer.

"These statistics for the chemotherapy arm are a sea-change in the treatment of cancer," Dr. Chabot said.

"But there's a disparity between the two groups in terms of numbers and staging," Nick said.

Cancer patients are "staged" in relationship to the severity and spread of their disease. Stage I denotes a cancer that is fairly self-contained with the best chance for patient survival, with stages II and III showing some metastasis to other organs and body parts and a lower patient survival rate. Stage IV shows significant infiltration of the cancer throughout the body with a low patient survival rate. In general, the survival rates for earlier I, II, and III stages of the disease is higher than stage IV cancer patients.

The protocol for the clinical trial eliminated stage I pancreatic patients who might be better helped through surgery. The early stage II and III patients and the late stage IV patients were to be balanced on both arms of the study. An imbalance of patients might give one arm an advantage over another in the final outcomes. For the first five years, Nick and Linda kept track of the statistics on their patients in the trial, calculating 38 admitted patients with a total of 76% in stage IV, and 24% in earlier stage II and III. These figures reflect the general pancreatic patient data at large. The chemotherapy arm had had only 14 members with 61.5% at stage II and II and 38% at stage IV.

"In terms of the staging, the chemotherapy arm had a clear advantage," Nick said. "Almost all of our patients were stage IV. The statistics for the nutritional arm mean nothing because so few of them complied with the treatment."

No one around the table disputed the compliance issue.

Dr. Killen argued with Nick about the staging issue. "All non-stage I pancreatic patients have the same life expectancy," Killen said.

"Correct," said Dr. Chabot.

"Nonsense," Nick said. "The medical literature clearly shows that patients with earlier stage II and III live longer than those with stage IV. Every oncologist knows that."

Back and forth, the debate continued into the afternoon, and when the meeting broke up, Nick and Linda hailed a cab and rode back to their office feeling frustrated. They had never before met Dr. Killen. With this change in administration, Nick and Linda clearly didn't have the kind of NCI-NCCAM support that they had once assumed they'd had. Nick and Linda realized they no longer seemed to be working with objective scientists there to study a treatment in a dispassionate way. The two alternative medicine researchers had to save the clinical trial from its demise.

Nick took the next three weeks to write a 29-page letter to Dr. Killen, filling him in on the details of the clinical trial. Nick was particularly bothered by

Killen's repeated remarks that they had to "counter the positive results of the pilot study." Nick wondered if Killen had been given any background on the study. So Nick outlined the whole evolution of the clinical trial, and its protocol, detailing all the players—from Dr. Ernst Wynder to Dr. Pierre Guesry to Dr. Julian Hyman—and how they assessed and corroborated the data to guarantee its validity. As a back-up to the human pilot study, Nick noted the positive results of the animal studies conducted at the Eppley Cancer Center at the University of Nebraska by Dr. Pour. Finally, Nick discussed the anecdotal evidence of successful use of pancreatic enzymes in treating cancer from John Beard to Dr. Kelley.

Next, Nick addressed the non-compliance problem with the patients in the clinical trial, and how most were simply too ill to follow the program. Those who were strong enough to have ordered the supplements often couldn't get them down. Nick emphasized that they had to rely on oral pancreatic enzymes due to the lack of availability of intravenous formulations. As a result, the patients had to have the ability to swallow.

In the 1960s, Nick continued, Dr. Frank Shively of Dayton, Ohio, had learned of Beard's work, and with the cooperation of a local drug company, created an injectable solution that he administered to patients with advanced cancer with unusual success. But in 1966 the FDA prohibited the use of injectables because they could not understand their need.

Nick finished his letter by addressing the staging issue in the clinical trial. He took up Killen's claim that staging has no effect on survival rate. Nick cited Dr. James Abbruzzese of the University of Texas MD Anderson Cancer Center, one of the world's leaders in the study and treatment of pancreatic cancer. In the well-known text *DeVita, Hellman, and Rosenberg's Cancer: Principles & Practice of Oncology*, Abbruzzese clearly laid out the survival rates of patients with pancreatic cancer. Patients with locally advanced, non-metastatic cancer (stage II, III) have a median survival of six to ten months. Patients with metastatic disease (stage IV) have a short survival of three to six months.

On January 7, 2005, Nick finished his letter and mailed it off to Dr. Killen with copies to Dr. Chabot and the chief administrators at NCI and NCCAM. Three weeks later he received a copy of a letter from Dr. W. Linda Engel, Special Assistant to the Director at NCCAM, written to Dr. Chabot. In the first paragraph of her letter, Dr. Engel told Chabot that Nick had "seriously misinterpreted the motivations for and beliefs underlying Dr. Killen's question to the group."

Engel surmised that Dr. Killen's style of questioning—attempts to clarify points of uncertainty—and also play devil's advocate may have led Nick to conclude that Killen had a totally different agenda. Engel then outlined Nick's allegations about the trial and its data, without disagreeing on a single point. She then questioned continuing the study in its current design, finally expressing her disappointment that the clinical trial had not yielded a clear answer to the question that it had posed—despite the best efforts of the team.

On February 2, 2005, Nick received a one-page letter from Killen himself, reiterating his devil's advocate role, and the fear that Nick had misinterpreted his motives. Killen professed his admiration for Nick and Linda's pilot study. He thought their promising results merited investigation. "I assure you," Killen went on, "that my intention was (and is) to understand as best we can all of the information that we have to date about the treatments under investigation in the trial."

Nick was anxious to hear Dr. Chabot's response to his letter and to confront Dr. Killen face-to-face at the next meeting on March 7, 2005. But when Nick and Linda arrived at Columbia, they were surprised to find Killen a no-show.

"In his letter, Nick has outlined the problems with the study," Dr. Chabot announced to the conference table. "Nick's missive will provide the basis for the paper that will be written about the project and its many difficulties."

Chabot then expressed his wish that Nick and Linda would remain fully engaged in the clinical trial. He hoped that with their cooperation and involvement, the team could address and correct the shortcomings of the study. Chabot especially hoped that more appropriate and compliant patients might be entered into the nutritional arm in the future, helping to insure more meaningful data.

Nick and Linda agreed to stay on board, but in the next passing weeks and months, the trial continued as before with many problems.

Nothing had changed.

Fearing the worse, Nick wrote a letter to Congressman Dan Burton, detailing the history and problems with the study. Finally, Nick concluded:

> *Frankly, at this point, despite my hope six years ago, I see no new era of co-operation between alternative researchers and the NIH and NCI. I have come to believe the study was set up to fail, it is failing, and there is the possibility the illegitimate results will be*

> *used to belittle my treatment, undermine my 20 years of hard work*
> *and research efforts.*

His frustration mounting, Nick emailed Dr. Chabot and the supervisory personnel before the June 20, 2005 meeting, including Dr. Jeff White and Dr. Wendy Smith of the NCI, and Dr. Linda Engel of NCCAM. Nick outlined problems with delayed payments, the long periods when the study was "on hold" when ideal candidates for the nutritional arm were turned away, and entrance of patients unable to comply with the treatment. Two days later, Nick received an email from Dr. Smith at the NCI commenting on Nick's issues without offering much help in getting them resolved. Dr. Smith hoped that they could discuss things further at the next meeting. She acknowledged Nick's frustration and assured him of NCI's support of the research.

On June 20, 2005, Nick and Linda steeled themselves for the next meeting. They were prepared to walk out if corrections weren't made. In the conference room at Columbia, Nick lead off with his most pressing concerns that he had outlined in his email. Once again, Dr. Chabot was conciliatory and hoped that Nick and Linda would stay involved.

"We'll accrue more patients into the nutritional arm—at least 15—to offset the compliance issues," Chabot said.

"But if those patients are too sick to do the program," Nick said. "We're back to muddled data."

Chabot agreed to listen more closely to Nick and Linda when they challenged the admission of patients to their arm. And Chabot promised prompt payment of all invoices. He even handed Nick a letter that he had written and signed to the effect. Chabot then announced a plan to counter any overt or subtle hostility to the trial on the part of the local physicians monitoring the trial patients.

With these olive branches in hand, Nick and Linda agreed to stay on the project, despite their six years of bad experiences. During the following week they awaited the minutes of the meeting with these assurances in writing. But after a month the minutes did not arrive, despite Nick's urging. And no new patients were admitted into the nutritional arm of the trial.

Nothing had changed.

* * * * *

On August 11, 2005, Nick received an unexpected email from Dr. Chabot:

> *Wendy, Nick and Linda. The IRB [Institutional Review Board] has*
> *reviewed our 6-month renewal application. They have closed the*
> *study to new accrual until the 10th death on the chemo arm and*
> *the interim analysis are performed. The study remains approved*
> *for ongoing data collection and analysis. jc*

Nick called Chabot that afternoon.

"Nick, I can only repeat that the IRB board felt the study had reached its conclusion. The chemotherapy arm was clearly superior. The board has shut down recruitment pending the tenth death in the chemotherapy arm. At that point, the IRB will analyze the data and make a final determination about stopping the trial for good."

"But did you let the IRB know of all the problems that have plagued this study?"

"No."

"Then how could the IRB make an informed decision?"

"They've made their decision."

"And what about the 15 additional patients you'd promised to enter into the nutritional arm of the study?"

"The IRB has made its decision."

Nick hung up and informed Linda of the conversation. They sat in Nick's office, staring out the window beyond the potted plant to the courtyard below.

Then Nick and Dr. Chabot fell into a familiar pattern of firing volleys back and forth, with Chabot finally labeling the problem a misunderstanding. On August 15, 2005, Nick wrote a lengthy letter to Congressperson Burton, summarizing the history of the clinical trial and the recent turn of events.

> *I am concerned, as I have been before, that 20 years of hard work*
> *is about to be destroyed, with no recourse on my part.*

Nick wrote to Dr. Smith of the NCI, asking that she try to figure out what was going on with the IRB. He wrote to Dr. Andrew von Eschenbach, the director of the NCI, summarizing the problems with the trial. Then on August

28, 2005 Chabot emailed Nick, stating that Nick had misunderstood the gist of their phone conversation. Chabot emphasized that the IRB did not consider the trial over—just that the study could not accrue any more patients until the interim analysis was done.

Nick continued to be frustrated about the managerial problems with the study. He still wasn't receiving his promised payments, and after three months, he and Linda hadn't received the official minutes of the June 20, 2005 group meeting. The next session was set for the afternoon of September 12, 2005. The NCI personnel had already changed the meeting date once, and they continued changing it, creating scheduling nightmares for Nick and Linda's practice. Finally, Nick couldn't rearrange the appointments of patients who had unchangeable plane tickets, so he sent word he couldn't attend the September 12 meeting.

On Sunday, September 11, 2005, Nick finally received the June 20 meeting minutes. Dr. Smith's summary of the meeting did not match Nick and Linda's recollection. Nick and Dr. Smith disagreed on the characterization of key issues: interruptions in accrual, entrance of patients unable to comply with the treatment, and contacts with local treating physicians. Too, no mention was made of the agreement to add 15 extra patients in the nutritional arm of the study.

On Tuesday, September 12, 2005, in hopes of correcting the official record, Nick composed a long email documenting the errors he saw in the minutes. He received no responses nor corrected minutes. But on September 23, 2005, Dr. Chabot announced that the Columbia IRB had suddenly re-opened the trial to accrual. On September 30, 2005, Nick replied to Chabot that before any more patients were entered into the study, he wanted the managerial problems and the disparities in the June 20 minutes addressed.

Nick and Chabot then emailed back and forth, with Chabot informing Nick that the data analysis was underway and that further discussion about accrual was pointless. On October 9, 2005, Nick shot back a response, again detailing his now familiar concerns. Chabot responded that he had resolved the staging problem with the admission of 11 chemotherapy patients. He had removed two earlier stage chemotherapy patients and added multiple stage IV patients to the group. And he had sent the trial to evaluation.

I do not understand what more you can ask for with regard to stage matching... The 10th death on the chemo arm occurred shortly after chemo started, however it is not likely to invalidate the statistical difference between the groups. We will need to follow the remaining patients on study before any final analysis but it is almost certain that accrual will cease. I will keep you informed of developments as they occur and I hope you will continue to be actively involved with the analysis. Jc

Nick replied with an email that Chabot still had not addressed the issues he had raised in his previous correspondences, problems that to Nick made the data meaningless. And, yet again, he requested the missing consent forms.

Five days later on October 24, 2005, Dr. Chabot said sent a short email:

Wendy and Nick, Please note that per the DSMB recommendation, the ICB has closed our study to further accrual. We remain open for followup [sic] and data analysis. jc

40

On October 26, 2005, Nick sat across from Iowa Senator Tom Harkin and two of his aides in a large office off the main Senate chambers in the U.S. Capitol. Senator Harkin had been instrumental in both passing the Americans with Disabilities Act and setting up the Office of Alternative Medicine which had evolved into the National Center for Complementary and Integrative Health, or NCCAM.

One of Nick's patients sat next to him. The patient, a resident of the Washington D.C. area and survivor of stage IV cancer, had already outlived by years a dire prognosis given at both Sloan Kettering and Harvard. Senator Harkin had called the meeting after having received an eight-page letter from Nick outlining the problems with the clinical trial. Harkin had asked Nick to bring along one of his patients.

Harkin furrowed his brow when Nick went down the list of the obstacles he had encountered in the trial.

"Tell me about your experience with Dr. Gonzalez' protocol," Harkin asked the patient. He listened intently to a personal story of healing and rejuvenation.

"I should have been dead years ago," the patient finished.

Harkin pushed back his chair. "I have to tell you that I'm concerned that NCCAM seems more determined to discredit alternative medicine than to evaluate them the way we had hoped—in a fair and objective manner."

Nick agreed, and on the train back to New York, he sank into the cushion relieved at Harkin's promise to write to NIH director Dr. Elias Zerhouni, expressing his worry about Nick's study and the direction of the NCCAM as a whole. Congressperson Dan Burton had also agreed to write to Zerhouni on Nick's behalf. Nick thought that the two legislators—on either side of the aisle—might muster enough political clout to persuade Zerhouni to investigate.

Burton's office had communicated to Nick that the congressperson seemed exasperated that the trial had become sidelined by managerial issues. He had hoped that Nick's study would be a breakthrough, a means to draw both conventional and alternative medicine researchers together for the benefit of science and patients. Burton wrote to Zerhouni:

> *...Unfortunately, despite the assurances from NCI, it appears from reports I have received that a fair and appropriate evaluation of this important protocol has yet to take place... Dr. Gonzalez believes that none of the data gathered is worthy of publication, and he is greatly concerned that individuals could use this faulty data to justify statements indicating a negative outcome, when no such outcome has been determined through valid scientific investigation.*

Twelve days later, Harkin wrote his letter to Zerhouni:

> *Congress did not create NCCAM with the intention that it would serve only to validate alternative medical treatments in every case, but there was the expectation that NCCAM would be an unbiased source of information ...Unfortunately, there is a growing sense in the alternative medicine community that this is no longer the case. And if practitioners of alternative medicine believe their treatments will not receive a fair and unbiased review form NCCAM, they will no longer agree to work with the Center, and consumers will lose what Congress believes would be the one independent source of information on promising alternative treatments.*

Meanwhile, the next meeting for the clinical trial team was scheduled for December 12, 2005. Nick and Linda had still not received any response to their September 2005 email asking for corrections in the minutes of the June 2005 meeting. So Nick and Linda decided not to attend any more meetings in person, but to place all future communications in writing with any personnel involved in the study.

Shortly after the December 12th meeting, Nick and Linda received a copy of the minutes from that meeting. No reference was made to their protest or the errors they wanted addressed in the minutes of June 2005.

A few weeks later, Nick and Linda received a copy of a four-page letter dated December 22, 2005, from Dr. Zerhouni to Congressperson Burton. Zerhouni denied that there had been any managerial issues or wrongdoing. He thought that the trial had been impeccably run, and that Nick's complaints were only sour grapes. Point by point, Zerhouni went through Nick's allegations and refuted each one including:

- NCI failure to notify oncologists of his cancer treatment protocol, thereby limiting patient recruitment for the trial.
- Physician bias against his treatment so strong as to cause subjects to withdraw from the study.
- NIH staff failure to ensure timely payments to the private clinic involved in the study.
- Scientific misconduct by Dr. Chabot and his staff.
- Referral bias in favor of the chemotherapy arm, including staging issues.
- Inappropriate admission of patients for the nutritional arm of the study.

Zerhouni concluded by urging continued communication and dialogue between Dr. Gonzalez and Dr. Chabot. He emphasized his commitment to a fair evaluation of potentially therapeutic alternative therapies. He stressed that the NIH staff had diligently managed the trial and had "provided the necessary support to ensure that the investigators can bring this trial to a statistically meaningful conclusion."

Nick absorbed the full implications of Zerhouni's letter and its failure to even entertain any of his concerns. He realized the letter did not take in consideration Dr. Engel's official letter that underscored the allegations of his 29-page letter of January 7, 2005. He was dismayed that Zerhouni had so easily backed-up the Columbia team and had not contacted him to document and weigh his side of the story. Nick surmised that the NCI and NCCAM staffers had not shared Dr. Engel's letter with Zerhouni.

Nick picked up the phone and called Congressperson Burton's office and spoke at length with an aide who strongly urged him to write a detailed rebuttal to Dr. Zerhouni, answering each and every point.

Tap, tap, tap. Tap, tap, tap. Head down, Nick immediately set to work at his computer in his office, working on his Zerhouni rebuttal. *Tap, tap, tap.* Fingers dancing furiously across the keyboard, he hammered home his arguments, making his case for his side of the dispute. Again, as he had had to do in so many previous communications, Nick attempted to explain the protocol. His treatment was far outside the conventional paradigm, but it had already saved a significant number of lives, and it had the potential to save even more.

Mornings, Nick dashed up his office steps, his hair still wet and slicked back from his shower, always a few minutes late to his appointments. All day he met with his normal patient load, finishing up the physical exam at the end of each office visit. "Do you have any more questions?" he asked.

Once final matters had been settled and the patient headed to the office manager's desk to pay the bill, Nick returned to his desk to write up the detailed notes he kept on each patient visit. The records complete, he returned to his rebuttal, squeezing in any bit of time—even ten to fifteen minutes—between patients. At the end of his patient day, after he'd returned numerous phone calls from patients all over the world, Nick worked well into the evening on his document. Home, he allowed himself Sunday mornings off when he read his Bible and he and Mary Beth enjoyed a more leisurely breakfast together. Then it was back to his office on Sunday afternoon to *tap, tap, tap.*

On the other side of the office wall, Linda surfed the web on a hunch that the clinical trial may involve some sort of conflict of interest. She searched the medical literature, and up popped information linking Dr. Chabot and the GTX chemotherapy regimen used in the conventional arm of the study. The GTX regimen had been developed at Columbia University by a colleague of Dr. Chabot's. On page 44 of an article in the March 2004 issue of *Oncology New International*, Dr. Chabot identified as an integral part of the research team that helped develop and test GTX.

By March 2006, Nick and Linda received word that another group meeting had been called for the twentieth of the month. Though they had not resigned from the trial, they had no intention of attending this meeting. They still had received no corrections to the June 2005 minutes, and were more convinced than ever that all communications with the group needed to be in writing. The minutes to the March 20th meeting arrived promptly, but did not mention the study's managerial issues, nor Congressperson Dan Burton's November 4, 2005 letter, nor Dr. Zerhouni's reply.

At this point, Nick and Linda began to suspect that the group was going to attempt to place an article about the study in a medical journal. In the minutes to the March 20 meeting, Dr. Smith wrote:

Dr. Chabot has not heard anything from Dr. Gonzalez but again welcomes his participation and continues to consider Dr. Gonzalez a part of the research team. Unless he hears differently from him, Dr. Chabot plans to continue to invite him and Dr. Isaacs to future meetings and to welcome Dr. Gonzalez' participation in the development of the manuscript as originally planned.

The rest of the minutes negated many previous objections that Nick had made to the protocol.

- The group had found no significant difference in the staging of the two groups of patients in the chemotherapy versus the nutritional arm.
- The group confirmed that two of Nick's patients had "walked-off" with their consent forms.
- Consequently, the investigators conducted the statistical analysis with and without these patients, concluding that these patients had no effect on the results.
- Dr. Smith did acknowledge payment delays, but she had been assured that Nick had now been paid in full.
- The group denied that any patient admitted to the trial had not met the entrance criteria.
- And the group confirmed that calls had been made to all hostile local treating physicians.

Nick scanned the minutes from the March 20, 2006 document on his computer screen. He jotted down notes to counter what to him only appeared to be another error-filled report.

A few weeks later, Nick received a short letter and a final data chart for the study from Dr. Chabot in the U.S. mail. The letter was dated April 22, 2006. Chabot conceded that Nick had been waiting for several years for a written response to several issues of concern about the study:

- In his January 7, 2005 letter, Nick had argued that three patients had been admitted to the study with strong histories of mental illness. Chabot addressed the issue of two patients who had been admitted to the trial with depression. Psychiatric disease was listed as an exclusion criterion in the study, but Chabot argued that the two patients had been treated.

- Nick had also described at least ten patients who could not eat at the time of entry into the study. One of these patients was taking Megace, an appetite stimulant used to treat wasting syndrome. On his initial visit, Nick had noted that this patient should have been excluded from the study. But Chabot argued that his appetite had improved steadily over the course of treatment. Nick noted the patient did improve for a few weeks, but generally he went downhill and died in three months.

- Chabot made no mention of the other nine patients Nick had mentioned with eating problems.

On the data sheet, Chabot showed that he had admitted 11 extra chemotherapy patients toward the end of trial accrual from March 9 through September 23, 2005. This number approximated the total number Chabot had admitted for chemotherapy during the first three years of the study. Nine of the eleven patients were classified as stage IV. He had eliminated two stage IV "Gonzalez patients" and down-staged five "Gonzalez patients" from IV to lower numerals. The result: the appearance that the nutritional arm patients were less advanced than the chemotherapy arm patients of the study.

Nick and Linda had never reviewed the actual charts of any of the patients in the chemotherapy arm to confirm the stagings of those patients. They only had Dr. Chabot's April 2006 data chart as their guide. In early May of 2006, after six months of hard work, Nick finished his 352-page response to Dr. Zerhouni's letter. After he summarized and explained the program itself, and detailed the pilot study and the subsequent problems he had had with the clinical trial, he gave a point-by-point rebuttal to Dr. Zerhouni's claims. He bound up 25 copies of the document and supporting materials, sending one to Congressperson Burton, and one to Dr. Zerhouni.

In his cover letter to Zerhouni, Nick again highlighted the issues in the study, in addition to Dr. Chabot's perceived conflict of interest and the staging problems that showed up on the data sheet. Nick petitioned Zerhouni to consider his cover letter a formal complaint against Dr. Chabot, Dr. Wendy Smith, and Dr. Jeff White of the NCI, and any other personnel both in the NCI or on Dr. Zerhouni's staff who had mishandled Zerhouni's original letter to Nick.

Several weeks later, Congressperson Burton also sent a copy of Nick's monograph and a lengthy cover letter to Dr. Zerhouni outlining the problems in the study and urging Zerhouni not to publish or make public announcements about the study until all questions in the letter had been addressed. "To do otherwise," Burton wrote, "would in my opinion, run the risk of perpetuating a grave injustice by misleading the public in general and the cancer community specifically."

Nick and Linda waited for a reply from Zerhouni but they didn't have high hopes that they would receive a satisfactory response. In the meantime, Linda pressed forward, researching their next step. She and Nick contacted two Washington D.C. oversight agencies, the Office for Human Research Protections (OHRP) and the Office of Research Integrity (ORI) both within the Department of Health and Human Services, the umbrella organization above NCCAM, the NCI, and the NIH. The OHRP and the ORI have the charge of investigating allegations of misconduct in federally funded research activities.

On June 19, 2006, Nick called the OHRP and reached the director of Compliance and Oversight who asked to receive evidence of protocol violations— especially the patients who were admitted to the trial without signed consent. Nick also reached the director of ORI's Division of Investigative Oversight. She assured Nick that she would coordinate efforts with the OHRP.

That same day, Nick composed a seven-page letter to the two agencies. Once again, he summarized his program and its history. He addressed the problems with the clinical trial and included Zerhouni's letter and his own rebuttal, attaching his monograph. Shortly after receipt of these materials, OHRP opened a formal investigation into the trial's management. But Nick feared he may have been too late. He suspected that the Columbia team was attempting to place an article on the clinical trial in a medical journal.

A June 22, 2006 email from Dr. Wendy Smith at the NCI announced that the next staff meeting for the clinical trial would convene on June 26, 2006 with these two items on the agenda:

1. Update on status of subjects in the chemotherapy arm.
2. Discussion of data analysis and the preparation of the study manuscript.

On June 30, 2006, Nick composed a letter to Dr. Chabot, sending copies to the rest of the Columbia team, and urging them to withhold any publication.

*Though you may all believe the study has been appropriately man-
aged, I have been in discussion with a number of regulatory agencies who do not share your perspective. I am aware that shortly,
two very serious investigations with the management of the trial,
and those involved with it, will be beginning.*

Weeks passed. Nick and Linda received no response from the Columbia team
to their June 2006 letter of warning. Nick and Linda thought that the proposed
publication had been called off in light of the pending OHRP investigation.

Nick and Linda couldn't have been more wrong.

41

Sunday, December 3, 2006, around 10:35 P.M. Nick and Mary Beth were about to retire for the night in their apartment in the Upper East Side when the phone rang. Nick stood in his bedroom in his blue Brooks Brothers bathrobe, the landline handset to his ear. It was Nick's answering service who had mastered the art of triaging his many calls, forwarding him the urgent ones, and letting the others wait until morning.

"A Dr. Boris Pasche from Chicago needs to speak to you right away," Nick's service told him. "It's urgent. You should return the call immediately."

Nick didn't have a clue about Dr. Pasche's identity or why he would be calling late on a Sunday evening. Nick thought that perhaps Pasche was a physician with information about one of his patients, so he called him right back.

"Thank you for returning my call so promptly," Dr. Pasche said.

Pasche explained that he was an oncologist living in Chicago, currently affiliated with Northwestern University. He had worked at Sloan Kettering and had known Dr. Robert Good. He had followed Nick's work for many years, including his efforts to have his treatment tested through a clinical trial. Pasche was now the Oncology Editor for *The Journal of the American Medical Association (JAMA)*.

"I have a manuscript on my desk submitted for publication to JAMA by Dr. John Chabot and other colleagues from Columbia University entitled "Pancreatic proteolytic enzyme therapy vs. gemcitabine-based chemotherapy for the treatment of pancreatic cancer."

Pasche explained that the paper had been tentatively approved for publication pending his final review and okay. He summarized the report's findings: For patients with pancreatic cancer, the Gonzalez program had shown no positive benefits in contrast to the GTX chemotherapy which had been shown effective.

The Gonzalez patients had not only failed to arrest their cancers, but had experienced a significantly worse quality of life.

"As I studied the paper carefully, I began to get increasingly concerned," Dr. Pasche said.

For starters, it appeared to Pasche that two experimental treatments were being compared—the Gonzalez program versus the GTX therapy, a still unproven regimen. In an appropriately designed clinical trial, the new treatment under scrutiny must be compared to the gold standard, the best treatment at the time, in this case, the single agent Gemzar.

"I'm also perplexed that you are not listed as an author," Dr. Pasche said.

Pasche said he was aware of the clinical trial and that it was designed to test Nick's program. Nick and Linda were clearly treating the patients in the nutritional arm of the study. But in a note at the end of the article, the authors claimed that Nick had withdrawn from the study and refused to cooperate with the preparation of the manuscript.

"Why would you quit a trial testing your own therapy and not participate in the publication of the data? There had to be some sort of conflict between you and the supervisory team."

After thinking about the situation, Pasche decided to call one of the Columbia team to find out why Nick wasn't listed as a co-author on a paper discussing a multi-year investigation of his program. The individual had insisted that Nick had withdrawn from the trial, refused to participate in the preparation of the manuscript, and had "disappeared" and couldn't be found.

Pasche, even more perplexed by this explanation, made a deliberate decision to call Nick at an inconvenient time, to find out how hard he was to reach. Pasche obtained Nick's office phone number off the internet, and was delighted to pick up Nick's call only five minutes after he had connected with the answering service.

"Contrary to what you've read in the postscript to the article, I never resigned from the trial. I have never seen the manuscript of the article, and had never refused to cooperate with its writing. I didn't know that the article even existed," Nick said.

Nick informed Pasche about the OHRP investigation and how, two months earlier, he had written all the members of the Columbia team, warning them not to leap to the publication of an article about a questionable trial. At Pasche's urging, Nick summarized all the problems with the study, including everything from the consent forms to the entry criteria of the patients, to patient compliance, to finally the conflict of interest linked to the chemotherapy arm of the research.

"I'm unhappy to hear that *JAMA* was never informed about Dr. Engel's letter or the OHRP involvement," Dr. Pasche said. He believed the paper should never have been submitted and believed it would be rejected by *JAMA*. "I will write to Dr. Chabot about my decision and advise him not to seek publication elsewhere."

Nick thanked him, and Pasche promised to email Nick a copy of the article the next morning.

Nick hung up the phone and was so angry he couldn't sleep through the night. At the same time, he was grateful to Dr. Pasche, obviously a man of great integrity, who didn't have to make the effort to track him down, or search for the other side of the story. Pasche was a conventional oncologist and the Columbia team was a group of well-credentialed Ivy League ensconced researchers. Nick was considered a renegade on the outside looking in.

The next morning, Nick found the article in his email in-box, containing all the errors that Pasche had outlined, and more. The article cemented in stone all the issues that Nick had objected to throughout the clinical trial. Again, reading through the manuscript, he was infuriated, but relieved that the manuscript had been rejected.

The publication of this article in *JAMA*, the premier journal in the medical world, would have instantly countered Nick's objections about the trial and killed his reputation. Nick sat before his computer screen envisioning the backlash against him should the article see the light of day. The media would be hounding him. His face would be flashed on screens throughout the U.S. accusing him of fraud. He would be accused of exploiting poor cancer patients.

Tap, tap, tap. Nick immediately set to work, sending the article and a cover letter explaining the inaccuracies to both the director of the OHRP and the ORI. Then Nick spent the next week writing a 14-page single-spaced letter of complaint to the Dean of the Columbia University College of Physicians and Surgeons, alleging misconduct on the part of Dr. Chabot. Nick detailed the Pasche call and countered all the misrepresentations in the article itself. He emphasized that he had not resigned or withdrawn from the study, explaining the precise reasons for his absences from the meetings. Nick bundled up his letter with sheaths of supportive documents and sent it to the Dean, and Dr. Chabot, on December 11, 2006.

The next day Nick's assistant put an urgent call through to him from Dr. Catherine DeAngelis, the Editor-in-Chief of *JAMA*. Dr. DeAngelis' attitude toward Nick was 180 degrees different from Dr. Pasche's. She recounted that she had contacted the Columbia team who had insisted that Nick had been fully informed about the finished article, but Nick had refused to cooperate with its writing.

"So I fail to believe that you knew nothing of the article until you spoke with Dr. Pasche," Dr. DeAngelis said.

Nick tried to remain calm, repeating what had by now become a broken record—that he had no knowledge of the existence of the article until Dr. Pasche's call.

"Did the Columbia doctors inform you about the federal OHRP investigation that is underway?" Nick asked.

"No."

Nick outlined in detail the history of the study and its many problems. He told DeAngelis how he had turned to Congressperson Burton, the OHRP and the ORI in frustration when his concerns went unaddressed.

Finally, Dr. DeAngelis admitted that given the current federal investigations of the clinical trial, the paper should never have been submitted to *JAMA* or anywhere else. Nick told her of his warning letter to Dr. Chabot in June of 2006 and of his formal complaint to the Dean of the Columbia medical school, offering to send her copies of the documents.

By February, Nick had received word from the dean of the Columbia medical school that his letter had been forwarded to the Executive Vice President of Research. He also received a letter from the Director of Research Compliance and Training and the Office of Research Integrity at Columbia that they were awaiting the outcome of the OHRP investigation before they proceeded with Nick's research allegations. Congressperson Burton and Dr. Zerhouni sent similar messages: All were waiting on the results of the OHRP findings.

On February 28, 2007, Nick's office phone rang and he picked up a call from Dr. Patrick McNeilly from OHRP, who had been assigned to Nick's complaint. McNeilly had been in communication with Dr. Chabot who claimed that Nick had assisted with patient selection throughout the study.

"Dr. Chabot said that if any patient failed to meet the entry requirements, then it's your fault. You were involved all along."

Nick explained that when the study began in 1998, Dr. Chabot's office conducted the initial interview of all potential trial candidates. Only after he had tentatively approved the candidates, could Nick and Linda veto the patients. But in July of 2000, the NCI turned around and excluded Nick and Linda from the whole admission process for both the chemotherapy and the nutritional arms of the study. Nick and Linda weren't even allowed to discuss the trial with any potential candidates. When they called on the phone, they had to immediately refer them to Columbia.

In further discussion, Nick discovered that McNeilly had never seen his lengthy Zerhouni document that he had sent to OHRP. Later that afternoon, Nick bound up and mailed the Zerhouni letter and other supporting materials to McNeilly. Then Nick waited for the wheels of bureaucracy to churn ever so slowly.

While he waited, Nick began to implement the principles of investigative journalism that he had learned at the feet of his mentor Byron Dobell.

"If there is a problem on the surface of the situation," Dobell had once said. "Usually the problem beneath the surface is ten times worse. A true journalist will keep digging until the last layer of the last problem has been unearthed."

Nick and Linda researched the clinical trial staff and discovered that Dr. Killen had served as director of the division of AIDS, NIAID (National Institute of Allergy and Infectious Disease) during the time of a tarnished HIV-Nevirapine study which ran from 1997–1999. After that study's completion, he had been transferred to NCCAM and ultimately to Nick and Linda's clinical trial. Other members of the Columbia team had only tangential ties or interests in alternative medicine. One was a psychologist, not an M.D. with an expertise in bio-feedback and no experience in cancer.

Quietly, Nick was approached by two NIH insider scientists. They told Nick that they had followed his work for years and had hoped for a fair evaluation of his methodology. But independently, they each warned Nick that NIH and NCI senior staff had little respect for him and the clinical trial. The senior staff had, in effect, inherited the study from departed senior managers. Furthermore, the insiders revealed that the Office of Cancer Complementary and Alternative Medicine had been set up for political, rather than scientific reasons, to appease congresspersons and senators like Dan Burton and Tom Harkin.

I was told by another person who had supported me at the NIH
that I shouldn't call him at his office, that he was afraid that his
line was tapped, and I should only call him at his home. That's how
insane the politics over this clinical study got. I couldn't believe it. I
just thought this was just something you'd read about or see on TV,
or someone paranoid or crazy would make up. Here I was living
it. Coming out of Robert Good's group, I don't say that to impress
people, but my background was so pure and conventional. It was
so unbelievable to see that the profession I respected and wanted to
join could behave like this.

Nick had no way to verify the insiders' reports, but he started to wrap his head around the idea that the clinical trial was just something that the senior managers hoped would go away. Yet he had no choice but to keep fighting for the legitimacy of the trial and its administration.

In the late spring of 2007, over a year after Nick had first contacted OHRP, Dr. McNeilly called. Dr. Chabot had countered Nick's allegations with three main points. First, that as far as he had known, no trial candidate had been admitted who did not meet the entry criteria. Second, that Nick had participated in the admission process throughout the entire trial. And third, that during the trial, neither Nick nor Linda had expressed any reservations about patients admitted into the nutritional arm.

Nick was taken aback by these rebuttals and explained that he could prove otherwise on all three points. McNeilly then asked Nick to put together documents to prove his points, including emails, letters, and notes in patient charts to provide evidence for his side of the argument. McNeilly also requested detailed documentation for the patients who had been admitted without consent forms.

Nick and Linda plunged in, creating another huge narrated document to answer McNeilly's questions. Nick worked in every spare moment between patients, in the evenings, and on the weekends. Nick reviewed everything—all the records, every bit of correspondence, meeting minutes, and patient charts that they had going back ten years. After three months, Nick and Linda had put together a manuscript—including 12 chapters that directly addressed Dr. Chabot's rebuttals.

By August of 2007, Nick had finished the first draft of the manuscript and was working on the rewrite when he received an irritated, urgent call from

Dr. McNeilly. Nick picked up the phone in the middle of an appointment with a patient sitting opposite him on the other side of the desk.

"Why haven't you sent the documentation like you claimed?" McNeilly demanded. "Your delay in response to my simple request is holding up the whole investigation."

Nick took a deep breath. He told McNeilly that he was finishing a narrative to accompany the documentation and needed a little more time to polish the writing.

"I don't need a narrative," McNeilly said. "I just need the documents. Send them immediately."

Nick explained that the narrative would make sense of the documents. They numbered several hundred pages and included complex information.

But McNeilly couldn't be persuaded. He wanted the documents the next day.

"I didn't know I had a deadline," Nick said. "From our previous conversations, I understood that I had time to gather all the materials necessary. Now I just need to edit and polish my writing."

"I don't need editing and polishing," McNeilly said.

Nick and Linda worked throughout the day—in between patients—to arrange and collate the documents. Then Nick typed non-stop through the weekend to finish his narrative. On Monday, the report was all but complete when his assistant put through another call from McNeilly demanding the documents.

Nick promised them in a couple of days, but McNeilly again insisted that they be delivered to the OHRP immediately. Finally, he confessed that he was leaving OHRP in two weeks and needed to finish the project. "Columbia," he said, "is pressing me to finish to get back to them."

Nick couldn't imagine why Columbia, the object of the investigation, was pressuring the investigator, but with an exhausted sigh, he and Linda bundled up the uncompleted manuscript and the documents and sent it to McNeilly. Once again, they waited for a reply. It would be posted, they were told, on the OHRP website.

42

On March 10, 2008, Nick sat in his office, scrolling through the OHRP website as he had done once a week for months searching for the response to his complaint. Finally, up popped a post addressing the management of the clinical trial at Columbia, dated February 25, 2008 and signed by Paul J. Andreason, Compliance Oversight Coordinator. The conclusions were two-fold, documented in a short one-page report.

First, the OHRP found that subject #113 was enrolled into the study more than eight weeks after undergoing biopsy of his pancreatic tumor, which was inconsistent with the criteria stipulated in the protocol.

Second, the OHRP noted that Columbia Medical Center found that 40 of 62 subjects had not signed a proper informed consent form prior to being treated in the trial.

The OHRP asked to be provided with a corrective action plan by March 21, 2008.

Nick read and re-read the report. After 600 pages of evidence, two monographs, and pages and pages of supporting evidence, his complaint had come to this?

Okay, at least OHRP had agreed that subject #113 had been admitted into the nutritional arm of the study beyond the eight-week cutoff from biopsy, a clear violation of protocol. But where were the two other patients who had been sent to Nick and Linda who had failed the eight-week rule? And where were the other 13 patients they had been sent who didn't qualify for the study? Eleven who couldn't eat properly, three with psychiatric problems, and one lacking social support? And what about the patients who waited for weeks for the determination of their eligibility?

Then, wow. There were ultimately 40 of the 62 patients who had not been properly consented? The consent problem was way worse than he had previously imagined. But the OHRP letter seemed to imply that eventually Columbia had obtained written consent for all of these 40 patients. Yet Nick and Linda knew that there were three patients sent to them without proper consent forms signed and returned. How well they knew that.

Nick pounded his fist on his desk. After all his work in gathering together evidence and documents, after all the months of waiting for an answer, the OHRP still hadn't done an adequate job. And there was something else distressing about the report. Nick was particularly bothered by the line that read, "Columbia University Medical Center (CUMC) found that for 40 of 62 subjects it appeared that informed consent was not documented." Did Columbia itself conduct the investigation? Investigating themselves? How objective could they have been? What were the ramifications of that scenario? And why wasn't Dr. Chabot named in the report? And why wasn't Nick cited as the complainant?

Well, at least Nick had been vindicated to a certain extent. The report admitted that at least one patient had been admitted beyond the eight-week biopsy cut-off, and other patients had been improperly consented. Yet the whole report left Nick upset. He fired off emails and letters to the OHRP, highlighting the errors in the report and requesting full explanations of the problems.

Six days later, on March 19, 2008, Congressperson Burton sent a letter to Secretary Michael O. Leavitt, Department of Health and Human Services. Burton called for an audit of the OHRP's investigation of the clinical trial, a review of Dr. Chabot's eligibility of Federal research funding in light of the report, and an immediate review of all NIH-funded research at Columbia to assure that the studies were being conducted in accordance with Federal guidelines.

On April 4, 2008, Nick received an email back from the OHRP stating that they made their decision based on the documentation that they had in their possession. If Nick wanted to see that documentation, he could file a Freedom of Information Act request, but it was unlikely the request would be filled until the case was closed. So the case was still open? Nick wondered. Open due to Nick's protest?

During the second week of June, 2008, Nick opened his mail and found a lengthy response from Dr. Paul Andreason, the administrator who had sent the original response from OHRP in February 2008. Dr. Andreason's letter, dated

June 3, 2008, sought to address Nick's additional charges and complaints. Nick read down through the letter, held in his frustration, and found some vindication in this second report.

In his first report, Dr. Andreason cited a single patient who had been admitted to the study after the eight-week cut-off point. The second report identified two patients admitted into the nutritional arm who had failed the eight-week rule.

And, Andreason again confirmed that 42 patients had been admitted into the trial improperly, and that the "principal investigator"—John Chabot—acknowledged "non-compliance" with federal requirements in his processing of multiple patients. Chabot's acknowledgement in this second OHRP report contradicted his repeated claims over the years that he had never admitted a single patient into the trial that did not satisfy the entry protocol. Columbia had also devised a retraining program for its staff in the tenets of research methodology. This action was a step beyond what had been described in Andreason's first report as simply "corrective action."

That was the good news. The bad news came as a series of denials in the second report. Nick couldn't believe this litany of rebuttals. Did no one read the documents that he had sent? Did no one care about the truth? For the sake of science and cancer research, you'd think that the investigation would have been more fair. Or, at least more factual.

Andreason denied:

- Nick's claim that a third patient had been improperly enrolled in the study beyond the eight-week cut-off point.
- Nick's insistence that the study had been terminated too soon, with only 62 of the minimum 72 patients enrolled. The report stated that the study had been halted "due to predetermined stopping criteria."
- Nick's allegation that at least eight subjects were admitted into the study who could not eat properly. The reported denied that any of these patients couldn't eat, and stated that their "appetite" and "eating" were adequate.
- Nick's assertion that at least one patient was admitted to the study even though she lived alone, a violation of the protocol. The report stated that she lived with her son, and her son and daughter were involved in her hospice care.

- Nick's contention that patients with significant psychiatric illnesses were included in the study in violation of the protocol.

Nick strongly disagreed with all the denials, but he doubted that Chabot would ever try to publish an article about the clinical trial again. Yet, Nick felt compelled to respond to the denials and set the record straight.

Tap, tap, tap. Nick went to work again and on June 15, 2008, he sent Dr. Andreason a lengthy letter addressing in specific, concrete detail all of his denials, from the missing consent forms to patients admitted beyond the eight-week post-biopsy period, from the entry of inadequate numbers of study subjects to the admission of patients who could not eat properly, from the patient who lacked family or social support to the patients with psychiatric illnesses. Nick reminded Andreason of Chabot's attempt to publish an article with *JAMA*, claiming the study had been run properly and that all patients had been appropriately admitted. In addition, Chabot had claimed that Nick was not listed as a coauthor because he refused to cooperate with the writing of the paper. Nick had no knowledge that the paper was even being written.

> *With all this in mind ... I am somewhat astonished that you apparently hold statements in Dr. Chabot's records sacred without a second thought, and apparently disbelieve mine. I would like an explanation why you selectively take as legitimate the records of Dr. Chabot, and disregard mine?*

Nick went on to profile patients who had been kept waiting for long periods of time before Chabot admitted them into the trial. Often, the patients became desperate and pleaded with Nick to treat them off-protocol. Patients usually go into rapid decline with pancreatic cancer, and treatment with the Gonzalez program needed to begin as soon as possible to be effective. Nick thought that these patients lost precious time in their treatment.

For example, patient #38 contacted Nick's office on March 12, 2001. Nick's staff, as required by the study protocol, directed him to Columbia, even though the patient was unaware of the clinical trial and had called to be seen directly by Nick or Linda. The patient contacted Columbia, but heard nothing, and sent Nick an urgent fax on April 5, 2001, 24 days after his original call.

Dear Dr. Gonzalez:

I am urgently in need of your assistance.

I am a ___ year-old male living in ____ diagnosed with pancreatic adenoductal carcinoma on February 27. I researched the treatment options available and decided that the proteolytic enzyme treatment you offer is the best option for me. I contacted your office and was told I had to apply for the clinical trial at Columbia Presbyterian Medical Center.

I contacted Dr. John Chabot's office on March 23 regarding the trial, providing information on my case. Since then, I've encountered one delay after another in getting approval for the clinical trial—even though I believe I meet all the eligibility requirements...

I was originally told by Michelle that scheduling an appointment would "only take a few days" once I was approved. However, the "paper work" obstacles have dragged on for almost three weeks now, putting me in an agonizing position of having to put my treatment program on hold.

I need to know where I stand regarding the clinical trial. I would prefer to see you directly, and as quickly as possible. I am prepared to come to New York at any time.

Dr. Gonzalez—can you please help me with this?

Nick did call Dr. Chabot's office on Patient #38's behalf, attempting to hurry Chabot along. Finally, on April 16, 2001, exactly five weeks after his first contact with Columbia, Linda met with Patient #38 to begin the program.

Though Patient #38 tried valiantly to follow his program, he eventually died in May, 2002, some 13 months after his first meeting with Dr. Isaacs. We suspect his chance for response had been unfor-

tunately compromised by the inexcusable five-week delay before Dr.
Chabot finally admitted him for treatment.

Nick also addressed the issue of stopping treatment, claiming that there had been a double standard in the clinical trial. When a patient in the chemotherapy arm of the study did not respond to the treatment, the Columbia doctors became more aggressive, adjusting the doses, and/or altering the sequence of the drugs. The doctors didn't give up, stop treatment, suggest another approach, or call in hospice. Yet when a patient in the nutritional arm did not respond or their disease worsened, they were often strongly urged by local physicians to move to chemotherapy. Or told to simply call hospice.

Ironically, the written protocol of the study of the nutritional arm clearly states that when there is a disease progression, the treating physician should:

> *Modify the doses of enzymes and other nutrients according to the*
> *protocol but do not discontinue protocol therapy except at the*
> *patient's request.*

Yet the treating physicians, who usually knew nothing of the Gonzalez program, often ignored the protocol, pushing the patients to change course. Nick wrote:

> *Unfortunately, Dr. Chabot's two sets of standards in this case, one*
> *for Dr. Fine and one for me, not only reflects a serious bias—and*
> *disregard for the written protocol—but also influenced, as his own*
> *statements demonstrate, the treatment course of nutrition patients.*

Finally, Nick argued that Dr. Chabot's conflict of interest should have been addressed. He reiterated that Chabot's involvement in developing the GTX chemotherapy arm of the study, should have disqualified him from his role as Principal Investigator in the trial. Nick was outraged that after 24 months of investigation, the OHRP did not investigate this problem, even after he had provided extensive documentation about the issue.

In conclusion, Nick vented his frustration concerning the whole investigation and posed pointed questions to Dr. Andreason:

Based on what appears to be either disregard or ignorance of the facts in this case expressed in your June, 2008 letter to me, I would like to know for the record whether you yourself ever read any of the documentation I provided your office.

I would like to know for the official record whether you and your OHRP colleagues fulfilled their mandated professional and ethical responsibility by conducting your own thorough investigation of the issues raised in this case. Or did you, as I suspect, rely primarily if not exclusively on the internal review conducted by Columbia staff.

Nick sent off his letter and waited. His answer to these final questions came in the form of a letter sent to Congressperson Burton on August 4, 2008 from Joxel García, M.D., Assistant Secretary for Health.

It is standard procedure for OHRP to ask the institution to conduct an investigation of the potential noncompliance and to report those findings, along with documentation, to OHRP for review. OHRP then makes determinations based on that documentation and other relevant sources.

A month later, on September 4, 2008, Dr. Andreason replied to Nick's June 2008 letter, claiming that the OHRP had done all it could within their jurisdiction:

We acknowledge that in your letter of June 15, 2008, it is clear that you are not satisfied with the outcome of our actions in this case; however, your June 15, 2008 submission does not provide us new substantive information regarding allegations of non-compliance with human research-subjects' protections regulations at 45 CFR 46. Our compliance oversight case with Columbia University School of Medicine regarding the above research will therefore remain closed.

43

"Babies calling Babies," Nick dialed Mary Beth on the phone at the end of the day on September 4, 2008. Both Nick and Mary Beth referred to each other by the nickname "Babies," and he always called her just before he was about to go out the door of his office and depart for home—often as late as 8:00 or 9:00 P.M. When Mary Beth received the call, she started steaming vegetables for their dinner, and as soon as he arrived, they would sit down to eat together.

Immediately, on the other end of the line, Mary Beth could tell that Nick was upset, more upset than usual in these long grueling years of the clinical trial. "What's wrong?"

"It's over," he said.

"The trial?"

"The trial, my research, my practice, my career. Take your pick."

"What happened?"

"Tell you when I get there."

Briefcase in hand, Nick walked up Fifth Avenue toward his apartment building as he did most nights, his shoes clicking the pavement of the sidewalk. Past Saks Fifth Avenue, Tiffany's, and Trump Tower, Nick got angrier and more worried with each step. The trial had already done damage to his reputation. The word was out about the purported results and his numbers of new patients were down. His expenses were up. The cost of his office suite climbed every year as did his malpractice insurance. His apartment, too, wasn't cheap. But most of all, his twenty years of research were over. Tanked.

And scores of cancer patients could potentially be denied a therapy that might save their lives. Science. He believed in the tenets of sound science with each molecule of his being. But was this clinical trial science? Or biased manipulation of the facts? Oh, yes, he knew what he was in for before he even hung out his

321

shingle. He'd seen what Kelley had suffered. He'd churned it over and over again in his mind throughout the years. Kelley was an eccentric dentist in Texas. Nick was an Ivy League-trained physician in New York City. A world of difference.

Nick loved and had the upmost respect for the medical field. He was part of the establishment. He wanted nothing more than to be a researcher at Sloan Kettering right now. Twice, not once but twice, Sloan Kettering had offered him that job that he so desired. But there were strings attached, always the same strings. He could only research conventional treatments, not this nutty Kelley thing that included coffee enemas. Oh, no, no, no, not enemas, heaven forbid! Tell that to Florence Nightingale. Nick had turned down the plush Sloan Kettering jobs to do his Kelley research. How could the medical world be so blocked that they would have no interest in a protocol that is saving lives? How could the medical world, the reputable, distinguished scientists behave this way? How could any human beings, period, behave this way?

With each step up Fifth Avenue, Nick was falling into a darker and darker mood, a mood that only Dr. Hans Moolenburgh had been able to address in the past. Yes, maybe he would try to call Hans tonight … On second thought, maybe he would just fold his practice right now. Call it quits for good. What was the use? Here he was left to fend for himself, to try to do his own research. How did he pay his bills? Not through the support of a grand institution with health insurance and benefits, labs and assistants, but through a private practice, a demanding practice filled with very ill patients who flew in to New York from all over the world. Here he was working day and night, every weekend and most holidays, to try to advance science. He just wanted a chance to prove his theory in a conventional way, through a clinical trial, through the rigors of the medical model. Then he wanted some free time, please God, just a couple of hours a day of free time to write about his program and get the word out to the public.

Mary Beth met him at the door with the "Babies dance," but she knew that as much as he loved the greeting, this time it wasn't working to elevate his mood. Nick slumped down at the kitchen table, and he and Mary Beth ate organic roasted chicken and steamed vegetables. He told her about Dr. Andreason's short response that he had received that afternoon.

"The OHRP has closed their case. There is no more recourse," Nick said.

Mary Beth knew full well the implications of the actions of the OHRP. This was the final appeal. The final bundle of documents supporting his case had been sent long ago. Now Nick could no longer throw himself into writing rebuttals. His work at the computer had been a stress release as well as a necessary defense. Now what?

After their meal was finished, Mary Beth thought a little television would take his mind off of work. She knew not to suggest they watch a movie as she didn't have anything on hand that she had pre-screened. So she clicked on Fox News. They sat together on the sofa and watched, but Nick soon became irritated and yelled at Bill O'Reilly on the T.V. set.

"What in the world are you saying?" he shouted. Nick, a Reagan Republican, thought the party had recently taken a wrong turn. He walked out of the room, leaving Mary Beth to click off the set.

It was too late to call Hans—still in the middle of the night in the Netherlands. So Nick sat in his study and took solace in his Bible, reading favorite passages that tended to calm him. The Psalms were usually his first stop. His Bible open on his lap, he let the words sink down into his body and his soul.

> *I want you to trust in times of trouble, so I can rescue you and you will give glory to me.*

(Psalm 50:15).

At last it was time for bed. Tomorrow was a busy day with patients and he knew he needed his rest. Mary Beth was already in bed, so he sat on the edge of the mattress and pulled out a stack of letters from the bedside table, cards of appreciation and letters of acknowledgement thanking him for what he had done patients and colleagues.

> *Dear Dr. Gonzalez:*
> *Thank you so much for your brilliance and guidance throughout my illness. I'm so thankful to be on the other side of it now...*

> *Dear Nick:*
> *Thank you for your dedication and hard work. You've done brilliant work in cancer research and deserve the Nobel Prize...*

On and on the letters went. Nick read through the whole stack, fingering their pages. He read some of them a second time. He smoothed the sheets and pressed the letters back into their envelopes. He arranged them in a pile, larger envelopes on the bottom, smaller ones on top. Finally breathing more deeply, he slipped under the covers next to his wife, as if he were folding himself into a sealed and secure space, drifting off to sleep.

*   *   *   *   *

A few weeks later, the stock market crashed on September 29, 2008, and an air of panic spread through New York City. Consumers all over the United States worried about their savings, their pensions, their mortgages, their jobs, and how they could make ends meet. People doubled up on housing. Young adults lived in their parents' basements. More homeless appeared on the streets. People everywhere tightened their belts and spent less. Many who had wanted to become Gonzalez patients, held off, due to the out-of-pocket expense. Once again, Nick thought he might just have to close his office.

But Congressman Burton wouldn't let Nick nor the case rest. In October 31, 2008, Burton, dissatisfied with the progress of the government investigations thus far, wrote to the Inspector General Daniel R. Levinson of the Department of Health and Human Services, the official with the power to authorize investigations of institutions and individuals engaged in government sponsored research. Burton summarized the history of the study, then requested the IG open a formal evaluation of the trial's management.

In the meantime, fired up again, Nick arranged a meeting with Dr. Josephine Briggs, the new director of NCCAM in Bethesda, and a date was set for December 12, 2008. Nick hoped to brief her on all the many snafus and in the trial, the OHRP report, and the managerial problems that had derailed the study. Nick also asked to bring along his patient in the Washington, D.C., area who had accompanied him to the meeting with Senator Harkin.

While preparing for the Briggs meeting, Nick received a letter from Dr. Dahlberg, the director of the Office of Research Integrity, a division of the U.S. Department of Health & Human Services to whom he had appealed in 2006. The ORI reported that Nick's concerns about the consent process, the changes in protocol, and the conflict of interest did not fall within the department's legal jurisdiction. Nick shook his head. He couldn't understand what he was reading. Where else was he supposed to go with these concerns?

Tap, tap, tap. Nick began again, drafting a 16-page letter to Dr. Dahlberg. Once more, Nick outlined, then carefully documented all the areas of concern, from the Columbia team's attempt to publish the article about the trial, to Dr. Chabot's false statements in the article that Nick had withdrawn from the study, to Dr. Chabot's inappropriate down-staging of five nutritional patients. Nick bundled up the material and sent them off to Dahlberg, settling down for what he assumed would be another long wait.

On December 12, 2008, Nick, accompanied by his patient, pulled open the heavy glass door to the NCCAM headquarters, located on the sprawling NIH campus in Bethesda.

"I was not aware of all these issues in your clinical trial," Dr. Briggs told Nick, sitting across from him at the table. Dressed in a smart dark suit, her blond hair parted on the side, gold earrings accenting her rounded face, Dr. Briggs was a pleasant, open-minded person who graciously discussed Nick's problems with the study. "No, I'm afraid I haven't been debriefed about your study. But I hope that we can all look forward instead of backwards from now on."

Nick explained out the basic protocol of the study, and Dr. Briggs did agree that clinical studies investigating nutritionally-based treatments for disease required a more flexible design.

"I don't think a simplistic comparison of Drug A to Drug B format would be suitable for evaluating your program."

Briggs then became intrigued by Nick's patient's story. She listened carefully to his tale of recovery from cancer through the Gonzalez program.

After forty minutes, Briggs concluded the session by turning to Nick and saying, "I hope that you will be willing to share your experiences with others at NCCAM and NIH, so that we might all learn from the mistakes made during your eight-year effort."

Several days later Nick wrote to Dr. Briggs thanking her for the meeting and enlarging on some of the points they had discussed. On December 30, 2008 she wrote back, thanking him for coming down to Bethesda:

I very much enjoyed our conversation. It is clear to me that you have a deep commitment to your patients and to exploring innovative methods to help with this terrible disease.

She then said that NCCAM was beginning its strategic planning process, and in the future, she would invite Nick to come and share his thoughts on how they might conduct clinical trials more effectively.

Nick replied that he was most willing to return to NCCAM and share his experiences with her staff.

But he never heard from Dr. Briggs again.

In late January of 2009, Inspector General Levinson wrote to Congressperson Burton. Levinson informed Burton that he had referred the concerns about the clinical trial to their Office of Investigations. Burton's staff told Nick that she thought this a good sign as the Office of Investigations, with limited funding, only pursued a small number of complaints.

Dr. Dahlberg's letter came next on February 2, 2009, responding to Nick's 16-page letter and supporting documents:

> *The Division of Investigative Oversight (DIO) within the Office of Research Integrity (ORI) has received your letter of November 24, 2008. While your letter contains information that could lead to an inquiry into research misconduct, that inquiry and the related fact finding must be conducted by the institution.*

So now we're going around in circles again, Nick thought. I'm to go back to Columbia? Columbia who was supposed to have investigated the trial for the OHRP? Columbia whom Nick hadn't heard from in two years? Even after he had written to them about the aborted attempt to publish the *JAMA* article?

"Babies," he said to Mary Beth that evening. "Babies, Babies, Babies. I've been sent on another wild goose chase."

After dinner and mulling over Dahlberg's letter for a while, he finally decided no, he wasn't going back to try to appeal to Columbia. He would leave the matter in the hands of the Inspector General.

Nick slumped down in front of the television set and yelled at Bill O'Reilly.

44

A sweet voice came on the phone line. "I know all about you. I've been following the progress of your clinical trial. I would like to write a chapter
about your work in a new book that I'm doing."

It was late February, 2009, and Suzanne Somers was calling and interviewing
Nick for a book on alternative cancer treatments for Crown Publishing Group, a
division of Random House. Nick, of course, knew Ms. Somers as a very successful
author, entrepreneur, and T.V. actor with a Las Vegas nightclub act. She had had
her own run-in with mortality when she was treated by surgery for localized breast
cancer followed by a course of radiation. Debilitated by the side effects of these
treatments, she turned down the recommended chemotherapy and launched
her own investigation of alternative cancer therapies. She had never seen Nick
as a patient, but she had consulted with several well-known unconventional
physicians who had guided her through dietary recommendations, supplements
and bioidentical hormones.

Then she became acutely ill, hospitalized with CT scans seeming to confirm
the diagnosis of widespread metastatic cancer with multiple tumors in her lungs.
Her doctors insisted that she begin chemotherapy at once. She resisted. It turned
out that she had been misdiagnosed. She had had Valley Fever (coccidioidomy-
cosis), a severe fungal infection that was cleared up with proper medication.
Somers re-emerged from the black hole of this experience determined to tackle
one of the most difficult of all medical topics for her next book—alternative
cancer treatments. She had run across Nick's work years earlier in a waiting room:

> *I was looking through medical journals and magazines left on my
> anti-aging doctors' office coffee table and came across a very inter-
> esting article written by Dr. Gonzalez about his cancer protocol.*

*I copied and filed it just in case I ever wanted to do a book on
non-drug cancer approaches, thinking he would be an interesting
subject. Little did I know this man was going to change my life
and affect me forever.*

Somers' initial interview with Nick lasted two hours, but over the course of
the next couple of years, they spent hundreds of hours talking together about
his work and program.

*He had passion for his beliefs and there was no one else who had
his courage to go against the big business of cancer. I was taken by
his sincerity, his incredible smarts, commitment and compassion.*

Nick and Linda couldn't believe this turn of events. They had spent their
professional lives developing their research and attempting to get it accepted
into the conventional medical model—only to no avail. Now the phone rings,
and a non-scientist, a celebrity actor, is on the other end of the line, planning
on sending out word to the public about the Gonzalez Protocol. Nick and Linda
crossed their fingers and hoped for the best, awaiting the publication of Ms.
Somers' book, slotted for the fall of 2009.

Throughout the spring and summer, Nick and Linda returned to caring for
their patients, having heard nothing from Dr. Briggs, NCCAM's new director to
whom Nick had appealed. Nor did he hear from the Columbia Dean, or NCI.
Nick assumed that the various institutions had put a stop to any second attempt
at publication about the clinical trial. Then on the afternoon of August 20, 2009,
Nick happened to go into Dr. Isaacs' office where she was sitting in front of her
computer, scrolling through her in-box, checking emails.

Suddenly, her hands went limp at her computer desk. She turned to Nick and
met his eyes. "I can't believe it," she said. "They managed to publish the article!"

There on the computer in the online version of *The Journal of Clinical
Oncology (JCO)*, was an article by Dr. Chabot and his Columbia University col-
leagues. The *JCO* is the official publication of the American Society of Clinical
Oncology, considered by some to be the premier oncology journal in the United
States. There was no mistake. "Proteolytic Enzyme Therapy Compared with
Gemcitabine-based Chemotherapy for the Treatment of Pancreatic Cancer," an

article analyzing the clinical trial of the Gonzalez Protocol, jumped out at Nick and Linda from the screen.

Nick's face flushed red, anger ricocheting through his body. He sat down beside Linda and they went over the article—a slightly different version than the one written by Dr. Chabot and the Columbia team, then rejected by *JAMA*. Nick noted the differences in the two versions. Every change made him even more angry.

For starters, the article detailing a clinical trial of the Gonzalez Protocol deleted Nick's name, only mentioning him in passing once in the entire document in the introduction:

> *The Scottish embryologist John Beard first proposed pancreatic pro-teolytic enzyme treatment in 1906 and soon after published a mono-graph, entitled The Enzyme Therapy of Cancer. In 1981, Nicholas Gonzalez began to evaluate the use of proteolytic enzyme therapy.*

Next, Nick found that Chabot had adjusted significant numbers, made errors and misrepresentations in most of the familiar areas including the consent forms and the number of patients appropriately entered into the trial. A new figure was given for the number of patients who "walked off" with the forms. The number of eligible patients enrolled after the eight-week cut-off rule was changed from the first article, Chabot's figures still not jiving with Nick and Linda's calculations.

No mention was made of Dr. Engel's letter or the fact that so many patients did not comply, or only minimally complied with the protocol. And the "Results" section reported that the longest-living patients had received chemotherapy, one dying at 39.5 months and another who was still alive at 40 months. There was no mention of Nick's nutritional-arm patient who lived 40 months from the time of his diagnosis. And of course, there was no mention of Linda's patient who was turned down for the study but treated off-trial and still alive at the publication of the article.

In addition, Nick and Linda wondered if any of Chabot's patients had undergone radiation and surgery in addition to their chemotherapy. An article published in 2008 in the *Journal of Gastrointestinal Surgery* coauthored by Chabot and Fine detailed the Columbia GTX experience. The authors laid out their goal of shrinking tumors to an extent to allow for "curative" surgery. In Nick's eyes, the article proved that Chabot worked very closely on GTX during the time of the clinical trial, and that involvement created a conflict of interest.

And the abstract of the Chabot and Fine article in the *Journal of Gastrointestinal Surgery* reported that from October 2000 to August 2006, "245 patients with pancreatic adenocarcinoma underwent surgical exploration" at Columbia. Of these patients, 78 had previously completed "neoadjuvant" chemotherapy with GTX" with the hope of shrinking the tumors to allow for surgery. Seventy-five percent of the GTX group had also undergone a course of radiation. The authors concluded that the patients who received chemotherapy and radiation before undergoing surgery survived longer than those who were not considered candidates for surgery. Nick wondered if any of the 23 chemotherapy-arm patients in their clinical trial had been part of this larger Columbia study on GTX, and if any of them, after receiving the chemotherapy, had been treated with radiation and surgery. But Nick had no way of knowing as he wasn't privy to the details of those patients' care.

Nick flew into battle, calling the editorial office of *JCO*. Yet again, he bundled up sheaves of supporting documents and attached them to an outline of the history of the trial. He explained how he had received the grant in the first place, and how he had remained engaged in the study from beginning to the end. He explained the *JAMA* submission and the action that journal had taken. Nick emphasized Chabot's failure to reference the OHRP's findings and his conflict of interest. To support his arguments, Nick sent: 1) copies of his June 30, 2006, letter to Chabot warning him not publish with a federal investigation underway, 2) his December 2006 letter of complaint to Dean Goldman at Columbia, and 3) his June 15, 2008, letter to Dr. Andreason at OHRP in response to their findings.

Scores of emails followed, but the *JCO* refused to honor Nick's request that the Chabot article be struck from their website. To make matters even worse, on September 8, 2009, the NCI posted a four-paragraph discussion of the Chabot article on its "Cancer Bulletin" site. In Nick's eyes, the posting treated the article as if it were reporting on a perfectly managed study, without controversy or problem. *Tap, tap, tap.* Nick fired off an email to the *Cancer Bulletin* editor, only to find that the NCCAM website, too, had provided a direct link to the *JCO* article.

Nick sent another email to NCCAM. He wrote Dr. Briggs, asking that the NCCAM link be removed from their site, or that qualifying information be added. A few days later, the NCI *Cancer Bulletin* editor replied that the newsletter would monitor the *JCO* article for updates, reports, and corrections. The NCCAM replied that they posted a simple citation and link to a peer-reviewed publication. They said they did not include any discussion of the article and would publish any updates that *JCO* might provide.

Nick was not happy. Neither institution—agencies who had been instrumental in funding and carrying out the study—would provide a link to the OHRP investigation. The internet buzz about the article grew louder each day. In an attempt to get their side of the story out to the public, Nick and Linda knuckled down and posted a 9000-word refutation to the Chabot article on their own website. They included scanned versions of all the important supporting documents.

In fairness to Suzanne Somers, Nick informed her of the publication of the *JOC* article and the developing controversy. He offered to withdraw from her book.

"I'm not surprised," Somers said and insisted that the book remain as written with Nick's chapter included. Somers' book had an October 20, 2009 publication date.

In late October of 2009 Somers published *Knockout: Interviews with Doctors Who Are Curing Cancer.* She included interviews of a spectrum of eleven different doctors whose cancer treatment methods ranged from the conventional, to the integrative, to the completely alternative. Within the 337 pages of the book, Dr. Stanislaw Burzynski, Dr. James Forsythe and Dr. Nicholas Gonzalez were the focal characters, with a chapter devoted to each accompanied by patient interviews.

There the reader could read the stories of former Kelley and Gonzalez patients. Arlene Van Straten, the mother of six and gas station owner in Wisconsin that Nick had interviewed years before when he was working with Kelley, made an appearance. Van Straten was diagnosed with stage IV pancreatic cancer when she was just 46 years old. At that time, she was on a steady diet of sandwiches, candy bars, ice cream and soda. She was told that chemotherapy and radiation wouldn't help and was advised to go to the Mayo Clinic. Mayo simply told her to go home and get her things in order and enjoy the time she had left.

> *Now I know I can talk smart, but really, I didn't know what my options were. My doctor told me I was going to starve to death, the shriveled-up shrimp that he was. I looked at him and said,*

> *"You are going to tell me that I weigh two hundred pounds and I am going to starve to death?" He said, "Yep." Well, guess what? It didn't happen… I'm still fat and sassy. And I never went back to the original doctor because he has been dead for a long time now.*

Instead, Ms. Van Straten wandered into the health food store in Appleton, WI and found Dr. Kelley's book *One Answer to Cancer*. She called Kelley's office and they referred her to one of Kelley's trainees practicing in Wisconsin.

> *The next week I was in his office and he looked at me and said, "You're not going to die," I then said, "Well Mayo just told me I was." And he said, "Do what I tell you and you will have good years ahead of you."*

Her blood work was sent into Kelley's office and the Wisconsin trainee went through the whole program with her, including her dietary instructions, all the supplements she was to take, and how to administer the coffee enemas. She had some initial difficulties adjusting to the program, but finally focused and took it seriously, even finding a way to eat the prescribed raw liver called for in her diet.

> *You can do anything you want, especially when you look at your options. Dead was my option. That's pretty motivating.*

At the end of October, 2009, Somers hosted a party for all the doctors in *Knockout* on her secluded estate nestled into the mountains and overlooking the desert near Palm Springs, California. The pink stone walls of the 10-bedroom house reflected the rays of the warm sun, the sky a radiant blue. A tram transported people up the hillside.

Nick and Mary Beth mingled with the other guests around the swimming pool surrounded with lounge chairs and wicker sofas accented with turquoise pillows. Dr. Burzynski, and Nick's old friend Dr. Jonathan Wright, the nutritional physician from Washington State who Nick hadn't seen in years, attended with their spouses. The party gathered on the patio for dinner next to Somers' personal bandstand. They were treated to a superb organic dinner, much of the produce drawn from Somers' own organic garden. Many crystal wine glasses were raised in toasts to the success *of Knockout.* One course after another appeared from the expanse of Somers' French country kitchen, copper pots and pans hanging from the ceiling beams.

Next, the party turned to the small natural amphitheater formed by the mountains where Somers entertained her guests with her nightclub act. She performed with her band accompanying her, and both Nick and Mary Beth sank back into their chairs, the sounds of Somers' voice, the freshness of the mountain air washing over them. It was one of the first nights of respite that they had had in years where, surrounded by like-minded friends, they felt safe from attack, and at ease from the battles of the cancer wars.

Somers sang, looking out on her guests, and realized that the answer to cancer was there in that collection of doctors who were visiting with each other and sharing their knowledge:

> We need to acknowledge that cancer just might have a simpler solution than chemical poisoning. Nick's protocol was the most daring in that he used/uses NO DRUGS. Yet his patients were surviving and emerging not emaciated but glowing with health.
>
> We dined that evening on organic beautifully prepared food, danced to the music of Jack Sheldon, formerly Merv Griffin's bandleader. I sang a couple of songs, but mainly I wanted to give homage to and about each magnificent doctor who was sitting at these tables—to give them the credit they deserved for daring to 'go another way'.

45

Knockout quickly hit the bestseller list. Somers was interviewed on all the media sources throughout the country, telling her own story and explaining the methodologies of the various doctors in her book. She took up the challenge of a book tour, staring into the T.V. camera, her blond hair framing her face and falling onto her shoulders, her large blue eyes open wide. She smiled warmly at her interviewers but was vocal about the failure rates of conventional medicine in treating most cancers (testicular, childhood leukemia, lymphomas and non-Hodgkin's, the main exceptions). She acknowledged that cancer therapy was a big business uninterested in disrupting the status quo. She suggested that "maybe we are barking up the wrong tree, that we should take a look at these little guys outside the mainstream who are getting better results."

Somers, of course, was opposed for her views by physicians and cancer researchers. But her readers were curious to learn more about cancer treatments that didn't involve chemotherapy and radiation. Like Van Straten, many of them had no hope but to search for something beyond conventional treatments. Nick's office began to get more and more calls from "Knockout patients."

Somers took Nick and Dr. Stanislaw Burzynski, M.D., Ph.D., two of the alternative physicians she had profiled in her book, with her to appear on the Larry King show on October 23, 2009. Dr. Otis Brawley, chief medical officer from the American Cancer Society, and Dr. Keith Black, chair of the Department of Neurosurgery and director of the Maxine Dunitz Neurosurgical Institute at Cedars-Sinai Medical Center in Los Angeles, CA, were also on the show to balance the discussion.

Nick was nervous, dreading the interview. He had appeared on many mainstream media shows in the past with mixed results, the interviewers usually latching on to the more esoteric aspects of his program. This time, Nick braced himself for the inevitable question about the publication of the article about his clinical trial.

Somers kicked off the debate by asking the question:

> *We're going to have Dr. Gonzalez on and Dr. Burzynski and other doctors I've interviewed for this book. Both of these doctors have said to me …we all know in the oncology world, absolutely, that chemotherapy does nothing whatsoever for pancreatic cancer … Why are they giving this it if it's not working for these cancers?*

Larry King countered by asking, "Are we saying that no none ever took chemotherapy and got better with that? You can't say that."

"No, no, no," Somers said, explaining that she was just saying that about pancreatic cancer. Then she cited the three kinds of cancer that do respond to chemotherapy.

> *They [the doctors she had interviewed] said that it [chemotherapy] is palliative, meaning it makes the family feel good. It makes the patient feel like something is being done, but it—extends life sometimes by a month, sometimes a little longer—poor quality of life.*

King turned to Nick. "Dr. Gonzalez, do you agree with Suzanne?"

Ironically, Nick then defended chemotherapy, but opened a wider lens on the issue:

> *I think there are cancers, unquestionably, for which chemotherapy works. And Suzanne named several of them. Hodgkin's disease—they can cure 80 percent early stage with chemotherapy; testicular cancer, 80 percent, at least; certain lymphomas. Childhood leukemia can be cured with chemotherapy. But for the mass—for the mass of cancers, the major killers, such as metastatic lung, metastatic breast, metastatic colon, metastatic pancreatic cancer, unfortunately chemotherapy really doesn't—it's not curative. It may prolong life, but it isn't really that beneficial. So, we need to look at new options.*

King pressed the conventional doctors on the use of chemotherapy. Dr. Brawley stated that there are, indeed, a few people who have metastatic disease who actually have long-term survival. He wouldn't say that they were "cured," but those whose quality of life, pain, and other factors are all improved by chemotherapy. But then he admitted that there are people who get chemotherapy who shouldn't:

> *Frequently, those people are getting treated because the patient wants treatment, because they don't want to die, and the doctor wants to give them treatment because the doctor doesn't want to tell them that they are dying. And we need to actually start looking—in the United States—into how we look at hospice and other things.*

Both Dr. Brawley and Dr. Black stated that they believed that diet and emotional support were good complements to cancer treatment, but that a patient should be under the supervision of a conventional doctor, preferably in a major cancer center like Sloan Kettering. But Somers thought that alternative physicians like Dr. Gonzalez and Dr. Burzynski were onto something more that adjunctive therapy.

> *If chemotherapy is the answer, then why do a half million people die of cancer each year? ... The New York Times said that "the war on cancer is a dismal failure."*

Dr. Black said that he found no scientific evidence that Dr. Burzynski's methods worked. And Somers asked:

> *Why is he in Phase II clinical trials then? Why is he starting Phase III? I mean to discount what Dr. Burzynski did, I think, is a great disservice to people listening also.*

The conventional doctors argued that patients with cancer get desperate and turn to alternatives doctors who give them hope, but ultimately just make money off of the unsuspecting. Somers emphasized that the conventional cancer industry was a $200 billion a year industry.

If these gentlemen are right, that means that business is in jeopardy.
And that's what we lay people need to understand.

Nick jumped in and said it's a mistake to believe that all conventional treatments have been proven effective. He gave the example of bone marrow transplant (which he himself as a young doctor administered) for breast cancer.

It is estimated that 40,000 women underwent that procedure. Ten to 30 percent died during the procedure. It cost up to $450,000. Oncologists did make money off of that. Hospitals made an enormous amount of money off of that. And when the NCI finally supported clinical trials after it was in common use around the country by practicing oncologists, they found out it didn't do anything. So, there's an example of a standard therapy that became insurance reimbursed and had no benefit and no evidence.

Somers concluded by asking why these doctors—conventional and alternative—weren't communicating with each other.

It's like Doctors Gonzalez and Burzynski are pariahs here. They are doing something incredible. Dr. Burzynski has found the peptide in the liver that is responsible for cell multiplication. You stop that, you stop the cancer. Why don't they want to know about it?

Black answered that conventional doctors were communicating with others:

We have meetings. We collaborate all the time, and I think again, it's important for our research scientists to be able to replicate one's results.... that's what you're hearing is the scientific process to really get to the answer so that we really have the truth that we can tell our patients.

In the end, Nick was relieved that the *JCO* article didn't come up. Instead, Dr. Burzynski's work took most of the focus of the discussion.

In later interviews, Somers was once again attacked for offering false hope. Critics accused her of simply wanting to hit the bestseller list with a book designed to make money off of cancer patients' desperation. Her opponents dismissed her cancer topic as a mere marketing tool to fuel her already thriving entrepreneurial business of selling and promoting beauty and anti-aging tools and remedies.

A November 8, 2009 article in *The Daily Beast* by Gerald Posner actually pushed this line of reasoning further asking, "Does Suzanne Somers Cause Cancer?" Doctors interviewed for the piece speculated that Somers actually caused her own cancer by taking bioidentical hormones.

"It's pretty scary," said Dr. Rahul Parikh, a California physician who writes *Salon's* popular "Vital Signs" column. "Bioidentical hormones are a multi-billion-dollar business and there's no science to back them up."

Physicians were even more infuriated by Somers' claim in *Knockout* that bioidentical hormone replacement is protective against cancer.

"If Somers were a doctor," Parikh added, "she'd be sued for malpractice."

Posner wrote that some of the physicians included in the book came from "checkered backgrounds." He highlighted the *JCO* article on Nick's clinical study and its conclusion that the chemotherapy patients fared better than those on the Gonzalez program, or the nutritional-arm of the study.

Dr. Timothy Gorski, a gynecologist and president of the Dallas/Fort Worth Council against Health Fraud, told the Houston Press that the patients treated by Burzynski were not much different from somebody "cured" by a televangelist or faith healer. In 2001, Gorski testified for the Senate committee, "Hearing on Swindlers, Hucksters and Snake Oil Salesmen." He specifically cited Nick and relayed comments by a Sloan Kettering Cancer Center doctor who called Nick's program "voodoo magic, silly, not scientific. Worse than not scientific. This is pure ridiculousness."

Dr. Parikh said:

> *"It's a hundred-year-old-phenomenon. She's [Somers] selling hope in a jar, the idea that you can control all your destinies and stay healthy and young. Snake-oil salesmen did it all the time, but this time we have a celebrity hawking it. And there is a risk that it could be potentially dangerous. In the modern media, people like Somers thrive."*

Posner concluded his piece with the speculation that many of Somers' readers will die sooner if they make the wrong treatment choices.

* * * * *

Out of the light of the television cameras and back at his desk in his office, Nick knew that his choices to defend his program within the bureaucracy of the academic and governmental worlds were narrowing. His plea to the Inspector General, sent him in circles, with promises of follow-up letters and a plan of action, but ultimately without results.

Then on March 10, 2010, up popped an email alert on Linda's computer. The *JCO* was about to publish the print version of the article on the clinical trial. Nick wrote yet another letter of protest to no avail. The *JCO* article was finally printed on April 20, 2010. To Nick's surprise, the journal published an accompanying editorial by Dr. Mark Levine of the Department of Oncology, McMaster University in Canada.

Without any apparent awareness of Nick's complaints or the OHRP findings, Dr. Levine questioned the study's finding based on the evidence presented in the article itself. Levine questioned the study's design and the uneven numbers of patients analyzed in each branch of the trial. Next, Levine wondered if baseline differences in the patients could have skewed the results.

> *One wonders whether there were more liver metastases in the enzyme-treated group than in the chemotherapy group, but this information is not provided.*
>
> *Chabot et al. should be congratulated on their persistence and determination to compare pancreatic enzymes versus chemotherapy. Can it be concluded that their study proves that enzyme therapy is markedly inferior? On the basis of the study design, my answer is no. It is not possible to make a silk purse out of a sow's ear.*

Levine's last line gave Nick some consolation, but that was about the only thing about the article that was comforting to Nick. What a terrible, damaging day, he thought. A very damaging day to his career. Suzanne Somers tried to help by contacting a producer she knew at NBC *Dateline*, the premier newsmagazine at the network. Again, Nick was hesitant to deal with the mainstream media, but Somers convinced him that her producer friend would handle the interview responsibly. As a result, Nick spent hours with the producer, explaining his research and program, connecting her to his past patients, and answering her questions.

"This producer really understands," Nick told Mary Beth one night when he arrived home from work. "She's the first journalist who has dug in and tried to wrap her head around my protocol. She asked for information on Beard, Kelley, and Dr. Good. She's reading and learning. This interview should be totally different from the rest."

The cameras rolled into Nick's office, capturing him with patients, stethoscope around his neck. The Dateline interviewer spoke to him in a one-on-one dialogue, then sought out other doctors to comment about Nick, including Dr. Andrew Weil, a well-known celebrity physician who advocated alternative medicine. At one point in the process, the interviewer asked Nick if he wasn't just in this "for the money."

Nick abruptly pushed his chair away from his desk, walked out of his office to his store room, circling back with his tax returns. He dropped the folder on his desk, revealing his previous year's income: $120,000—barely enough to live on in New York after he paid his enormous expenses for the rental of both his office and for malpractice insurance. He often saw patients free of charge or let them pay on installment plans. Linda, who kept the books, fretted that they simply couldn't afford to continue those practices.

Through emails and phone calls, the producer came back and back to Nick, asking for more information until he felt very comfortable with and reassured by her. They had established a good rapport. He looked forward to the broadcast.

On February 20, 2011, the *Dateline* show aired. Nick and Mary Beth sat on the couch together and clicked on their T.V. The show began by profiling Somers and her book.

> *She is a woman on a mission. She champions doctors promoting alternatives. One with special proteins. Another doctor uses pig enzymes, coffee enemas and a hair test.*

Nick's face paled. He knew right away that this show wasn't going to be what he'd hoped. His image was being broadcast to over two million viewers at this very moment who were forming an opinion of him, his program, and alternative cancer treatments in general. And there would be no information about John Beard and the pancreatic enzymes, no mention of Dr. Kelley and how he had cured his own cancer.

Is Suzanne Somers offering real hope or selling something else?

The show picked up the familiar refrain of worthless alternative treatments offering false hope, of kindly but shady doctors providing placebos while they robbed patients of their money. First, the spotlight was on Dr. Burzynski and a child he had cured of a cancerous tumor on his brain stem. "He saved my life," a young woman said who had also seen her brain tumor shrink under Burzynski's care. In the next frame, Dr. Burzynski was dancing with the woman at her wedding. But a voiceover undercut the joy of the moment:

> *Yet for over a decade, the F.D.A. and the Texas Medical Board doggedly but unsuccessfully pursued Dr. Burzynski in an attempt to shut down his practice. In 1995, a federal grand jury indicted him on 75 counts, including marketing an unapproved drug, criminal intent, and mail fraud... Eventually all the charges were dropped except for one, on criminal intent. On that Dr. Burzynski was acquitted.*

Oh, boy, Nick thought, squirming on the couch. He knew what was coming. Next, his face flashed across the screen. Then Ann Cooper's face, explaining that she had been given up for dead, and that she was now nine years out from her original diagnosis of pancreatic cancer.

> *I celebrated my 69th birthday. I celebrated my 50th year wedding anniversary. No doubt in my mind, I've been cured. No doubt.*

The reporter went into the demands of the program, and the number of supplements taken. The coffee enemas were mentioned with a clip of Andrew Weil stating that they had no efficacy, that they were just an old hippie remedy. Then the hair analysis test became the focus, with questions of legitimacy and accuracy, critics comparing the instrument used to a Ouija board. Next, the reporter brought up the publication of the clinical trial article. And again, the hair analysis and the woman who performed the test. *Dateline* had filmed her with a hidden camera. Finally, the reporter mentioned Nick's brush with the New York State Medical Board. The reporter asked:

> *How, if you were doing everything right, did you come so perilously close to losing your license?*

A headshot followed of Dr. Julian Hyman, the oncology physician who had monitored Nick after the New York State Medical Board:

> *I would say there's a place for Dr. Gonzalez' practice of medicine combined with standards today.*

Other oncologists disagreed, with shots of them dismissing Nick's methodology off hand. Then it was a cut to a commercial break, advertising Turbo Tax. And Somers returning to hold off more criticism by the reporter.

But Nick couldn't stand any more of it. He clicked off the T.V., stood up and briskly walked out of the room, leaving Mary Beth sitting alone on the couch.

46

In early December, 2011, Nick's assistant put through a call from a reporter working for a major Midwestern newspaper.

"I would like to interview you," the journalist said, "for an article I'm doing about NCCAM, highlighting you and the problems with your clinical trial."

Oh, no, Nick thought. By this time in his life, he reacted to reporters as if they were "rabid rattlesnakes"—cautiously, quietly, while moving away as quickly as possible. But the more the reporter talked, the more Nick realized she had done her homework. At least she realized the study had been mismanaged.

"Okay, I'll give you an interview to tell my side of the story."

The reporter informed Nick that the FDA had conducted and completed its own evaluation of Chabot's supervision of the trial. And they had found it lacking.

"What? The FDA?" Nick asked. Nick had no idea that the FDA had been involved.

Nick completed the interview, then immediately pulled up the link the reporter had provided. The FDA had done their inspection on September 2, 2009. There was Chabot, John A., MD cited with four deficiency codes, including inadequate informed consent form, failure to follow investigational plan, inadequate and inaccurate records, and failure to list additional investigators on 1572.

Nick didn't know what the "inadequate consent form" meant and why Chabot hadn't been cited for "failure to obtain and/or document subject consent." And, Nick didn't understand what "failure to list additional investigators on 1572" meant. Nick scoured the website but couldn't find any evidence that the FDA had levied any penalty upon Chabot. But overall, Nick finally felt vindicated that a major governmental agency had confirmed at least some of his issues with the study.

And in the long run, despite the *JCO* article, Nick's office had never been busier, and he had never felt more successful with his treatment. *Knockout* patients kept calling. In an email to Suzanne Somers, Nick expressed his thanks for her publication of her book and gave her a couple of examples of patients with good outcomes:

> *Today I saw during a routine follow up office visit a patient diagnosed with advanced pancreatic cancer, who has now been with me as of this past April two years, and he is approaching two and a half years since diagnosis, with a prognosis at the time of diagnosis of maybe six months. He is now in his eighties, does the program perfectly, is doing wonderfully, and continues to run his family business. He has been a perfect patient, great attitude, the entire family is supportive—and comes in with him for every visit with me. He learned about us through Knockout and would have been dead except for your book.*
>
> *Last week a woman patient originally diagnosed with terrible breast cancer came in for her two-year visit, she read the book when it first came out, when she had just been diagnosed and had undergone breast surgery. She refused chemotherapy and radiation, chose my therapy, had a great attitude, took responsibility for her decision, has never once wavered about her choice, complies perfectly and is doing wonderfully—she says her health has never been better. She wants to write you a letter of thanks, which if she does, I will send on to you.*
>
> *So we are starting to see long term survivors who came via Knockout, we call them "Knockout patients," and I will keep you posted on such people. The book saved many from certain demise. And we're still getting patients in from the book—including a new one just today. The book had an enormous impact on many desperate lives, for which you should be very proud.*

At the tail end of the clinical trial debacle, Nick had turned his attention to his own books. During the years of turmoil with the study, Nick had been offered a large advance for a popular book about his program. He worked on the manuscript diligently, pausing only to observe the little glimpses of nature he could catch from his office window—the falling leaves and the memory of the owl outside his office in the tree. Yet when he submitted the manuscript to his editors, they only came back to him asking for a rewrite with a "self-help" approach.

"Cancer treatment is not a do-it-yourself project," Nick protested. "Patients need the guidance of a skilled physician."

Nick's editors suggested that he reshape the book to allow readers to begin his program on their own.

"Impossible," Nick said. "That's malpractice."

When his editors insisted, Nick stood up and abruptly walked out of the room. Later he reimbursed them for the advance, and never returned to that manuscript.

But after the stress of the trial was past, Nick decided that the only recourse he had was to write up case studies of his patients and publish the history of the protocol.

In 2009 Nick and Linda began a publishing company called New Spring Press. The first book they published was *The Trophoblast and the Origins of Cancer*, a volume that Nick and Linda wrote about John Beard, explaining his underlining theory behind the use of pancreatic enzymes in the treatment of cancer. The entire office staff helped with the project, Linda collaborating with Nick on the editing and handling of the orders, the assistants doing much of the proof reading. Even Judith Pryor, Mary Beth's mother, read through the manuscript, helping with style, and organization of ideas and chapters.

The Trophoblast and the Origins of Cancer detailed not only Beard's discoveries but Nick and Linda's own perfection of the pancreatic enzyme formula. With a blurb by Suzanne Somers, and a long acknowledgement page, the book reflected many of the people who had aided Nick over the years. He thanked everyone from Dr. Pierre Guesry to Dr. Hans Moolenburg, from Dr. Jonathan Wright whose columns Nick read in *Prevention Magazine* before he even went to medical school, to Sally Fallon Morell, the nutritionist and chef whose cookbook, *Nourishing Traditions*, he recommended to his patients. Fallon had worked ceaselessly to advocate for healthy fats, healthy soil and organic farming and to promote the work of Weston Price. Nick had spoken at her Wise Traditions conference, giving a 90-minute talk titled "Enzymes and Cancer," in which he had laid out the scientific support for his treatment of cancer and other degenerative diseases.

And in the book, Nick gave a big, loving thank you to Mary Beth, the tribute opening a window into their personal world:

> *…who has lived through years of my hard work with virtually no complaining, enduring my writing late into the night and on weekends and putting vacations aside as I toiled on my various writing projects, the first of which is this book. It isn't always fun, being married to a driven, hardworking physician-scientist who seems to have been placed in the position of taking on the academic medical universe, but she understands completely the seriousness, and ultimate value, of this difficult and consuming task.*

With both Dr. Kelley and Dr. Good now deceased, Nick decided to publish his monograph that he had written years before in medical school, the book that had gained only flat-out rejection letters in the past. Nick and Linda published *One Man Alone*, an updated version of the five-year study of Kelley, in January 2010. Published first as a soft-cover book, it would later be republished in 2016 in hardcover. The book included 50 representative case histories of cancer patients, including relevant medical records. After all those years of struggle to bring Kelley's work to the public, Nick was thrilled to finally hold the heavy book in his hands.

In addition to the writing and publication of his books, Nick resumed his lecture schedule not only in the United States, but in Europe. In 2009, he travelled to London, England, to speak for nearly seven hours at a seminar sponsored by Nutri-Link LTD and held at the Royal Society of Medicine. As always, without even a single note card, he whizzed through the history of the program at galloping speed. Mary Beth, who supervised all his appearances, prepared his PowerPoint, as he was never one to spend a lot of time on computer proficiency. She handled his book sales, and during the break, he asked Mary Beth to get him food.

"Meat," he said. "I need meat."

Nick, of course, knew his own metabolic type (balanced, but leaning toward alkaline) and his own dietary needs. The stress of the lecture, he knew, would push him more alkaline, but the meat would bring him back into balance.

At the conclusion of his London lecture, he received a standing ovation with the audience pressing toward him, curious with questions and admiration.

Soon after, he was invited to lecture to a group of physicians at an oncology clinic in Germany who greeted him with the opposite response. They had little patience for the history of Nick's program, demanding he skip the information on Weston Price, John Beard, Dr. Kelley, and the rest of it. Instead, they wanted Nick to simply tell them what to prescribe. When Nick protested that they must understand the theory behind what he was doing, they started pounding on the table, demanding the "fix."

Yet despite all the other positive publicity and media attention that Nick was now getting, he liked nothing more than to hole up in his office, writing his books. He had hit his stride, combining his two great gifts and interests—journalism and medicine. From his notes and the buckets of documents that he had prepared during the clinical trial battle, he began work on a book about the clinical trial called *What Went Wrong: The Truth Behind the Clinical Trial of the Enzyme Treatment of Cancer.* He set about the task of documenting everything—all the people, events, phone calls and emails that were involved in the ordeal, nailing down names, dates, times, places, and outcomes in the complicated and convoluted tale.

"Oh, just let that trial go," Dr. Sweat had advised him.

But Nick refused. "It's a story that needs to be told," he said. *Tap, tap, tap.* He had the book together in record time, releasing the 583-page tome in 2012. Ann Cooper, Linda's pancreatic patient who had been denied admission but who had been treated off-trial, wrote the foreword to the book.

"Dr. Gonzalez asked me to write about my experience for the foreword. I'm not a writer, so I didn't know if I could do it," Cooper said. But Nick had every confidence that she could.

With the publication of *What Went Wrong?* Nick made the rounds of the alternative medicine talk shows, publicizing his book. He was interviewed on *Conscious Talk Radio* with Brenda Michaels, a former patient, and Rob Spears. In 2013 he also appeared with Kat James, the award-winning nutritional author and radio host. In the interview Nick laid out how he had chosen to go to Cornell Medical School because it was associated with Sloan Kettering, the prominent teaching hospital, and had hoped to stay there the rest of his life, working as a research scientist in a lab. He never thought he would be seeing patients. And then he stumbled upon Kelley's work, and described his reaction to his research:

I'm very data driven. I learned as a journalist that you can't go into a story with pre-conceived notions or you'll never get to the truth. Your prejudices will cloud your vision. So I put all my prejudices about nutrition and coffee enemas aside.

Nick spoke of how he had become better known over the course of the last twenty years. More patients came to him early on in their diagnosis, instead of waiting to see Nick as a last resort. Nick said that he now had a very cordial relationship with some doctors at Sloan Kettering who were following his patients. "Then there are other doctors who would just as soon I was hit by a bus."

*   *   *   *   *

Nick also began work on collecting data for a book of his 100 best cases, documenting their progress, including their initial diagnosis, their medical backgrounds and records. He knew that when it came to cancer research, clinical trials were the gold standard for proving new treatments. They generated more reliable data and were more accepted by the medical establishment than narrative case studies. But all Nick had left were case studies, so *tap, tap tap,* he wrote and documented his patients, and documented and wrote, at first meticulously detailing pancreatic and breast cancer patients, then widening his scope to include everything from adenoid cystic carcinomas, to ovarian, prostate, and uterine.

...no conventional journal would publish anything from me, as you will recall my mentioning, I did a major effort some years ago and didn't get a single response, not even a formal rejection. I knew at the time it would lead to nothing, but did the experiment just so I could say I had done the experiment.

Most alt med journals don't like me either, I don't follow the fads and trends. About eight years ago I did publish a whole series of cancer cases in Alternative Therapies, to his credit Mark Hyman, then editor, approved them all. They were published and nary a ripple followed. No one cared particularly.

That's why I am concentrating on the book(s) of 150 cases, then people can take it or leave it. It will all be there, from beginning to end, cancer to diabetes, and everything in between.

Beginning in 2011, Nick became a frequent guest of Robert Scott Bell's radio show, explaining his program, but also taking on topics such as vaccines and abortion. Listeners asked him to speak about his religious views and he brought his considerable Biblical scholarship to different verses in the sacred text.

"Dr. Nick is here to answer your questions," Bell said. "From health to the Bible."

Through his friendship with Bell, a well-known homeopath and advocate of alternative medicine, Nick began to slowly shift his affiliation from the Republican to the Libertarian party. Ultimately, Nick found that Libertarians were more tolerant of an individual's freedom to choose his or her own health practitioners and treatments.

Nick jumped from radio appearances to television with repeat appearances on Carol Alt's *A Healthy You* show on the Fox News. Alt had been one of Nick's patients and she credited him with saving her life. Linda Isaacs also found herself on Carol Alt's show, marking perhaps the first time a physician had explained coffee enemas on national television.

Nick was filmed by Ty Bollinger for his show *The Truth about Cancer* that profiled doctors like Nick and Dr. Stanislaw Burzynski who were practicing alternative approaches to the disease. Bollinger, a CPA and former competitive body builder, watched his whole family die of cancer, their bodies diminishing while his grew in muscle mass. To address his loss, he dedicated his life to finding better cancer treatments than those that had devastated his family members.

Bollinger was able to launch a detailed and wide-ranging interview with Nick with one question, "Tell us about yourself and how you became a medical doctor involved in cancer." What followed was a concise history of Nick's life story, from his days at Brown University and his writing career, to Dr. Kelley and Steve McQueen, to Dr. Good, to one of his own first patients that he treated with inflammatory breast cancer who survived over 26 years with the condition. Bollinger sat in the "patient's chair" across from Nick in his office, the potted plant in the window providing a backdrop for the video shot. The two bonded over their Christian faith, and later Nick sent Ty a Bullinger Bible.

In 2014, Nick had given a lecture at the Functional Medicine Forum in New York City. With lightning speed, Nick, dressed in his signature brown Brooks Brothers suit with a matching brown and red tie, gave a history of his program and his practice in ten minutes, nearly gasping for breath at the end of his long sentences. In the audience that night sat Dr. Kelly Brogan, a New York psychiatrist. Like Nick, she too had a medical degree from Cornell University. In recent years, she had become more and more interested in holistic treatments for mental conditions.

Later that week, Nick took a call from Brogan who wanted to study with him.

"I will pay you for your time, exactly what your patients do."

Nick took her on and from January 2015 until July of that year, Brogan appeared in Nick's office every Friday afternoon to learn about his program and witness the miracles he was working in his office. They sat down together for one-on-one tutorials, then followed up with daily phone calls and emails. Brogan had already become disillusioned with the medical model approach to psychiatric illness that had become more and more oriented toward pharmaceuticals.

She did her residency at New York University Bellevue hospital and had been trained to view psychiatric illness as a chemical imbalance of the human body that only drugs could address. So she wrote prescription after prescription with few positive results. Instead, she noticed that her highly creative patients (the parasympathetic dominants) would improve by eating more meat. Nick's research explained and provided a theoretical framework for her own observations. Soon, she was at work on a book called *A Mind of Your Own* about women, depression, and holistic ways to heal the whole body.

"Nick was a scholar of everything," Brogan said.

> He was non-collegial, confined to his own isolated research silo, but his mind was one of the most expansive I've ever encountered. He knew everything from soil science to the zodiac. He was a closet spiritualist, like a sage, and knew that true scientists eventually find God and embrace faith.
>
> My seven-month mentorship by Nick was like drinking from a fire hose but every minute was somehow a transcendent experience. I knew, almost instantly, that this man represented the single most powerful force —and inspiration —to lead us out of darkness. His moral compass, his brilliance, his compassion, his unerring intuition, his fire all packaged into someone who could deliver a four-hour lecture without a single note, a man with an

impeccable pedigree, a clinician who fought for his patients, knew them, loved them.

He was a healer, a prodigal intellectual, an activist, and a visionary.

Once, when Kelly herself was in a state of existential angst, Nick wrote her words that would carry her through her struggle for years to come:

We are in "times of trouble" to be followed by the light of peace, the calm of hope realized, the transcendence of truth. Not now, not yet, but soon. We are in the Suntaleia, the Greek term for Consummation of the Ages, a time of confusion, political strife, hatred of truth, governmental oppression and the rise toward one world dictatorship. Then comes the destruction of truth's enemies, the restoration of the earth and recognition for those that gallantly stood firm for the truth and its always righteous application. So do not despair, it isn't necessary to do so, the plan is falling into place, these times are but the birth pangs of the glorious world that will follow.

47

I last saw Dr. Gonzalez in March of 2015. I had flown to New York City, as I had every six months for the last 20 years, for my semi-annual re-evaluation. By this time, I knew the drill. Make certain I wasn't hitting spring break time for colleges and universities., then call for an appointment at least three months in advance. Make my plane reservations with my credit card rewards, reserving my lodging with a cheap hotel I'd used over the years which was within walking distance of Nick's office.

Over this 20 year-time span, 75% of my symptoms had cleared.

"Your neck injury is never going to improve much more," Nick said. A whole array of orthopedic surgeons and neurologists had agreed. So, unlike cancer patients who were cleared up in a relatively short time, I made slower progress, and stayed on the program for maintenance. Although I had a rollercoaster of ups and downs, including an attack of transverse myelitis that had landed me in a wheelchair for months, I had been able to stay employed full-time, productively teaching and writing books.

Nick greeted me that March day as he always did, walking out to the waiting room with my scores in his hands, escorting me back to his office.

There, I was struck by his change in appearance. He had put on weight, his small, tight physique looking puffy. His hair, always dark, curly, and bushy, with only flecks of gray, looked limp and completely faded. It had only been six months since I last saw him, but in that period of time, he no longer looked like a short stop, but more like a distinguished judge sitting behind his oak desk. Oh, he's finally aging, I told myself. Always, in the past, he seemed like he was still 35 years old. I sat opposite him, as we had done forty times in the past twenty years. We went over my scores, but there was a spark missing from our interchange. I traced my finger down one side of the sheet of paper as Nick called out my numbers. We flipped to the other side.

He asked about how I was feeling and how my professional life was evolving. He encouraged me in my writing as he had done in the past. Over the years we had bonded over the protocol. But we had also found common ground in our mutual work as writers, and in our childhood Catholic upbringings. Finally, we had both left the fold of strict medical-model believers to become more open-minded explorers in human health. We also shared a love of nature and he loved to hear stories of the different varieties of vegetables I grew in my garden, and how my dog could fetch my trowel.

My physical exam was quick but thorough. He covered all the usual bases, but spent more time on neurological tests than anything else. Pick pricks and cotton swabs, *This side? Then this side?* were part of my usual testing routine. *Now follow my finger, follow my finger,* my eyes moving this way and that.

Nick ended our session with his usual, "Do you have any questions?"

I thanked him for his good work and expertise.

I paid my bill and headed out the door to treat myself to lunch at my favorite New York organic restaurant. I sat at a table by myself, the noise of the city humming around me, and found myself struggling to come to grips with mortality. We're all aging, I told myself, not just Dr. Gonzalez. I look a lot different than I did 20 years ago, too. At the time, I didn't know that Nick knew that something was wrong.

"I just don't feel up to par," he had told his colleagues.

He was experiencing severe itching of his skin, and tingling from his neck down his arms. He knew he was sensitive to EMFs, or electro-magnetic fields, generated by electronic devices including cell phones. He had the EMF levels checked in both his office and his home. They were high. He tried to eliminate as many fields as he could. He also went for an exam by a cardiologist, but nothing showed up.

Then four months after I had last seen him, on the evening of July 21, 2015, he called Mary Beth to notify her that he had finished at the office for the day.

"Babies calling Babies," Nick said playfully into the phone. "I'm coming home."

Briefcase in hand, Nick walked up his usual route along Fifth Avenue through the New York City summer heat thinking of the patients he had seen that day, their progress, and how the program and enzymes were working for them. Always thinking about enzymes.

Mary Beth got the salmon ready to pop into the oven, then met Nick at the door with the "Babies dance." Nick was as pleased as ever with the greeting. He went into the kitchen and made the salad for their dinner, the two of them sharing the news of their days.

After dinner, they sat on the sofa and tried to watch a movie. Even though Mary Beth had previewed the film, it still didn't have enough action for Nick's taste. So they shut it off and began looking at a book Mary Beth had made for Nick for his 65th birthday. The pages were filled with photographs of his family and pieces of personal writing he had done for the Pryor family newsletters.

Nick looked at pictures of his mother and grandmother, and a flood of memories rushed toward him of Italian food, camping trips and Lake George. He lovingly touched a photograph of his mother—a woman who was still alive—and said, "She was a good Mommy." He stared at photos of his father and grandfather. There was Guillermo at his cello, Guillermo in the Mexican revolution with his hat shading his eyes from the bright sun with Generalísimo Carranza. Pancho Villa and his revolutionaries rode through Nick's consciousness.

There was his grandmother Luz at her harp, the scores of Bach and Beethoven rising from the strings, the strings that were drawn so tight. There was a picture of Nick's father, William, in his army uniform during World War II, home from India. There was even a picture of Nick himself as a young boy in his baseball uniform, the bat cocked behind his shoulder. His ancestors' deeply-set eyes held him in their gaze. His whole family of musicians came together in the scrapbook, a symphony of warm reassurances drifting toward him. He was in Queens. He was in Mexico hearing his cousin play *Rhapsody in Blue*. He was at his wedding reception with Mary Beth listening to Peter Duchin's band play *The Way You Look Tonight*. He was standing in front of St. Matthew's Episcopal Church, the handsome couple smiling and so much in love, surrounded by their two families and a gathering of friends to support them.

The evening was getting late and Mary Beth was feeling tired, so she retired to bed. Nick sat in the den. He wanted to do just a little more work and watch a little T.V. before he joined his wife. She drifted off to sleep, then was awakened by a loud crashing sound. She jumped up and found her husband collapsed on the floor in the bathroom. Immediately, Mary Beth called 911 and began CPR until the first responders arrived and took over the task. They pulled Nick into the living room to create more space around his body and to get more leverage. When their efforts weren't succeeding, they called for an ambulance and sped him to the hospital with Mary Beth at his side.

In the emergency room, a team of ten doctors circled his body and again tried to revive him. The head doctor called Mary Beth into the room then asked the others, "Is there anything else anyone can think to do?"

Mary Beth looked into the doctors' faces and screamed, "You have to keep trying. You don't know who he is!"

Finally, they had to admit it was no use.

"Keep trying," Mary Beth sobbed. "You have to keep trying."

But it was too late. Dr. Nicholas James Gonzalez, the man who fought so hard for an alternative medicine program that saved so many patients' lives, enabling them to live years beyond their prognoses, the man who put his whole heart and soul into the development of his enzyme protocol, was dead at 67 years old.

Mary Beth removed his wedding ring from his finger and slipped it onto hers.

At first, the attending physician thought that Nick had had a heart attack. Mary Beth insisted on an autopsy. The results came back "inconclusive," a heart attack ruled out. More tests were run, the results still inconclusive. Nick Gonzalez' death has remained a mystery to this day.

Epilogue

The funeral for Nicholas James Gonzalez, M.D., was held on July 28, 2015, in St. Matthew's Episcopal Church, Bedford, NY, the same church where he was married. The sun shone brightly on a hot, windless day. Reverend Terry Elsberry, the same minister who had married Nick and Mary Beth, performed the funeral service, the light streaming through the Palladian windows.

The church began to fill with mourners, many of them former patients of Nick's, an hour before the service began. Elsberry opened the service with the words recited at the beginning of every Episcopal funeral, "I am the resurrection and the life. Whosoever believeth in me shall never die." The readings were selected by Judy Pryor and Dr. Hans Moolenburgh. Nick's brothers-in-law and Carol Alt read the selections.

Suzanne Somers, her husband Alan Hamel, and Kelly Brogan all gave eulogies. Nick's niece and goddaughter Jeanne Marie Miller played the violin and sang "Farther On." Finally, Mary Beth gathered herself together, rose and gave her tribute to her husband, ending with "Dear God, let me not die while I am alive."

Elsberry concluded with a eulogy about Nick, questioning the suddenness of his death. "How do we understand this? Why? What do we do? The Answer: We give it to the Lord." And Elsberry closed with "Nick is still sharing the blazing light of his knowledge and his power and his love from that realm to this. God reigns. Nick lives. The healing continues."

Nick's organic, non-toxic casket followed the cross down the aisle, followed by Mary Beth and the three hundred mourners. They walked together to the gravesite, the last plot left in the cemetery, in the corner of the churchyard. Nick was buried in his favorite blue suit with his blue shirt and red tie. In the casket were placed photographs of Mary Beth and of Nick's parents, a letter from Mary Beth and a lock of her hair, an American flag and a baseball. Long stemmed white roses handed out by the funeral director were placed on the casket, more prayers were recited. All gathered sang *God Bless America* to the sounds of the roaring brook in the valley below.

At the reception, patient after patient shook Mary Beth's hand, each with heartbroken condolences, each with a story of healing and survival from a deadly cancer or other hard-to-treat disease. Mary Beth, who had lived a life of relative seclusion with a husband who never socialized, was astounded by this outpouring of support.

* * * * *

To advance Nick's legacy, Mary Beth Gonzalez set up The Nicholas Gonzalez Foundation, a 501 (c) 3, and a website called The Gonzalez Protocol (https://thegonzalezprotocol.com). The Foundation board includes physicians, an award-winning marketer, an educational research professional, successful business executives, and devoted former patients.

Immediately after Nick's death, Dr. Linda Isaacs admitted some of Nick's patients into her practice. A few years later, she moved to Austin, TX, where she sees patients, treating them with the protocol. She has written numerous medical journal articles, set up her website, and has granted interviews and given lectures throughout the United States.

Dr. Kelly Brogan's *A Mind of Your Own: The Truth about Depression and How Women Can Heal their Bodies to Reclaim their Lives* was published by Harper Wave in 2016. It was embraced by the alternative medicine underground and hit *The New York Times* bestseller list.

Mary Beth Gonzalez continued to publish Nick's writing posthumously through New Spring Press (https://www.newspringpress.com). In 2016, she brought out a book of case histories that Nick was working on when he died: *Conquering Cancer: Volume One: 50 Pancreatic and Breast Cancer Patients on the Gonzalez Nutritional Protocol*. In early 2017, Mary Beth brought out the second book, *Conquering Cancer: Volume Two: 62 Patients on the Gonzalez Protocol*. This book was closely followed by the publication of the manuscript that Nick had written for a popular audience called *Nutrition and Autonomic Nervous System: The Scientific Foundation of the Gonzalez Protocol*. In 2019, New Spring Press reissued *The Trophoblast and the Origins of Cancer*. That same year, Mary Beth collected Nick's original presentation of his 25 best cases that he made to the National Cancer Institute in 1993 in a book called *Proof of Concept*.

In the hopes of making the program more accessible to a greater number of patients, Mary Beth is working with a team of physicians to educate doctors in the Gonzalez Protocol.

* * * * *

Soon after his funeral, the Nicholas Gonzalez (physician) Wikipedia page was updated to include his death day: July 21, 2015.

Acknowledgements:

I owe deep gratitude to Mary Beth Pryor Gonzalez who spent hours with me interviewing and retrieving documents, providing perspective and insight into the life of her husband. She supported Nicholas J. Gonzalez, M.D., throughout their marriage, and she has done a heroic job of making certain that his legacy will be preserved into the future. After her husband's death, Mary Beth assumed the editorship of New Spring Press. She has worked tirelessly to assure a readership for her husband's work, the protocol he developed, and its theoretical background.

I am also indebted to Linda Isaacs, M.D., Dr. Gonzalez' colleague, who has continued the challenges of her practice and has shone a new light on the years of research that they did together. Many thanks to Dr. Isaacs for the information she contributed to this book and the encouragement she has given me.

I thank Dr. Nicholas Gonzalez' family who opened their living room to me, sharing stories from their youth and filling in biographical background information about their brother, brother-in-law and uncle.

I thank Dr. Gonzalez and Dr. Isaac's office staff who generously gave of their time to describe the unfolding of their office days. The staff were more than helpful in understanding Dr. Gonzalez' work habits and the intricacies of his busy schedule.

Thanks are also due to Dr. Gonzalez' many colleagues who supported him through his trials and triumphs. They were able to give me a grounding into not only the science behind the protocol but the spirit behind the man who carried this research forward.

I thank Monica Leo for your artistic work and the moral support she gave me during the writing of this book.

And finally, a round of applause here for all the patients who had the bravery and determination to attempt the Gonzalez program. They stood alone, often without the support of colleagues, family or friends, and had the courage to step into a new paradigm, a path that they thought best to address their health challenges. Many outlived their prognoses by years and were alive to describe their journeys to me with joy and thanksgiving for the man who guided their remarkable recoveries.

References:

Chapter 1:

Gonzalez, Mary Beth, interview with the author, May 23, 2018.

Brogan, Kelly, interview by the author, New York, December 4, 2017.

Dubos, R., *Man, Medicine and Environment*, New York: New American Library, Inc., 1969.

Gonzalez, Nicholas J., "A Walk on the Battlefield," *Cancer Wars: Messages from the Front*, unpublished memoir, 2007.

Gonzalez, Nicholas J., "Revisiting the Sympathetic and Parasympathetic," *Nutrition and the Autonomic Nervous System: The Scientific Foundations of the Gonzalez Protocol*, New York: New Spring Press, 2017, pp. 132.

Gonzalez, Nicholas J., "Conclusion," *What Went Wrong: The Truth Behind the Clinical Trial of the Enzyme Treatment of Cancer*, New York: New Spring Press, 2012, pp. 564–570.

Howard, Albert, *An Agricultural Testament*, Oxford, UK: Oxford University Press, 1940.

Price, Weston A., *Nutrition and Physical Degeneration*, Lemon Grove, CA: Price-Pottenger Nutrition Foundation, 8th edition, 2009.

Chapter 2:

Gonzalez, Bill, Letter from Bill Gonzalez to Mary Beth Gonzalez, September 14, 2017.

Katz, Friedrich, *The Life and Times of Pancho Villa*, Stanford, CA: Stanford University Press, 1998.

Chapter 3:

Gonzalez, Nicholas J., "Dr. Beard and the Placenta," *Nutrition and the Autonomic Nervous System: The Scientific Foundations of the Gonzalez Protocol*, New York: New Spring Press, 2017, pp. 9–10.

Gonzalez, Nicholas J., letter to Dr. William Kelley, August 14, 1987.

Moss, Ralph W., "The Life and Times of John Beard, DSc (1858–1924)," *Integrative Cancer Therapies*, Vol. 7, No 4, December 2008, pp. 229–251.

Chapter 4:

Gonzalez, Bill, Letter to Mary Beth Gonzalez, September 14, 2017.
Segretto, Dana, John, and Michelle, interview with the author, New York, December 2, 2017.

Chapter 5:

Price, Weston A., *Nutrition and Physical Degeneration*, Lemon Grove, CA: Price-Pottenger Nutrition Foundation, 1939.

Chapter 6:

Gonzalez, Nicholas J., "Baseball," *Top Pryorities: The Pryor Family Newsletter*, Vol. X, September 2013.
Gonzalez, Nicholas J., "My Father," *Top Pryorities: The Pryor Family Newsletter,* Vol. VIII, April 2013.

Chapter 7:

"Francis Pottenger Sr., An Authority on TB, Dies at 91." *The New York Times*, Sunday, June 11, 1961.
"Pottenger's Cats—Diet Will Affect Future Generations," La Mesa, CA: Price-Pottenger Foundation, https://www.youtube.com/watch?v=OvQ5F6GCfgI.
Pottenger, Francis M., Jr. M.D., *Pottenger's Cats: A Study in Nutrition*, edited by Pottenger, Elaine and Pottenger, Robert T. Jr., Lemon Grove, CA: Price-Pottenger Nutrition Foundation, second edition, 2017.
"The Pottenger Sanatorium for Diseases of the Lungs and Throat, Monrovia, California, U.S.A." *The British Journal of Tuberculosis*, July, 1911, Vol 5., pp. 228–230.

Chapter 8:

Gonzalez, Nicholas J., "Memorization," *Top Pryorities: Pryor Family Newsletter*, Vol. 2012, October 2012.
Segretto, John, Dana, Michelle, interview with the author, New York, December 12, 2017.

Chapter 9:

Gonzalez, Nicholas J., *One Man Alone: An Investigation of Nutrition, Cancer, and William Donald Kelley*, New York: New Spring Press, 2010.

Gonzalez, Nicholas J., *Nutrition and the Autonomic Nervous System: The Scientific Foundations of the Gonzalez Protocol*, New York: New Spring Press, 2017.

Chapter 10:

Gonzalez, Nicholas J., "Revisiting the Sympathetic and Parasympathetic," *Nutrition and the Autonomic Nervous System: The Scientific Foundations of the Gonzalez Protocol*, New York: New Spring Press, 2017, pp. 210–212.

Manchester, Melissa, interview with the author, December 13, 2017.

Oberlink, Mia, interview with the author, December 18, 2017.

Powell, George, interview with the author, August 7, 2020.

Segretto, Dana, John, and Michelle, interview with the author, New York, December 12, 2017.

Chapter 11:

Gonzalez, Nicholas J., "Dr. Kelley's Mother," *Nutrition and the Autonomic Nervous System: The Scientific Foundations of the Gonzalez Protocol*, New York: New Spring Press, 2017, pp. 16–42.

Gonzalez, Nicholas, J., "The 'Kelley Program' as Therapy," *One Man Alone: An Investigation of Nutrition, Cancer, and William Donald Kelley*, New York: New Spring Press, 2010, pp. 7–35.

Chapter 12:

Dienstag, Jules, "Stress Fractures: Are Stories of Notoriously Difficult Interviews for HMS Applicants Fact or Fiction?" *Harvard Medicine*, Autumn, 2018.

Gonzalez, Nicholas J., "Revisiting the Sympathetic and Parasympathetic," *Nutrition and the Autonomic Nervous System: The Scientific Foundations of the Gonzalez Protocol*, New York: New Spring Press, 2017, pp. 210–17.

Gonzalez, Nicholas J., "My Career," *Top Pryorities: Pryor Family Newsletter*, Vol. V, July 2012,

Gonzalez, Nicholas J., "My Father," *Top Pryorities Newsletter*, Vol. VIII. April 2013.

Gonzalez, Nicholas J., "Showdown at Sands Point," *New York Magazine*, July 31, 1972, pp. 36–43.

Chapter 13:

"Doctors Treating Actor Steve McQueen in a Mexican Hospital," UPI, October 9, 1980.

Gonzalez, Nicholas J., *One Man Alone: An Investigation of Nutrition, Cancer, and William Donald Kelley*, New York: New Spring Press, 2010, pp. 38–47.

Gonzalez, Nicholas J., "The Real Story behind Steve McQueen," interview with
    Ty M. Bollinger, *The Truth about Cancer* video, July 17, 2015. https://www.
    youtube.com/watch?time_continue=19&v=GXxNgWJDGko&feature=emb_logo
Seiler, Michael and Warga, Wayne, "Actor Steve McQueen Dies in Juarez Hospital,"
    Los Angeles Times, November 8, 1980.

Chapter 14:

Gonzalez, Nicholas J., "Two Lawsuits," *The Cancer Wars: Messages from the Front,*
    unpublished memoir, 2007, pp. 99–112.
Isaacs, Linda, interview with the author, December 1, 2017.

Chapter 15:

Ackerknecht, Erwin, *A Short History of Medicine,* Baltimore, Maryland: The Johns
    Hopkins University Press, second edition, 1982.
Fernández-Armesto, Felipe, *Near a Thousand Tables: A History of Food*, New York: The
    Free Press, 2002, pp. 21–54.
Pole, Sebastian, Ayurvedic Medicine: *The Principles of Traditional Practice*, London:
    Singing Dragon, 2006.
Tannahill, Reay, *Food in History*, New York: Three Rivers Press, 1988, pp. 224–229,
    363–364.
Schmid, Ronald, *Traditional Foods Are your Best Medicine*, New York: Ballantine
    Books, 1987, pp. 6–33.
Yanchi, Liu; Vian, Kathleen; Eckman, Peter; Gastel, Barbara (editor); Tingyu, Fang
    (translator,) *The Essential Book of Traditional Chinese Medicine,* New York:
    Columbia University Press, 1988.

Chapter 16:

Gonzalez, Nicholas J., "One Man Alone: My Investigation of Dr. William Donald
    Kelley," *The Townsend Newsletter*, Aug./Sept., 2009, pp. 1–12.
Gonzalez, Nicholas J., "Revisiting the Sympathetic and Parasympathetic," *Nutrition
    and the Autonomic Nervous System: The Scientific Foundations of the Gonzalez
    Protocol*, New York: New Spring Press, 2017, pp. 218–223.
"Toward Cancer Control," *Time Magazine*, March 19, 1973.

Chapter 17:

Chowka, Peter Barry, "Nicholas J. Gonzalez, M.D., in Conversation with Peter Barry
    Chowka," *Alternative Therapies in Health and Medicine: The Gonzalez Protocol,*
    Egan, MN: InnoVision Professional Media, 2016, pp. 45–55.

Gonzalez, Nicholas J., "Revisiting the Sympathetic and Parasympathetic," *Nutrition and the Autonomic Nervous System: The Scientific Foundations of the Gonzalez Protocol*, New York: New Spring Press, 2017, pp. 220–221.

Gonzalez, Nicholas J., "A Walk on the Battlefield," *The Cancer Wars: Messages from the Front,* unpublished memoir, 2007, pp. 8–10.

Gonzalez, Nicholas J., "My Father," *Top Pryorities: The Pryor Family Newsletter*. Vol. VIII, April 2013.

Chapter 18:

Gonzalez, Nicholas J., "A Walk on the Battlefield," *The Cancer Wars: Messages from the Front,* unpublished memoir, 2007, pp. 10–23.

Gonzalez, Nicholas J., "One Man Alone: My Investigation of Dr. William Donald Kelley," *The Townsend Newsletter*, Aug./Sept., 2009, pp. 1–12.

Isaacs, Linda, "Part One," The Hearthlight Event, November, 27, 2016. https://www.youtube.com/watch?v=2ByFyofhG9s.

Chapter 19:

Gonzalez, Nicholas J., interview with Ty Bollinger, The Truth about Cancer, A Global Quest 2015. https://www.nde.life/library/health-nutrition-vegetarian/ttac/189-ttac-agq/16894-video-the-truth-about-cancer-interview-with-dr-nicholas-gonzalez

Gonzalez, Nicholas J., phone call to Dr. William Kelley, September 12, 1985.

Gonzalez, Nicholas J., phone call to Dr. William Kelley, September 23, 1985.

Gonzalez, Nicholas J., phone call to Dr. William Kelley, October 30, 1985.

Gonzalez, Nicholas J., "Postscript to the Kelley Study," *The Cancer Wars: Messages from the Front,* unpublished memoir, 2007.

Isaacs, Linda, "In Memorium: Nicholas J. Gonzalez, M.D.," *Townsend Newsletter*, January, 2016. pp. 14–19.

Isaacs, Linda, email to the author, Sept. 20, 2018.

Chapter 20:

Fisher, David W., letter to Nicholas Gonzalez, June 12, 1986.

Friedman, Fredrica S., letter to Julian Bach, Feb. 10, 1987.

Gonzalez, Nicholas J., "Postscript to the Kelley Study," *The Cancer Wars: Messages from the Front,* unpublished memoir, 2007.

Gonzalez, Nicholas J., "Dr. Kelley and Ethylene Dichloride—One Era Ends, Another Begins," *Nutrition and the Autonomic Nervous System: The Scientific Foundations of the Gonzalez Protocol*, New York: New Spring Press, 2017, p 85.

Isaacs, Linda, "In Memorium: Nicholas J. Gonzalez, M.D.," *Townsend Newsletter*, Jan., 2016, pp. 14–19.
Kelley, Kimberly S., letter to Nicholas Gonzalez, May 23, 2011.
Nemethy, Sonia, interview with the author, March 5, 2018.

Chapter 21:

Gonzalez, Nicholas J., "More Making of an Enzyme," *Nutrition and the Autonomic Nervous System: The Scientific Foundations of the Gonzalez Protocol*, New York: New Spring Press, 2017, pp. 74–83.
"The Willner Chemists Story," https://www.willner.com/content/About1103.pdf.

Chapter 22:

Anonymous, interview with the author, July 13, 2020.
Mackintosh, Enoch Sherwin, interview with the author, June 14, 2018.
Gonzalez, Nicholas J., "Fats and the Pancreas—a Closer Look," *Nutrition and the Autonomic Nervous System: The Scientific Foundations of the Gonzalez Protocol*, New York: New Spring Press, 2017, pp. 99–101.
Isaacs, Linda, interview with the author, December 1, 2017.
Isaacs, Linda, "Why I Offer this Treatment Protocol" September 19, 2017. https://www.youtube.com/watch?v=_mJyiAVkUA8
Johnson, Lisa, interview with the author, September 24, 2018.
Savino, Raphaela interview with the author, December 18, 2017.

Chapter 23:

Gonzalez, Nicholas J., "A Planned Attack," *The Cancer Wars: Messages from the Front*," unpublished memoir, 2007, pp. 63–64.
Gonzalez, Mary Beth, interview with the author, August 7, 2017.
Good, Robert, letter to John H. Renner, Consumer Health Information Research Institute, August 20, 1991. https://www.cancertreatmentwatch.org/reports/gonzalez/good.pdf
Good, Robert, notarized statement about Dr. Gonzalez, March 14, 1988, https://www.cancertreatmentwatch.org/reports/gonzalez/good.pdf.
Good, Robert, letter to Saul Green, Ph.D., January 29, 1991. https://www.cancertreatmentwatch.org/reports/gonzalez/good/green.pdfs
Isaacs, Linda, "In Memoriam," *The Townsend Newsletter*, January, 2016, pp. 14–19.
Johnson, Lisa, interview with the author, September 24, 2018.
Specter, Michael, "The Outlaw Doctor," *The New Yorker*, February 5, 2001, p. 61.

Chapter 24:

"Ernest Wynder, Pioneer in Preventative Medicine," *Cancer Network: Home of the Journal Oncology*, Vol. 8, Issue 8, August 1, 1999.
Gonzalez, Nicholas, *The Cancer Wars: Messages from the Front*, unpublished memoir, 2007 pp. 35–45.
Kluger, Richard, *Ashes to Ashes: America's Hundred-Year Cigarette War, The Public Health, and the Unabashed Triumph of Philip Morris*, New York: Alfred A. Knopf, 1997, p. 236.
Wynder EL, Graham E (1950). Tobacco smoking as a possible etiologic factor in bronchiogenic carcinoma: a study of 684 proven cases. JAMA. **143** (4): 329–36. doi:10.1001/jama.1950.02910390001001. PMC 2623809. PMID 15415260.

Chapter 25:

Moolenburgh, Hans, letter to the author, November 23, 2017.

Chapter 26:

Gonzalez, Nicholas, "Chocolate, and other Swiss Gifts," *The Cancer Wars: Messages from the Front*, unpublished memoir, 2007, pp. 49–59.
McNair, Mary, interview with the author, January 16, 2018.
McNair, Mary, "Remarks," Proof of Concept: 25 Best Cancer Cases Presented to the National Cancer Institute, New York: New Spring Press, 2019, p. xxix.

Chapter 27:

Gonzalez, Nicholas, "A Planned Attack," *The Cancer Wars: Messages from the Front*, unpublished memoir, 2007, pp. 60–71.
Sorvillo, Andrea, interview with the author, August 11, 2018.

Chapter 28:

Chowka, Peter Barry, interview with the author, September 7, 2017.
Chowka, Barry, "One Man Alone," *Alternative Medicine*, April, 2002.
Gonzalez, Nicholas, "A Very Strange Year," *The Cancer Wars: Messages from the Front*, unpublished memoir, 2007, pp. 70–78.
Isaacs, Linda, "In Memorium: Nicholas J. Gonzalez, M.D.," *The Townsend Newsletter*, January, 2016, pp. 14–19.

"Matter of Gonzalez v. the New York State Dep't of Health," A.D. 2d, 232 A.D. 2d
    886 (1996). https://www.leagle.com/decision/19961118232ad2d8861237.
Moolenburgh, Hans, interview with the author, November 23, 2017.

Chapter 29:

Gonzalez, Nicholas J., "Two Lawsuits," *The Cancer Wars: Messages from the Front,*
    unpublished memoir, 2007, pp. 99–112.
Charell v. Gonzalez (June 10, 1997), 173 Misc. 2dm227 (1997) sc2d2271372,
    Leagle.com. https://www.leagle.com/decision/1997400173misc2d2271372.
Charell v. Gonzalez (June 9, 1998) New York Personal Injury Lawyers, National
    Association of Personal Injury Lawyers. http://wwwNAPIL.com.
Gonzalez v. Ellenberg, Justia, (2004), New York Other Court Decisions, New York
    Case Law, pp. 1–20.

Chapter 30:

Gonzalez, Nicholas J., interview with Carol Alt on *A Healthy You* & Carol Alt, *Fox
    News,* September 21, 2013.
Landsman, Jonathan, interview with Nicholas Gonzalez, M.D., "The Truth about
    Chemotherapy," *Natural Health 365,* reposted July 26, 2015.

Chapter 31:

Gonzalez v. Gray, 69 F. Supp.2d 561 (1999) pp2d561 1580, Leagle.com, https://
    www.leagle.com/decision/199963069fsupp2d5611580
Gonzalez, Nicholas J., "Two Lawsuits," *The Cancer Wars: Messages from the Front,*
    unpublished memoir, 2007, pp. 99–112.
Moolenburgh, Hans, interview with the author, November 23, 2017.
"N.Y Doctor Found Negligent in Unusual Cancer Treatment Case," *The Los Angeles
    Times,* April 21, 2000.

Chapter 32:

Gonzalez, Mary Beth Pryor, interview with the author, April 15, 2018.
Gonzalez, Nicholas J., "A Beginning and an End," *The Cancer Wars: Messages from the
    Front,* unpublished memoir, 2007, pp. 89–94.
Gonzalez NJ, Isaacs LL: Evaluation of pancreatic proteolytic enzyme treatment of
    adenocarcinoma of the pancreas, with nutrition and detoxification support.
    Nutr Cancer 33 (2): 117–24, 1999.

Gonzalez, Nicholas J., "The Truth Conquers All, Sometimes," *The Cancer Wars: Messages from the Front,* 2007, unpublished memoir, pp. 79–88.

Isaacs, Linda, interview with the author, December 1, 2017.

Lampe, Frank and Snyder, Suzanne, "Nicholas J. Gonzalez, MD: Seeking the Truth in the Fight Against Cancer," *Alternative Therapies,* Jan./Feb., 2007, Vol. 13, No. 1., pp.66–73.

Moolenburgh, Hans, interview with the author, November 23, 2017.

Chapter 33:

Chabot, John, "Proceedings from the White House Commission on Complementary and Alternative Medicine Policy," May 16, 2001, p. 1.

Chowka, Barry, "One Man Alone," *Alternative Medicine,* April, 2002.

Gonzalez, Nicholas J., "Historical Background," *What Went Wrong? The Truth behind the Clinical Trial of the Enzyme Treatment of Cancer,* New York: New Spring Press, 2012, pp. 3–16.

Gonzalez, Nicholas J., "Summary of Major Problems Affecting the NCI-NCCAM Study," *What Went Wrong? The Truth behind the Clinical Trial of the Enzyme Treatment of Cancer,* New York: New Spring Press, 2012, pp. 17–47.

Gonzalez, Mary Beth, interview with the author, April 15, 2018.

Okie, Susan, "Maverick Treatments Find U.S. Funding," *The Washington Post,* January18, 2000.

Specter, Michael, "The Outlaw Doctor," *The New Yorker,* February 5, 2001, p. 48–61.

Chapter 34:

Gonzalez, Mary Beth, interview with the author, March 26, 2018.

Gonzalez, Mary Beth, "How We Met," email to the author, March 22, 2018.

Gonzalez, Mary Beth, "Engagement Story," email to the author, March 22, 2018.

Pryor, Judith, interview with the author, May 25, 2018.

Chapter 35:

Cooper, Sarah Ann, interview with the author. December 12, 2017.

Chapter 36:

Gonzalez, Mary Beth, interview with the author, May 23, 2018.

Sweat, Roy, interview with the author, February 14, 2018.

Chapter 37:

Gonzalez, Nicholas J., interview with Dr. Joseph Mercola, April 23, 2011. https://mercola.fileburst.com/PDF/ExpertInterviewTranscripts/Interview-Gonzalez-on-Alternative-Cancer-Treatments.pdf.

Gonzalez, Nicholas, "Failure in Handling Informed Consent," *What Went Wrong? The Truth behind the Clinical Trial of the Enzyme Treatment of Cancer,* New York: New Spring Press, 2012, pp. 49–58.

Wunderlich, Chelsea O'Connor, interview with the author, January 8, 2018.

Yoffie, David, interview with the author, February 14, 2018.

Anonymous, interview with the author, March 2, 2018.

Gonzalez, Nicholas, "A Case of Insulin-Dependent Diabetes," *Alternative Therapies in Health & Medicine: The Gonzalez Protocol*, Jul/Aug., 2016, Vol. 22, Issue 4, pp. 24–35.

Chapter 38:

Gonzalez, Mary Beth, interview with the author, April 15, 2018.

Gonzalez, Mary Beth, interview with the author, May 23, 2018.

Gonzalez, Nicholas, *Nutrition and the Autonomic Nervous System: The Scientific Foundations of the Gonzalez Protocol,* New York: New Spring Press, New York, 2017, pp. 120–121.

Pryor, Judy, interview with the author, May 25, 2018.

Chapter 39:

Gonzalez, Nicholas J., "The December 13, 2004 Group Meeting," *What Went Wrong? The Truth behind the Clinical Trial of the Enzyme Treatment of Cancer,* New York: New Spring Press, 2012, pp. 59–84.

Gonzalez, Nicholas J., "The Problems Worsen," *What Went Wrong? The Truth behind the Clinical Trial of the Enzyme Treatment of Cancer,* New York: New Spring Press, 2012, pp. 85–102.

Chapter 40:

Gonzalez, Nicholas J., "Dr. Chabot's April 22, 2006 Letter," *What Went Wrong? The Truth behind the Clinical Trial of the Enzyme Treatment of Cancer,* New York: New Spring Press, 2012, pp.185–196.

Gonzalez, Nicholas J., "Dr. Zerhouni's Answer," *What Went Wrong? The Truth behind the Clinical Trial of the Enzyme Treatment of Cancer,* New York: New Spring Press, 2012, pp. 111–117.

Gonzalez, Nicholas J., "The Battle Continues," *What Went Wrong? The Truth behind the Clinical Trial of the Enzyme Treatment of Cancer,* New York: New Spring Press, 2012, pp. 197–201.

Gonzalez, Nicholas J., "The Battle Heats Up," *What Went Wrong? The Truth behind the Clinical Trial of the Enzyme Treatment of Cancer,* New Spring Press, 2012, pp. 179–184.

Gonzalez, Nicholas J., "The Battle Moves to Washington," *What Went Wrong? The Truth behind the Clinical Trial of the Enzyme Treatment of Cancer,* New York: New Spring Press, 2012, pp. 102–110.

Gonzalez, Nicholas J., "The Feds Step In," *What Went Wrong? The Truth behind the Clinical Trial of the Enzyme Treatment of Cancer,* New York: New Spring Press, 2012, pp. 203–206.

Chapter 41:

Gonzalez, Nicholas J., "A Closer Look at the NCI and NCCAM Supervisors," *What Went Wrong? The Truth behind the Clinical Trial of the Enzyme Treatment of Cancer,* New York: New Spring Press, 2012, pp. 251–264.

Gonzalez, Nicholas J., interview with Dr. Joseph Mercola, April 23, 2011. https://mercola.fileburst.com/PDF/ExpertInterviewTranscripts/Interview-Gonzalez-on-Alternative-Cancer-Treatments.pdf.

Gonzalez, Nicholas J., "My Growing Concerns about OHRP," *What Went Wrong? The Truth behind the Clinical Trial of the Enzyme Treatment of Cancer,* New York: New Spring Press, 2012, pp. 427–429.

Gonzalez, Nicholas J., "My Report to Dr. McNeilly," *What Went Wrong? The Truth behind the Clinical Trial of the Enzyme Treatment of Cancer,* New York: New Spring Press, 2012, pp. 279–281.

Gonzalez, Nicholas J., "The Attempted Publication by Chabot et al," *What Went Wrong? The Truth behind the Clinical Trial of the Enzyme Treatment of Cancer,* New York: New Spring Press, 2012, pp. 207–211.

Gonzalez, Nicholas J., "The OHRP Investigation Continues," *What Went Wrong? The Truth behind the Clinical Trial of the Enzyme Treatment of Cancer,* New York: New Spring Press, 2012, pp. 239–241.

L'Heritier, Nancy, interview with the author, February 1, 2018.

Chapter 42:

Gonzalez, Nicholas J., "My June 15, 2008 Letter to Dr. Andreason," *What Went Wrong? The Truth behind the Clinical Trial of the Enzyme Treatment of Cancer,* New York: New Spring Press, 2012, pp. 463–494.

Gonzalez, Nicholas, J., "Some Vindication, but the Battle Goes On," *What Went Wrong? The Truth behind the Clinical Trial of the Enzyme Treatment of Cancer,* New York: New Spring Press, 2012, pp. 457–494.

Chapter 43:

Gonzalez, Mary Beth, interview with the author, March 26, 2018.
Gonzalez, Nicholas J., "More Letters and More Meetings," *What Went Wrong? The Truth behind the Clinical Trial of the Enzyme Treatment of Cancer,* New York: New Spring Press, 2012, pp. 507–514.

Chapter 44:

Chabot JA, Tsai WY, Fine RL, et al. Pancreatic proteolytic enzyme therapy compared with gemcitabine-based chemotherapy for the treatment of pancreatic cancer. *J Clin Oncol.* 2010;28(12):2058–2063.
Gonzalez, Nicholas J., "Hollywood Comes to the Rescue," *What Went Wrong? The Truth behind the Clinical Trial of the Enzyme Treatment of Cancer,* New York: New Spring Press, 2012, pp. 515–520.
Gonzalez, Nicholas J., "The Journal of Clinical Oncology Article," *What Went Wrong? The Truth behind the Clinical Trial of the Enzyme Treatment of Cancer,* New York: New Spring Press, 2012, pp. 521–537.
Gonzalez, Mary Beth, email to the author, March 31, 2020.
Somers, Suzanne, *Knockout: Interviews with Doctors Who Are Curing Cancer and How to Prevent Getting It in the First Place,* Harmony Books, Crown Publishing Company, 2009.
Somers, Suzanne, interview with author, April 30, 2018.

Chapter 45:

Dateline NBC, Feb. 20, 2011, 7:00–8:00 pm PST. https://archive.org/details/ KNTV_20110221_030000_Dateline_NBC
Gonzalez, Nicholas J., "The Journal of Clinical Oncology Article," *What Went Wrong? The Truth behind the Clinical Trial of the Enzyme Treatment of Cancer,* New York: New Spring Press, 2012, pp. 537–542.
Somers, Suzanne, interview with Larry King, *Larry King Live,* CNN, October 23, 2009.
"Suzanne Somers Throws Knockout to Cancer," Interview with Kathleen Walter, Newsmax T.V. February 12, 2010.

Chapter 46:

Bell, Robert Scott, interview with the author, December 13, 2017.
Brogan, Kelly, interview with the author, December 4, 2017.
Brogan, Kelley, *Eulogy of Dr. Nicholas Gonzalez*, https://kellybroganmd.com/eulogy-dr-nicholas-gonzalez/
Gonzalez, Mary Beth, interview with the author, June 26, 2018.
Gonzalez, Nicholas J., interview with Brenda Michaels and Rob Spears on *Conscious Radio,* October 20, 2010.
Gonzalez, Nicholas J., interview with Kat James on the Kat James Show, September 21, 2013.
Sweat, Roy, interview with the author, February 14, 2018.

Chapter 47:

Gonzalez, Mary Beth, interview with the author, December 18, 2018.

Epilogue:

Pryor, Judith, "Memories of Nick's Funeral Service, St. Matthew's, Bedford, NY, July 28, 2015," August 1, 2015.

Books by Nicholas J. Gonzalez, M.D.

Available on Amazon

The Trophoblast and the Origins of Cancer, 2nd Edition

One Man Alone: An Investigation of Nutrition,
Cancer and Dr. William Donald Kelley

The Enzyme Treatment of Cancer and Its Scientific Basis
by Dr. John Beard, foreword by Dr. Nicholas Gonzalez

What Went Wrong: The Truth Behind the Clinical Trial
of the Enzyme Treatment of Cancer. *Independent Book
Publishers Association 2013 Silver Award Winner*

Conquering Cancer: Volume One—50 Pancreatic and Breast
Cancer Patients on The Gonzalez Nutritional Protocol

Conquering Cancer: Volume Two—62 Patients on The Gonzalez Protocol

Nutrition and The Autonomic Nervous System:
The Scientific Foundations of The Gonzalez Protocol.
2018 Book Excellence Award Winner for Diet and Nutrition

Proof of Concept: 25 Best Case Reports
Presented to the National Cancer Institute

New Spring Press

New Spring Press proudly publishes books and videos in the fields of health and nutrition and their impact on disease.

We are the exclusive publishers of the scientific work of Nicholas J. Gonzalez MD and Dr. John Beard, the British scientist who pioneered the therapeutic uses of pancreatic enzymes.

In addition to offering Dr. Gonzalez's award-winning books, we offer his lecture recordings. New Spring Press accepts direct orders via email at custsvc@ newspringpress.com and will ship anywhere in the world.

To learn more, visit www.newspringpress.com.

NEW
SPRING
PRESS

newspringpress.com

The Nicholas Gonzalez Foundation

Founded in 2015, The Nicholas Gonzalez Foundation is keeping the brilliant, healing work of Nicholas J. Gonzalez, M.D. alive today and for generations to come. The foundation fuels the future of Dr. Gonzalez's legacy by preserving, promoting and propagating his holistic individualized nutrition protocols in the education about the treatment and prevention of cancer and other degenerative diseases as well as general wellness.

This non-profit, 501 (c) 3 foundation strives to inspire, guide and educate professional healers and patients on their path to discovering and adopting effective nutritional protocols for prevention and disease treatment.

There is a treasure trove of free information and videos about Dr. Gonzalez and The Gonzalez Protocol® at http://www.thegonzalezprotocol.com/

The Author: Mary Swander

Mary Swander is the co-founder and executive director of AgArts, a non-profit designed to imagine and promote healthy food systems through the arts. She is also the artistic director of Swander Woman Productions, a theatre company that tours plays about agriculture and the wider rural environment. Swander is an award-winning author of poetry, non-fiction and drama, and is best known for her books *Driving the Body Back*, *Out of this World*, and *The Desert Pilgrim*. She has published widely in such places as *The Nation*, *The New York Times Magazine*, *The New Republic, and Poetry Magazine*.

Swander lives in an old Amish one-room schoolhouse, and raises sheep, goats, and a large organic garden. www.maryswander.com, www.agarts.org.

Index

Functional Medicine Forum, 351
fungi, 60
Funkenstein, Daniel, 74–76

G

Galen of Peragmon, 108–110
García, Joxel, 319
garpike (*Lepisosteus osseus*), 17, 45
gemcitabine, 241, 247, 261, 305, 328, 376
Gemzar (see gemcitabine)
Georgia Tech, 138
germ cells, 15, 16, 18, 19
Gerson Clinic, 230
Gerson, Max, 57
Goddard College, 62
Gonzalez, Bill, 12, 13, 79, 80, 365
Gonzalez Protocol, 97, 98, 162, 169, 172,
    224, 233, 235, 244, 247, 249, 259,
    262, 263, 265, 276–299, 301, 316,
    318, 325, 327–329, 356, 358, 360,
    361, 363, 365–370, 374, 379, 383
Gonzalez-Isaacs clinical trial, 247, 263, 301,
    317, 328, 360, 363, 368–372
González, Francisco Ignacio Madero, 9, 10
González, Gustavo, 10, 11, 22
González, José, 9, 22, 239
Gonzalez, Mary Beth (Pryor), 251–254, 265,
    269, 285, 286, 305, 323, 343, 347,
    356–359, 361, 363, 365, 370, 372–
    374, 376, 377
Gonzalez, Sr., William, 23–26, 35, 36, 45,
    56, 63, 80, 123, 124, 239
Good, Robert, 114, 115, 118, 127, 132, 180,
    239, 305, 310, 351, 370
Gori, Gio, 238
Gorski, Timothy, 339
Grant, William, 210

Gray, Jack, 229, 233
Green Revolution, 5
Guesry, Pierre, 189–191, 199–201, 206–208,
    219, 232, 233, 239, 248, 249, 291,
    347

H

Hahnemann Medical College, 278
Hamel, Alan, 359
Harkin, Senator Tom, 208, 297, 298, 309,
    324
Harvard University Medical School, 74–76,
    114, 181, 230–232, 248, 297, 367
Health Revelations, 161
Hemingway, Ernest, 62, 73, 75, 76, 78, 113,
    137
herbal remedies, 97, 102, 106, 108, 155, 190
Herbert, Victor, 247, 248
herbicides, 5, 62, 97
Hippocrates, 107, 108
Hodgkin's Disease, 226, 229–231, 335, 336
holistic view (of health), 7, 8, 158, 352, 383
Holocaust, 57
hope, 55, 56, 87, 147, 163, 186, 230, 246,
    278, 335, 337, 338, 339, 342, 353,
    361
hospice, 209, 315, 318, 337
Howard, Sir Albert, 5, 365
Howell, Edward, 67
Huerta, Victoriano, 11
humors (four), 107, 108
Huxley, Thomas Henry, 16
Hyman, Julian, 210, 211, 232, 235, 291, 343
Hyman, Steve, 211
hypericum perforatum (St. John's Wort), 156
hypothyroid, 278, 279

I

immunology, 114, 137, 170
Indian (system of medicine), 104, 105, 106, 108, 110,
iodine, 65, 153
Isaacs, Linda, 95, 99, 133, 134, 137–139, 207, 246, 247, 263, 317, 328, 351, 360, 363, 368–372
Italian heritage, 3, 23–25, 33, 76, 357

J

James, Kat, 349, 377
Jefferson University Hospital, 278
Jefferson, Thomas, 46
jellyfish, 17
John of Gaddesden, 109
Jonas, Wayne, 193, 209, 238
Jones, J.P., 269
Journal of Gastrointestinal Surgery, 329, 330
Journal of the American Medical Association (JAMA), 16, 29, 178, 240, 305, 307, 308, 316, 326, 329, 330, 371

K

Kapha, 105, 106
Kelley, William Donald, 53–58, 65–70, 75, 83–89, 99, 101, 102, 107, 110, 116–119, 121–127, 129–135, 137–145, 147–157, 159, 161–163, 165, 166, 172, 174, 177, 179, 180, 184, 186, 187, 190, 208, 209, 219, 224, 239, 253, 263, 275, 291, 322, 331, 332, 341, 348, 349, 351, 366–369, 379

Killen, Jack, 289, 290, 291, 292
King, Larry, 335, 336, 376
Klauser, Richard, 238, 239
Knockout, 331–333, 335, 346, 376
Know Your Body Campaign, 182
Knox gelatin, 159

L

La Roche, Hoffman, 190
laetrile, 88, 204, 229
Lake George, 4, 45, 46, 48, 60, 129, 357
Lampe, Frank, 237, 373
Landon, Michael, 165, 269
Landsman, Jonathan, 224, 225, 372
Leavitt, Michael O., 314
Leo, Monica, 363
leukemia, 84, 121, 171, 225, 226, 275, 335, 336
Levin, Ezra, 153–160,
Levine, Mark, 340
Levine, Stephen, 159, 160
Levinson, Daniel R., 324, 236
Levitt, William, 179
Lister, Joseph, 174
love (*philia*), 107
Luckenbach, Edgar F., 79
lupus, 84, 93, 278
Lyme, 93, 277–279
lymphoma, 84, 166, 225, 226, 335, 336

M

Mackintosh, Sherwin, 165, 166, 370
Madero, Francisco, 9–11, 13, 22, 63
magnesium, 42, 54, 57, 68, 71

Manchester, Melissa, 16, 77, 367

Manhattan, 4, 77, 81, 99, 113, 118, 132, 162, 164, 165, 179, 189, 201, 204, 228, 265, 271, 284, 285

Maori, 7, 28

Marine Biology Research Center, 62

Maxine Dunitz Neurosurgical Institute, 335

Mayer, Robert, 248

Mayo Clinic, 27, 143, 262, 331

Mayo, Charles, 27

McNeilly, Patrick, 308–311, 375

McQueen, Steve, 86, 87, 101, 116, 117, 119, 351, 367, 368

Medical Tribune, 245

Medieval Church, 110

Megace, 302

melanoma, 191

Merck Manual, 57

metabolic types, 69, 71, 73, 83, 84, 101, 102, 104, 107, 157, 180, 184, 219, 265, 280, 348

metabolism, 40, 41, 69, 97, 283

metagenesis, 17

metastatic breast cancer, 93, 184, 194, 202, 226, 327, 336

metastatic colon cancer, 93, 184, 226, 336

metastatic lung cancer, 134, 162, 184, 202, 204, 226, 327, 336

metastatic pancreatic cancer, 93, 134, 162, 184, 291, 336

Mexican heritage, 3

Mexican Revolution, 9, 10, 12, 13, 15, 21, 22, 63, 126, 357

Mexico City, 10–13, 63, 64, 74

Michaels, Brenda, 349, 377

microbiology, 7, 113

migraine, 46, 57, 166

Miller, Jeanne Marie, 359

Miller, Sandy, 177, 179, 181, 240, 241

Monrovia, 39, 366

Moolenburgh, Hans, 183, 184, 187, 212, 213, 232–234, 236, 237, 239, 287, 322, 359, 371–373

Morell, Sally Fallon, 347

Morris, Philip, 178

Morrison, Carol, 148

Moss, Ralph, 238, 365

multiple sclerosis (MS), 277

myasthenia gravis, 278, 279

Myasthenia Gravis Specialty Center, 278

myeloid leukemia, 121

N

National Cancer Institute, 99, 149, 190, 192, 199, 200, 243, 246, 247, 274, 360, 371, 379

National Center for Complementary and Alternative Medicine (NCCAM), 202, 208, 209, 243, 246, 289, 290, 291, 293, 297–299, 309, 324, 325, 326, 328, 330, 331, 345, 373, 375

National Inquirer, 88, 150

National Institute of Allergy and Infectious Disease (NIAID), 309

National Institute of Mental Health, 211

native diets, 7, 29, 30, 44, 102

Natural Health Magazine, 245

NBC Dateline, 340, 376

Nemethy, Sonia, 150, 369

nervous system, 17, 18, 40, 41, 58–60, 62, 63, 68, 70, 74–76, 97, 105, 117, 131, 141, 277, 360, 365–370, 374, 379

Nestlé Corporation, 99, 189–191, 199–201, 207, 219, 232, 248, 253, 332

Nestorian monks, 109

Netherlands, 183, 186, 187, 212, 232

neuroanatomy, 123

CROSSWAY BOOKS
38 De Montfort Street, Leicester LE1 7GP, England

First published under the title The Engaged couples Handbook *in
1992.*
Reprinted as Preparing for Marriage: An A-Z Handbook *in 1996.*

British Library Cataloguing in Publication Data

A catalogue record for this book is available from the British
Library.

ISBN 1-85684-126-X

Typeset in Great Britain by Nuprint Ltd, Station Road,
Harpenden, Herts AL5 4SE.

Printed in Great Britain

Contents

A
is for
Adventure

THE DAY IS SET. Invitations are chosen, written and sent. Tours of likely hotels and halls for the reception are completed and the final choice has been made. Final adjustments are made to her dress and a desperate search is carried out for a suit that fits him. Wedding rings need to be chosen. There's always something we forget.

Sounds familiar? It's the well-worn path countless couples have travelled as they prepare to enter 'the estate of holy matrimony' or marriage as it is more commonly described.

What lies the other side of the 'big day' as everyone insists on calling it, with a knowing look in their eye and a strange leer of the lip? Certainly the preparations are fun, but they are also exhausting and sometimes extremely stressful. Indeed, the very energy required in setting up the day can obscure our focus on the marriage which is to follow. Several months of expectation, concentration and hard work building towards an occasion will give way to a lifetime together.

Have we got what it takes? Do we have any idea what it will require? Has our experience in our parental home

4

been happy? Is there a role model for us to follow or are we learning from scratch?

Many couples today do not have a very positive picture of marriage to carry with them as they begin a committed relationship, and in many cases one blessed by the church in a service which has more to do with tradition than a meaningful kick-off to the marriage. And yet the truth is each partner's mind is filled with questions. Will it last? If it doesn't work out, can I get a divorce? Am I becoming a piece of property—losing my independence and individuality?

That's the great thing about marriage. It is an adventure; and what adventurer ever knows on setting out if they will complete the challenge before them? So with marriage; it is a challenge. A journey that will require great stamina and strength from both partners. An adventure which has the capacity to become the most exciting and challenging task ever undertaken by two individuals, one which will demand sacrifice, develop character and enrich each person's experience of life. The challenge of the adventure called marriage is whether together the couple can discover the resources to complete the course successfully.

Each couple will face different set backs. No two marriages are the same. Circumstances will vary and yet the objective is the same: to stay together, discovering that neither could have chosen a route leading to a more fulfilled experience of life.

In the next few pages we hope to provide helpful insights for those preparing to take the plunge. These emerge from our own experience and from talking to countless couples both before they marry and following them through the heights and depths of their marriage experience.

Organised as an 'A—Z', it is aimed to become a helpful bedside reference book for the months leading up to the wedding and also, we dare to suggest, into the first few years of marital bliss. The advice given is very practical; from bride's hairdo to contraceptive wisdom. It is our hope that the few words of encouragement found in this book will prove helpful as you struggle to resolve that first argument; weep as the tension builds towards the wedding day; sort out with whose parents Christmas will be spent.

Each section is short, punchy and easily read. Where appropriate, basic guidelines are provided, for example in how to find a mortgage or budgeting the household finance week by week.

Albert Einstein, the famous scientist, once expressed the view that the average person only ever uses 10% of his mental powers. We believe that many couples only ever achieve the same percentage of their marriage potential. Just as improving the mind takes a measure of disciplined commitment, so does marriage. No relationship just happens.

Marriage should be seen as an ongoing, lifetime relationship. Each partner is an equal shareholder, equally responsible for the shape and direction of the relationship and equally committed, no matter what the circumstances or discoveries along the way. When we discovered that we had a less than 1% chance of having children, our commitment to each other and hence our marriage was tested. Our marriage withstood, and is withstanding, the test but only due to a level of commitment attained through honest talking and learning to understand and appreciate each other in new ways.

When pressure comes, as indeed it will, it is important to remember that you need your partner at that point. There is no room for a mindset that sees a failure and a need to start again. No; rather as obstacles are encountered during the voyage of discovery marriage provides, the partners together find the way to overcome and go on. It is more a continuous journey than a series of episodes. Just as a car will tend to fail you at the most

6

inopportune time unless it is regularly serviced, so a marriage will run into problems unless it receives constant maintenance; and both wife and husband are the mechanics. Though there may be times when the help of the marriage garage may be appropriate!

As you read and consider the following pages please remember we do not have a series of solutions; rather, helpful principles which we have discovered and practise ourselves. They have also been taken up and used by many other couples we have had the privilege of preparing for marriage.

As you move into marriage remember the experience of Christopher Columbus who set out not knowing where he was going, arrived not knowing where he was and returned not knowing where he'd been. In this way he discovered America. I bet he'd have appreciated an 'A—Z' guide to recognising foreign countries. This is the Christopher Columbus guide to marriage. Do yourself a favour and start reading.

Before reading further, however, complete the following questions and discuss your answers with your partner.

A. Why do you think now is the right time to marry? (Tick as many as you like.)

☐1. I'm old enough
☐2. I'm in love
☐3. I want to leave home
☐4. I've found the right person
☐5. I can afford it
☐6. Most of my friends are engaged or married
☐7. I want security
☐8. The sooner I'm married the better
☐9. I could never find anyone else as nice

B. Of all the boyfriends/girlfriends I've known my partner is special because ....
C. In what ways do you think you will be happier as a married person than as a single person?

7

is for Bride

THE WEDDING DAY is often said to be 'the Bride's Day'. The bride is certainly the centre of attention in many ways. It is also a very special day for the bride's parents, not least because they are seeing their daughter leave their care to start a new life with someone else. This is true even if the bride to be has been living away from her childhood home for several years. The bride's mother has usually been very involved with all the preparations for the wedding day, so in many ways it can be seen as her day too.

There are many factors to occupy the bride's mind and energy in the run up to the wedding, and many things must be considered in plenty of time.

The dress

The wedding dress is usually the most expensive single item necessary for the day, but do not panic; you need not buy. There are a few options available:

    (a) Buy a gown
    (b) Hire a gown

(c) Make a gown
(d) Borrow a gown

A dress which is bought will obviously belong to the bride. However, ask yourself what you will do with the dress after the wedding day. It may be altered so that it can be used again (perhaps as a baby gown), kept for posterity or sold.

There are many specialist shops where you can buy your dress—national chains and local independent stores. Department stores often have a bridal department too. Trying on wedding dresses can be great fun but it is also tiring. Make sure you are wearing white underwear, and take someone with you who will be level headed and honest about the dresses you try on. It helps to have a second opinion apart from the assistant who is probably trying to sell you the most expensive dress in the range!

A dress which is hired works out more economical for one day's wear. And you may be able to choose a style which is more extravagant. There is no problem about what to do with it after the big event. *Yellow Pages* lists hire companies, national and local, under Wedding Services.

A dress which is made can be made to fit exactly (as long as the bride's weight doesn't fluctuate dramatically near the wedding day!). It can include personal touches (like royal wedding dresses often do) and can also be tailored to suit the purse.

Borrowing a gown is also a viable option, similar to hiring. There may be a particular gown which is, or is becoming, a family heirloom. A friend may have a gown which you particularly admire and would enjoy wearing on your wedding day. This is often the cheapest approach to acquiring a wedding dress but provision must be made for cleaning the gown afterwards.

However you acquire your dress it is important to try it on with the other accessories, ie underwear and shoes. The height of the shoes should take into consideration your height, the groom's height and also comfort. It's a long day with a lot of standing, so it is important to be comfortable. It may be romantic to wear a garter but be sure it doesn't show through your dress, particularly if the garter is black!

It's not essential to wear a traditional wedding gown. They can be expensive and of very limited use so you may decide to wear a smart dress or suit which will be serviceable afterwards. Remember, it's your day so you can wear what you want to.

Hair

Hair is a very important component of our overall appearance. Obviously the headdress will dictate what hairstyle will be worn on the wedding day. Again there are various options:

(a) A veil which can be worn over the face at the beginning of the service and then off the face
(b) A veil which is off the face all the time
(c) A hat
(d) A headdress without a veil
(e) No headwear

Once the decision about headgear is made, plans should be made concerning hair dressing. If you are planning a radical change for the wedding day a rehearsal is essential. Perhaps you are planning to have a perm. If so, one to two months before the wedding would be a good idea. If you are having a trial run, we would encourage you to take your headgear to show the hairdresser so that he/she knows what the final aim is. Katey had fresh flowers in her hair and she practised with the comb to which they were attached. Remember that life does continue after the wedding service so plan how you will wear your hair when going away. Katey's hair had been so severely lacquered that she had no option!

Make-up

If you are wearing a traditional gown which is full length and white you need to adjust your make-up accordingly. One full rehearsal is essential so that you know what you are doing. Many hair salons also offer a make-up service, as do many department stores. The choice is yours but it is important to book hair and/or beauty treatments well in advance. Don't forget that bridesmaids will also need to be beautified!

Some hairdressers and make-up specialists will come to the house. This can save a lot of hassle and unnecessary travelling on a busy day.

Bride's timetable

The details of every wedding day are different but there are some 'landmarks' which are always there. This timetable is for a 1.30pm wedding but adjustments can easily be made to fit in with your day.

8.00am	Get up. Breakfast and bath. Time with family.
9.30am	Pick up headdress of fresh flowers and fresh flowers for top of the wedding cake from the florist. Deliver cake flowers to the reception venue.
10.00am	Arrive for hair and make-up appointment. Hair washed, make-up applied, hair styled and headdress fitted.
11.00am	Driven from hairdressers to home where a light lunch is consumed.
12.00pm	Bridesmaids arrive to get ready. Bride and bridesmaids help each other with bride's mother.
12.45pm	Bride gets into dress. Leave this as late as possible to avoid accidents.
1.00pm	Various photographss taken at bride's home, eg bride, bridesmaids and bride's parents.

1.10pm	Bridesmaids and bride's mother leave for the church.
1.20pm	Car returns to pick up bride and father.
1.30pm	Bride and father arrive at church.

Behaviour

In celluloid epics the bride is often portrayed as a 'spoiled brat' ruling the roost on 'her' day, getting all and sundry that she requests, whether reasonable or not.

A bride should remember that the wedding day can be traumatic for her parents. They have cared for the bride since babyhood and now they are witnessing her about to begin a new life in a home of her own with another man. Parents therefore need to be treated gently with sensitivity, even though the bride also needs careful treatment. It is a good idea to celebrate together in the morning over events like breakfast. Perhaps with a little thought the bride can make this an extraordinary time with special touches.

A mother often likes to perform a last duty to her daughter by helping her dress and prepare. The father also enjoys the special time when he and his daughter travel alone to the wedding. These are often treasured memories the bride will take with her into marriage.

It is a lovely touch for the bride and groom to acknowledge what they owe to their parents by presenting each set of parents with a small gift. This can be done at the reception, at a private meal just before the great day or at some other time when parents and children are together.

A bride should aim at making this a day to remember for everyone involved. This can be done with just a little forethought.

Flowers

Traditionally brides carry a bouquet of flowers. The time of year and the amount of money you wish to spend will govern what flowers you choose. Florists usually have photos of bouquets they have made up and will also advise on choice of flowers. The shape of the bouquets for bride and bridesmaids needs to be considered as well. A small bridesmaid often copes better with a ball of flowers on a ribbon rather than a bouquet. Baskets or hoops are other popular alternatives. These days silk flowers which are, of course, everlasting are very popular—especially if the bride wants to keep her bouquet.

Buttonholes for the men involved should also be ordered well in advance. The colour and the type of flower need to be decided upon. A colour contrasting with or matching, for example, the bridesmaids dresses can help to give a co-ordinating look. Buttonholes or corsages should be provided for each set of parents, best man and ushers. More can be provided. The list is open-ended but grandparents and godparents are often included, as are special friends or anyone who has been particularly involved in the wedding.

Do turn to 'W is for Wedding Day' for a full explanation of all participants' responsibilities running up to and on the day of the wedding itself.

is for
Contraception

A REGULAR SEX LIFE is an essential ingredient to a satisfying and healthy marriage. If there are problems in this area please turn to 'S is for Sex'.

Our forefathers (or should it be foremothers?) demonstrated this by the fact that it was quite normal for a child to be born every year. Today, we are not so much in the lap of the gods. We have the benefits of contraception. But it is not always plain sailing.

Contraception, the means by which we seek to prevent the fertilisation of the female's egg by the male's sperm, should be openly and fully discussed by every engaged couple. This must be done in good time before the wedding so that plans can be acted upon before the honeymoon. It is not now so socially acceptable to bear a child every nine months; nor can many couples afford it.

Discussing contraception and the sexual dynamic of your relationship will provoke a healthy discussion about children. Do you like and want children of your own? In an ideal world, when would this be? Are there financial implications for your lifestyle and aspirations? What are they? It would be appropriate to turn to 'O is for Offspring' at this point for further discussion on the subject of children.

Contraception can appear a very confusing subject at first glance. However, be assured there is a lot of useful advice available to you both. We stress *both* since you will both be involved in sex, so it is as much his as her responsibility. Somehow, because most contraceptives apart from the sheath involve women, men seem to think it is a matter for women only. This is untrue. Men should accompany their wife to be to the GP or family planning clinic to be as involved as possible in this part of preparing for marriage.

Books

These provide a useful source of information. There are many free pieces of literature available from your GP or family planning clinic and you would be well advised to get hold of these. Some books cover specific forms of contraception. Reading widely can present you with conflicting information, for example on the side-effects of the pill, so make sure you can take your questions to your doctor or that you can handle the various viewpoints. Your local library will have a number of books that you can borrow or any good bookshop should carry some.

Friends

Close friends in whom we have confidence are also a great asset. They can hopefully speak from experience and give personal insights. This is often more reassuring than any piece of literature or the GP with whom we may not be especially relaxed.

GP/family planning clinic

This is one visit you should certainly make; if only for the free samples! Here you can talk through all the various methods of contraception, what is involved, their reliability in preventing conception and any possible side-effects. They will be able to instruct you in their use and their suitability for you.

Some of the more 'mechanical' methods such as the IUD will need to be professionally fitted, which will be done on just such a visit.

A woman asking for family planning advice will almost certainly be given a full internal examination. This is nothing to be anxious about and it does help to relax for it. This is purely a routine measure. Indeed, in the years ahead an internal will become the norm for checking that cervical cancer has not found its way into your system.

Methods available

So what are the methods of contraception available to us? Consider the following chart to get an outline of methods, suitability, practical use and reliability.

Methods of birth control

Method	Who for?	Medical advice needed?	Reliable?	Comments
The Pill	Her	Yes	Very	Not suitable for all women
Intrauterine Device (IUD) (permanently fitted in womb)	Her	Yes	Very	Fitted by doctor– only yearly check needed. Removed by doctor when you want a baby
Cap	Her	Yes	Very– especially when used with spermicidal cream	Doctor or nurse chooses right size. Put in vagina before intercourse.

16

Sterilization	Him/her	Yes	Completely–permanent	Operation required. Only suitable when family complete
Condom (sheath)	Him	No	Fairly	Can be purchased at most chemists or prescribed by Family Planning doctor
Creams, foams, jellies	Her	No	Moderately	Available at chemists and Family Planning centres
Safe period		No	Only if calculated on a regular cycle	Advice and special temperature charts etc. from FPA or CMAC

You can find the address of your local Family Planning Clinic in the telephone directory. Drop in or phone during the hours that your clinic is open and make an appointment.

The pill. There are different types of pill available. The pill must be prescribed by a doctor. Taking the pill regularly means that you should have your blood pressure tested from time to time.

The pill is taken by the woman every day for twenty-one days. During the following seven days the woman will menstruate. On the twenty-ninth day (day one of the next cycle) a new packet of pills is started.

The pill works by suppressing ovulation and is a highly reliable method of contraception providing the woman remembers to take it. It is also the husband's responsibility to remind her.

There may be a few side-effects since the pill does not suit everyone. However, your GP can advise you here and even let you try out different types of pill to find one that suits you.

Aesthetically the pill is the most pleasing form of contraceptive. However, some women can't get on with it or carry anxieties about health risks that have been identified with it in the press. Therefore you must decide if you are both happy with this method before proceeding. If you do adopt the pill as your method of contraception then it is a good idea to begin taking it three months before your wedding day so that any problems can be dealt with and you are comfortable with it as you depart for your honeymoon.

Intra-Uterine Device (IUD or coil). An IUD is a mechanical device inserted into the woman. It must be fitted by a doctor and stays in place permanently. It should be checked annually. Some people have a moral problem with IUDs because they enable conception to take place before preventing the egg embedding in the lining of the uterus. Again, an IUD is painless and makes no difference to sexual intercourse. It is also very reliable.

The cap. The cap is another method of contraception to be used by the wife. It is carefully fitted so that it fits tightly into the vagina thus preventing any of the man's semen entering into the woman and leading to fertilisation. It must be inserted into the vagina prior to intercourse. This can be done as a matter of course every night or can be incorporated into lovemaking. It should be used with spermicidal cream to make it more effective and should be left in position for some hours after intercourse. This can be a very effective method of contraception.

Sterilisation. The husband or the wife can be sterilised. It is a smaller, more straightforward operation for the man involving local anaesthetic, whereas for a woman it is quite a major operation. This method of contraception is 100% effective and should be considered to be irreversible. It is not a method of contraception which should be considered by young newly weds.

Sheath. The sheath or condom is a method of contraception used by the man. Sheaths are widely available at chemists and most supermarkets. They are also available at family planning clinics. The sheath is fitted over the man's erect penis. The idea is for it to contain the man's semen thus preventing conception. Condoms should be used in conjunction with spermicides to ensure a higher level of contraceptive protection. Some people find condoms a real 'turn off' because they appear to be so very unnatural but others find them very acceptable.

Creams, foams and jellies. These are available at chemists and family planning centres and need no medical advice. They are used by the woman but some find them messy and therefore distasteful. They are only moderately reliable.

Safe period. The safe period relies on accurate prediction of when the woman ovulates. By avoiding intercourse around that time conception is avoided. It is very helpful if the woman has a regular monthly cycle! No medical advice is needed but advice and a special temperature chart are available from the Catholic Marriage Advisory Council (see *Yellow Pages* for address and phone number). The woman must take her temperature every morning before she gets up and plot it on a graph. Upon ovulation the temperature rises and stays at the higher level. A benefit of this method is that it is completely natural. If used carefully, and calculations are made accurately, it can be a good and fairly reliable method of contraception.

Whichever method of contraception you decide to use, it is important that you both assume corporate responsibility for the situation. Each method puts more responsibility on one of the partners but it is still a joint responsibility.

Some couples do decide to give contraception a miss and leave it up to God. If you decide to do this, you must be prepared to have a child nine months after you marry!

19

D

is for
Daily Budgeting

IN 'F IS FOR FINANCE' we will take a full look at the whole area of money matters. However, this section deals with the issue of money management. Every day we need to spend cash. Housekeeping, necessities, luxuries: all demand our income. There is nothing wrong with this but if we do not monitor it carefully it will run away with us.

Money cannot look after itself. It is an essential friend and a ruthless enemy. Once our financial affairs begin to get out of hand we are often fighting a losing battle to recover solvency and order in our financial affairs.

Money management is a vital skill that we all need to acquire. If, like Mike, you are innumerate, never fear. There are very practical guidelines to be followed and they are explained in this section. Furthermore, it only takes one of you to manage the money side of the relationship. Nevertheless, both of you must be able to take over from each other at a moment's notice.

For either partner not to know your joint financial situation is unacceptable within marriage. All income is joint no matter who earns it; no matter who generates the most. For years Katey earned more than Mike but he was happy to be a kept man. In real terms though we both knew what our financial position was, where the loot was stashed, and each had access to all accounts.

If you have not done so before, answer the following questions together with your partner.

A. My wage/salary each week/month is ....
B. My savings amount to £................................
C. My bank is ....
D. My account is a
    (1) Current account
    (2) Deposit account
    (3) Other (please specify)
E. My other accounts, eg building society, are ....
   (please specify).
F. My shares are .... (list all shares together with values and average dividend payments).

It is as well to start as you mean to continue and there should be no financial secrets between you. If you have financial liabilities as a result of family, friends or business connections you should also come clean on those so that your partner knows precisely what (s)he is marrying into. Lack of clarity at this stage on this issue can lead to difficulties not long into marriage itself.

One of the key things about money is that it needs constant attention. While this may be obvious if you are trading with billions on the stock market, it is equally true that your rather small household budget requires regular attention. However, we are often very sloppy in this whole area of money management.

We are all aware of what happens if we neglect the family car. One day we leave the house, climb into the vehicle, turn the ignition key and nothing happens. If a car is not regularly serviced, don't be surprised if it fails you; and usually at the most inconvenient moment.

So it is with our family finances. Ignore them, or assume the bank manager is keeping a helpful eye over your financial affairs, and you will end up in trouble.

21

What's required is some practical administration of your financial affairs.

Income

First, you will need to establish the total income you and your partner are receiving. Then you will have to calculate your expenditure before comparing the two and discovering if you can afford to live!

To compute your earnings, both you and your fiancée should consult your pay slips which you should receive from your employer. This gives you a lot of information but all you are interested in is the net or take home figure. This relates to the amount of cash put into your hand at the end of each week or deposited in your bank account at month's end.

If you are paid monthly multiply the net figure by twelve to see how much you earn in a year. This is purely for your own information as we will be working on the monthly sums for the purposes of this section. On the other hand, if you are paid weekly then multiply your weekly income by fifty two (number of weeks in a year and hence your annual take home pay) before dividing by twelve (the number of months in a year thereby giving you an average monthly income figure).

$£^{**} \times 52 = ? \div 12 = ?$ average monthly income

There may be other sources of income which are received on a regular basis (social security benefits, child allowance, building society interest, shares, etc). All these figures need to be entered in; but remember: average them out over the year so that you get a monthly average. The following chart will help you here.

Item	Amount earned	Payment date	Average monthly value
Employment:			
Husband			
Wife			
U/e benefit			
Other benefits:			
(a)			
(b)			
(c)			
(d)			
Building society interest			
Share div.			
Other			
TOTAL			

Obviously, if you are self-employed your earnings may be more difficult to establish but from your previous books you should be in a position to set down your average monthly income.

Expenditure

When it comes to the money you spend each month (your outgoings) there are two aspects to consider: regular and irregular payments. Now by 'irregular' we do not mean backhanders, so do not be alarmed!

Regular expenditure is the payment of set amounts which are made each month such as your mortgage repayments. The only variant here is the rate of interest charged and you will be forewarned about any increase in payments.

Irregular expenditure includes fuel bills (higher in winter than in summer), house repairs, Christmas, etc. You might also include trips to the dentist and the like here which may prove an unexpected extra one month. This irregularity of outgoings explains why one month you are apparently wealthy, enjoying a surplus, and the next you are in deficit!

Practical and simple administration of your finances can iron out hiccups and enable you to be aware of an anticipated surplus and therefore utilise it to cover the known deficit in another month.

Having listed your income, you should now work through the following charts and assess as accurately as possible your expenditure. Before you do so, however, you will need to approximate some of your irregular outgoings. You may not spend what you allocate but at least you won't be spending money you haven't allowed for.

To make this approximation look at last year's bills, or if you are buying or renting a property request the vendor or landlord to give you the figures and adding them together divide by twelve to give you a monthly average. Do likewise for other anticipated expenditure. Decide on a sum to cover the cost of birthday presents for example, then divide by twelve and see what the average monthly total is. Obviously you won't spend that amount each month but you will be able to compare your average monthly expenditure with your average monthly income.

Now complete the following tables.

AVERAGE MONTHLY EXPENDITURE

ITEM	Amount paid	How often	Date of payment	Who is paid	Amount/ mth	Notes
Rent/Mortgage	£				£	
Rates	£				£	
Water rates	£				£	
Ground rent	£				£	
Service charge	£				£	

Community charge	£	£
Insurance schemes	£	£
Pension fund	£	£
Electricity	£	£
Gas	£	£
Oil	£	£
Coal	£	£
Telephone	£	£
Maintenance payments	£	£
House repairs	£	£
Redecoration	£	£
Car loan	£	£
Car fuel	£	£
MOT	£	£
Road tax	£	£
Vehicle insurance	£	£
Car repairs	£	£
Public transport	£	£
Groceries	£	£
Other housekeeping	£	£
Kid's pocket money	£	£
Childminding	£	£
Pet food	£	£
Vet bills	£	£
Clothing	£	£
Laundry	£	£
Regular prescriptions	£	£
Dentist	£	£
Optician	£	£

TV licence	£	£
TV rental	£	£
Video rental	£	£
Christmas	£	£
Birthday presents	£	£
Holiday	· £	£
Trips and outings	£	£
Sporting activities	£	£
Hobbies	£	£
Records and tapes	£	£
Toys and books	£	£
Drinks	£	£
Cigarettes/tobacco	£	£
Newspapers	£	£
Other	£	£
	£	£
	£	£
	£	£
TOTAL	£	£

MONTHLY CREDIT REPAYMENTS

ITEM		Amount paid	How often	Date of payment	Who is paid	Amount/ mth	Notes
Mortgage		£				£	
Second mortgage		£				£	
Secured loans	1	£				£	
	2	£				£	
Unsecured loans	1	£				£	
	2	£				£	
	3	£				£	

Credit cards	1	£	£
	2	£	£
	3	£	£
	4	£	£
Storecards	1	£	£
	2	£	£
	3	£	£
	4	£	£
Catalogues	1	£	£
	2	£	£
	3	£	£
Local moneylender		£	£
Hire purchase	1	£	£
	2	£	£
Others		£	£
		£	£
		£	£
		£	£
		£	£
TOTAL		£	£

You are now in a position to do some simple sums. Take your combined totals from your expenditure table and debt repayment table, add them together and subtract their combined total from your income total. If you still have money to spare then you are in credit and are living within your means. If not then you need to do a bit of pruning.

Pruning

What we mean here is that if you are spending more than you are earning when you have completed the above steps, then you need to return to your expenditure table to prune it. Work through each item and identify what is essential expenditure and what is unessential. It is the unessential items that will need to be cut. For example, fuel is an essential item but clothing can be trimmed. We have also found that when under financial pressure, working hard at when we have hot water and the amount of heating we have on during the day makes a significant difference to the size of the fuel bills.

Work through your expenditure table doing some ruthless pruning. Be fair to each other. What you may see as inessential may be life's blood to your partner; therefore work on this together and negotiate. Remember, however, that you are seeking to get to a balanced budget where income meets expenditure.

If you find that you are seriously in debt then seek advice. Your local Citizens' Advice Bureau (details in your phone book, *Yellow Pages* or from your local library) will assist you. Below is a further chart that you should fill in if you find yourself already owing a lot of money that you have previously taken out on credit terms. Complete this if appropriate and take it with you when you visit the CAB.

DEFAULT DEBTS

ITEM	Amount owed	Interest rate (APR)	Notes
Mortgage arrears	£	%	
Second mortgage arrears	£	%	
Secured loan arrears	£	%	
Rent arrears	£	%	
Rates arrears	£	%	
Electricity arrears	£	%	
Gas arrears	£	%	
Outstanding Community Charge	£	%	
Water rates arrears	£	%	

Income tax arrears	£	%
Credit card arrears	£	%
Storecard arrears	£	%
Hire purchase arrears	£	%
VAT arrears	£	%
Unpaid fines	£	%
Maintenance arrears	£	%
Bank overdraft	£	%
Other	£	%
	£	%
	£	%
TOTAL	£	%

When dealing with debt remember to be honest about your situation; first with yourself. It's easy to stick bills unopened into the desk drawer; to continue to live as if you have no financial worries. Admitting to yourself that you have problems is the start to getting rid of them.

Secondly, talk with your partner. They share the consequences and indebtedness anyway. Hopefully you are both fully aware of the household financial state so will be in touch with the debt problem.

Thirdly, let the people to whom you owe money know your situation. Inform your bank manager and also the building society or whomever you have a mortgage with, if you have one at all. It is worth noting that you need to deal with those creditors (the people to whom you owe money) who can take most from you first. The building society could take your house from you. Therefore communicate with them and keep them informed. The CAB will help you devise a plan to organise your debts and seek to protect you and your family as much as is possible.

Controlling your finance

You will need to decide whether you will share a joint account or both operate independent accounts. For years we operated separate accounts because we couldn't effectively regulate a joint one. We found it impossible to co-ordinate our expenditure and we would go overdrawn, with one spending without the other knowing that the balance was reduced. With separate accounts we could take responsibility for avoiding being overdrawn.

We now have a joint account into which both salaries are paid and from which all standing orders are paid. We also have a second joint account to cover housekeeping. Each month a sum is paid over into this account and we can effectively budget the housekeeping. If we only have £10 for the last week of the month, that is all that is spent.

We also operate a joint, high interest building society account with immediate withdrawal facilities which provides us with a means of saving. Rather than buy on credit we save for the purchases we want to make. Katey also has her own building society account into which she pays birthday money and other financial gifts and then spends on what she wants whenever.

All our social spending comes out of the main joint account. In our early years of marriage, Katey operated this and did all the finances. However, she sneakily passed it over to Mike a few years ago and has so far successfully resisted taking it back!

Finally, we do have a high interest, withdrawal with ninety days' notice without penalty, building society account. This is for unexpected sums or when we have a surplus one month. It is for unexpected expenditure, eg a new roof. Every so often we intend to pay off some of our mortgage if it builds up to suitable proportions.

Money saving hints

1. Don't buy cheap clothes! Sounds crazy but Katey's mum always says: 'Poor people can't afford cheap clothes.' Now you may get a bargain but there again it may fall apart within a year. Mike buys quality Clarks shoes with commando soles. He has two pairs; one brown and one black. The brown pair he bought eight years ago and they are still not worn out and have not needed re heeling or soleing. This is good value for money.

2. Don't neglect the second-hand market. Good bargains can be had, but only buy what is useful. A bargain is only such if it is something you need and will use.

3. Buy to suit your income. Is the house you are considering easy to keep warm, easy to maintain and within walking distance of shops and school? Think before you purchase anything. Is it the best and most practical buy?

4. Save now and buy later. Avoid the pitfalls of credit by organising your own regular saving plan and delaying purchase until you have the cash available. Then negotiate a cash discount!

In these ways you can gain control of your money and budget effectively. You may not have the lifestyle that you observe in all the glossy magazines but you will have one that you can afford. As for quality of life, this is always improved through avoidance of debt and all the stress and hassle that it can produce.

We are grateful to the book *Credit & Debt. Sorting it out* by Michael Schluter and David Lee for the tables printed above and would commend this helpful book to you.

31

is for
Engagement

TRADITIONALLY THIS IS that period of time between asking your girlfriend to marry you and the wedding day itself. Once engaged your partner is known as your fiancé(e).

The actual word 'engaged' refers to a formal promise or covenant. Basically, a commitment has been entered into by the man to marry and take responsibility for the woman. In medival times this period was a most important time. The promise having been accepted it was then the responsibility of the man to demonstrate to his intended's father that he had a job generating sufficient income to provide for his bride following the wedding. She was not at risk from being purloined by someone else since a public commitment had been made.

Today this is no longer the case. It is more a social convention and often the length of the engagement is dictated by the financial needs of the couple in providing accommodation in which to begin their married life. However, it is a special period and there is certainly a change in the intensity and nature of their relationship once people get engaged.

Approaching the intended's father

Although engagement is a far more informal affair today it is quite appropriate to approach the bride's father and request the hand of his daughter in marriage, as the time honoured form of words runs. This is no more than a matter of courtesy and makes a statement about the measure of respect you have for your intended father-in-law. It may therefore have diplomatic aspects to recommend it!

All eager young men should reflect on the fact that many fathers struggle at the thought that they are going to be replaced as the major male decision maker in their daughter's life. The way the proposal is handled can have a marked impact upon the character and quality of the future relationship with the young lady's parents.

Today, with many children growing up in broken families, it may prove more difficult to follow the above course of action. However, be inventive and if your fiancé(e) has been brought up by her mother and there is no real bonding with her natural father then request her mother's permission. The whole object behind the tradition in today's society should be to express respect to the parent(s) and value in the intended.

When we decided to get engaged we chose Christmas Eve. Mike, aware that Katey was particularly concerned about various informal anniversaries, chose carefully, knowing he could remember Christmas Eve. He had learned from frequent failure to recall the date we started going out together when questioned by Katey. The same mistake would not be made again.

A few days before this he visited Katey's father to request his permission to marry her. Knowing Katey was out he arrived on his motorbike, rang the door bell and waited. Katey's father came to the door and immediately informed Mike that his daughter was out. Now Katey's father is somewhat deaf due to an industrial accident. On explaining that he knew Katey was not in her father then

33

asked if there was something wrong with the motorbike. This was a natural question since Mike's knowledge of things mechanical was negligible and Katey's father was an engineer who had proved most helpful in the past. On realising there was no easy entrance to be gained to the house Mike raised his voice and shouted: 'I would like to marry Katey if you are agreeable.'

The whole neighbourhood was informed along with Katey's dad who happily at that point responded: 'I think you had better come in.'

Mike went in, and fortunately Katey's father was in full agreement.

Making the announcement

Once the bride to be's father has been approached, a decision needs to be made about whether an announcement should be placed in the newspapers. This decision is often taken out of the hands of the engaged couple by overjoyed parents who assume all their friends avidly scan the 'hatches, matches and despatches' columns and feel the world in general ought to enjoy their good news.

If you are placing the announcement in the newspaper phone in and get a costing before dictating your chosen form of words. Have this written down before you phone as the paper will take it down during the call, read it back to you, confirm the appearance date and either send you an invoice or take details of a suitable credit card for payment.

Choosing the ring

It is today unusual for the man to arrive with a ring already purchased to place on his betrothed's finger. Strange though it may seem she has quite set ideas about the type of ring, the setting and the stone(s), and enjoys being involved in trying on various rings and making the choice with her intended.

It is worth noting that the lower the carat of the gold the tougher it is and the better it will withstand rubbing against the wedding ring once married.

There are also lovely rings available second hand which will certainly provide financial savings. Alternatively, this is the way to obtain an antique ring if that is your preference.

Increasingly common today is the giving of an engagement present by the girl to her betrothed. This should reflect the financial realities of her situation. A wallet, tie clip or a signet ring are popular choices. This is not however mandatory.

The engagement party

This is traditionally held on the day the engagement is announced. There can be difficulties—especially if the couple hail from different geographical locations. At least seek to get the parents together to celebrate the occasion.

Often the bride's parents meet the costs of this party, though again couples are increasingly taking this responsibility themselves. Traditionally the bride's father makes the announcement of the engagement at a suitable moment. The couple and their friends may well move on to a night club later leaving the family members to continue at a pace more suitable to their age.

Engagement presents

It may well be that family and close friends wish to give you a present to mark the occasion of your engagement. They will often ask if there is anything in particular you would like. Assuming that the wedding is not too far distant it may be appropriate to request one or two small items for your future home together. When we got engaged we received a hand mixer, casserole dishes, brandy glasses and similar items.

However, if finance is the most pressing need don't be afraid to request cheques towards a home of your own or some large item, such as a washing machine.

Being engaged

Once engaged the relationship takes on a whole new feel. There is an increased intensity. Why this should be we do not know but in the majority of cases this is what people testify to. As a result it is important to think through how you intend to handle life during the engagement. This is the final stage of growing towards marriage and habits learned now will be hard to shed later.

There are three fundamental areas you will need to address regarding your relationship. These are the social, the sexual and the spiritual.

Social. By this we mean the maintenance and development of your relationships with your wider circle of friends. It is most unrealistic to believe that your fiancé(e) and future spouse will meet all your social needs. You should seek to retain a good and active contact with your special friends.

Traditionally this has been the preserve of the 'lads': off playing football all winter and cricket all summer, this is frequently interrupted by trips to the pub. However, women also need their free time with their mates and the men must learn to accept and help this to happen.

Then there are those shared friendships. Eating, drinking and generally socialising together creates an important further forum for enriching your relationship. It's amazing how much you learn by observing others. Things you want to emulate, things you want to avoid and things that cause you a sigh of relief because you are not the only ones struggling with a particular issue.

We all need friends. Our partner should be our foremost and best friend. But we do need other friends of the same sex as ourselves with whom we can sound off, seek advice and generally unwind. It is important that we retain a measure of discretion and trustworthiness in such relationships as we are acting as friends and not enemies. Talking over personal conversations with others later is not the action of a friend.

Sit down and talk through how you will work out this social dimension during your engagement. This is a good preparation for marriage and helps you to discover each others views on each other's friendships and the shared social element you want to develop. It also means you don't hive off on your own all the time, increasing the intensity and ultimately the isolation of your relationship.

It may help to list your current friends below and identify those you want to build with together. Then answer the following few questions and discuss your answers.

Her friends   *His friends*   *Our friends*

1. How often do you like to go out socially during the week?
2. Where do you like to go?
3. What does the weekend mean to you?
4. Do you like entertaining at your own place?
5. How much do you spend socially over a week? (Include the cost of entertaining friends at home.)
6. Do you find mixing with new people difficult?
7. Do you like your fiancé(e)'s friends?

8. Is there one friend who acts as a confidante for you?

Once you have thought through your answers, discuss them with your partner, but do avoid a slanging match! Simply learn more about each other. If there are friends of yours whom your partner doesn't like, then seek to establish the reasons why. It may well be that they feel insecure or even threatened by them. Better to learn honestly now than through painful experience later.

Sexual relationship. By this we obviously mean the physical side of the relationship. This is dealt with in far more detail under 'S is for Sex' and 'C is for Contraception' but at this point we want to talk briefly about establishing the parameters for this important side of the relationship.

Although in our society it is now assumed that all couples have sex before they are married, this is not everyone's chosen course. In an age when pornography is so readily available and we appear to have achieved the ultimate in sexual freedom, the majority are struck dumb when asked to talk about their own sexuality, that is, sexual likes and dislikes.

Hence it is important at this stage to have some honest talking. The ideal from our point of view is to look to marriage itself as the place for sexual intercourse. This will no doubt to a degree depend upon your value system, so consult the section 'V is for Values' for a fuller discussion on this. At all costs talk through carefully what you are looking for from your sexual/physical relationship. If it simply boils down to self-centred pleasure you will quickly grow tired of your partner and look for ever-increasing amounts of stimulation. However, if it is to give as much as to take pleasure, and to respect the human dignity of your partner, then a full and exciting life lies ahead of you.

It is also important to talk through previous sexual encounters, fears and expectations so that you are communicating and understanding each other in what can prove a more complex area than it at first appeared.

Spiritual relationship. By this we mean those inner aspirations that motivate you. To discover that your fiancé(e) is an entrepreneurial land developer, while you are a major campaigner for Brazilian rain forests, can lead to tension.

It was St Augustine who pointed out that within every individual there is a God-shaped gap. It is what goes in that gap which counts at this level of relationship. Therefore, some honest talking about what and why you believe things is essential. The section 'V is for Values' should also be consulted here.

Again it would appear that such talk of God is somewhat scorned today. However, we all have values which motivate us. If we don't share the same values we will find conflict at times of pressure and perhaps an inability to take clear decisions with which we both agree.

We share a Christian faith which at times of conflict or stress has proved invaluable in finding a way forward. To recognise that there is a God who loves, cares for and originally created us and to grow to know Him personally is a wonderful experience. To be in a position to pray together strengthens the marriage. To read the Bible and discover a common value system is marvellous.

A successful marriage will enjoy a shared spiritual base. If you want to know more about how we have worked this out we would be pleased to send you a copy of our book *Praying Together*. This gives details of developing a spiritual life together, costs £3.25, including postage and packing, and is available from the publisher's address at the back of this chapter.

Expectations of marriage

This period of engagement is also a time when you should personally identify your expectations of marriage and as ever talk them through with your betrothed. By 'expectations' we mean what your ideal for your marriage is and what you will therefore be looking for.

Each of you take a moment now to jot down your expectations. Then compare notes. You should consider how you anticipate beginning and ending each day (one of Katey's expectations was that we would always retire to bed together), the level of support you expect in your job from your partner, how you envisage running the home (chores, shopping, etc) and the amount of time spent together and apart.

Some years after we married we discovered that we had both entered marriage with low expectations of success and enduring happiness. We only discovered this when talking it through unexpectedly one day during a conversation as to how surprised we were at the level of happiness we had from being married to each other.

There are basically three types of marriage to aim at.

The first is a marriage of *minimum involvement*. This is common today in our culture; especially where both partners are pursuing careers outside the home. Such a relationship makes few demands and hence there are few expectations to fulfil. It is a perfectly adequate form of marriage so long as both partners are in agreement. The danger comes when changes occur in circumstances, for example with the arrival of the first child, and one partner is no longer working full time outside the home and feels a sense of loss of social contact and mental stimulation.

Therefore, in such a marriage, beware the impact of changing circumstances and take the necessary preparatory steps to embrace them.

The second is a marriage of *maximum involvement*. This is the favourite option for idealistic couples. It involves a decision by the couple to share their lives together as completely as possible. Equal value and status are attached to the personal and vocational needs of each other. The interpersonal relationship between the couple is the greatest objective for this type of marriage.

To sustain such a relationship, a high price has to be paid. Our culture does not favour it and it has been estimated that only 5-10% of couples achieve this type of marriage.

The final is a marriage of *measured involvement*. This is a more realistic goal and we highly recommend it. In this type of marriage a high level of individual freedom is maintained while enjoying a reasonable amount of togetherness. It gives marriage a worthy place among the couple's commitments but does not award it an unrealistic priority.

Consider what you intend to aim at as a couple. Ask yourselves the following two questions:

1. What are we aiming at?
2. What framework will we establish to redefine our aims as our marriage matures and circumstances change?

It cannot be stressed too strongly that establishing an effective process for discussing where each of you feel the marriage is at, and to take stock of the potential impact of changes in circumstances, is essential for ensuring that a marriage will grow ever stronger and both partners feel fulfilled and active participants.

Finally, it is worth remembering that you will need to talk through the wedding day together. It is *your* wedding. Parental desires may need to be considered seriously but your own preferences are paramount. Think about and discuss your personal aspirations for the day. This may include constructive conversations with parents but aim to include the elements that will make the day special for you both and a day worth remembering. See 'W is for Wedding Day' for further comments on this.

Praying Together is available in bookshops or from Kingsway Publications, 1 St. Anne's Road, Eastbourne, East Sussex BN21 3UN.

is for
Finance

'INSTANT CREDIT!' 'BUY NOW; pay later!'
'Increase your spending power now!' These and
similar messages greet us in high street windows,
magazines, newspapers and TV commercials. And yet
the sad truth behind such statements is that there is no
such thing as free money. You pay for everything you
purchase; sometimes at a price you never imagined and
certainly cannot afford.

Today many young couples are languishing under an
intolerable burden of debt which they see very little
opportunity of paying off. The consequences are tension,
stress and, unfortunately, marriage breakdown.

Why is it that so many difficulties arise concerning the
household finances?

As we prepare many young couples for marriage, most
are carrying a level of debt into their marriage with them
from day one. This is often in the form of outstanding
credit card debt (Visa, Access, etc), monies owed on
storecards (Next, Benetton and the like) or bank loans
taken out for that irresistible sound system or some form
of 'wheels'.

All of us need to recognise that there is great pressure
to purchase a vast range of so-called 'essential' goods in

society today. The advertisers are dedicated to ensuring that their clients outsell their competitors; and sell to *you*. Everywhere we turn there are appealing pictures with the hidden message that we are somewhat incomplete or second class if we are not the proud owners of whatever is depicted.

This is where the problem begins: other people convincing us of what we need. You will no doubt have discovered already just how many people are interested in your wedding. They try to sell you this outfit, those floral arrangements, that honeymoon package. Usually each item is just slightly beyond what you said you would like to spend. Yet it does look so lovely and, after all, it is only *just* beyond what you were thinking of spending.

Then of course there is the argument, presented with a real smooth and sentimental tone: 'Well, you only get married once and it is a very special occasion for you both,' as though such reasoning will of itself add money to your bank account which is currently groaning under the weight and number of demands already being placed upon it.

Of course they say that love is blind and at times the whole momentum that builds up around the wedding preparations can generate a false sense of security. We lose touch with reality. Although we can't afford, we spend. Our concentration is entirely focused on the wedding day, with little thought for the months and years beyond. Beware, for this is a trap which every couple should resist falling into.

It is not that such luxuries are somehow evil. But in the early years of marriage particularly, income levels can be stretched. Furthermore, it is easy to forget that alongside the special purchase of luxuries there are the ongoing costs for heating, lighting, telephone, etc. So often a couple's plans are thrown out by the arrival of the quarterly gas bill which had been left out of the financial computations.

What is credit?

Very simply, credit is a way of enjoying goods or services before we have paid for them. The most obvious illustration in the UK is a mortgage, where a building society or bank advances the capital sum required to purchase a house, and you, the mortgagee, agree to pay a set sum each month for a period of, on average, twenty-five years. Hence you enjoy the benefit of what is called 'a home of your own' but at the discretion of the lender.

In return for this financial service, and the opportunity to occupy your own house, you pay a rate of interest for the money borrowed. This rate is referred to as the mortgage rate and represents how much in real terms the house is costing you.

For example, you purchase a £40,000 house and borrow £30,000 to do so. If the mortgage rate stayed at 12% you would in fact pay £159,000 over twenty-five years for your £30,000. Obviously, however, mortgage rates vary so it is never quite as simple as this illustration but the point is made. It costs money to borrow money. Credit can be very expensive. (See 'M is for Mortgage' for more on the subject of house purchase and house rental.)

The reason why so many people purchase their accommodation by means of a mortgage is that property generally tends to appreciate in value. It is what one calls an appreciating asset. Unfortunately, the majority of goods (cars, furniture, electrical equipment) are depreciating assets. They lose their value over a period of time and in times of financial difficulty you are unable to sell for anything like their original value, let alone with the cost of borrowed money added as well. A house, however, can usually be sold and provide sufficient finance to pay off the lender (eg building society) and hence leave no outstanding debts.

Therefore 'credit' is really a polite way of describing debt. Of course, no one wants to consider themselves in debt, so calling credit cards 'debt cards' would not make commercial sense. Hence the adoption of the user-friendly term 'credit'. It's amazing what difference a word can make.

Let Mike illustrate. He travels widely with his work. As a result he needs to purchase railway tickets, petrol and airline tickets regularly. The simplest way to do so is by means of a credit card. However, having made his purchases he is not in credit to British Rail, but in fact in debt to them. If he doesn't clear his credit card account by the due date he incurs interest charges, so begins to pay extra for the services he has already used. Working with an expense account from his employer he is in a position to cover the monthly accounts on time, so it is a useful and convenient way for him to organise his business finance.

So why do people pay by credit?

Obviously the advertisers are at work to convince us that we need things we as yet don't possess. Never underestimate the desire to own. It can remove all rational argument at times.

It is also a very convenient way of paying. Passing over a credit card is far more painless than parting with cash or even a cheque. It should also allow you to spread your payments to match your cashflow, although you must exercise good discipline at this point for such an argument to prove valid.

In recent years, those offering credit have also tried to link possession of their credit card with a sense of being a cut above the rest of society; attaching status to card ownership and offering a short cut to improving your self-image.

Finally, an offer of a small financial contribution to

your favourite, environmentally friendly charity each time you use their card is the latest inducement to encourage people to adopt credit as a way of life.

If you can see beyond the marketing, and with a clear head consider what is really convenient to your household's budget, then you will handle the credit question very well.

One final point here. You will need to distinguish between fixed term and revolving credit. For fixed term credit you will be told as you make the agreement what the repayments will be and when you are to make them. These will in fact vary slightly because of changes in the Annual Percentage Rate (APR) (see below).

Revolving credit is what most store and all bank credit cards and charge cards offer. In brief, a fixed credit limit is set for the cardholder and interest is charged at the end of each month on the outstanding credit. However, the interest charged at the end of month one is added to the credit outstanding figure and contributes to the amount of interest charged at the end of month two and thence subsequent monthly accounts.

With revolving credit the danger is that the amount outstanding is so large that the interest grows at a faster rate than the repayments. You cannot escape from your indebtedness.

Where does credit come from?

There are four major sources from which credit can be obtained: finance companies, banks, credit cards and stores. It would be worth considering from which of the above sources you enjoy credit. Also, jot down the amounts owed so that you get a picture of your indebtedness; how much you owe.

A fifth source of credit is the mail order catalogue which a large number of folk use to purchase items of clothing, etc, from the comfort of their own front room.

Generally, payment is made by putting a small sum down and then paying regular amounts on a monthly or weekly basis. It is worth noting in passing that items purchased in this way are often more expensive than when bought directly from the shops.

When we consider the four major sources of credit we also discover that storecards are underwritten by finance companies' schemes and that the banks issue credit cards, eg Visa, Access.

Whenever you are considering credit remember three key points:

One: You are committing yourself to spend as yet unearned money.

Two: You are most likely to be purchasing luxury items, not everyday essentials.

Three: Borrowing money is expensive: the retail price plus the interest charges, which increase the longer the period you elect to pay over.

The cost of credit

As we have pointed out, nothing is free in this life. Credit costs. To find out how much it will cost, you will need to do a number of small sums each time you consider a credit purchase.

First, you will encounter the letters APR. These letters stand for the Annual Percentage Rate. Government demands that anyone offering credit must inform the customer what the APR is. And this provides you with the real cost of the goods you anticipate buying on credit.

If you are intimidated by mathematics, as we are (Mike still counts using his fingers!), you should ask the retailer to compute the APR for you. If he won't, purchase elsewhere.

In simple terms, the higher the APR figure the higher the amount of interest. Also, the shorter the period of the loan the cheaper it will be, even though the monthly payments on a long term loan are apparently so much smaller.

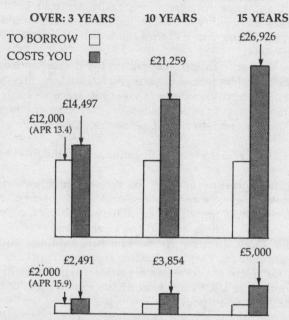

DIAGRAM 1: CREDIT AND DEBIT

OVER: 3 YEARS   **10 YEARS**   **15 YEARS**

TO BORROW ☐
COSTS YOU ▨

£26,926

£21,259

£14,497

£12,000
(APR 13.4)

£2,491   £3,854   £5,000

£2,000
(APR 15.9)

Consequences of credit

If you fail to make your credit payments you become what is known as a 'defaulter'; that is, you have defaulted on your commitment to pay. You will receive a *default notice* terminating your agreement, usually within seven days. The lender or creditor demands full and immediate payment on the outstanding sum and will charge *default interest* on whatever isn't repaid.

Furthermore, he is entitled to repossess goods if you have them on a hire purchase agreement. Or, if you had taken out a secured loan, he can take what security you

49

had agreed in order to get his money back. Beware the small print on any loan agreement, especially those wonderful newspaper ads offering to pay off all your existing debts in exchange for one more easily serviced debt. Often they demand your home as their security, and should you default you will find the roof over your head being removed.

If you do not or cannot respond to the default notice, the creditor will be forced to take you to court. As this is risky from the creditor's point of view you are more likely first to face a process of intimidation: the threat of court action, unpleasant letters and phone calls, often late at night.

Should you end up in this situation, apply the following rules:

First, tell someone outside the immediate situation. Not just anyone but someone who understands debt and will listen with a sympathetic ear. There are many locally based debt counsellors around the country today. Contact your local Citizens Advice Bureau (address and phone number in *Yellow Pages* or *Thomsons Local Directory*). Or many churches now provide help and support. Contact the UK Evangelical Alliance on 071 582 0228 for details of help in your area.

Secondly, alone with a close friend, confront your desire for purchasing all the luxuries. What is it that really affords you fulfilment and satisfaction in life? If you can break from finding your identity in what you possess, and cease comparing yourself with those around you and what they own, you will have taken a major step forward in avoiding further or future debt.

is for Groom

THE GROOM OR BRIDEGROOM is so called because his is the privilege of attending to the bride—for the rest of their lives together. Indeed, the wedding day really is the first day of the rest of your lives.

Compared with the bride's responsibilities the groom gets away pretty lightly. His specific tasks are as follows:

1. Choosing a best man or groomsman
2. Selecting ushers
3. Selecting and booking the honeymoon
4. Purchasing the wedding rings
5. Tipping where appropriate
6. Organising the departure from the wedding reception

Use the above checklist as a guide as you make all the necessary arrangements for your wedding. The specific responsibilities are outlined below.

Choosing a best man

Obviously the groom will want to select someone trustworthy to fulfil this essential task. The answer to a smooth running occasion and a stress free groom is a competent best man.

When Mike played this role first time around, on arrival at the hotel for the reception he made immediate contact with the maitre d'hotel. Requesting details of who would be making announcements and guiding the guests to their places, and who would be announcing the arrival of the bride and groom, he was surprised to learn that it was all down to him.

This entailed maintaining a watchful eye on the photographs in the hotel grounds so that on their cessation he could move the guests through to the wedding breakfast. All went well until he requested the gathering to be upstanding to receive the bride and groom, and the door opened to reveal the bride's brother returning from a comfort break.

A secure, responsible individual is indispensable since they may well have to problem solve on the run without alarming the immediate family nor enabling the guests to spot anything is out of place.

Quite frequently the groom may request his brother to fulfil the role of best man. Alternatively, it could be a good friend of long standing. It is a good idea to let your future bride know your proposed choice of best man ahead of time to get her perspective. It is worth bearing in mind that although the wedding is only one day, the marriage extends for quite a few years beyond that. To select a best man who is a good friend and who will continue to build a relationship with you and your wife over the years following is a good idea.

Mike chose a college friend to act as best man. Although we now live in different parts of the UK we keep in contact and the friendship is such that we can take up from where we left off whenever we meet up. We have also taken an ongoing interest in what the other is doing.

Once the best man is chosen, an informal invitation,

eg a phone call, should be extended. This should be done a good few months before the wedding in case he declines or is unavailable. Believe it or not some grooms don't get around to finding someone until a few days before the wedding. This is unhelpful as it leaves the groom carrying all the responsibilities for the wedding.

It is important to ensure that the best man is available on the day before the wedding ceremony. He is the means by which the groom guarantees to retain his sanity and is assured of a spare pair of legs to run around looking after him.

The best man is responsible for organising the stag party (more of which below). However, his main responsibility throughout is to attend to the needs of the groom. Therefore, ensure he is fully briefed on the day's arrangements. A visit to the reception location and an introduction to the manager can prove most helpful. Also, a conversation with the bride's parents will reassure them that you have selected a reliable individual. Hopefully they will like him as well.

If the wedding is a formal occasion and morning suits are to be hired then the best man should accompany you to Moss Bros (or similar hirer) and take responsibility for returning hire clothes afterwards. If it is less formal, then it is a good idea to invite your best man to accompany you when you go to purchase your wedding outfit. It is increasingly fashionable to match in some way, by sporting the same tie for example.

Of course the budget may not extend to purchasing. This does not matter. Hiring does work out very reasonably at around £40.00 for the weekend. Suits can be picked up the day before the wedding and returned the next day the shop is open. Alternatively, invest some money in a striking new tie or shirt to give a little extra lift to an existing suit. Or wear a flamboyant buttonhole. Of course, you could be completely radical and adopt jeans and a T-shirt but check the disposition of the bride's mother first! You could set off on entirely the wrong foot with your future in-laws.

Once the day of the wedding arrives the best man becomes indispensable. It is he who dashes out to purchase anything that you have neglected, such as cufflinks for that shirt you hired with the morning suit. When your fingers refuse to work as you get dressed it is he who secures your shirt buttons. He also protects you from unexpected and/or unwelcome visitors.

If the wedding is in the afternoon it is customary for the best man to organise a light lunch for the groom in a suitable, pleasant location. This is essential if the reception is late in the day and there is a danger of the groom passing out during the service through the deadly mixture of hunger, heat and excitement. An invitation to the groom's parents to join the lunch party is most acceptable.

Selecting ushers

Apart from the best man the groom must ensure that the ceremony itself is well stewarded. Obviously a registry office requires nothing in comparison with Winchester Cathedral. So the issue is wholly dependent upon the type of ceremony selected.

The tasks that need to be covered are:

1. Handing out orders of service
2. Escorting guests to their seats
3. Answering guests' questions
4. Directing guests for the photographs
5. Ensuring guests find their way to the reception
6. Meeting the needs of the wedding party

The ushers are usually friends or relatives of the groom. They operate under instruction from the best man. The best of ushers have the capacity to use their initiative, having been clearly briefed by the best man.

Their duties do not cease until the last of the guests have left the reception.

The importance of good ushers becomes clear once the wedding ceremony begins since both groom and best man are fully involved and cannot deal with anything apart from the business of the marriage service.

Selecting and booking the honeymoon

Consult the section headed 'H is for Honeymoon' for further, detailed information. Suffice to say here that it is the groom who must ensure all honeymoon arrangements are made.

This involves confirming bookings, collecting tickets, organising passports and valid visas where appropriate, and organising foreign currency and traveller's cheques and checking on arrangements to and from airports if relevant.

The one golden rule which cannot be stressed enough is make sure you book your honeymoon well in advance.

Purchasing the wedding rings

Before you can buy your intended her wedding ring you first have to find out what her preference is. If she has an engagement ring the wedding ring should complement it. It should be of the same material and, if gold, the same carat. She will have very set views no doubt on whether it is to be plain or patterned, thick or thin and various other aspects. Never did buying a ring appear so complex. It will also need to fit her finger and hopefully you will remember the size from purchasing the engagement ring.

Today, most fiancées accompany their bridegroom to be to purchase the ring so that a number can be tried on to see how they sit alongside the existing engagement ring.

Although gold is expensive, if you are prepared to

shop around a good deal should be found. Sometimes you will find a high street jeweller who will give you a discount if you purchase the engagement and wedding rings from the same store. Also, it is well worth while considering second hand purchase.

Finally, it will need to be decided whether the groom will also wear a wedding ring. This is becoming a very common practice today.

Both rings are entrusted to the best man on the day of the wedding and he produces them when asked to by the person officiating at the wedding ceremony.

Tipping where appropriate

It is essential to establish before the wedding if the chauffeur, for example, will expect a small tip. Mike well remembers one wedding when the groom pushed some money into his hand and said in a stage whisper, 'Go tip the driver.' If there are such tasks, equip the best man with the necessary funds and instruct him to act as appropriate.

Organising the departure from the wedding reception

Very simply, this is the area where the groom needs to prepare carefully in advance. If you are leaving a disco late at night to travel to your honeymoon hotel for a romantic first night together as Mr and Mrs, then you do not want the car so impaired that you need to stop and clean it off within a mile of leaving the waving hordes whom you imagined were your friends until you saw the vehicle.

Make sure your best man knows when you intend to leave the reception and on the day give him a half hour warning. Also, ensure that he is in charge of the car decorating ceremony. Give clear instructions as to what is and what is not permissible; this will test his leadership skills.

The greatest danger is of people tampering with your luggage, so take steps to protect yours and your wife's. Having changed into going away outfits entrust any baggage to your best man to organise taking to the car.

At the time of departure steer your wife on your arm through the revellers to both sets of parents to say farewell. Escort your bride to the car and open the door for her, ensuring she is comfortably ensconced before shutting the door. You might have prewarned her to lock it as soon as it is closed! Then get in yourself and drive off—carefully.

The stag party

This is traditionally the bachelor's last fling of freedom before entering the shackles of marriage. Fortunately, in these days of sexual equality, such sexist perspectives are disappearing. However, the idea of a night of celebration with one's male friends is still worth indulging in.

The arrangements are the responsibility of the best man. A short list of the groom's friends should be drawn up. This should also include brothers of the bride, if appropriate. The tradition of only unmarried males being eligible has largely disappeared, although women are still regarded as most inappropriate.

Invitations are informal and made by means of a phone call most conveniently. The location should preferably have a private room for such an occasion to prevent boisterous behaviour annoying other diners. The proprietor should also be informed that the booking is for a stag party. Some establishments may refuse you on that basis and it is better to arrive to a friendly welcome if the evening is to prove successful.

The cost per head is a most important item as it may limit peoples ability to attend. Since the objective is fun and frivolity, then a gourmet meal is probably unnecessary. Many restaurants are prepared to provide a set meal for a reasonable price which means the party members are aware of their costs ahead of time. It is the best man's responsibility to organise the collection of the money and payment of the bill.

Obviously the cost of the groom's meal is met by the others. After all, this is their send off to him. However, the groom may like to buy a round of pre-prandial drinks as people arrive. Indeed, the groom should ensure he is first to arrive in order to welcome his friends. He can leave the best man to worry about the practical details throughout the evening.

It is also traditional for a couple of brief speeches to be made. The first, by the best man, is to say a few words of fond farewell to the groom as he leaves bachelordom and enters the ranks of the married. It may include references to unusual and embarrassing events in the groom's life and should be humorous but never unkind.

The groom then responds, acknowledging his changing state, requesting financial assistance and doing all with a humorous air.

It is then quite appropriate for two or three other contributions from the floor. These should again be short yet amusing.

Following the conclusion of the meal the party carries off the groom to carry out some awful rite of initiation of their own choosing. Stories of grooms placed on ferries to the continent or having legs put in plaster are hopefully more apocryphal than real. However, they illustrate what should *not* be done. A bit of fun, such as a dunk in the sea or a frozen trout down the trousers, brings the stag night to a satisfactory conclusion.

The reception speech

Briefly and finally, the groom does have the privilege of making a speech at the reception. This is a nerve-wracking experience for those unused to speechmaking. However, a bit of thought ahead of the occasion can spare a lot of nervous tension.

Of the three speeches traditionally made (bride's father, bridegroom and best man) the groom's is second, following the bride's father. He is introduced by the best man.

The areas normally covered in what should be a short speech are:

1. Thanks to parents
2. Appreciation for in-laws
3. The story of how the couple met
4. Some affirmation and compliments to the bride
5. Thanks to the best man
6. A comment on the beauty of the bridesmaids
7. A toast to the bridesmaids

You don't have to be humorous. The best advice is to prepare something before the reception, stick to it and be yourself. Surprisingly, when we are true to ourselves people take to us much more easily and the speech is not an ordeal. The time honoured wisdom of 'Stand up, speak up and shut up' is worth paying heed to. In other words, make sure you can be seen by all, heard by all and are sufficiently brief so as not to bore all!

You are now set up to prove a most effective bridegroom.

A
is for
Honeymoon

ORIGINALLY 'HONEYMOON' REFERRED to the first month after marriage. Now it is used to describe the holiday taken by the newly-married couple immediately after their wedding. However, if both partners hold active and demanding jobs, a holiday proper may be delayed until some mutually convenient time in the not-too-distant future, and this again will be described as the honeymoon.

Some of you may feel it's a shame that employers are not sufficiently enlightened to restore the word to its true meaning and grant a full month off after the wedding. With the wedding day itself completed one could be forgiven for thinking that a month was not really sufficient time to recover one's energy and emotional stability after the manic attentions of parents, in-laws and assorted relatives. The stress of 'the big day' has to be experienced to be believed!

The honeymoon, therefore, is a first-class opportunity to rest and recover, as well as the start of a lifetime's commitment to each other.

Where to go

This depends on the state of your pocket and each partner's preference. Let's begin with the pocket, or the cost of the honeymoon.

Basically the sky is the limit. As you prepare for your wedding you will no doubt discover that you are very popular. You read magazines on marriage, largely filled with advertisements of what the happy couple will seek to furnish their home with. Likewise, the department store(s) handling the wedding list will also shower you with splendid magazines highlighting all the material resources the 'normal' couple require in setting out on their marriage. Hence you become prime targets for those selling holidays: '...champagne awaiting you in the bedroom, corner bath, revolving bed, eighteen course "morning after!!" breakfast', etc.

Weddings are expensive. You have also probably just undertaken a mortgage and it is only the excitement of the wedding which has prevented you from acknowledging its crippling effects. There *is* life after the honeymoon, and life that will involve expenditure. The first question therefore is: What can you afford?

Decisions on honeymoons can be taken, and are advisably taken, nine to twelve months before the wedding. This means there is no last minute rush and plenty of time to secure what you want and not settle for anything that is left. This also gives you time to save something for the cost both of the honeymoon and spending money while away.

It is at this point that you need to settle on your preference. One may like the Lake District, the other the Greek Islands. While traditionally it is the groom's responsibility to organise and pay for the honeymoon, in these enlightened days it is constructive to do some detective work, ie have a conversation about preferences. If the bride in question has a phobia about flying, take it into consideration. Such a conversation does not prevent the setting up of a surprise honeymoon but does save the awful sense of disappointment with all the related stress that brings to the relationship.

Organising the honeymoon

Having determined to what part of the world you are going, and having set a budget which you can afford and which the most persuasive travel agent will not be able to push you beyond (even though he is armed with a case of free wine and six free entry competitions promising 'the lucky winners' time share for life), you are ready to start searching.

Begin by taking advice from friends. They may have discovered the ideal honeymoon island. They should be able to direct you to a good travel agent. Remember, this is your honeymoon, so however inferior you feel stepping through the doors of the travel agents you are the customer and the customer is always right.

Decisions do not have to be made on the spot, and indeed are best not made then. Take away brochures. Ask about any little extras that will make it special for you. It does pay to let the hotel know you are a honeymoon couple, however embarrassed you may feel, since you will often benefit from special treatment. Mike well remembers discovering our hotel room filled with fresh flowers which were a delight. What's more, Katey gave him all the credit which he gladly received. It's only now she's discovered the truth!

Enquire whether your hotel is surrounded by discos that will blare out music all night so that you can avoid these if you want to. It is often a good idea to write out a list of questions before you go so that your mind doesn't go blank in the middle of a discussion with the travel agent.

Remember you will be tired. The week preceding the wedding and the day itself are demanding, physically and emotionally. Therefore organise flights sensibly. The last thing you want is to be sitting in an airport lounge at 1.00am waiting for your 'discount' flight.

By planning ahead you may choose to spend the first night at a hotel near the airport of departure or a few miles into your journey if staying in Britain. This means you have the minimum of hassle once you have got away from the celebrations, especially sensible if you will be having a disco or evening party following the reception for all those friends you were unable to invite. *The honeymoon is for your benefit so plan accordingly.*

If you are planning to honeymoon in UK, then visit the reference section of your local library. They have all the hotel, Bed & Breakfast, camping and such guides. They can also give you a pen and paper to take notes. With your preferences in mind, study the relevant key page explaining the symbols used throughout the guide. This is essential when pricing each lodging. You can find good deals to suit your pocket and meet your criteria (from city to rural isolation).

Once you have made a selection, phone the proprietor to check the guide's details remain as read, and place a provisional booking which should be followed up with a written confirmation. This can increasingly be faxed through in most cases today.

Preparing for the honeymoon

If you are travelling abroad do check with your GP or health centre nurse whether vaccinations are required. You will often need to begin these eight weeks before departure. Sometimes vaccine will need to be ordered so get organised early.

Passports are also essential for the world traveller. We know of one couple who missed their honeymoon when a helpful official *at the airport* pointed out that one of the passports was out of date. Imagine their disappointment.

We also know of a couple who successfully completed their honeymoon only discovering on their return home that one passport was beyond its expiry date. Two cases known to us, so it does happen. Check dates and details now.

Also, if you are applying for your first passport or a renewal do leave plenty of time. Bureaucracy can move exceedingly slowly and never appears to recognise special cases, however hard you argue. It is worth noting that the woman can apply for a passport in her married name before the wedding.

Many banks or travel agents require you to order foreign currency several days in advance. Work out how much you want to carry. It's convenient to carry large amounts in the form of traveller's cheques. Banks and building societies will issue these and you will need your passport with you when collecting them. The advantage of traveller's cheques is that they can be cancelled if stolen, saving you from losing your holiday money. Once abroad you can cash them at banks and many shops; always keep an eye out for the best rate of exchange and check if there is a service charge involved (usually a percentage of the amount you are changing).

It is worth talking with others who have visited your chosen romantic location to find out if it is better to carry sterling, as the exchange rate may well be in your favour within the country rather than 'cashing up' before leaving Britain.

If heading for sunny climes remember sun tan lotion, sunglasses and something for upset stomachs and headaches (the real and not the excuse type!). If remaining in Britain take suitable clothing for the unpredictable weather.

On arrival

Check into your hotel or pick up the keys to your self-catering cottage or apartment, and ensure that what you ordered or were told would be there is there. If not, summon up the courage to mention anything you are unhappy about to the reception desk or equivalent. Remember, you have paid your money so ensure you get what you have paid for. Don't just moan and complain to each other in the standard British way.

If in a hotel discover where the dining room is, how room service works (and what charges are applied when you order via room service), where the swimming pool is and what time it opens. Check meal times, morning tea/coffee, etc. If hungry on arrival order a meal.

If abroad make enquiries for maps, public transport arrangements, hiring cars, cost of taxis, etc. These details will help you to become acclimatised very quickly. Look through tours on offer or places of interest worth visiting and talk through a schedule for your honeymoon. It's good to provide some definition as to how time is to be spent; if you are both sun worshippers and there's an abundance of sun then you won't require any other diversions.

Obviously the honeymoon is about making love together; beginning a physical partnership which is akin to a journey. Over the years you will discover more about each other and what pleases your partner, and you will become increasingly expert and confident in the art of sex. (Read 'S is for Sex' for further information on this essential topic.)

The honeymoon should be the time for laying an initial foundation to your marriage. Whatever else was true about your relationship before your wedding, it was not a marriage. Now you have publicly committed yourselves to each other for life and need gently to build a strong relationship. Don't rush—you have a lifetime ahead of you. This is the start of the greatest adventure of your lives!

Honeymoon disasters

Now, for your encouragement, everything is not guaranteed to go right as you depart on your honeymoon. So if you have a disaster, don't panic; chalk it up to experience.

One couple, having left their reception, were looking forward to disappearing off to some far flung overseas location. On arriving at the airport all flights were fog bound so they spent their first night in the departure lounge. Perhaps not the most auspicious location for the first night of your honeymoon.

Another couple we know arrived safely at their destination and, having consummated the marriage, fell fast asleep only to wake with a scream when their bottoms touched in bed.

Yet another couple had the difficult task of explaining to the hotel how it was they had come to break their bed.

Perhaps the most awful experience belonged to the couple who were distressed to hear the hotel fire alarms go off five minutes after consummating their marriage. That really is a poser; do you trust it is a false alarm or do you evacuate your room?

As for us, we arrived at our hotel. Katey had a temperature of over 100° and went to bed. Mike ordered a large meal courtesy of room service and watched TV. I don't think the porter could quite believe his eyes when he entered the honeymoon suite!

J

is for
Insurance

THIS MAY SEEM a strange heading to come across
in a book on preparing for marriage. Yet very soon
you are going to commit yourself to someone else's
welfare, 'for better for worse, for richer for poorer, in
sickness and in health'. These are significant promises
and commitments to make.

Of course when we marry we basically believe it's for
better, richer and health. Naturally we don't assume it is
for calamity. If we did we wouldn't get married in the
first place. However, it is important that we think
through carefully what financial provision and protection
we are to invest in as a precaution against future difficulties.

There is nothing worse than being struck by sudden
unemployment or having your residence burgled and
discovering there is no means of meeting the financial
consequences of such events.

No doubt you will have read all sorts of newspaper ads
offering everything from car insurance to life assurance.
Alternatively, you may have been canvassed by phone or
at your door by enthusiastic and persuasive salespersons
seeking to sign you up for a policy of one sort or another.
Since their income depends a great deal on commissions

paiu out by companies on policies they have sold, it is little wonder they are so pushy.

So where do you turn to for advice? Open up your *Yellow Pages* or equivalent and turn to 'Financial Services'. You will find a list of financial advisers. You will then seek out a suitable adviser who meets certain important criteria.

First, you will want to ensure that they display a logo that tells you they are 'A FIMBRA Member'. FIMBRA is a regulatory body which everyone who wishes to offer financial advice on life assurance, pensions, investment, etc, must be registered with. The qualifications for membership are: relevant experience and a well run, financially sound and efficient business. These ground rules have been laid down by the Financial Services Act.

Secondly, you need to check that they are operating as an independent financial adviser. If they are, they will display the IFAP logo. Such an adviser is obliged by law to research the relevant policies offered by different companies and then advise you on the most beneficial course of action for your circumstances.

If you make an approach direct to a specific company, or take the advice of a broker who may be operating an agency for a certain firm, such an individual may only be operating such an agency on a part-time basis as a means of generating extra income. Alternatively, at worst they may in fact be no more than a 'cowboy' whose advice is hardly worth the paper it is written on.

It is also worth stating that if you are self-employed then the whole question of insurance is one you should get advice on as you are in a vulnerable position if you find yourself unable to work at any stage.

When it comes to insurance there are basically two types: insurance of yourself and insurance of your possessions. We are usually better acquainted with the second type.

Insurance of yourself

1. Life assurance. This, as its name suggests, is an insurance payable in the event of your death. At present, death is probably the last thought going through your mind; and quite rightly. However, it is advisable to consider the circumstances in which your partner will be left should you die. Initially, with you both earning, the only consideration may be the outstanding mortgage. You were no doubt offered a mortgage protection scheme to cover this eventuality. Basically the insurance is to pay off the mortgage in the event of the death of one of the named owners. This means no more mortgage payments and a chance to take stock. Most building societies and banks include it as part of the package. However, you don't need to take the package they offer and can seek independent financial advice for the best deal. You do not need a mortgage to take out life assurance. Most couples think more seriously about it once children arrive. If one partner were to die the sum payable would contribute towards maintaining the children, especially as one parent finds it hard to act as breadwinner as well as look after the kids. In order to obtain life assurance you will be expected to fill out long and detailed forms. All serious illnesses or existing health problems will have to be declared. Failure to do so may nullify the policy and prevent payment. Also, height and weight relationship will have a marked impact upon the premiums, so diet if necessary before you fill out the forms. Finally, the younger you start the cheaper the premiums will be.

2. Pensions. While many firms used to run a variety of pension schemes for their staff, increasingly a measure of flexibility is being introduced to enable individuals to take out their own pension scheme and transfer it with them when they change jobs. You will need to see what pension provision your place of work offers you, if any.

Again, talk of retirement and pensions may seem somewhat irrelevant but not to make some form of financial provision for later years is irresponsible. Many schemes are on offer and expert advice should be sought. With increasing concern about the environment, a growing number of companies are offering environmentally friendly policies. By this they mean they will not invest your monthly contributions in companies that do not meet the criteria they have established. Again, this may not be on your immediate priority list but should concern you both at some point in the not-too-distant future.

3. Health. This is of course much more politically sensitive and you may well have very set ideas already. Just to say health plans are available and if you have a measure of disposable income you may want to consider investing in this area. However, be careful to consider the areas of exclusion in any policy you look at.

4. Credit. We have looked at the subject of credit under the title 'F is for Finance'. However, you are able to take out insurance to cover your outstanding credit payments should you suddenly lose your job or be unable to work for some reason. This may be the sort of financial provision that makes sense in your circumstances and does mean you are not left heavily in debt if life takes a turn for the worse.

On all these types of insurance there are income tax benefits to be gained and an independent adviser can explain these to you.

Insurance of your possessions

This covers the more everyday aspects of cars and household contents. Suffice to say for such insurance you can shop around the high street or approach an independent broker. Often this will prove to be someone other than the person you have found specialising in life assurance and the like. However, such an individual can easily advise you on who to turn to.

Again, if you go for a mortgage you will probably be offered a household contents insurance deal along with the insurance you have to take out to cover the rebuilding costs of your residence should it be destroyed.

With contents insurance you may get cheaper rates if window locks are fitted or a burglar alarm is in situ. Indeed, some companies insist on these precautions in areas deemed to be high risk as far as break-ins are concerned. Also be sure to check at what value individual items need to be separately insured. When Katey's engagement ring collapsed we claimed the repair on the insurance. A letter informed us that due to its value it was not covered under the basic terms of the policy and should have been separately itemised. Fortunately, the company made an *ex gratia* payment to cover the repair, but we had discovered something new and very important.

In this whole area of insurance the principles are threefold:

1. What is relevant to our situation?
2. When does it become relevant, eg immediate need or next year?
3. How much can we afford?

Do take the budgetary question very seriously. Everything is available for a price, but can we afford to pay the price—regularly?

At all times openly discuss the provision you are making. Ensure that you both understand the policies. This is rather important if at some point one of you is left on your own. And, finally, at all times ensure that you are in full agreement.

is for
Jokes

A BRIEF RESPITE now follows. It is customary that humour is a part of the traditional speeches on the wedding day. In a moment you will find a number of jokes accumulated on our travels which may be of assistance. Mike's favourite when acting as best man is to rise to his feet and begin: 'Ladies and Gentlemen, I wish to begin by congratulating the groom on his wonderful, nay exquisite, choice of (*dramatic pause here*) best man. I know of no one who could do it better.'

The aim of all such humour is to relax people and add interest to the speeches. At a wedding, although you do not want to come over as a professional comedian, whatever your role, there is a requirement to keep an air of informality, indicating a real relationship with the bride and groom on what is their day.

Also, remember that this is not the occasion for either lewd or personal humour. The embarrassment of either bride or groom is totally unacceptable here. Hence try to include one or two funnies, as well as some words of positive affirmation, to send the bride and groom on their way.

A few funnies

'The groom had a distinguished academic career. When a visiting lecturer arrived to speak on the dangers of alcohol, he used a vivid illustration to make his point. He placed a live worm in a glass of water and one in a glass of whisky. At the end of his lecture he drew attention to the two glasses. The worm in the water was still wriggling about; the one in the whisky was stone dead.

'Turning to his audience he said: "What can be learned from this demonstration?"

'The groom, always a keen student, immediately replied, "If you want to avoid worms, drink whisky." '

'The groom is also a master of logic. On one occasion, entering a chemists to purchase some rat poison (college accommodation really is bad these days), the assistant informed him: "I'm sorry, we don't stock it. Why not try Boots?"

'Our intelligent groom replied somewhat bemused: "I want to poison them not kick them to death." '

'The groom is well known for his compassionate nature. His love for animals is perhaps not quite so well known. Travelling on a bus the other day with a baby alligator in his arms the conductor enquired if he was taking it to the zoo.

' "Don't be silly," he replied, "we are going to the cinema. We did the zoo yesterday." '

'The bride and groom have just invested in a new car and called it Daisy. Some days it goes and some days it don't. It's replaced their old car called Connie, short for constipation. It strained and strained and passed nothing.'

'The groom is certainly a man of creativity. He was seen the other day sitting in a train carriage tearing bits of newspaper up, screwing them into small balls and then throwing them out of the window. When asked what he was doing he replied: "It keeps elephants away."

' "But there aren't any elephants," his companion replied.

' "I know,' the groom responded, "It's very effective isn't it?" '

These can all be chopped and changed around with suitable comments addressed to the bride to the effect that does she really know what she has taken on board?

With one good funny well prepared, whether you are best man, groom or bride's father, you can survive the speech ordeal and come out with flying colours. Just remember to keep it short.

is for
Keeping House

OWNING OR RENTING a property carries with it a number of other responsibilities. Not all of these are that attractive at first glance; cleaning, decorating, gardening to name but a few. Yet these and many other tasks are involved in keeping house effectively. How do the newly-married couple work these issues out?

Priorities

There are a vast array of what might be termed labour saving devices currently on the market. No doubt you have either had these thrust before you in innumerable magazines and handouts designed especially for those preparing for marriage or have dreamily window shopped together through large department stores.

It is also apparent that most newly-married couples carry with them the assumption that they will begin life together at the same material point that their parents have currently attained. It may come as some surprise but parents have had quite a number of years working, earning and saving to arrive at their present financial state. Furthermore, with children beginning to spread their 'independence wings' and leave the family nest, parental overheads are diminishing—and not before time many a loving parent would gladly sigh!

As newly weds you need to establish what your disposable income is going to be; not what it might become but what it is now (see 'D is for Daily Budget'). You may well have been given many useful household items as wedding gifts (See 'W is for Wedding Day'), but you will certainly still require certain tools to enable you to keep house effectively, efficiently and conveniently.

When we were married we received £100.00 worth of gifts among our wedding presents. With Katey teaching full time, as well as Mike working in a job which entailed travelling away from home, we decided to invest the money in an automatic washing machine. This meant great excitement for Katey who came from a home where all washing had been done by hand! Indeed in our discussions it was Katey's persuasive logic that carried the day, pointing out as she did that such a labour saving device would ease our life considerably; Mike arriving home with luggage full of dirty washing and in need of an instant turnaround; Katey exhausted from teaching and running a home with three lodgers.

A washing machine was a priority for us. Indeed we got it for exactly £100.00 since we inherited a broken washing machine in the house we purchased which was worth £20.00 in exchange for a new one. It's wonderful what a bit of bartering can achieve.

So what are your priorities? List them individually and then compare lists; it can make for interesting reading and explosive conversation. Having written down your lists and compared them, work out which items are a priority and which a luxury. Luxuries are nice but may not be appropriate if the choice lies between eating an evening meal or steaming in a jacuzzi bath!

Another question worth asking is: Are you able to secure them second hand? A glance through the 'For Sale' ads in the local newspaper or cards in your local news-agent can save you pounds and give you the necessary breathing space to save for its eventual replacement with something of your choice. We were very grateful for the gift of a reconditioned vacuum cleaner which gave sterling service until it was eventually killed off by dog hairs following the purchase of a gorgeous golden retriever puppy. It then took two further vacuum cleaners to discover one that could cope with mounds of dog hair; not because we don't vacuum but because the dog moults a lot.

So don't seek to emulate the parental home immediately. The dishwasher may just have to wait. Do not get taken in by glossy adverts or smooth talking salespeople who infer that you are somehow not quite together if you are not surrounded by the most up-to-the-minute high tech paraphernalia. Rather, spend to your budget, cut corners where you can, ensure you can distinguish between a necessity and a luxury, and relax into being the couple you are and establishing the style of home you both want. The advertisers exist to market and sell. If that involves undermining individuals' self-esteem and self-confidence they will do it. So don't fall prey to their marketing skills. Retain your individuality and make your own choices in line with your budget.

Planning

So what are you most likely to need?

Vacuum cleaner, dusters and floor mop of some suitable type.

Scourer and suitable cloth for washing up. As for tea towels the rather plain 'glass cloths' have proved best value for us. Long lasting and excellent at drying, the shine on glass has to be seen to be believed!

Food processor or equivalent, depending on culinary habits.

A washing machine. A tumble dryer if you are in a flat with no garden or a studio flat (ie the bedroom and lounge are one, and space is therefore at a premium); in other instances we think this is a luxury initially.

Iron and ironing board. Clothes horse (essential throughout the winter months). Outside, we are great advocates of the old-fashioned washing line rather than rotary dryers.

Garden spade, fork, trowel and rake if you have a garden. A mower if you have a lawn, although you may be able to borrow one initially. When purchasing, go for the best mower you can. We tried several of the smaller ones (around £60.00 mark) and found them useless and a lot of hard work. We now have a motor mower which means the grass is cut in fifteen minutes and is therefore no longer the fortnightly chore it once was. The initial outlay was high but the ease of use has more than repaid us for that cost.

The above constitutes the very basic requirements for running a house effectively, efficiently and conveniently. We take it for granted that you will have a cooker and fridge. A freezer is a useful tool if organised and run efficiently; more so if you like to feed off instant convenience foods. A microwave is primarily a tool for dealing with convenience foods from the freezer and is not really an essential part of any house. However we have done away with our traditional cooker and only have a combination microwave which gives us the benefits of microwave and traditional cooking. It also takes up less space in what is a very small kitchen area.

Partnership

It's all very well having the equipment, but who is going to operate it? As yet we are not in the age of the automatic robot, and while servants are making a rapid return you are still very fortunate if you are in the income bracket which enables you to employ such (that is if you agree with the principle in the first place).

There are two routes you may choose to follow.

Route One. You identify the various tasks that need doing and allot each task to husband or wife.

Route Two. Having identified the tasks that need performing regularly, both partners co-operate in an informal way to ensure they are fulfilled.

The second route obviously requires more trust, but does have the benefit of flexibility. If one partner is over-tired, the other can perform tasks without feeling 'hard done by' or unhelpfully self-righteous. Or if one finds they are in from work early then they can get on with sorting the house rather than thinking, 'Well, I've done my tasks so I'll put my feet up and wait for dinner,' only for the other half of the relationship to charge in from work and virtually break his or her neck trying to complete unfinished tasks. This route also enables couples to maximise their free time together since they work for each other in this informal arrangement, and they have more chance of both being able to relax together than when one party still has some tasks remaining.

Success in this area does also depend on one person in the marriage being an organiser; not of their partner but of the tasks that need doing. If neither of you is a natural organiser (you don't salivate when given a Psion or Filofax) then you need to get hold of a small notebook and write down days of the week and allot specific tasks to each day. Then either partner can pick up the book and perform their allotted task (*route one*) or whatever is waiting to be done (*route two*) and mark it off as completed. Believe us, a little organisation saves a multitude of arguments.

Before we set out a hypothetical plan for the week we

want to stress that there are no tasks which are either masculine or feminine. There was a time when gardening was his affair and ironing hers. Fortunately, we now live in more enlightened times and marriage is a partnership jointly owned between husband and wife. Therefore both partners contribute to its success, and performing household tasks is part of the price of a successful marriage. So husbands and wives will have to pay the price if they are to succeed. However, you may dislike certain tasks. This is not wrong, but necessitates honest negotiation. Mike hates ironing and has taken full responsibility for the toilets in order to be relieved from wielding the iron.

Hypothetical weekly task plan

Sunday	Church, relax.
Monday	Grocery shop (usually the quietest night at the supermarket, only check times of closing first).
Tuesday	Vacuum (downstairs only). Dust.
Wednesday	Wash (overnight is a good idea and hang out next morning before work).
Thursday	Iron. DIY tasks. Baking for weekend.
Friday	Vacuum whole house and dust ready for weekend. Clean bath, sink and loo.
Saturday	'Top up' shop for weekend. Gardening.

Generate a list to include a plumber, odd-job man, gas engineer, electrician, and any other useful person. Also have a torch, candles and spare fuses easily accessible.

Finally, try to find a local window cleaner to look after the outside windows. There are a number of gadgets on the market promising to make this difficult task easy but they only seem to complicate it further. Support local industry; get a recommended window cleaner (seeking recommendations provides a good way to get to meet your neighbours).

Ten basic helps to keeping a happy house

1. Never put anything down when you can put it away.
2. Always replace the bin liner on emptying the bin.
3. Always replace the loo roll.
4. Keep a running shopping list of items to be replaced in a prominent place (and take it to the shops when you go!).
5. Use the correct tool for the job, ie screwdriver to change plugs not the nearest knife!
6. Put dirty washing in the linen basket—don't use it as an extra decoration to the bedroom.
7. Maintain a stock of spare lightbulbs and fuses in a convenient cupboard.
8. Soak saucepans immediately after use and stack crockery to save kitchen becoming an apparent junk yard.
9. Put cap back on toothpaste after use, clean discarded stubble from sink, clear away hair from plughole after washing and unblock sink or loo if you are the culprit.
10. Apologise to your partner rather than invent an elaborate excuse when you make a mistake or forget to complete some task.

is for
Leisure

IT SOUNDS SOMEWHAT inappropriate perhaps to put the question: 'What do you intend to do with your leisure time?' to a couple preparing for marriage. Yet once the novelty of being married has worn off there are quite a number of years ahead with hours to be filled.

Many couples we discover have never discussed their hobbies and interests together. Often such activities appear somewhat irrelevant during the first flush of excitement as the relationship blossoms and then wedding preparations fill every hour of the day and, so it would appear, night! Yet it is often in this area that the cracks and fissures which can lead to break up first appear.

We once had reported to us that a minister preaching from his pulpit used this area to illustrate a somewhat strange and to our minds unhelpful point. Talking on marriage he suggested that in today's 'high tech' society it was exceedingly naive to expect two people to stay together 'till death did them part'. With the increased pace of life people's interests were changing repeatedly through their lives so that the person one married could not be said to be the same person several years on. His conclusion was that we should expect to marry around three different individuals during our adult life; not at the same time of course but following 'amicable' divorces.

Obviously this is not the most wholesome of thoughts to enter marriage with. Certainly we change as the years move on. This is because of experience, circumstances, personal choices and the like. However, with clear communication there is no reason why a marriage should not mature and change along with the two principle characters. Indeed a measure of the quality of the marriage is just such an ability. This demands a commitment to effective communication (see 'P is for Partnership') and an active interest in each other's new and ongoing hobbies.

When we married we did not have much of an idea about each other's leisure interests. Mike was a reader and sportsman; Katey enjoying a strong social life, music and all gregarious activities. This indeed was one of the areas Mike found most difficult since he was not then a particularly sociable character.

Our relationship developed while we were at college. Katey's room was invariably filled with hordes of friends—something which was not to Mike's liking. In fact he felt he needed to book an appointment to have some time with Katey on her own. His reaction was often to get frustrated and moody, and failure to communicate the cause of this frustration did not help Katey to understand his condition nor allow them to talk it through to a suitable resolution. Many hours of non-communication were spent with Mike disappearing to prowl around unhappy, while Katey was trying to analyse what she had done to upset him.

It was only as we learned to discuss together and discover our different interests in life that such unhealthy and time-wasting breakdowns in communication were avoided. As a result Mike confessed his lack of social skills in company hence his insecurity when confronted by a social scene. Katey expressed her lack of interest in reading and sitting for long periods apparently doing nothing, and doing it in silence.

This was important as we entered marriage since Katey insisted that we went to bed at the same time (a practice we continue today), while Mike had to explain that he often liked to read after retiring, which had severe implications for Katey's intended late night witterings! We therefore developed a process where we retired together and Katey would go to sleep after a brief witter, leaving Mike to read. The compromise was that Katey had to learn to sleep with the light on!

These may sound very trite issues but they are the bread-and-butter issues of marriage.

As the years have passed we have discovered interests that we can share together. Mike's first attempts at gaining Katey's interest were fairly high risk and reveal a lot about Mike's lack of diplomacy.

The first occurred while living in Wolverhampton. Celebrating Katey's birthday Mike booked up a meal at a local restaurant. All went well and Katey was delighted with the romantic setting and the thoughtfulness of her partner. Having been promised a further treat after lunch, Katey left the restaurant with a spring in her step and anticipation in her heart. Her excitement turned to horror when she found herself passing through the turnstiles at Molyneaux with the expectation of watching Wolverhampton Wanderers v Norwich. (A soccer match for the uninformed!) Always positive in outlook Katey did appreciate the legs of the players for a full ninety minutes of play!

A similar and second such incident occurred in celebration of one wedding anniversary. Living in Leeds at the time Mike whisked Katey off to Headingly for the day. For those who are not quite sure, this is the home of Yorkshire cricket and also a test match ground. Katey was to have the privilege of seeing the third day's play between England and New Zealand. What had appeared very promising, with a large hamper being loaded into the car, appeared to be turning into a nightmare. However, a strange metamorphosis took place and Katey actually enjoyed the day. Since then she has very much taken to cricket and in this dubious way we discovered a shared interest. Football remains a no go area!

It is advisable to avoid such high risk strategies in discovering shared interests. Not that you will want to do everything together; nor should you. Mike enjoys bird-watching as a hobby. It's not something Katey has any great aspiration to get into. It also affords Mike time and space to himself which he appreciates and needs in order to retain his sanity. So how is it you establish what your and your partner's leisure pursuits are? How do you determine areas of shared interest?

Below is a short questionnaire. Each of you should complete it and then talk through your answers together.

LEISURE QUESTIONNAIRE

1. How many close friends do you have?
2. How often do you see them?
3. Where or in what context do you see them (eg pub, football training)?
4. Does your partner know/like your friends?
5. Will they be welcome in the new home you'll be sharing together?
6. If not, why not?
7. What is your favourite memory from childhood?
8. What were your hobbies as a child?
9. Do you still maintain any of these hobbies? Which ones?
10. Why did you stop them (eg boredom, time factors, grew out of them)?
11. What leisure interests have you now?
12. Does your partner know/share them with you?
13. How do you unwind?
14. Do you enjoy your own company?
15. How do you spend spare time?
16. List in order of preference the following activities:

(a) Board games
(b) Reading
(c) TV
(d) Videos
(e) Music—type and bands
(f) Sport—type and frequency
(g) Walking
(h) Theatre
(i) Gardening
(j) Other (identify)
17. Where do you like to holiday?
18. What do you like to do on holiday?
19. What would you do with a free evening?
20. Do you have a regular day off each week?

Now you have talked your answers through you will have a far fuller picture of what your partner's leisure interests are. It might also have proved helpful in shedding light on your own pastimes.

It is worth looking at why you finished with some of your childhood hobbies. Obviously we grow up and out of certain activities. (Mike no longer races Corgi cars!) However, sometimes the increased pace of life that usually accompanies teenage years (exams and social life) and then entry into the world of work can squeeze hobbies out.

Mike certainly found this true in his experience. A marvellous teacher called Mr Talents captured Mike's imagination with the world of nature. He remained interested in animal and bird life for most of his childhood. However, as he grew up, partly because it wasn't very 'in' to discuss the mating habits of the badger and partly through lack of time, this interest fell into disrepair. Only in the last few years has he taken up this interest again and found it affords as much pleasure today as it did then.

Sometimes we need to make time to enjoy ourselves. We must all find effective ways to unwind. Often it costs very little to indulge our leisure interests. Increased stress through work and life in general requires that we learn how to rid ourselves of tension and rediscover that life is good on balance, and that we make time to appreciate ourselves as well as each other. The growing incidence of stress-related illnesses, such as ME, indicates that we cannot ignore making time to unwind and relax.

However, it is not always easy to relax. Time on our hands without knowing what to do can lead to pressure and argument. So knowing how we like to relax individually and together helps to ensure that we maximise any leisure time we have. Although it might sound a little contrived, it is important to think about and talk through how to spend free time. Nothing is more frustrating than the feeling that a day together has been frittered away to no purpose. Alternatively, it is equally distressing when one partner is participating in an activity under sufferance, wishing they were doing something else.

So how do we avoid such pitfalls? We always agree how we will spend time off. Imagine that we have a day off together coming up. We know what our interests are, both individual and joint, and so we run through the list to see what grabs us. To illustrate, consider the following list:

Mike's Interests	Katey's interests	Day off activity
Birdwatching	Gardening	Tiredness level
Reading	TV	Weather
Photography	Cooking	Personal space
Walking		Outstanding chores
Cycling	Cycling	Family
Cricket	Cricket	Friends
Historic buildings	Historic buildings	Funds
Public gardens	Public gardens	
Music (classical)	Music (classical)	

Let us concentrate on the final column. These are factors that will enable us to select what we want to do with leisure time.

Tiredness level has a direct bearing on what we feel able to do. If we have been very busy we will not want a long drive. We will probably decide to 'get up slow' as we say. Alternatively, if Katey is tired Mike may opt to get up early and go birdwatching, hence not infringing on time together later.

Weather also has a bearing. A good day suggests a visit to a public garden. A bad day in spring demands a birdwatching trip before breakfast and after tea. Cool but fine may entice us to cycle out for a pub lunch and a cream tea.

Personal space causes us to check how much space we each feel we need to do our own thing. Mike might read for a couple of hours in splendid isolation. Katey may wish to repot a few house plants.

Outstanding chores requires an honest consideration about what ought to have been done around the house from a six-foot lawn and fortnight's ironing to repairing the washing line or installing the smoke alarms.

Family is a check to ensure we haven't ignored parents and assorted kith and kin. We try to make visits to maintain good contact and to keep in touch with all family developments.

Friends often get drawn into our time off. Some enjoy historic houses, others birdwatching or cycling. All enjoy a meal and we often conclude a day off by inviting friends around. It is important to get the balance right between time together and time spent socially. Given what we said above it's worth pointing out that Katey has successfully socialised Mike; a leopard can change his spots with care, craft and a willingness to enrich the marriage relationship.

Funds are often the critical question. A day out without any spending money is a disaster. Every trip needs to be budgeted. It's no good finding that antique light oak bureau on an expedition and either bankrupting yourselves or returning home disappointed, having missed the chance to get something special for the house. Funds have implications affecting whether, when driving any distance, we take sandwiches or plan for lunch out, for example.

Take time to create three similar lists for yourselves. Add your own name and remember to review these lists on, say, an annual basis.

A further area which does require much discussion is holidays. Some like to lay for hours under the sun. Others choose to explore local towns. Yet others struggle with the heat and would prefer Iceland. Additionally, hay fever or some such allergy may prove a factor in choosing locations.

A holiday is for relaxation, rest and recuperation. Therefore both partners must be happy with destination, location and planned activity. Skiing may be wonderful for her but an absolute nightmare for him. Come to a conclusion on what sort of holidays you plan for.

Katey loves to stay at home. If away, she gets bored after a maximum of ten days. We build our holiday plans around these factors. Mike likes to rot and do nothing. That provides another factor. Neither of us likes lazing in the sun; although Mike definitely likes water activities more than Katey does.

If you are an avid skier or yachtperson and your partner does not share your passion then consider taking a week at some point in the year to disappear to indulge your passion. But make sure your spouse has the finance and opportunity to enjoy themselves back home. Perhaps they can visit friends or go on their own special holiday as well.

Be aware of the temptation which can lurk on such solo holidays and don't get caught up in a short-term extra-marital affair. Make sure you maintain some form of contact, either by phone or regular and inventive correspondence.

One final point. With both of us having full-time jobs it is easy to get into diary mismanagement. Katey can invite people who arrive to meet the guests Mike has offered a meal to. This can prove both a source of embarrassment and antagonism. Hence we do seek to get our diaries together on a monthly basis and learn what each other is doing. This also means that if we know the other won't be in for a particular evening one of us is not waiting around for a romantic evening.

What's more we can also plot in our days off throughout the year ahead, and make the most of our time with each other. A day off is sacrosanct so nothing or no one intrudes without mutual agreement.

is for Mortgage

EVERY COUPLE NEEDS somewhere to live. Finding a place of your own must be a priority especially when the wedding day looms nearer and nearer!

There are two obvious choices: (a) to buy; (b) to rent.

Some couples do not manage to find accommodation of their own and end up living with one or other set of parents. This situation is not one to be encouraged as it can present a whole host of problems and pressures. Part of marriage is leaving your parents' home and setting up home together in a new household. It is important to establish your own identity as a couple. If you live with parents you may still be seen very much as children. Obviously house buying can be a very stop-and-start business and you may need somewhere to live for just a week or two. We would still encourage you to make this as short a time as possible.

So how do you go about buying a house? Most of us are not in the position to buy a property outright so we need to arrange a mortgage. We remember when we did this. All of a sudden we felt very grown up, It must have been the idea of borrowing all that money!

Taking out a mortgage

The first step. The first step in the mortgage maze is to find out how much money you can borrow. In order to do this it will be necessary to visit the building societies and banks in your area. Some will see you without an appointment but others prefer an arranged time. It is a good idea to dress fairly smartly and have the relevant facts, like your annual salaries, easily accessible (a monthly pay slip will do), so that you can answer any questions you may be asked.

When we tried to get our first mortgage we walked up the high street visiting all the building societies. It was very depressing when we were refused at every society. There was one more to try and we went in holding out very little hope. Amazingly enough we were offered enough money to enable us to go for the house we had seen. It is always worth trying all the possibilities.

These days most building societies will lend two and a half times the joint income. For example:

His salary	£10,000
Her salary	£ 7,500
Total	£17,500 x 2.5 = £43,750

This couple could expect to borrow £43,750 from the building society on a mortgage. It is not necessary to buy the most expensive house that you can afford. Remember that mortgages have to be paid every month!

The second step. You now know your price range. Now is the time to go house hunting. There are many estate agents who will be able to furnish you with house details. Know in your mind what type of property you would like, eg flat (purpose built or converted), house (terraced, semi-detached or detached). Decide upon the area(s) you would like to live in and go to the estate agents in the same area. Most agents make an appointment for you to view a house; some accompany you.

When viewing a property it is a good idea to take the details with you and to jot down anything which strikes you while wandering around. If you look at a lot of properties it is amazing how easily you forget what they are like. Interior decoration can be changed quite easily and comparatively cheaply. The important points to look for are: is the house laid out as you would like it; is there enough room and moreover do you like it?

When you have found a house you like and can afford, make an offer. Don't be afraid to return to the house again to view it for a second or third time. You will be spending a lot of money, after all! The offer should be made to the estate agent either in person or by phone.

The next step is up to the person selling the house (the vendor) to accept or decline the offer. If accepted it is all systems go. You need to instruct a solicitor to act for you. You do this by phone, by letter or in person. Your building society or bank can recommend a solicitor if you do not have contact with one.

The third step. You will need to provide 5% of the selling price of the house as a deposit. The rest of the money is usually provided by the building society as a mortgage. Approach the building society and ask for a firm mortgage offer. Remember, you may not need or want to borrow the maximum. The more you borrow, the higher the monthly repayments. Think very carefully before finally deciding.

Types of mortgage available

Repayment mortgage. The capital sum borrowed plus the interest are repaid, normally over twenty-five years, but the length of time can be flexible. You also pay for a

Mortgage Protection Policy which gives life insurance cover.

The advantage of this type of mortgage is that if you get into financial difficulty you can extend the term and therefore reduce the payments, or you can defer payment on the capital and pay the interest only for an agreed length of time.

The disadvantages of this type of mortgage are that you don't get full tax relief for the whole period of time and there is no savings element.

Endowment mortgage. You pay the interest only on the amount borrowed. At the same time you pay money into an endowment policy which accumulates over the period of the mortgage. At the end of the term there should be enough money to repay the initial amount borrowed with some money left over.

The advantages of this type of mortgage are that you get full tax relief for the whole period, the endowment policy is portable and can go with you each time you move, this method is designed to be a way of investing.

The disadvantages of this type of mortgage are that there is no guarantee the outstanding balance will be paid back, if you get into financial difficulty there is little you can do but convert to a repayment mortgage; when interest rates are high this can be more expensive.

Pension plan mortgage. If you have a Personal Pension Plan you can link it into a mortgage. It would be a mortgage where you paid interest only and instead of having an endowment policy the PPP is used. At the end of the term the proceeds from the PPP are used to pay off the outstanding balance on the mortgage and you can opt either for a cash lump sum or a pension at retirement age.

Extra costs.

* Buildings insurance—this is obligatory.
* Contents insurance—this is optional (see 'I is for Insurance').
* Payment protection plan against accident, sickness or unemployment. This is again optional.
* Valuation fee for building society survey—this is obligatory.
* Indemnity premium—one-off payment payable at completion.
* Solicitor's fees.
* Private survey—this is in addition to the building society or bank survey and is optional. Ensure that you get a figure quoted to you before issuing instructions to carry out the survey. It is usually quite expensive, but advisable, especially on an older property.
* Stamp duty

The fourth step. Once you have decided which type of mortgage to go for the building society or bank will, in due course, issue an offer of advance in writing. Then all you have to do is wait for the completion of searches and for the exchange of contract date.

Solicitors normally take a minimum of six weeks to execute the legal work and need to be regularly chased by you if you are in a hurry. The offer of advance normally takes about two weeks. The solicitor needs written confirmation of the advance before the completion can take place.

You will be given the key to your property by the estate agent upon completion. The house is then yours (and the building society's, of course)!

Renting

Many young couples start their married life renting their accommodation. There are agencies dealing solely with rented accommodation and some estate agencies have a department which deals with renting.

Once you know which area you would like to live in find the appropriate agencies and visit them. They will be able to let you know what is available and to arrange viewing. It is important to make sure that any agreement entered into is on a legal basis. Alternatively, you may choose to enter into a private renting agreement. Again, this must be done on a firm legal footing.

Decor

When you take possession of your new home it may not be decorated quite as you would like. It is important at this stage not to attempt to do too much at once. If you are near the wedding you do not want to exhaust yourself by decorating morning, noon and night.

As a couple you need to decide what colour schemes you would like to follow in which rooms. We took possession of our first home about ten weeks before our wedding. We wanted to do everything before we were married but soon realised that we couldn't. Therefore we decided to decorate our bedroom and spent a long time choosing wallpaper, paint and curtains. It was a large room and wasn't finished before the wedding day. However it didn't matter. Decorating together it was Mike who demonstrated the expertise. Once finished we loved it and it was very much our room.

In order to change the appearance of a room you do not need to spend much money. Lining paper and paint, with perhaps an attractive border, can make all the difference, as our current residence demonstrates. Old and somewhat tatty furniture can be transformed by throwing over brightly coloured blankets or sheets. Floor coverings can be very expensive but stripped and varnished floorboards are very attractive (and fashionable) with scatter rugs. Curtaining is expensive but charity shops, jumble sales and relations often supply excellent bargains.

If possible concentrate on colour which can give a unifying appearance to bits and pieces around the house. Whatever the decor it will always look better when everything is clean and sparkling, so make that your aim.

The bare necessities

Having acquired your house you will now need to start thinking about what you will require when you live there. Starting from scratch is very exciting but can also be expensive. It might be a good idea to add one or two ideas to your wedding list such as a box of basic groceries, first aid kit and cleaning materials.

We have listed some basic necessities in order to act as a rough guide and prompt to your own thinking. Please play around with this chart, adding or subtracting as you choose.

Tinned goods	*Household goods*	*Dry goods*	*Groceries*
Tomatoes	Matches	Tea	Vinegar
Baked beans	Tin foil	Coffee	Instant potato
Tuna	Greaseproof	Salt	Oxo cubes
Pie fillings	Paper towels	Pepper	Cereal
Fruit	Dish cloths	Flour	Mustard
Kidney beans	Scouring pads	Rice	Dessert mixes
Various veg	Washing liquid	Sugar	Marmalade
	Toilet rolls	Herbs	Jam
	Soap	Spices	Marmite
	Toothpaste	Cocoa	
	Candles	Spaghetti	
	Bin liners	Pulses	

N
is for Negotiation

U NDER 'P IS FOR PARTNERSHIP' we deal with the whole issue of communication. In this section however we wish to look at the ways in which at times we must negotiate with one another in order to take decisions with which we both agree.

Depending upon your strength of character, education and upbringing you will find it either easy or difficult to take decisions. It really doesn't matter where you find yourself here. Nevertheless, you will very quickly discover that life turns on decisions. While as a single person you could regret but get away with bad decisions, once you are married your decisions affect someone else.

Mike is a very decisive person. He has not always been so but as he has matured he has developed a capacity to decide something and go with it. There is one situation though in which he detests making decisions. That is when he is relaxing. As far as he is concerned, once he is not working he doesn't want to be decision-maker.

Katey on the other hand prefers someone else to take the lead. Partly this is because it was the role Mike adopted from early on in their married life and she didn't challenge it but rather went along with it and actually found that she quite liked it.

Difficulties arose when Mike would ask Katey what she fancied doing on a day off. He wanted her to be the decision-maker, but she replied that she didn't mind. This frustrated Mike and led to argument, atmosphere and the waste of a good chance for a relaxing day together. What could make it worse was if Mike took the initiative at that point and at some time during the day Katey made reference to the fact she'd rather be somewhere else. Guaranteed thermo-nuclear explosion from Mike!

In discussion together we aired the problem (in similar terms to those above) and came to some practical conclusions:

For Mike:
A bad decision was better than no decision at all.

He really wanted to organise something Katey wanted to do and not assume that what he initiated was OK.

He couldn't abdicate all responsibility for decision-making just because it was a day off.

For Katey:
Decision-making was as much Katey's responsibility as Mike's, and not just limited to days off or when Mike felt like sitting back.

She must communicate her preferences in order that Mike could see he was investing time in a way that pleased her.

Decisions had to enjoy the clear support of both Mike and Katey.

As a result some very healthy talking went on. In order to achieve what we had identified, a number of practical steps were introduced. For example on days off, or as one approached, Mike would list a number of options with a request that Katey either choose one or play a random card and go for something completely different of her own making. Alternatively, he would ask Katey to think through and organise the day off. This also meant that surprise was reintroduced into Mike's life since he would be entirely in Katey's hands.

This is an outline of what we understand by the term

negotiation. Much as some politician or diplomat there are occasions when we cannot assume our way is the right or only way. We must consider our partner and *create space for debate and discussion before reaching our decision.*

This subject of negotiation is particularly important in six key areas. We have set them out below:

1. Career/Vocation

At the start of your marriage you may both be working. You may be in the fortunate position of enjoying your job. Again, you may be pursuing a vocation such as nursing or teaching. This is fine until one of you is offered promotion which entails a geographical move. Is the promotion sufficient reason on its own to move? Is the partner who stands to lose their job through the move prepared for that?

When after three years of marriage Mike considered a request from his employers to move, he first took it to Katey. She was at the time teaching in a comprehensive school in the Midlands and doing very well. After discussion we decided to move with Mike's job which meant Katey resigning her teaching job.

The consequence was that she was unable to find another teaching job and had to teach supply which she finds most dissatisfying. So there was a cost for her. It was essential therefore that the decision had been discussed and agreed before any action had been taken.

Of course, not to accept promotion might mean either retrenchment or even redundancy. Sometimes such are the costs involved in maintaining a strong marriage. The number of divorces as a result of job relocations is appalling. If you cannot move in agreement either wait till you can or stay put.

What if the children are grown up and the wife is considering a return to work? Traditional thinking that the wife's place is in the home may need to be challenged. Also, many women returning to work face a crisis of confidence and husbands will need to be attentive, sensitive and supportive.

Finally, if one of you is made redundant or is unemployed there is a need to be sensitive to the stress of that situation. Often the unemployed partner can feel they are not contributing effectively to the household and are in fact the weak link in the relationship. The 'working' partner, if we can put it like that, needs to be practical and caring in the way he or she involves the unemployed partner in the daily decision making and invests them with dignity.

2. Relocation

We have looked at moving house in the light of promotion or a change at work. However, there is great importance in involving your partner in all aspects of moving house. We heard of a couple where the husband went ahead with buying and selling the family home without telling his wife. You can imagine her shock when she suddenly learned her home was sold and that she was moving to a property she had never seen!

Often more is invested in the bricks and mortar than pounds and pence. Individuals develop a sense of security in where they live and in their neighbours round about. Therefore it is important that you come to a common mind when considering moving.

3. Finance

It is important that each partner in the marriage is free to spend the 'loot'. In 'D is for Daily Budgeting' a lot of this ground is covered. This is a reminder that all major purchases should be discussed together and agreement reached on the item in question, and the price band in which to spend.

Mike has an interest in ornithology and regularly looks at catalogues of birdfeeders as he seeks to attract a wider diversity of birds to the garden. However, he will always talk it through with Katey before he makes an order. Likewise, Katey will check with Mike the budget she has on going to the sales or out to look for a new outfit. In fact Mike often goes along as well as he enjoys picking clothes for Katey.

4. Leisure

Again this is covered in its own section yet we need to be sensitive to each other. A couple we know well are affected at this level. The husband is a keen and devoted carp fisherman. This entails sitting at the lakeside night and day, the worse the weather the better, in the hope of hooking a large fish. Once landed, weighed and photographed the fish is returned to the water. Well, it takes all sorts! In order to follow that interest they sit down and plan the fishing trips into the diary ahead of the season. Time is negotiated and set in place. Each knows the score and life goes on untroubled.

It is essential that our partner at no time feels they are being replaced by a hobby. Agreement is essential therefore over time allocations to our leisure pursuits. We must turn the tide on computer widows/widowers and ensure our hobbies refresh us and enrich our marriage.

5. Role

Entering marriage we may carry a load of unhelpful assumptions concerning our expectations of our partner; for example, she will cook my meals and wash my socks; he will plumb in my washing machine and decorate my house. The problem may be that neither of you have the skills nor inclination to meet your partner's expectations.

The idea is that in marriage you should complement each other. To do that you first have to establish what each other is gifted in. Then identify what each other is interested in exploring.

When we first married Mike never cooked. But over

the years he has developed both an interest and a skill in that area. Katey meanwhile has taken to exploring gardening. Often, once the mystique is removed it is easy to apply ourselves to something we have never tried before. We know of couples where she is the best decorator and odd job person; he is best deployed cooking and child minding. We must talk these things through and not assume. We must not criticise our partner on the basis that they are not fulfilling what we assumed they would, and we must become creative at inventing alternative lifestyle patterns.

6. Preferences

Both partners in any relationship will have preferences with regard to how they envisage the marriage developing. There will be aspirations as to what they see their partner becoming in the years ahead. These can act as a trap. You must own your aspirations for your partner and yourself as these will subtly affect your thinking and influence your decisions.

One of the most difficult problems in any marriage when there is an unresolved dispute is to avoid getting locked up to each other. When each of you is convinced that, finding a *modus vivendi* is virtually impossible.

We are always struck by the fact that of the many couples who come to us because their marriage is apparently failing, the first contact is made only when the situation is well out of hand. It's like the fire brigade being summoned to a burning building, but on arrival discovering that the fire has such a hold they cannot extinguish the blaze.

In preparing couples for marriage we always advise them to seek out a couple known to and trusted by them both, who have several quality years of marriage under their belts. We encourage them to develop this friendship so that at moments of stress they can go and get advice and assistance. So often the bleakest of situations lightens once shared with reliable friends.

There are certain ground rules to be observed. Never talk about an issue outside of the marriage without your partner knowing that you are going to do so. You do not require their permission but it is important that you do not act in an underhand way. Often the very fact that you mention speaking of the issue outside the privacy of the marital home is sufficient to provoke the situation to an amicable resolution.

Also, never confide exclusively in a member of the opposite sex. The hackneyed phrase 'You see, my wife doesn't really understand me' has been the beginning of more extra-marital affairs than one cares to mention. The objective of calling upon the wisdom of others is to strengthen your marriage; not to solicit sympathy or recruit supporters.

With the loss of the extended family in our society and the common practice of children marrying and moving some distance away from their parents the informal network of advice has all but disappeared. Therefore we must recognise that we cannot survive on our own, nor are we intended to. We can learn a lot from others, and relationships with other couples can provide a wealth of helpful hints through to advice which will help our marriage at difficult points.

We have appreciated the advice and support of trusted friends at times of difficulty or pressure, such as the time we had to contend with the thought of remaining a childless couple. Therefore seek out such friends and do not be afraid to call upon their help. If you do find that you have no one to whom you can turn then contact the organisation Relate. Their address and phone number are in the phone book under Relate. However, you may need to wait several weeks before an appointment.

𝑶

is for Offspring

C HILDREN ARE STILL assumed to be very much a consequence of a successful marriage. Ever since on their creation God instructed Adam and Eve to 'be fruitful and multiply' in the opening chapter of the Bible, this has happened with almost monotonous regularity! However, children do present us with some important questions. There are significant repercussions to what can appear a relatively simple decision to have children. They can prove to be an impossible strain upon the relationship as easily as they can prove a source of delight.

At this point pause to complete the following questions. Each of you should complete it independently by placing ticks in the appropriate column. At the end of these questions further direction will be given.

	Very much	A lot	OK	Not a lot	Dislike
I want kids.					
I enjoy kids					

I enjoyed
my child-
hood

I like my
parents

I liked
school

You should both have a completed table of ticks. They
will provide you with ample material for talking together
as an entry point into the whole subject of children.

It cannot be assumed that everyone both likes and
enjoys children. Sometimes one partner can express a
strong affection for kids which the other partner feels it
impossible to do anything but assent to. Then several
years into marriage the issue of going for a baby causes
both tension and disagreement, simply because the subject has never been discussed.

We have had young marrieds with a couple of years'
marriage under their belt come to us and with a certain
amount of nervousness enquire if they are wrong
because they do not feel they want to have a family. Our
response is to check carefully the reasons, but if they
have properly thought and talked the issue through we
have no difficulty with a conscious decision not to start a
family. Such decisions are not final and can and should
be reviewed from time to time. Many such couples have
devoted the time which would have been invested in
children to community service, either within the UK or
overseas.

Sometimes, however, our experiences of childhood
can themselves deeply affect our view of parenting; both
our desire to become a parent and our sense of ability to
carry such responsibility. If we have had difficult childhood experiences we should communicate them to our
partner. He/she is marrying into our history as much as

our present and the consequences of past experiences have a significant impact on the marriage we will build.

Therefore, in the light of the above chart, talk through parents, school days and childhood experiences and memories. If there are real bleak spots which are a source of emotional pain you may be advised to get some professional help from a counsellor. This could be organised through an informal conversation with your GP or your local church leader. Alternatively, a conversation together with a trusted and mature friend can release a lot of the emotions which have been bottled up for years.

We have known someone who was totally unable to bring herself to talk about her childhood years. She never recalled stories from the home she had grown up in and gave no indication of having any affection for her parents. It was as though there was a whole portion of her life over which a curtain had been drawn. As a result she was determined to avoid creating the same climate for her own children yet, having never talked the issues through, she was totally dependent on her wisdom alone in handling their upbringing.

The difficulty became acute in her children's teenage years when a serious break occurred, similar it turned out to the one which she had experienced herself. It took many years of hard work to recover the relationship between her and her children. Perhaps some of the pain could have been avoided through frank talking at an earlier stage. The family home could have been better prepared and the couple better equipped for parenting. Talking together and learning from each other can help us all to avoid repeating the mistakes we felt we were subject to.

As we pointed out in the section on engagement, our childhood and teenage experiences can severely shape our perceptions and determine our ability or otherwise to handle relationships. Our partner must know who they are marrying, and the question of children often brings anxieties to the surface.

Once you have established your personal view on children you may need to engage in discussions as to how your personal and different perceptions can be brought together. Do not bring children into a divided household. They will pick up and eventually play on the differences between you. Even where you take a radically different view on some action taken by your partner (eg a disciplinary issue), wait until you are alone before discussing it. *Do not disagree in front of the children.*

Starting a family

Agreement over the timing of this is essential. The trend is to leave starting a family later and later. This enables both partners to pursue a successful working life before babies arrive. With modern methods of contraception available, control over the timing and number of children is in most instances in the hands of the couple themselves.

This has obvious benefits, yet there are hidden difficulties. When for example children are delayed until the quality of life desired has been established by the couple, the children ultimately may be expected to 'fit in' to the dream lifestyle existing within the imagination of the couple. Unfortunately babies seldom do. They will play havoc with your SPALA (Stripped Pine And Laura Ashley)* home. The quiet evenings disappear and life begins to be dictated to a necessary degree by the routine of the child.

You both need to be honest about how selfish you are. Are you available to serve one another by each fulfilling

---

*We are indebted to Phil and Julie Stokes for this helpful descriptive item.

turns with the baby. Are you creating space for this infant to express itself in your home or more concerned about maintaining a sense of sterile cleanliness throughout ensuring your house reflects the centre spread of *Homes & Gardens* rather than a family residence? Toys and a measure of untidy chaos will enter your home together with that new babe.

You will need to reorder your lifestyle. Perhaps both of you have worked up to this point. Now the child will prevent this; it requires attention and care twenty-four hours a day. The following must be given some thought. Will you:

1. Take a traditional line and allow the wife and mother to continue at home to invest in bringing up the baby?
2. Act radically and explore role reversal with the husband and dad leaving work to look after the baby?
3. Follow the increasing trend to each follow your careers and employ a nanny to take responsibility for the child?
4. Involve immediate family members (grandparents, for example) to provide support in the child's upbringing?

These issues should be well discussed in the early years of marriage. Many men retain a very traditional view of family and are threatened by the thought of working mothers. This can prove aggravating to women who feel totally frustrated by childrearing. It may well have a bearing on geographical relocation should that mean moving away from close family.

Obviously there are laws concerning maternity leave for which the wife will continue to receive a measure of income. Some enlightened companies are also offering paternity leave these days!

Each of the above approaches is workable but which best suits your personality, objectives and budget?

Preparing for a family

Once you have decided to try for a family then preparations need to be made. Is there sufficient space in your accommodation? If you are not planning to have a 'family bed' it is helpful for the child to have a room of its own. This retains your own distinct relationship as a married couple and creates a sense of space and territory for the baby.

There is no need to invest in all the sentimental nonsense that is all part of the baby industry today. You will obviously want to make the nursery special, but this is far more for your satisfaction and enjoyment than for your offspring's since they won't notice if the walls are white woodchip or Peter Rabbit! However, some form of visual stimulation is recommended for the baby's benefit.

It is essential to draw up a budget for the baby's arrival or you may be surprised by the costs. We have drawn up a list of essential items below. Take a trip to your local supermarket and discount chemists and price the items so that you begin to see the real costs of preparing for Baby.

The Jayne Scott basic baby list

Baby
6 babygrows for use day and night (cheaper on packets of three)
4 bodysuits (vests) (cheaper in packs of two)
3 cardigans
2 pairs of mittens
1 bonnet (2 if a winter baby)
1 pramsuit if winter
1 sun hat if summer
1 shawl

Changing
changing bag

changing mat

Nappies

(a) Terry nappies

24 terry nappies
4 pairs of waterproof pants
200 disposable nappy liners
nappy pins
nappy bucket with lid
1 kilo sanitising powder

(b) Disposable nappies

(These vary in price and size. A newborn gets through
between 5-8 a day. They are cheaper when bought in bulk.)
nappy sacks

Bath

2 hooded towels
1 baby bath

Toiletries

top and tail bowel
zinc and castor oil
cotton wool balls
cottonbuds
baby wipes
baby talc
baby soap
baby shampoo

Feeding

(a) Breast

2-3 good fitting nursing bras
nipple cream
disposable nursing pads

(b) Bottle

6 bottles (cheaper in packs)
spare teats
cold water steriliser (alternative steam steriliser)
bottle brush

sterilisation tablets
6 bibs

Miscellaneous
baby nest
brush and comb set
baby chair/bouncer

Finally, be assured Baby's arrival will also affect your current lifestyle. One of you will need to stay in of an evening to care for Baby. You are therefore not as mobile as you were; especially as a couple. Of course over the first few months Baby can travel with you and it is worth while borrowing or buying second hand a travel cot for this purpose. Once a little older your wings will be clipped unless you have a long line of willing babysitters.

Also, you will be on night duty, and interrupted nights of sleep lead to tiredness and irritability. Most mothers we have spoken to speak of feeling desperate for sleep at times, and support for them from sensitive husbands is essential. This is when family members living close are invaluable.

There will also be the need to guarantee space away from Baby in order to retain sanity. Plan carefully to get out together and keep enjoying your relationship. Also, keep up your social friendships. If Mum (or Dad) is with Baby all day she (or he) will need adult stimulation at regular intervals.

Childlessness

Of course there is the possibility that you may discover that you are apparently unable to have children. The likelihood is one that slowly dawns as you keep trying to conceive but don't.

If you have been trying to start a family for a year without success it is worth while making contact with your GP. Initially, he or she is likely to have a friendly conversation with you and ask several questions about your sex life with your partner. It is helpful if you can attend the surgery together for mutual support, but beware many men feel highly threatened by the thought of not being able to father children.

The initial test will normally be a sperm count to check the viability and motility of the man's sperm. This involves masturbating into a glass jar and can be done at home or at the surgery or hospital if you have been referred to an infertility clinic at that stage. The only important factor is to get the glass jar to the laboratory (all organised by GP or hospital) before the sperm dies.

If the sperm passes, then a referral to the infertility clinic will enable further investigations to discover why conception is proving a problem. This may involve surgery. If there is little that can be done surgically there is today the possibility of 'test tube' babies. There are moral and financial implications to a decision to proceed in this direction, and you and your partner will have to talk seriously about such matters.

The overriding impact of infertility, especially for the woman, is the emotional consequences. This can lead to irrational and extreme behaviour and requires great support, strength and understanding from the husband. It is a circumstance which will test individual character and the commitment of the couple to their relationship. It is essential not to keep silent but to find sensitive and trustworthy friends in front of whom you can be yourselves and who can provide a measure of external support.

If you do face infertility, and just because you have one child it does not mean you won't face secondary infertility, then there is an organisation you should contact for information and advice. This is: National Association for the Childless, 318 Summer Lane, Birmingham B19 3RL. There is also a helpful book detailing our own experiences in this area entitled *Two's Company*.

Testament of Childlessness published by Kingsway Publications or available from the EA, Whitefield House, 186 Kennington Park Road, London SE11 4BT. You may also choose to explore the possibility of adoption or fostering, and again the infertility clinic should be able to provide you with information to begin that process.

Along with childlessness there is the possibility that you may give birth to a handicapped child. Everyone carries a level of anxiety on this issue, especially during pregnancy. It is essential that as a couple you have talked about your attitude and approach to such a situation should it occur. Own your fears and anxieties. These are not intrinsically evil. Again, each situation cannot be faced in reality unless it occurs, but to have aired your thoughts and fears is helpful. Should you produce a handicapped child there are specialist societies and self-help groups, details of which will be available through your GP, Citizens Advice Bureau or local library.

If the principles of honest communication are retained then all further issues such as the children's education can be worked through effectively.

We have not dealt with divorce, and children from a previous marriage at this point, as it is dealt with specifically in 'U is for Unfaithfulness'.

is for
Partnership

MARRIAGE INTENSIFIES THE boy/girl relationship. Together under one roof wedlock enables your relationship to become more intimate, more continuous and more demanding. We discover things about each other that we had never even slightly suspected before. The way he sits on the bed and picks his toes; her litter of dirty laundry decorating every surface of the bedroom. These are the issues that bring tension and argument.

It sounds obvious but in marriage we must learn to accept each other for who we are. Mike remembers an earlier relationship with a girlfriend where he thought she had all the potential to be shaped up to become a most suitable companion for him. However, he learned the hard way that people are not lumps of modelling clay to be shaped by the master potter. Rather they are individuals with a past and a history of experiences which have formed their personality and character. To treat someone as a thing to be modelled to meet our personal requirements is an abuse of their humanity and must be avoided at all costs.

The whole purpose of marriage is not to manipulate and control our partner. We are called to be liberators, not dictators. This involves the challenge of creating space for each other and allowing individuals to be who they really are. Yet a number of us have very little idea of our partner's character and personality in detail. We simply know that we have met someone whose company we enjoy and with whom we have fallen in love.

Below, you will find several questions which we would like each of you to answer honestly and then discuss your answers together.

1. Family Background:
(a) What elements from my family home do I want to bring into my marriage?
(b) What elements do I want to leave out?
(c) What is my happiest childhood memory from home?
(d) What is my unhappiest childhood memory from home?

2. Social Adjustment:
(a) On a scale of 1-10 (10 being excellent) how do I rate my ability to relate socially?
(b) How do I react to other people?
(c) Do I talk positively or negatively about people I've met socially?

3. Intellectual Development:
(a) Am I more or less intelligent than my partner?
(b) How many books do I read in a year?
(c) Do people with qualifications threaten me?

4. Vocational Development:
(a) What is my work?
(b) Am I happy in it?
(c) What I would really like to do is ....
   (fill in the blank).
(d) Do I see myself pursuing a career?
(e) What am I prepared to sacrifice for my career?

5. Leisure Interests:
(a) How do I use leisure time?
(b) My favourite hobbies are . . . . (make a list).

6. Spiritual Development:
(a) Am I more or less spiritual than my partner?
(b) The type of spirituality I enjoy most is . . . .
    (fill in the blank).
(c) What are my gifts?
(d) What is my spiritual objective?

7. Sexual Experience:
(a) How have previous sexual experiences affected me?
(b) Are there areas I should communicate to my partner?
(c) Am I relaxed or tense with regard to sex?
(d) Am I worried about anything related to sex?

8. Physical & Mental Health:
(a) Have I suffered from any serious physical or mental
    illness?
(b) On a scale of 1-10 (10 being excellent) how would I rate
    my health?
(c) Do I find the thought of any particular illness difficult
    to contend with?

When we marry we need to remember our partner's history as well. All of us have been shaped by our experiences; psychologically, emotionally and spiritually. These experiences leave their mark and may trigger certain reactions to a given set of circumstances. This can be most disconcerting for our partner. Therefore it is essential that we understand as much about each other's past as possible.

Marriage is a relationship; indeed a lifetime's relationship. Hence it is most important we take seriously the relational experiences we have each had. These more than anything else can cause friction within the present relationship we are seeking to build.

While we are all *products* of our history, we need not

be *prisoners* of our history. Through owning the areas where we have been scarred growing up, we can find ways forward together which will lead to great personal fulfilment for each partner, and a cracking good marriage relationship.

A marriage relationship should afford sufficient security to enable each partner to drop their defence mechanisms and feel entirely safe. This should be your aim.

Conflict

Conflict is an inevitability of any relationship. Marriage is no exception. The nonsense propounded by the film *Love Story* that 'love is never having to say you're sorry' has to be ignored. Love is very much about the willingness to say, 'I am sorry,' and to mean it. This is the true stuff of romantic love and is essential to establishing an effective relationship together within marriage.

The problem with conflict is that we often feel guilty or ashamed of the fact that there is conflict within our marriage. Sometimes we pretend everything is wonderful when we have spent the whole of the previous night in tears. Relationships will inevitably produce wounds. Wounds lead to resentment. This in turn generates hostility and this hostility can precipitate a war. The problem with all wars is that they lead to fatalities and our society is fast becoming littered with the debris of broken marriages.

The answer is to avoid the war. This is easily said, but how do we do it?

One story which highlights the humorous side of these situations was related to us by the wife of a couple with whom we were staying. In the early years of their marriage she had become irate with the way her husband came home from work, picked up the newspaper and ignored her. She therefore decided to ignore him entirely. After several days, during which time he had apparently failed to notice that he was being ignored, she gave up on this approach feeling even more rejected than when she'd started! Instead she decided to raise the issue and they were able to talk it through constructively. He hadn't considered she might feel ignored. He was simply doing what he'd always done and needed a dose of progressive education!

Again, several days before our first wedding anniversary, Mike, was telling a joke to a couple of friends as we stood around drinking coffee in the kitchen. Katey made the unfortunate mistake of interrupting to give the punchline. Mike saw red, reacted and threw boiling hot coffee over Katey. She left in tears, the couple diplomatically excused themselves and Mike had to decide whether to stand his ground or follow his wife upstairs, eat humble pie and apologise, seeking to explain why he had overreacted to such an extent.

Fortunately he followed the latter course of action and sought to put things right. A wrong decision at that point could have led to a major problem. The ensuing conversation helped Mike to explain his sense of anger at being upstaged and Katey's embarrassment that here was a joke that had been regularly trotted out by Mike and no doubt everyone had heard. Reconciliation was achieved and an area of the relationship that needed working on identified.

Interestingly we were censured by another couple who heard about the incident. The friends who had witnessed the whole thing and had made such a tactful withdrawal were engaged to each other. We were told that our behaviour in front of them would not have helped them get a proper view of marriage. They are now successfully married and have been for a number of years. We believe they got an honest insight into the realities of wedded life which did them no harm.

Throughout marriage we need to learn to recognise the verbal and non-verbal messages our partner is sending. Mike knows from the tone of voice when called to

119

table if he can afford to finish what he's doing or needs to attend forthwith. Again at a party he can recognise instantly what is being said to him across the room by the look in Katey's eyes. We do well to learn to pay attention to such signals. In so doing we can avert conflict most effectively.

At all times conflict arises out of choices. On all occasions we are responsible for the choices we make. This is helpful. The cries of: 'It's all her fault'; 'He's totally unbearable!' and the like seek to lay blame totally at someone else's door. This is a somewhat selfish and naive approach. Two people involved in a relationship must accept mutual responsibility for the situations they find themselves in.

Hence we can choose if we are going to allow the conflict to develop or nip it in the bud. Each of us can take personal responsibility for the scale and nature of conflict within our marriages. After all, it's not conflict but rather the ability to recognise and resolve it that matters in the end.

Each of you should make a commitment to the other that you are more interested in resolving conflicts than furthering them. Whether they involve the replacement of the toothpaste cap or changing jobs, discuss how you will find ways of approaching the other and airing your grievance, justified or not, in the interests of maintaining an honest relationship.

For many years it has been recognised that sharing life in depth with another person is the solution to most of our human problems. It is in loving and in being loved that we find real meaning in life. However, seeking such closeness which is in itself an answer generates conflict. The consequent disillusionment can make or break the relationship. This is why active communication is so important.

At this point it would be good to do a brief exercise together.

1. Together, identify those incidents and factors which generate conflict within your relationship.
2. Identify, in as far as you can, the sequences which generate such conflict, eg mood, tone of voice, behaviour pattern, etc.

Affirming each other

Many of us have grown up under constant disapproval. From parents, teachers, employers and friends we have developed a strong picture of our weaknesses and what we can't do rather than our strengths. We in our turn find it easier to criticise than to affirm people. Most of our conversations over lunch or out for a drink involve pulling people apart rather than speaking warmly about them.

The tragedy is, many of us are as much victims as perpetrators of this. When we come to marriage we hear all too clearly the negative comments and fail to pick up the word of encouragement. All of us in our marriages need to take a definite decision to compliment and build up our partner. This affirmation generates trust within them for us, creates a greater measure of security within the marriage and helps us to begin to think rightly about ourselves. We take on board more of what people say about us than we can imagine, so let us not add to the load that has been built up over the years.

When Mike was growing up he well remembers it was generally joked, 'Don't let Mike carry the plates; he'll drop the lot!' The concept that he was clumsy stuck with him over the years and he would refuse to undertake certain tasks because he was clumsy. One of these was a reticence to hold very young babies. Now, while this is somewhat lighthearted, it well illustrates the point about the importance of what is said to us.

However, this is not a licence to go around saying all sorts of positive things for the sake of it. We need to be realistic and address obvious weaknesses as well, in case we should become resentful at what appears to us our partner's apparent non-performance in certain areas.

As a start, try the following exercise together. You will each need a piece of paper and a pen. Write your answers down privately and read the instructions before sharing together.

1. List three strengths you recognise in your partner.
2. List three weaknesses you recognise in your partner.

Instructions for sharing.
Strengths: Guys should share the strengths they have identified about their partner first; then girls should follow suit and share with their fellow.
Weaknesses: Girls go first this time and fellows follow on.

The reason for this order of communication to each other is to underline the point that men are so often slow in encouraging and affirming their wives. It is good to take time to communicate those qualities you appreciate; to notice special additions around the house.

When it comes to weaknesses men are the worst at receiving criticism, however kindly it is meant. Wives know their husbands best and if the men can hear what their wives see as weaknesses, which everybody else has probably noted anyway but is too inhibited to tell them, then husbands can be creatively shaped to become more whole human beings.

This process is one that should be regularly repeated throughout marriage as it provides a good basis for healthy communication.

Finding ways to communicate

1. Interrupt the sequence leading to conflict. This may take courage, but get into the habit of doing it. We struggled over the way Mike picked his nose and the way Katey ate an apple. Mike would suddenly get a

sharp rap across his picking hand and as Katey nibbled away endlessly Mike could feel his blood boiling. We therefore learned to acknowledge our weaknesses and request we were given a warning or expressed our frustration early and without any edge.

2. We must exercise trust and confidence in each other. Mike is no TV lover. He prefers reading but cannot concentrate when the TV is on. However, if he asked whether the TV needed to be on, or left the room to read elsewhere, Katey felt he was making a statement about her watching TV and what she was watching. Therefore Mike mentions he is leaving to read or enquires if Katey is using the TV for anything more than moving wallpaper, while indicating verbally that he has neither a problem with her watching or the programme.

3. We must learn to apologise and take responsibility for our bad behaviour. In the early years of marriage Mike would often storm out of the room and disappear off out of the house. When he returned there was no word of explanation. Katey was left with an awareness that she had upset Mike, but didn't know whether or not she was culpable. Learning to say sorry and to acknowledge to your partner that you are out of order is essential.

4. We must work through the possibility of rejection and the increased hostility such rejection can produce. There are times when an apology has been thrown back by one of us in the other's face; there are occasions when the process of defusing a situation has been hijacked by the refusal to co-operate on the part of the other. This is the learning curve we need to ascend. Remember, there is no gain without pain and it is the truly tough who get going when the going gets tough!

5. Learn to decode each other's verbal and non-verbal messages. Tones of voice and knowing looks can

aggravate or educate; probably they do both. Wisdom leans towards treating such indicators as educational tools in order to prevent the deterioration of the situation into all out war. The passage of time allied to experience is the great secret here. Mike recently returned home from church much later than Katey, who was feeling unwell and had opted to go to bed early and catch up on her sleep, had expected. The tone that greeted him as he came through the door immediately alerted him to the fact that he was walking into an ambush: one false move, or word, and he would be dead. He therefore kept it lighthearted, refused the bait, went out of his way to be helpful and survived. Several days later he challenged Katey who acknowledged she had felt aggrieved and fancied a fight. Apologies made, another lesson learned and no casualties!

6. We must always remember that we are building a relationship and serving our partner over and above ourselves. Many have made the mistake of winning the argument but losing the person. We cannot afford to behave in this way.

7. We must recognise the true nature of stress in order to deal with it effectively. The question is: 'Do we have stress or does stress have us?' It is our perception of people and issues which finally counts. That is what causes us to act in certain ways. Mike still can't walk into a school building without his stomach knotting up. His childhood perceptions persist to this day. Practical advice and help from our partner will not go amiss here. They may not know all the intricacies of the situation, but they do know us and they can help reflect back to us on an issue from outside the situation.

Learn these communication skills together and enrich your relationship.

is for Questions

WE HAVE GATHERED together some of the most pressing questions that may occur and given a brief way forward to help you on your way to finding an answer. There will be things that cause us anxiety during our marriage. To sit and stew over these generally does little to help us. If we do not feel talking it through with our partner has eased the problem then we should look outside the marriage for help. But always with our partner's knowledge.

Obviously our partner may not want us to talk to anyone apart from themselves. However, not to do so courts disaster for the very relationship itself. Often, to have a helpful perspective from a neutral reference point can help put things into perspective. We stress *neutral* because it is all too easy to get support from a close friend who totally accepts our position and gangs up with us against our partner.

Someone who is neutral can help you as a couple by reflecting back what is going on between you both; things you cannot see because you are too close to the situation. One of the saddest experiences is talking with individuals whose marriages have failed but who with the benefit of separation and distance from their spouse

125

can see all the half-truths they accepted without challenge and how they were manoeuvred by the one they loved. A neutral sounding board would have helped the couple to recognise this while there was still time to do something about it, or revealed that one partner (or both) did not have the will to work at repairing and renewing their marriage.

What is marriage?

This is an essential question. Our answer will in many ways determine the extent of our commitment to making our marriage work and succeed. Our view is that the central meaning of marriage is covered in the text of the Christian marriage service. If this is the way we have chosen to begin our marriage together it is not inappropriate to understand a little of the thinking and convictions which lie behind the words we will be using.

In the first book of the Bible you will discover God creating mankind in His own image. 'So God created man in his own image, in the image of God he created him; male and female he created them' (Gen 1:27). Hence both the man and the woman are God's image bearers. They were also created for each other (Gen 2:21–23), and the words associated so closely with marriage are also found in the early chapters of Genesis: 'For this reason a man will leave his father and mother and be united to his wife, and they will become one flesh' (Gen 2:24).

These words apply to both members of the partnership; not just the male. In other words, at your marriage there is intended to be a leaving of the parental home and all it represents. You as an individual break from the protection and provision of your parents— always assuming this was something you had known which is not a foregone conclusion by any means today—and commit yourselves to provide provision and protection for each other.

Not to sever the links with the childhood realm in this way is disastrous. It leaves the door open to either side's parent(s) having an unhelpful level of access into your relationship. It also means you have not totally committed yourself to your partner and have left room for a retreat back into your childhood home as and when convenient.

The intended process is *to leave* the influence of parents while entering a new relationship with them as a couple. You are *to cleave* or commit yourselves so closely together that nothing can be driven in between you to act as a wedge and force you apart. This includes work, friends and leisure activities. You are also *to become one flesh*; to begin a sexual relationship together which is exclusive to you and your partner in marriage. However, the 'one flesh' principle extends beyond the realm of sex to include an equality of opportunity and leadership within marriage. (See 'X is for Xantippe' and 'P is for Partnership'.)

If we were to continue with our look at the Bible we would also discover that the concept of marriage, that is 'leaving, cleaving and becoming one flesh', preceded mankind's estrangement from God. Therefore it is God's intention for men and women to work out their relationship together within the context of marriage.

The church has often been accused of having a negative attitude towards sex and sexuality. On the contrary, God invented it and always intended that sexual union should be fully enjoyed but within the context of an exclusive and committed relationship. It was not limited to marriage because mankind's corrupt nature meant that a containment strategy had to be developed to deal with his sexual appetite. Rather marriage predates man's fall into sinfulness in the biblical record. We should therefore accord both marriage and our sexuality a high view. Mankind was designed for a lifelong monogamous relationship with a member of the opposite sex.

The Bible goes further. It also lays out clear parameters

within which marriage can be worked out successfully. Many of us think we know best or that we can work things out for ourselves. Unfortunately, given the high divorce rate and the loss of Christian faith within our society, to hold such a position is increasingly untenable. Not many of us would consider repairing a car engine without a trusty Haynes manual. The Bible is just such a manual for life in general and marriage in particular.

Always remember that marriage is not simply a piece of paper, ie the marriage certificate, nor simply a rather grand ceremony. It is a relationship intended for life which requires hard work and commitment within a clear framework. We believe that the Bible gives the best framework within which to establish a successful and enjoyable marriage.

Where do I get help?

We hope this won't be a regular cry of anguish within your marriage. However, you may meet a period when for various reasons what you had has gone a little sour; you are not apparently getting on as well together; some issue has arisen which is causing you some grief.

Elsewhere we have mentioned how to handle marital conflicts in detail ('N is for Negotiation' and 'P is for Partnership'). Broadly speaking, there are three routes:

1. Consult a trusted and unbiased friend. There is a lot of accumulated wisdom in people, but we don't have many contexts in which we can draw upon it. Do not consult someone who is strongly biased towards your opinions or who is not committed to seeing your relationship succeed. For some, a parent can play this role and traditionally that is where you would have gone for help. However, be careful that you are not giving an unhelpful lever which could threaten your relationship long term.

2. Make contact with the local church leadership. Most have a fund of experience in matters concerned with relationships and spend a good proportion of their time giving practical counsel to married couples. This is a further informal way to get assistance.

3. Contact Relate. If you want a more professional approach then contact Relate. Details can be found in your telephone directory, from your local Citizens Advice Bureau or from your GP. The only difficulty is that you may have to wait for an appointment. All counsellors have been trained for the work of marriage guidance and will probably want to work with you both over a period of time.

There is no shame in seeking advice as a married couple. Neither is it a sign of weakness. However, neither of you should engage in seeking significant counsel without your partner's knowledge. The pressure of the situation may demand that you do it without your partner's consent, however.

We would say you ought to talk with someone if you feel that you have made a mistake in marrying the person you have, find difficulties with sex, or your partner begins to hit you. Misplaced loyalty which suggests that to seek help is to betray your partner is a nonsense. Relationships reveal different strengths and weaknesses in us all and we may need advice on how to turn a weakness into a strength.

Finally, the people you speak with as suggested above will not think any the less of you because of your situation. They are prepared to listen and counsel primarily because they are committed to marriage, and successful marriage at that.

Cross-cultural marriage

With a shrinking world more people are marrying someone from a completely different culture from the one in which they grew up. This offers some special opportunities (some might say difficulties but we are optimists) in working out a marriage relationship.

If you meet your partner overseas and decide to get married be aware that you will have to contact the Home Office in the UK to check out their status and right of entry to the UK. This should create no problems, but we have talked with folk for whom this has meant some work before everything was ready to roll.

You would also be advised to learn as much as you can about your intended's culture. Read about it; look at an atlas; find communities of their culture and background within the UK.

There are special issues raised by cross-cultural marriages, not least in learning to understand each other and how most appropriately to communicate. Your British culture might mean you are fairly clear in saying what you feel. Your partner may come from a culture where you don't express things directly but only by inference. These are the areas of learning that lie before you both. Take your time and get help from those within the same culture as your betrothed.

Also, don't assume your partner is either familiar or comfortable with the way of life in the UK. Everything needs adjusting to from visiting a GP to running the bank account.

Financial difficulties

Consult chapters 'F is for Finance' and 'D is for Daily Budgeting'.

Miscellaneous

Adoption. You will need to make contact with adoption agencies. Many will write back with pro forma letters saying they are not looking for parents at present. This can prove very disheartening but will test your resolve to adopt. Eventually you will be accepted, then a long series of interviews will be the order of the day while you are both assessed as to suitability. If eventually you are successful you will need to wait until a baby/child is available and the society thinks it is a suitable match to you and your partner. Stamina is most definitely required.

Adopting from overseas is still frowned on by social services in the UK. If you intend to go down this route then you will have to be prepared to deal with a lot of red tape, and to defeat every bureaucratic barrier that is raised, and many will be, to obstruct you. If you decide upon a cross-cultural adoption you must discover all you can about the child's cultural roots so that as he grows up you can help him discover something of his national identity.

Of course, if you are in a position to adopt a child with a handicap then you are likely to be welcomed with open arms.

Fostering. Contact your local social services and they will advise you of the way forward. Details are to be found in the telephone book.

Bereavement. Contact your local GP for advice and referral for more specialist counselling. It is not unusual to go through quite a period of mixed emotions. Sometimes there are physical ramifications as well. This is a period during which your partner will need to be exceptionally sensitive and patient. It is also a time when expressing what you feel, from anger to despair, is essential, and your marriage is a safe environment in which to do this.

is for
Relocation

THERE ARE VERY FEW people who move into their first home, raise their children in it, become grandparents while living there, enter retirement and end their days still in the same house. Society is very mobile these days so we can expect to move house every so often. Your type of employment has a direct bearing on this.

When we first married, Katey was teaching full time and Mike was employed by British Youth for Christ. Mike's job involved a move every eighteen months fow a while and so we became experts at relocating. There are many issues involved. We had to decide whether we were both happy with the pattern we were establishing. For example, it made it quite difficult for Katey to keep changing jobs and she didn't always manage to secure a new post. We talked this through and Katey decided that she was quite prepared to resign from teaching in order to follow Mike's job around the country. When things got tough, it was important that Katey had to come to the conclusion on her own and was not just toeing the line put forward by Mike.

So you have to move. How do you go about it? The first decisions you have to make concern area, housing

132

and how to afford it. The section 'M is for Mortgage' goes through house buying with a mortgage in detail. Once you know where you are moving to, if you have a property to sell this should be well underway. It is vital to co-ordinate buying and selling so that you (a) don't end up living on the streets or (b) end up with two mortgages to pay—even for a few days this can be very expensive. The solicitor doing the legal work should be able to work towards simultaneous exchange of contracts.

When everything appears to be set up and going smoothly you must consider the actual move. There are a few more decisions to make. Are you going to move yourselves or are you going to employ professionals? We have moved ourselves once and used a removal company every other time! From that I think you can guess our prefence.

Moving yourself can work very successfully. It is often done because it appears to be very much cheaper. You need to look very carefully at all the costs to work it out:

Hire of van
Petrol
Lunch for helpers
Tea, coffee, etc
Breakages

We also think that 'wear and tear' on the personnel involved should be added as a legitimate cost.

Professional moving costs tend to be a one-off payment which covers moving costs and insurance. You need to add the cost of refreshment breaks.

We have tended to move nationally rather than locally which also adds a time factor which your helpers should consider.

So, if you are to move yourselves you need to book a van in good time. If you are having a removal company you need to contact them three to four weeks before your projected moving date. It is good to get at least three estimates so that you can compare prices and the service they offer. In order to arrange for an estimate ring the removal companies. They will ask for your projected date and destination and arrange for an estimator to call. This person has a quick look around your house, and makes notes on what is to be moved. It is important to tell him what is and isn't going to be moved. Don't forget the contents of the shed, the garage and the loft.

Removal companies also offer other services such as packing china and breakables, packing books or even packing everything! Obviously these services have to be paid for, but you may find that you want to use some or all of them. Removal companies provide packing cases or tea chests.

When you have decided on which company to use, book it! Removal companies are accustomed to dates changing, but you must keep them informed. Some companies offer a 'free removal package' with every estimate. Katey always gets one of those estimates because she likes playing with key bags and sticky lables!

As moving day looms you have to get organised. Now is the time to sort through all your possessions. There is a rule in our house that if it hasn't been worn or used for a year it's out!

If you are moving yourselves, or at least doing all your own packing, you have to decide when to start. Some people have the space to pack and put all the packing cases into a spare room. Other houses do not afford this luxury so it seems like you are living 'in limbo' for weeks. We have always tried to pack up in just two days. It is two days of chaos, but we find that preferable to four weeks of semi-chaos.

The most nerve-wracking part of moving is packing breakables. The answer is plenty of newspaper! Do not skimp on this because it is the cushioning of the newspaper which can stop breakages. Do not pack boxes or cases too full.

What about books? Our house has always been full of books. We both did history degrees and have books to cover most historical periods. Our first mistake was to fill large boxes to the top with books. Even Tarzan would have struggled to lift those boxes! We always like to label each box with its general contents and to which room in the new house we would like the box to go. If, for example, your new kitchen is too small to accomodate all the boxes, direct them to another room nearby.

One point is to remember is that some removal companies like to take their packing cases away with them so they will have to be emptied on arrival. We also find large bin liners invaluable for packing lighter, softer things as cushions, towels and linen.

Make sure that the last items packed, and therefore the first to be unpacked, are the kettle, mugs, coffee, tea, milk and sugar. (Removal men need to keep their sugar level up—it's hard work!)

Removal men take full responsibility for packing the van. We remember one removal man who wanted to saw our sofa in half to fit it in the van (it was a joke—we think). If you are doing it yourself, take advice on how best to pack the van with all your worldy goods.

So, those are the mechanics of moving. There are, however, other jobs to do. When leaving one house it is important to inform all the people who supply any services. This means th at you will eventually receive at your new home final accounts which need to be settled. The following authorities need to be informed:

Gas
Electricity
Water
Telephone
Community charge

Also inform:

Banks/building societies
Credit card companies
Storecards
Library
DVLC

You will be visited by officials the morning you move to take the final meter readings. They are quite used to the chaos in which you will no doubt find yourselves.

It's important to inform friends and relations of your new address. Most removal firms can supply you with change of address cards. Otherwise you can buy them or design your own. Our last move was a week before Christmas so we enclosed our new address with the Christmas cards!

Moving is not an easy pastime. Katey finds the whole event very traumatic whereas Mike embarks upon it as a new project which needs creative solutions.

The end of moving day needs very careful planning. It is not the time to invite friends and relations to see your new home. You need to have a good meal (courtesy of friends or the local take-away), ensure the bed is made up and have an early night. Tomorrow you can start to play house.

is for Sex

THIS OF COURSE may seem the most obvious of the subjects to be covered in this book. After all, sex is as easy as falling off a log! Unfortunately, this is not what every couple discovers.

We have counselled couples who have enjoyed an active sex life with various partners before their marriage but have struggled to sustain any sexual activity within the relationship. Others have never got off the starting blocks, and yet others have established a pattern whereby the man is happy having an orgasm but gives no thought either to giving his wife pleasure or avoiding causing her pain. It is not perhaps quite so simple.

If you have any questions about the mechanics, ie where everything fits, then get advice. Either get a graphic book on the subject or talk together with your GP. It amazes us that in an apparently so liberated society as far as sex is concerned, we are so reticent to talk about it in any other terms apart from real or imagined conquests. There is no shame in acknowledging that you are a novice as far as sex is concerned, and we recommend that you enter marriage with your virginity intact. It was intended to be preserved for the marriage relationship and society would be the better for an outbreak of sexual morality.

Once the mechanics are clear talk about what you intend for your first night away after the wedding. We give guidelines for this in 'H is for Honeymoon'. However, as far as sex is concerned be aware that you will have had an exhausting day. The thought of sex may be not the most delightful, especially in comparison to a good night's sleep. There is no failure in this. It is plain realism. If you are tired, sleep. Ending the wedding day with sexual intercourse is not a prerequisite for a successful marriage.

Plan the first night together beforehand. Express any embarrassment you may feel at the thought of peeling off your clothes in front of your partner or having your partner remove them for you.

It is also a good idea to take a honeymoon support package. You may find a tube of 'KY' jelly or equivalent proves useful in providing lubrication for sexual union. This can be applied to the penis and the vagina as part of the foreplay. It is also good to be aware that if the sheath is not being used you will discover a wet patch appear in your bed after sex as seminal fluid runs back out of the vagina. In the interests of equality, make him lie in the wet patch from time to time! Tissues are also therefore helpful.

Never rush at sex. Learn to appreciate your own and your partner's sexuality. This will require exploration of each other's bodies; discovering what pleases. This also means talking to each other and explaining verbally what is good and what is not quite so good. Learn to communicate freely during your foreplay. It took Mike a while to adjust to the fact that Katey would often crack a joke at what appeared to him to be an inopportune moment. In fact it took Mike a couple of years to learn how to relax fully into sex. But it was time well spent and an important lesson!

Sex itself is intended as a developing experience. It is quipped from time to time that if you were to put ten pence in a jar every time you made love in the first year of your marriage you would spend the rest of your married life emptying the jar. There is a measure of truth in this. Sex is meant to be a journey of exploration together. If it is simply about 'getting one's end away' then the whole act has been robbed of its purpose in securing and deepening the marriage relationship.

As one lays down good wine, likewise sex is intended to improve with age. We have gone through periods when we have neglected our sex life. This is very easy to do and very quickly it falls into disrepair. We are both so often shattered at the end of the day that the thought of lovemaking then is not that exciting. Therefore we have to plan mornings and other parts of the day carefully so as to find the right time for sex.

It does not matter who initiates sex. Gone are the days when the male initiated and the female lay back, closed her eyes and thought of England! Both partners should initiate. It is very disconcerting if the male is always expected to initiate. He can begin to feel that his wife doesn't really love him because she is making no advances towards him. Hence the importance of mutual responsibility in this area of initiation.

Again, it does not need to be left to bedtime. A suggestion that sex would be fun can be communicated early in the evening, and the evening can slowly lead in that direction. Alternatively, surprise each other by organising a romantic meal. Creativity and fun are the order of the day.

Throughout our marriage each of us is to be experience not performance orientated. The idea is to give pleasure to each other. Seeking to emulate some film star stud is not the best way forward. It's not making the earth move but your partner happy that counts in the end. Therefore don't be afraid to express what pleases you and keeps you interested in sex.

We have learned from an excellent book written by John and Christine Noble called *Hide and Sex* a most important phrase when it comes to sex. It is simply this: 'As long as you break no bones everything is permissable.' Obviously your partner needs to be in full agreement, and you both need to be supple enough to explore various positions. In the book *Hide and Sex* and the manual *A Touch of Love* by John Houghton, a number of intricate positions are detailed for your amusement and enjoyment.

A word here however on fantasy. It is unhelpful to become controlled by your fantasies. Your partner should provide sufficient stimulation for you. If they do not you are likely to have problems. So be clear to whom you are making love. For this reason we are not in favour of dressing up or bondage sex since it begins to move you away from the reality of deepening a relationship with your partner and entering a realm of unreality.

Problems

With regard to problems that may occur, time is usually the way to discover the answers. The man may find a problem with premature ejaculation. This will settle down once you develop your experience in sex. It is very common in the early stages of marriage, but as the man becomes more skilled he will be able to control the moment of orgasm and indeed should so that he ejaculates as and when his wife is happy. Often simply slowing the pace down and taking your time helps on this issue.

Female orgasm is another area of concern. We recognise that all women can achieve orgasm but that it is not essential to successful lovemaking. Again, exploration will enable you to discover together how to attain this. Don't be surprised if it doesn't happen overnight.

Also men can experience periods of impotence when they cannot sustain an erection. This is often related to times of stress. Do not be alarmed; it will pass. If you are concerned then have a chat with your GP.

You may discover that you find it impossible to penetrate with your penis. In this case persevere using fingers to help gently stretch the vagina. Also use KY jelly as a lubricant. If you still fail to couple successfully both pay a visit to your GP for some advice and help.

Finally, what if you decide you don't like sex and don't want sex? We would advise that you visit your GP to explain the situation and seek referral to a sex counsellor. Often our attitudes to sex have been set in place through upbringing and experience, hence we may need to unlearn some attitudes before we can proceed. Obviously it is not healthy to decide to exclude sex from the marriage.

It is also worth noting that some women go off sex altogether after having a baby so you will need to talk extensively at such a time and together determine how best to go forward.

Conclusion

It is worth remembering that when we get married we give our bodies away to our partners. They are not ours any longer. Therefore we cannot use sex as a means of control over our partner. The Bible, where we have turned to before for advice, points out that neither the husband nor the wife can withhold themselves from each other. So don't use sex as a means of reward. This is an abuse of your partner.

is for Troublespots

WHEN WE GET MARRIED we have to remember that we are marrying each other's backgrounds, upbringing and past experiences. We are each an amalgam of what's happened to us, how we've been treated and our opinions. This means that there are more than likely to be areas of conflict because of different understandings and perceptions. These need to be confronted head on before they develop into full-blown 'no go' areas. We have pinpointed a few such areas which may well emerge!

In-laws

There are many 'music hall' type jokes about in-laws which are, to say the least, unhelpful. When you marry, your relationship with your parents enters a new phase. You are no longer a child, therefore the ground rules for a successful relationship need to change. Upon marriage, of course, you also enter into relationship with your partner's parents on a new level. These relationships need to be handled carefully but clearly from both sides if success is to be achieved.

Clarity in a situation and in relationship helps to keep

things on a good footing. It is well worth communicating clearly so that everyone knows where they stand. Prevarication on an issue will often lead to a very tangled web. By being clear you are being fair to yourselves, your parents and your parents-in-law. Clarity also suggests forthrightness. It is impossible to be clear and yet not put your opinion or position in a forthright way.

Having said this, it is important not to be aggressive for the sake of being aggressive. It is possible to present a point of view and have a discussion in a mature adult way. It is through such discussions that all concerned can come to an understanding of a positive relationship. It takes time and energy but it is well worth it.

To reach a relationship of this type it is tempting, on occasion, to give in in order to keep the peace. You are bound not to agree on everything immediately, but do not be tempted just to give in. You will not always be right but neither will your parents. This relationship is one where no one should rule anyone else. Parents should not rule children but children should not rule parents either. Parents and children should seek to set each other free within the newly-formed relationship. It is lovely to see parent-child relationships having developed into really good solid friendships!

On occasion you may feel that there is a conflict of loyalty between your partner and your parents. It is important to remember that your first loyalty must always be to your partner and therefore he or she should be put first.

A discussion point which often arises in a marriage, later rather than sooner, is what will happen to my/our parents when they get older? It is impossible to tell any couple what they should do because each situation is so very different.

There are various options which it would be good to discuss with your parents if that is possible. Do they want to relocate, and if so where to? They may want to live near one of their children but much consideration has to be given to moving. It means leaving friends and neighbours who have, perhaps, been a part of their lives for a long time. Familiarity can be a great comfort and this is also true of surroundings, so have the people concerned considered the major change such a move will involve?

If a move to a remote or coastal area is considered, have they thought about what life will be like in such a community in the winter? It may have been a lovely holiday spot, but day-to-day living tends to be different.

How will they react if the relation they have moved to be near then moves? The motivation for moving must be clear and not dependent on other people's actions.

One possible scenario which must be considered is how would one parent cope if the other died and one person was therefore left alone?

There are no right or wrong answers to these questions, but they need to be discussed and considered, in advance if possible.

The situation of having parents to live in your house with you may well arise. It really should be discussed openly and honestly with all concerned. It might well involve other brothers and sisters who will obviously be concerned about their parents. Before having parents to live with you do consider these points:

1. Is your house big enough to sustain a good relationship together?
2. Will you be able to accept each other's lifestyles?
3. What financial arrangements have you made?
4. What arrangements have you made with regard to domestic matters?
5. As a family (you, your children, your brothers and sisters), are you happy with the situation?
6. Are your parents happy with the situation?

Stress/illness

Living life at the end of the twentieth century means that we are often subject to stress. Stress is defined in *The Shorter Oxford English Dictionary* as 'force or pressure'. Stress is a common complaint these days so it is as well to have considered how to avoid it and also how to deal with it.

We had been married for three years and were living in Milton Keynes. Mike began to experience inordinate tiredness and lethargy. We put it down to early mornings, late nights and lots of hard work in between! As the weeks passed there was no improvement; in fact Mike appeared to have even less energy. Eventually a visit to the doctor was arranged. We were shocked by the diagnosis and also the treatment. The doctor suggested that Mike was suffering from an unknown virus and that he needed complete rest. Well, complete rest for a human dynamo like Mike is not a very welcome suggestion. This situation, unfortunately, lasted for about six months. During this time Mike was not 'ill' in the classic sense of the word, but he needed looking after and encouraging a lot of the time. One Christian visited him and as his parting shot told Mike to 'pull himself together' and get back to work! Not a very helpful suggestion. Days seemed very long with no pattern to them. He would walk to the paper shop, buy a paper and sleep off this major exertion. Thankfully, the test matches were on TV so Mike could wile away the long days playing armchair cricket.

Katey had a lot of adjusting to do during this period. Having been used to a husband who was always in control and taking a lead she now had to take over as the number one decision-maker. Both of us found this a difficult situation which naturally created its own level of stress. Dealing with this stress was valuable experience, although at the time we didn't quite see it that way! Some of the lessons we learned were:

1. Be honest about how you are feeling, to yourself and your partner.
2. Don't be afraid to take time out by yourself.
3. Make sure you have someone to whom you can talk freely and honestly about the situation you find yourself or yourselves in. This is not failure, it is sensible use of friends.
4. Find an activity you find to be a real stress reliever—walking, running, cycling, listening to music.

After six months Mike eventually received prayer. This finally sorted the situation out and Mike returned to work. It had been a valuable time—we'd walked, talked, picked blackberries, shared our frustrations and learned a little about stress!

Christmas

You may think it odd to have included Christmas in the troublespots section. This is because such an important celebration can often be the cause of so much argument. One of the reasons for this is that we each have our own expectations for the festive season, usually derived from our childhood experiences.

Our first Christmas together we decided to spend alone in our own home. We told both sets of parents in good time so they knew what was happening. We also made arrangements to see them soon after Christmas for family celebrations, but we wanted to be together, just the two of us, on December 25th.

This was where the fun began! We both had set ideas on how Christmas should be celebrated and proceeded to plan, each of us on our own, what would happen. We bought a seven foot Christmas tree and trundled back with it through the streets of Wolverhampton. We had bought a few decorations and some lights for it and proceeded to dress the tree. As a child Katey had not often been allowed to decorate the tree as she was the youngest of three and had to fight to make her presence felt, but now that she could decorate at her leisure the thrill had gone!

The next 'problem' was when and where we should open our presents. We discovered that we each had different expectations for this great event. What we should eat and when we should eat it was a problem to be discussed and what we should do with all the time Christmas Day affords. Looking back we realise how important it is to talk such issues through and then to begin to establish new traditions of your own.

Mansion/detached/semi/terraced/flat/bedsit

Where you will live as a newly-married couple needs a lot of consideration. There are lots of factors to take into consideration:

1. Geographical area
2. Type of home
3. Money available

Getting a mortgage and renting are dealt with under 'M is for Mortgage' but you still need to decide on the type of home you would like. Many people automatically choose a similar home to that of their parents, but does it really suit your lifestyle? A large family house may be necessary when children come along but a flat can be easier to keep clean and tidy for two; especially when they are out working all day. It is also cheaper to run, which may prove significant.

The choice of living accommodation must be a joint decision so that husband and wife will both feel that they had a say in where they set up home together.

The size of the accommodation must also be determined by the volume of possessions needing to be housed. Also, are you intending to have visitors to stay regularly? Will you be entertaining folk at meals? These questions should all have a bearing on your choice of property.

We started out married life in a four bedroom, detached house in Wolverhampton. It was a bargain due to its location. Five weeks after our wedding three people moved in to share our home with us! Obviously we couldn't have lived like that in a one bedroom flat! Decide on your accommodation/lifestyle priorities and then select the type of housing that will enable you to fulfil those aspirations at a price you can afford.

Decorating your new home is one way of setting your stamp upon it. Finance again enters the equation but imagination can cut a good number of corners. One word of caution: don't strip the walls from top to bottom of the house in one go unless you know you can complete the job of redecorating immediately. Living in undecorated accommodation for a long period of time can prove most dispiriting. We once lived for four months with wallpaper stripped from the kitchen (an everyday room), so we know. Remember, a little and often is a most acceptable route forward. Unless you're intending to move on in six months.

With the redecoration you can find creative ways to express your personality in the house. Make sure you are in agreement about the final decisions and that each of you makes a contribution.

The place to start with decorating is to choose the colour scheme. The actual decorating can lead to all sorts of fun and games. Katey brought no decorating experience to marriage, while Mike with his little knowledge cast himself in the role of expert and perfectionist. The first room we decorated was the bedroom. Mike allowed Katey to paint the skirting boards—a backbreaking job which few visitors comment upon—with two undercoats and two topcoats. She was closely supervised throughout! Mike hung the paper, with Katey's assistance of course, and during which time he shouted at her not a few times. He also did the rest of the painting. However, as time went on Mike mellowed and Katey spoke out and she was entrusted with more difficult tasks to execute and through which she could express herself and make her own contribution. We learned how important it is to give each other room to develop and practise new skills.

Diet

Before marriage you may have been living in your family home, on your own or with mates. Wherever it was a pattern of eating was established with likes and dislikes, together with favourite dishes. Now you are to share both mealtime and food. Your partner's food fancies may not coincide with yours; you're a red meat devotee, he's a vegetarian. Accommodation of each other needs to be made. When presented with something which has made you heave since infancy, please be tactful; never compare the platter of food you receive unfavourably with what you were used to in the parental home.

It is important to eat a healthy diet. It is reckoned most men accumulate the weight they later seek to lose, often under medical instruction, within the first two years of marriage. This is through contentment. It is worth taking steps to avoid this if you can.

We are not of the school that sees the wife's role as including shopping, cooking and washing up. If both partners are working it is even more ridiculous to think roles can be established in such a way. Turn shopping and cooking into a corporate activity if you want some fun. Alternatively, indicate which of you is taking responsibility for which areas, and swap around regularly to save getting into a humdrum rut. Indeed, trouble-spots should provide an effective challenge to keep you from becoming boring and settled. So be encouraged.

u

is for Unfaithfulness

PERHAPS THIS IS something of a negative section to include in a book which is looking forward to and encouraging us into marriage. However, it is clear that many people enter marriage with a measure of fear for the future. Indeed every one of us should be realistic. Unfortunately, when we get married our interest in the opposite sex does not disappear or become wholly absorbed in our partner. If this is a shock to either of you then you had better start talking earnestly.

Today in England nearly two out of every three marriages are ending in divorce. This has serious consequences; first for the couple who have observed their relationship come apart before their eyes. There are large areas of emotional hurt to work through; bitterness to be confronted and dealt with; often an overwhelming sense of guilt to contend with.

We have stood close to a collapsing marriage on more than one occasion. The pain is intense and the road to healing is often long and arduous.

Secondly, if there are any children they too are deeply affected by the divorce. They have lost the stability of having two parents under the same roof. They will lack either a male or a female model. They will also be unable to observe how marriage works and so have no role model to guide them when they approach an adult relationship with someone of the opposite sex.

Apart from the chaos this introduces to society at large it leaves deep psychological and emotional scars on us all. It is therefore because of increasing incidence, likely contact with marriage failure at some point in our history and in the interests of being able to take steps to prevent it that we have included this section on unfaithfulness.

Obviously it is essential to be honest about any fears we may have with regard to our partner's potential marital unfaithfulness. Raising the issue should not threaten the relationship nor be interpreted as an accusation by one or the other. If we fail to acknowledge our fear we will discover we are watching our husband or wife with eyes like a hawk and seeking to circumscribe their activities. We will find it hard to believe they are really going out for a drink, or to visit a friend. Everything in us will try to probe and in every way but directly indicate we don't trust them. Since all relationships grow out of the soil of trust we begin to destabilise our marriage without even realising it.

Jealousy is an emotion which we all need to guard against. It is neither healthy nor helpful. It leads our imagination in all sorts of directions; none of which enhances our respect or love for our partner. There is nothing worse than returning home with a spring in your step and looking forward to seeing your partner, only to be met by a string of questioning that makes the gestapo appear moderate in approach. Immediately, tension is introduced and what should have been a good evening together relaxing is lost.

The only way to avoid jealousy is to keep an open account between yourselves. If you have suspicions, mention them. If you are attracted to someone else, be honest about it. Once something is aired it has far less ability to harm us. However, do be thoughtful about how and when you communicate. The style can determine the reaction. So learn to be wise.

In our early years of marriage Mike travelled extensively with his job. This meant he was away from home for several days at a time. While away he would be meeting people and naturally found some of the women very attractive. However, the ground rule laid down by us was that Mike would phone home every day and talk to Katey. This actually meant organising his time and locating a phone. Also on returning home Mike would tell Katey what he had been doing and also say if he had felt tempted at any level. This was helpful and non-threatening to Katey and strengthened the relationship.

One other lesson we learned early in marriage is the potential harm words can do. The old adage 'Sticks and stones can break my bones, but words can never hurt me' is totally false. Words go deep into us and wound. What's more we can begin to believe what is said and live under its shadow becoming an embodiment of someone else's opinion about us. Do not at any time privately or especially publicly, pull your partner apart verbally. No matter what the provocation, save it until you are on your own and sort it out then.

A programme of monitoring and accountability like this, established with the agreement of the couple, is an excellent safeguard for marriage. Talk through how you will act as a safeguard for each other in this area.

In the church where we are involved we each have friends to whom we can also be accountable in areas of weakness. Hence we have an extra safeguard for our marriage and a framework within which to talk through any areas of weakness within our moral character.

At all times the watchword for avoiding marital unfaithfulness is 'opportunity'. If we ensure that we are *avoiding every opportunity*, ie being alone in the office with that attractive young lady from personnel or allowing ourselves to be driven home by that handsome hunk of a manager, then we are building practical safeguards against anything untoward.

A final word on this is that boredom often leads to opportunity. If we fail to pay attention to our partner and create quality time together with them then problems can emerge. For example, if our work absorbs a large proportion of both our time and our energy, and we find we are leaving home early, returning late and always exhausted, then it is little wonder that our partner begins to lose interest in the relationship we have promised to build together. No relationship can be adequately sustained by one member. Should someone begin to flatter or spend time with the one who feels deserted or rejected in favour of work, do not be surprised if an extra-marital affair is born.

This is why it is so essential that we take time to relax together and discover activities that we enjoy doing as a couple. Look up 'L is for Leisure' for more on this particular subject.

Background

A word or two here about background. It may well be that you are a product of what is called a broken home. Your own parents failed to make marriage work and you were brought up by a solo parent. Obviously the timing of your parents' separation is important as to the effect it will have had upon you. Regardless of that, however, you will carry a greater anxiety about marriage failure than others. It is tragic how breakdown and divorce increasingly runs in families.

Having observed a marriage breakdown you have also been prevented from seeing a marriage worked out or modelled before your eyes. You will have seen the parents of your friends, but they were no doubt on their best behaviour when you were around. You will have heard about the rows they really have from your same friends.

But you won't have seen anger dispersed and dispute resolved. This is something of a handicap.

Therefore you must be clear about your aspirations for the marriage and the ideas you have formed about how it all works. If the reality does not live up to the imagined ideal then you have a problem.

Alternatively, you personally may have experienced a marriage breakdown. As you prepare to enter marriage again all sorts of spectres may have to be faced. You will need to have talked through in detail the causes of the previous failure. Also, it is essential that the emotional hurts have had time to heal and that bitterness and resentment have been laid aside. We are convinced that bitterness and resentment can produce severe physical symptoms if they are not dealt with properly.

You will also need to talk through with your partner your fears and anxieties as you are on the verge of re-entering marriage. These fears may be quite irrational but if they are real then you must address them. You will also need to confront areas where bad memories are resurrected, for example the whole sexual relationship may need to be thought about carefully.

If you will be bringing children with you into the new marriage then they too must find time and ways of bonding with your new partner. The relationship should be between all members of the new family.

Reconciliation

What happens if you discover your partner has been unfaithful?

First, you need to establish if they are prepared to be honest about it. If you have had your suspicions and discover that there is an adulterous relationship taking place, you need to establish if your partner will acknowledge it. You then need to establish if this adultery will end or if your marriage will be sacrificed. It is at this time that wise, external counsel can be helpful since you will both be boiling over with emotions of various sorts.

Alternatively, your partner may have come to you and confessed their misdemeanour. Obviously this is slightly better since they are seeking to put the marriage back together.

To recover from such a betrayal of trust, which is what adultery comes down to, takes a big heart and a lot of courage. However, it *can* be done and many can testify to a successful marriage retrieved from the dust of unfaithfulness.

What is required is an honest apology and an offer of forgiveness. There is no way that such unfaithfulness can either be justified or ignored. What's needed is a breaking off of the extra-marital relationship and a clear, unequivocal apology. The boot is then firmly on the foot of the injured party. Will they find it within themselves to forgive?

Now forgiveness cannot be conditional. All sorts of thoughts flow through your mind but you can only forgive and forget. Obviously for the relationship then to develop effectively new ground rules will need to be established. These are rather like a cane that is used to support a plant that has been knocked over, in order to enable it to grow again. It is unable to support its own weight immediately.

If forgiveness is extended then full reconciliation can be achieved. It will take time to recover trust in each other. There will be painful conversations together and probably tears as well. But slowly the marriage will recover and have every opportunity to flourish again. However, the idea is never to get into this situation. Prevention is always better than cure!

v is for Values

GATHER ANY GROUP of people together and raise a controversial subject such as capital punishment and you very quickly discover everyone has an opinion. Some opinions are strongly held; others less so. At times these opinions have been carefully thought through and are well argued; alternatively they are merely a cocktail of various threads of ideas accumulated over time and regurgitated with passion.

These opinions provide each of us with what is called our worldview. This very basically is our assessment of how things ought to be in the world in which we live; what we think is just and unjust; what we think is right and wrong. It affects our view of society in general and also our own personal morality, eg if there's no ticket collector at the station I won't pay my fare.

Our worldview provides the foundations upon which we build our life. It's illustrated by the following story: 'A wise man built his house upon the rock. The rain came down, the streams rose, and the winds blew and beat against that house; yet it did not fall, because it had its foundation upon the rock. But a foolish man built his house on sand. The rain came down, the streams rose, and the winds blew and beat against that house, and it fell with a great crash.'

Such simple wisdom highlights how important it is that we build upon something substantial. There is no sadder sight than a demolished house. In such a state it cannot fulfil the purpose for which it was intended and is of no real value. It reflects what it might have been but in reality is no more than a pile of rubble.

It is therefore important that we think carefully about the worldview we will adopt, and recognise that opinions can change. New information can mean we see things in a different light; experience can redefine the parameters of our beliefs. At all times it is important to engage in constructive discussion with a wide range of people as this helps us to appreciate their worldview and to apply our perspectives to what we hear from them. It also provides an opportunity to communicate what we believe and why.

During your courtship you and your partner may well have discovered that you have violently divergent views on certain subjects. Hopefully you do disagree in some areas or else the whole relationship will be very monochrome in a technicolour world. Divergent views enable us to discover creative forums for debate. Always remember we have two ears but only one mouth; try to listen twice as hard as you try to enforce your viewpoint.

When we were going out together we found ourselves radically disagreeing on a whole host of issues, many of them moral. We would talk late into the night, neither of us prepared to give ground. It was part of the learning experience for Mike that he could learn from Katey; he didn't need to win every argument.

Having majored in history at school and then university Mike's view of debate was to win. Katey often expressed the fact that if necessary he would argue white was black; and win! However, winning an argument is not necessarily the most creative approach to issues of fundamental belief.

On the other hand Katey had to discover a greater confidence in her opinions and to stick to her guns when arguing. She was always far more teachable than Mike and not at all fussed about winning arguments.

Through discussing such differences of opinion together you will discover to what extent you are threatened by someone else challenging your views. You will also learn how to engage in healthy dialogue over points of disagreement; again an essential marriage skill.

Below you will find an extensive questionnaire asking for your views on various issues. Go through and answer the questions independently of each other before joining together to discuss your answers with each other.

QUESTIONNAIRE

Belief

1. Do you believe in God?
2. Describe the God you believe in.
3. How do you know this God is real?
4. Are there others who share the same confidence in the same God?
5. Does this God take an interest in people in the world today?
6. How, and in what ways?
7. Do you communicate with this God?
8. How, and in what ways?
9. As far as you know does your partner share your faith in this God?
10. If so how do you express the reality of this shared faith together?

Morality

1. How do you decide if something is right or wrong?
2. On what basis would you be prepared to do something you knew to be wrong?
3. If your view is challenged, to what do you refer to support your view?

4. Is there, in your opinion, a final authority in all issues of morality? What is it?
5. What are the three most important moral issues that concern you today?
   (a)
   (b)
   (c)
6. Is your morality influenced by your belief or your belief by your morality?
7. Are there situations in your life where you have taken a decision or acted in a way which is against your moral code?

In discussing your answers together explore the question of the basis on which you made your answers to the questionnaire. Remember to listen to your partner's perspective; don't seek to correct them from your point of view. You are learning about each other.

Today we are increasingly confronted by a society which has adopted a morality of means to establish its values. It can be summarised with the phrase: 'If it feels good, do it.' The major problem with such a viewpoint is that it is primarily selfish. I see myself as the centre of the universe and so long as I am happy with my decisions then I will proceed. This individualism which pays only lip service to the fact that we live in a communal society is the seed of society's eventual destruction. With a shrinking world, the so-called global village, we must take a responsible position and realise that we are in fact our our brother's keeper and our decisions have an impact upon others' lives. We must therefore take others into consideration when we make both our public and private decisions. Indeed, our private world is directly related to the public and will determine how valuable a member of society we will be.

Where does worldview come from?

Parents: We owe more than we might care to admit to the values of our parents. We observe them more than any other individual in the earliest and most impressionable years of our lives. Mike can still vividly remember his father discovering he had been given too much money when cashing a cheque at the local bank and returning to give it back to the cashier.

The way our parents react to and handle situations makes a deep impression upon us and may well shape the way we react in similar circumstances as we pass through adolescence into adulthood.

It may also surprise you to discover that the majority of people adopt the political persuasion of their parents. So again, the deep influence of our parents is evident.

Reflect on the values that were paramount in the home of your childhood and identify the good from the bad; the ones you would want to emulate and those you would want to avoid. Also consider your own opinions and actions, and decide on those you are comfortable with and those you either want to change or subject to close scrutiny, uncertain whether you are keen on them or not.

Media: TV, newspapers and magazines all help form our opinions. It is a standing joke that you can tell someone's political leanings by the newspaper they read. Working in schools it is all too evident to what extent lightweight news programmes on the TV present young people with a set of opinions on contemporary moral issues which they immediately adopt.

It is inevitable that with the amount of television people watch their views are being set by what they observe. It's not just the news programmes. Soaps such as *Neighbours* also give a set of values by which a fictitious set of folk work out everyday life; resolving conflict, falling in love and building relationships.

We can be convinced that what we see on our TV screens is total truth. We can aspire to live as the fictitious characters we watch live; or be convinced that a certain viewpoint is the *only* viewpoint because of the way a programme is made. The media have an increasing role in giving us our opinions without us having to think about them.

Friends: Obviously we take very seriously what our friends think. Mike remembers vividly how hurtful it was when one of his friends dropped him once he discovered Mike had decided to become a Christian.

Especially in our teenage years friends' opinions matter and we talk more openly and honestly than at perhaps any other period in our lives. What our friends think of us is important. Among our friends we will find those who emerge as the opinion setters of the group. We disagree at our peril. Yet we must always be sure that we agree with what we are doing or participating in—even if such participation is passive.

Have you talked through to what extent your opinions are your own or just your friends'?

Observation and experience: We also pick up our value system in this way, often without realising it. This brings to mind the experience of a friend. Queuing with his son for some event, a couple pushed in front. This triggered the boy's sense of justice and he suggested to his father that they should force their way in further up still. However, his father addressed some significant and wise words to his son. He expressed his view that he did not want to have his behaviour dictated by the behaviour of others; that is, he was more than capable of forming his own opinions and determining how he would live— even if it meant standing at the back of queues.

All the above illustrate how important it is to set our own value system. We have found personal fulfilment through the Christian faith. The teachings of Jesus, which we quoted earlier in the chapter, provide a sure foundation for both private and public morality. We have also discovered a firm foundation on which to build every element of our individual and married life, and heartily commend it to all readers. We would be happy to send some literature on becoming a Christian to anyone who chose to write to the publisher requesting it.

We can also put ourselves under great pressure in forming and having confidence in our worldview. If we are either particularly insecure or ambitious we are likely to mould our values to suit our insecurities or ambitions.

Learning to know what we think and why we think it helps us with our insecurities. Then we have something to contribute to discussions with friends and can participate in setting the values in place for our marriage.

Ambition also needs to be recognised and rightly handled. Many folk have betrayed their values in the interests of personal ambition. This materialistic worldview must be both resisted and challenged. Each of you can maintain a healthy watching brief on each other to ensure that ambition does not take over.

It is important to have a clear and mutually agreed worldview as a couple. This will set the framework for your marriage in general and specifically when it comes to taking decisions with regard to work, education and use of holidays.

is for
Wedding

THE WEDDING DAY is the big event everyone works towards, and there is much to be done before the day arrives, so that it runs smoothly and legally! Depending on where you marry, and in what tradition, not all of the following will apply to your situation, but you will find the information you need to make the day run smoothly.

Church ceremony

In the Church of England there are four ways in which a marriage can officially take place. These are:

1. By Banns
2. By Common Licence
3. By Special Licence
4. By certificate issued by a Superintendent Registrar

1. Banns. These must be read on three successive Sundays in the parish church of each partner's parish. Application is made to the vicar of the church where the couple wish to marry. He will require certificates certifying that the banns have been published.

If no objection is raised, the marriage may be solem-

163

nised between 8am and 6pm on almost any day in the following three months.

2. *Marriage by Common Licence.* This is where the three weeks necessary for the reading of the banns are not available for some reason. One of the couple needs to live in the parish where the marriage will take place, and the residential qualification is only fifteen days immediately prior to the application. One day's clear notice is necessary for the ceremony. The licence is valid for three calendar months. Application for a Common Licence is made to the vicar of the church where the wedding is to be held. Only one person need apply for the licence.

3. *Marriage by Special Licence.* This is fairly unusual, and a Special Licence is issued on the authority of the Archbishop of Canterbury through:

> The Faculty Office
> 1 The Sanctuary
> Westminster
> London SW1

This licence is issued usually because neither of the couple fulfils the residential qualifications or because the wedding is to be held in a place not usually authorised for weddings. This may be because of serious illness (ie in hospital).

4. *By certificate issued by a Superintendent Registrar.* Such a certificate is not binding on a vicar who may still insist on the Common Licence being obtained. If such a certificate is available no other legal documentation is necessary. The bride and groom must have resided not less than seven days in their own districts immediately before the notice is entered by the registrar. The certificate is valid for three months. Cost depends on where each of the couple resides.

Civil ceremony (Register Office)

A totally non-religious wedding may be chosen because one or both of the couple may be divorced and therefore not able to marry in church; the couple may be of different religious beliefs or, as in our church, there is no licenced building for us to use, so couples marry in a civil ceremony as a formality and then hold a Christian service of their own. They can write their own vows and organise the celebration from start to finish.

In order to marry in a register office, notice must be given to the Superintendent Registrar in the district where the couple live and where they intend to marry. An application form also needs to be completed. Names, ages, addresses, marital status, occupation, where the marriage is to take place and how long each person has lived in the area are required, along with a declaration stating there is no lawful impediment.

In the case of either the bride or groom being under the age of legal consent (ie eighteen years of age) the consent in writing of both parents/legal guardians is needed. The bride and groom must have lived in the district where they wish to marry for at least the seven days immediately before giving notice to the Superintendent Registrar. In the case of each of the couple living in different districts, applications must be made in each district. If the bride or groom has been married before, a death certificate or decree absolute must be shown to the Registrar.

If no objection is received within twenty-one days, the certificate will be issued by the Superintendent Registrar. The couple may then marry.

It is possible to marry within the twenty-one days if application is made to the Superintendent Registrar for marriage by Certificate and Licence. Only one of the party needs to give notice and only one needs to have resided in the district for at least fifteen days. If no objections are voiced a certificate will be issued one clear working day later and the marriage can take place in the Register Office within three months.

If you are involved with a church which is not Church of England, consult the leadership for advice about the way forward.

Invitations

Having arranged the wedding venue and formal arrangements it is time to send out the wedding invitations. Traditionally the bride's mother arranges the choosing, printing and sending of the invitations. Invitations should be sent out at least six weeks before the wedding but can be sent earlier if desired.

Many stationers provide a printing service and will have several examples of what is available, showing layout and style. A very popular format is:

Mr and Mrs John Smith
request the pleasure of the company of

. . . .

at the marriage of their daughter
Susan Jane
with
Mr George Alan Jones
at All Saints Church, Jamestown
on Saturday 30th April 199X at 2pm
and at a reception afterwards at the
Belvedere Hotel

98 Castle Avenue   R S V P
This quick brown is being used for testing purposes.
Jamestown Sussex

If the bride's mother is dead the invitation will read:

Mr John Smith
requests the pleasure...

If the bride's father is dead the invitation will read:

Mrs Gillian Smith
requests the pleasure...

The invitations may be sent from parents who are divorced and should read:

Mr John Smith and Mrs Gillian James
request the pleasure...

Invitations to a Register Office wedding follow the same format.

If neither parent will be hosting the wedding the names of the hosts for the occasion should be at the top of the invitation.

It is essential to include RSVP because the hostess needs to know how many guests to expect and cater for. Replies should follow the same format as the invitation. For example:

[Address]

Mr and Mrs Simon Jones
thank Mr and Mrs John Smith for their kind invitation to their daughter's wedding at All Saints Church on Saturday 30th April and to the reception afterwards and are happy to accept.

15th March 199X

No signature is necessary.

Separate invitations may be sent for an evening reception, again following the same format.

Mr and Mrs John Smith
request the pleasure of the company of

. . . .

at the marriage of their daughter
Susan Jane
with
Mr George Alan Jones
at All Saints Church, Jamestown
on Saturday 30th April 199X
at 1.30pm
and at an evening reception at the
Belvedere Hotel
from 7.30pm

98 Castle Avenue   RSVP
Jamestown
Sussex

Prior to sending invitations a comprehensive guest list needs to be compiled. The invitations are sent by the bride's parents and therefore the groom's parents need to supply them with the names and addresses of relatives and friends they would like included.

Present list

At the same time as sending out the invitations a present list needs to be compiled.

Many large stores have a facility to hold your wedding list for you. This means that a list is compiled by you in consultation with the store. It is a detailed list giving specific designs and makes of items, and whenever an item is purchased for you at that store it is crossed off the list. It goes some way to ensuring that you don't get six toast racks or twenty-four assorted egg cups! Some people make someone responsible for the wedding list (eg chief bridesmaid, one of the mothers, a good friend) to whom all communication over presents should be made. Again, this can be a most efficient method.

A detailed list needs to be drawn up. It should give product, manufacturer, style, colour and where it is obtainable. It can also be most helpful to give the price (or approximate price) of each item. It is easiest to list requirements room by room. Here are some of the items you may wish to include on your list:

Kitchen
Refrigerator
Freezer
Washing machine
Tumble dryer
Cooker
Kettle
Coffee maker
Knives—various
Bread board
Bread bin
Toaster
Slow cooker
Microwave
Mixing bowls
Saucepans and frying pan
Tea towels
Oven gloves
Can opener
Cooking utensils
Scales
Pressure cooker
Storage jars
Trays
Wooden spoons
Rubbish bin
Washing-up set
Casserole dishes
Spice rack

Bedroom
Bed
Pillows
Sheets

Living room
Suite (chairs, sofa)
Vases
Lamps
Cushions
Occasional tables
Clock
Rugs
TV

Dining room
Table
Chairs
Place mats
Tablecloth
Dinner service
Tea service
Everyday china
Salt and pepper pots
Cutlery
Glasses—sherry, wine, tumblers
Sideboard
Candlesticks
Hot serving plate

Miscellaneous
Vacuum cleaner
Sweeping brush
Dustpan and brush
Garden tools
Garden furniture
Barbecue
Wastepaper bins

Duvet
Duvet covers
Pillow cases
Blankets
Bedspread
Electric blanket
Radio alarm/tea maker

Luggage
Mower
Ornaments

Bathroom
Towels
Mirror
Bathroom cabinet
Linen basket
Bathroom scales
Towel rail

Cheques are always very welcome as you can then buy what you need and want.

This is by no means exhaustive but it gives a good basis from which to work. It is a good idea to include items of varying price to suit all pockets.

Cars

Traditionally the bride's mother is responsible for ordering the wedding cars to take the bride and her father, the bridesmaids and herself to the service. The bridegroom should arrange transport for himself and the best man to the church, and the 'going away' transport for himself and his wife. If the reception is not within walking distance of the church the best man should arrange for the transportation of all guests from the church to the reception. This can usually be done quite informally but the best man should ensure that no one is left behind. Usually the car which transported the bride and her father to the church now takes the newly-wed couple to the reception. The bridesmaids travel in the car in which they arrived. Everyone else travels in their own cars, the bride's parents having arranged for their card to be at the church!

It is not necessary to pay a lot of money and hire cars. Friends will often oblige and use their cars, beautifully cleaned and bedecked with white ribbon. Specialist cars are, however, available to be hired.

Flowers

Flowers are a traditional part of all weddings nowadays. There are flowers to be carried, flowers to be worn and flowers to be displayed. Again the bride's mother is responsible for the wedding bouquets, buttonholes for the men involved and corsages for the two mothers. These can be ordered from a florist or made at home. Care should be taken to co-ordinate colour. There are also church decorations. These need not be on a very grand scale and often there are church members who are willing to use their skills in this way. Attention should be paid to the overall colour scheme.

Table decorations at the reception are also the bride's mother's responsibility and again either a florist or talented relations or friends will do this task. These floral arrangements should be at the reception venue on the morning of the wedding.

Many brides like to have fresh flowers adorning the wedding cake and these should be delivered at the same time as the reception flowers.

Fees

A wedding entails various fees depending on where you marry and in what tradition. These fees do change from time to time and should be checked to ascertain the exact amount payable. Church authorities will be able to let you know this, as will civil authorities. However much payable it is important that the bridegroom has either cash or a cheque book to clear any outstanding debts.

Ushers

The ushers are chosen by the bridegroom from among his male friends. It is also common to include male relatives of the groom and bride. Depending on the size of the church, four are normally sufficient. They should arrive at the church first and hand an Order of Service to each guest. Guests should be shown to their seats, the usher having first ascertained whether they are relatives or friends of the bride or groom. (Seating arrangements are explained later.)

Ushers dress in similar clothing to the bridegroom and best man, ie in morning suits or lounge suits. They are provided with buttonholes.

Music

The music for a wedding is entirely up to the bride and groom in consultation with the church musician(s). It is necessary to choose music to be played before the ceremony; for the bride and her father to walk in to; hymns and songs during the service; music to be played during the signing of the register, and music to leave the church by. There are many 'traditional' pieces which are very popular but some couples choose music which is special to them.

Rings

Traditionally the groom buys a ring for his bride and these days many brides also buy a ring for the groom. It is important for the engagement ring and the wedding ring to be the same carat gold so that one does not wear the other away.

At the service the best man is the custodian of the ring(s) until called upon by the officiating minister. They are then usually placed on a prayer book or Bible. The bride should wear her engagement ring on the third finger of her right hand during the service but she should tell the groom beforehand so he doesn't get confused.

Seating at church

As guests arrive at the church, they should be greeted by an usher and handed an Order of Service if one has been printed. If the guests are unknown to the usher he should enquire whether they are the bride's or groom's guest and he should then escort them to the appropriate seats. Relatives and friends of the bride sit on the left facing the front of the church and relatives and friends of the groom sit on the right. The closer the relationship, the nearer the front the guests should sit.

It is a good idea to reserve seating for young attendants who may find it too long to stand during the whole service. If there is to be an address, chairs or pews may be needed for the bride and groom on the groom's side of the church.

Order of Service

A printed Order of Service is optional but many young people like to keep them as a lasting momento of the occasion. They may be obtained from the same outlets as invitations. The front cover may be a design similar to the invitations. The Order of Service should clearly state what is happening when, and can also contain additional information such as what music is being played and who is taking part in the service. Hymns may be printed in full or hymn books used with just the number given in the Order of Service. If you are having them printed in full, bear in mind that newer songs/choruses are usually copyrighted and permission to use them needs to be sought. This is usually granted free of charge but an acknowledgement is required. It is important to leave enough time for the printing of the Order of Service.

Witnesses

In order to comply with the law a marriage must be witnessed by two people over the age of eighteen. It is customary for the best man and chief bridesmaid to 'do the honours' of signing the register as witnesses but any adults are eligible to do so. If you are choosing other people they must accompany you to the vestry for the signing of the register. Do ensure that there is a working pen for this deed!

Confetti

Many churches object to confetti being thrown within the church grounds. Find out beforehand and spread the word. It is often a good idea to ensure that instructions are given either at the beginning or end of the wedding service. A good alternative (and cheaper too) is rice (not the tinned, creamed variety) or fresh rose petals, both of which are biodegradable! Confetti is thrown as the bride and groom leave for the reception and also when they leave for their honeymoon. It may be a lasting memory, especially as it takes years finally to get rid of every last bit!

Who stands where?

The bride enters the church on her father's right arm. They are followed by page-boys(s) and bridesmaids. The groom stands at the front of the church towards the right, with his best man on his right and slightly behind him. The bride and her father walk down the aisle to the front.

The bride stands next to the groom and passes her bouquet to a bridesmaid. The bride's father stands to her left and slightly behind.

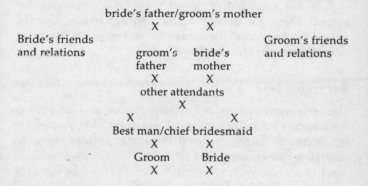

When leaving the church, the positions are as follows:

Photos/video

Every new bride enjoys looking at the photos of the big occasion. In years to come the album may be quite an historical archive denoting changes in fashion!

Professional photographs are expensive but look good. A photographer will often start at the bride's house, photographing the radiant bride and her father, before going to the church to photograph the groom, best man and other attendants. Some photographers will also photograph the guests arriving. This all, of course, has to be paid for. Many people these days also have a video of their wedding day. There are many professional video companies to be found in *Yellow Pages*. Some churches allow photography and filming during the service, but do check first. After the ceremony, many group photos are taken. A little thought and a carefully drawn up list can result in a very interesting photographic record. Depending on your guest list, of course, how about a group of groom's friends and bride's friends with the newlyweds, or school friends of the couple? Most families like to have traditional groups as well.

One factor to consider is how long the photography will take. It can be very tedious and tiring.

It is not essential to spend a lot on a photographic record. There are usually many amateur photographers snapping away and there may be one who could act as official photographer for the day.

Receiving line

Once everyone has arrived at the reception it is time to be 'received'. This is very informal and gives an opportunity for everyone to say hello to the main personalities. A receiving line is composed thus:

Bride's mother	Bride's father	Groom's mother	Groom's father	Bride	Groom
X	X	X	X	X	X

The best man and chief bridesmaid may also be included but the best man is often busy at this time and the chief bridesmaid is looking after any small attendants.

A receiving line is not absolutely essential and at a very informal wedding may be dispensed with.

After the receiving line guests are offered sherry or a soft drink and move towards the meal.

Seating at the reception

Many receptions are of an informal buffet style. Even at these events there is usually a 'top table' where the main characters involved in the wedding sit.

The bride and groom sit at the head of the table, the bride on her husband's left. The parents and chief attendants make up the rest of the top table:

(A) Chief bridesmaid
(B) Groom's father
(C) Bride's mother
(D) Groom
(E) Bride
(F) Bride's father
(G) Groom's mother
(H) Best man

X	X	X	X	X	X	X	X
A	B	C	D	E	F	G	H

If the parents wish to sit next to each other this is quite permissible. At a formal wedding the other guests are seated according to the wishes of the bride and groom. There should be a clear seating plan displayed and place names at each setting.

At an informal buffet it is important to provide chairs for flagging guests, even though they are not allocated.

Speeches

At the end of the meal the best man takes on the role of toastmaster. He calls upon the father of the bride. If the father is not available, or is reluctant to give a speech, a close friend or relative may step in. The speech is kept fairly short and can be quite humorous, referring to episodes in the bride's life. It is also usual to welcome the new son-in-law into the bride's family. Other jovial comments may be made and amusing incidents related before the toast of health and happiness of the couple.

The groom replies on behalf of his wife and himself. He thanks everyone for coming, his parents for bringing him up, his in-laws for their daughter and the wedding. He concludes by proposing a toast to the bridesmaids. The groom's speech can be humorous or more serious, but again should not be lengthy.

The best man responds on behalf of the bridesmaids. His speech should be light and definitely humorous. There is rarely any serious content in this speech and it may well recount incidents in the groom's life. A wedding is a happy occasion so there should be no nasty comments. The best man concludes by reading messages of congratulation which have been sent. The major point is always to avoid longwindedness and therefore boredom.

The cake

The wedding cake is often displayed as the centrepiece at the reception. Traditionally this is a rich fruit cake but we have been to one wedding where the cake was an ice-cream gateau and to another where one tier of the cake was sponge because the bride didn't like fruit cake. A wedding cake can be one, two, three or more tiers and it can be any shape. Only small pieces are served.

The cake is often made by one of the mothers and could be iced by them or done professionally. It is worth making a fruit cake three months before in order for it to mature.

The cake is cut after the speeches. The bride and groom place the tip of the knife into the middle of the bottom tier and make a cut. There is usually much posing for the photographs! At this point the cake is removed and cut into pieces which are distributed by the brides-maids.

Cake is often sent, in small boxes available from the stationers, to people unable to attend the wedding. The bride's mother is responsible for this. It is traditional to save the top tier of the cake as a christening cake for the first child.

Evening reception

Many young couples also hold an evening reception. This enables more people to come and join the celebrations. Food of a snack nature is usally provided, as is drink, but often a bar is in operation.

The bride and groom need to change from their wedding finery into 'going away' outfits. A room should be available for this. The best man should ensure that the groom's clothes are either taken to his new home or returned to the hire shop. The bride's mother should take care of her daughter's wedding clothes.

When the time has come for the couple to leave the reception they should bid farewell and then leave. In many cases the car has been lavishly decorated but hopefully not mechanically interfered with. It is a great relief to drive away together leaving everyone else behind!

The guests may now drift away, having thanked their hosts (the bride's parents) for a most enjoyable day.

is for
Xanthippe

WELL, WHEN YOU NEED an appropriate word beginning with 'x' you have to settle on something. It wouldn't be a bad idea for you to take a guess at the meaning before reading on to the next paragraph where all will be revealed.

It would be lovely to hear all the imagined meanings, but the word is actually a name. It is the name of the wife of Socrates. We never met the woman since Socrates actually lived from 470-399 BC His wife's dates have eluded us. For some reason his wife's name has found its way into the English language and is defined as, 'a shrewish wife.' This itself being translated suggests she was given to scolding a lot and hence not very nice to live with. There is no mention as to whether Socrates deserved it. One thing's for sure: it is rather shrewish and no doubt the RSPCA will take up this issue on behalf of our animal friends in due course.

So why is it included in this book, interesting though such information is? Quite simply because in these days of sexual equality it is essential to address the whole sexist issue and explore contemporary role models for effective marriages. Have you discovered each other's perspectives or prejudices about the other sex? Work through the following statements individually answering 'yes' or 'no', then discuss your answers. It is important to be honest rather than give what you assume will be the right or acceptable answer.

1. Women are irrational
2. Men are impatient
3. Women are the weaker sex
4. Men are the major breadwinners
5. Women should look after the home
6. Men must exercise ultimate financial responsibility
7. It doesn't matter if the woman doesn't enjoy sex
8. The car is the man's but the woman can use it
9. The kitchen is the woman's domain
10. Sex is initiated by the man
11. Women want to be dominated
12. Men are looking for a substitute mother

It is very easy to pick up stereotypic views about the opposite sex. Growing up, we are surrounded by many exasperated and often negative comments about our fathers by our mothers and vice versa. In an increasing number of situations mums have been left. Homes have entertained a succession of 'uncles', all interested in the carnal delights of the situation, none wanting to accept responsibility for the situation and the people caught up in it.

It is our view that men and women are coequals with gender distinctives and as such none of the above statements can be said to be true. We have found that we complement each other; Katey's strengths compensating for Mike's weaknesses and Mike's strengths for Katey's weaknesses. As one example of this, when Katey met Mike she discovered he was a liability in company. He had no small talk and when he did get involved in conversation it was to argue some keenly felt political point with a passion and commitment which frightened the rest of the company from wanting to risk speaking to him again.

For Katey, who was a most sociable animal, this was somewhat awkward. However, using her skills and experience she took Mike in hand and helped him to own his insecurities and recognise he lacked very much experience in how to act in a social gathering. She also explained that the ferocity and intensity of his conversation made people anxious about chatting with him, so he became something of a social pariah. In spite of the intricate difficulties of communicating this, and regular irrational explosions from Mike, Katey stuck to her task and Mike is now quite well socialised; he is also not uncomfortable in company. A weakness has been converted into a strength. This is one of the benefits of partnership and is a sure sign of a strong marriage.

Interestingly, although the Christian church has often been accused of sexism, when one turns to the Bible one discovers that God, whatever else He might be, is no sexist. In Genesis, the first book in the Bible, it is clear that God made mankind in His own image: 'So God created man in his own image, in the image of God he created him; male and female he created them' (Genesis 1:27).

Therefore at the heart of the Christian faith, which has down the centuries shaped the culture and society of the UK, is the clear recognition that men and women are coequals. Neither is more significant or greater than the other. In fact they are created for mutual interdependence or as a team!

While society at large struggles to respond to the challenge that it is sexist from top to bottom, ie that women occupy very much second place from the world of work to life within the home, our marriages ought to be the place where the coequality of the sexes is practised. Hence prejudices revealed through the statements at the start of this chapter will need to be addressed and dealt with.

For this to operate at any practical level we will need to challenge each other when such prejudices reveal themselves. We should also take initiatives to help change our own mindset where we discover it is suspect.

When we were first married Mike would only allow Katey to help with the decorating by painting skirting boards. These were virtually unnoticeable and so if badly done wouldn't be of any significance. Mike operated on two assumptions: (a) Decorating is men's work not women's, (b) Katey therefore would be less competent than he was.

Such assumptions create attitudes and these attitudes, communicated indirectly, can hurt and rob our partner of their self-worth and dignity. In this case it also meant the decorating took much longer. To change, Mike had to unlearn his assumptions and get rid of his prejudice. Ask yourself whether there are things within your new home together that you wouldn't trust your partner with doing or believe that they would not make as good a job of it as you. A pause for reflection and perhaps discussion might prove constructive!

Marriage is intended as a partnership—both parties co-operating in shaping a relationship, making a home and sustaining friendships. Set views about the general weaknesses of women or men can seriously interfere with the ability of such a partnership to develop real-istically. If unresolved, many nagging tensions emerge and one or both members of the marriage are forced to look outside the relationship in order to find approval and value in those areas in which their partner is unable to provide it.

Role models

Most of our prejudices are revealed by our behaviour and values (see 'V is for Values'). Hence when most couples get married they carry into their marriage the prejudices that they have grown up under in their family home and what they have observed in the circles within which they mixed. However, there is no guarantee that such patterns practised by parents are the sum total of correctness or the only model upon which to work out life.

Returning from a trip to Nigeria some years ago, Mike learned from Katey while travelling in the car from Heathrow Airport that she had signed up for a TOPS course in shorthand typing. This raised some interesting questions. We were living in a rented flat at the time and had monthly overheads of rent, bills and housekeeping to meet. Mike was self-employed and generating enough income most months on which to live. Katey had been assisting in the administration side of Mike's work as well as running the flat.

In discussion together we decided to reverse roles. Katey would be paid a small amount while studying and would need to work evenings on homework in order to keep up with what was a short-term, high pressure course of only twelve weeks. That's where the fun really began.

Each morning Mike dutifully drove Katey to the station before returning to housework, shopping and preparing that evening's meal. Late afternoon he would return to collect Katey from the station. Often we would be having guests around to eat during the evening. Whenever Katey got back into the flat she would start ferreting around in the kitchen, anxious about what we would be eating, more for our guests' sake than her own. Mike would have to sternly order her out of the kitchen and, placing a cup of tea in her hand, tell her to have a rest before getting down to the homework.

This went very well, apart from the fact that Mike was not such an economical shopper as Katey was! Over this period Mike's confidence in his cooking skills blossomed and he has continued to be very active in the kitchen. Not just cooking exotic social feasts but the basic everyday meals. This has been helpful as Katey is teaching full time again now so whoever gets in first or is least tired gets together a tasty bite to eat.

It is helpful to explore different role models to those with which we were surrounded as we grew up. At time of writing our household has grown to include a solo mum and her daughter. Deserted by her husband when seven months pregnant she turned to us as friends and we said, 'Come and join the family!' This has meant many more changes, including a move of house to accommodate us all the more easily. Unusual it may be but better by far than a solo mum struggling to bring up a child completely on her own with the minimal income that maintenance affords. As a family we have one budget from which we all live. We believe this model needs to be adopted more widely in order to respond to the type of society that disintegration of marriages and families generates.

Exploration of such models enables others around us, including our own children eventually, to see what it is to live a radical married life in active co-operation and partnership with our husband or wife.

In conclusion we may discover that we find ourselves living under the shadow of our family upbringing— unable to break from certain patterns of behaviour, even though we would like to; locked into certain prejudices we can't shed. If this is the case then we should honestly talk things through together and get some advice and help from a trusted friend. We have found the counsel and prayer of mature Christian friends to help us at this level and would commend talking to a committed Christian leader. Details of someone near you could be provided by writing to us care of the publishers.

is for Year

I T IS OFTEN REMARKED that the first year of marriage is the hardest. This no doubt sounds a little daunting as you are about to set out on your marriage. However, there is a measure of truth in the statement.

We believe that marriage has got easier the longer our relationship has run. On reflection the first year was the hardest of all, yet this is hardly surprising. Two people are suddenly forced to work out their lives together under one roof and with a publicly expressed commitment to each other.

It is certainly only once we are married that a number of the personal habits and attributes of our partner become apparent. How could we have been so blind up to this point, we ask ourselves? All the processes of communication and negotiation are being set in place. The novelty of being married soon wears off. It now comes down to grit and determination. Our commitment to both our partner and our marriage is placed under the microscope.

In our first year Mike had to learn how to control his temper (overreaction and unkind retorts to Katey were the norm over that first year). This demanded a strong commitment to sustaining the relationship. It also caused us both to explore precisely what we meant when we said we loved each other. Was this love capable of absorbing the hurtful things we did to each other?

The Bible helped here when we discovered the characteristics of love:

> Love is patient, love is kind. It does not envy, it does not boast, it is not proud. It is not rude, it is not self-seeking, it is not easily angered, it keeps no record of wrongs. Love does not delight in evil but rejoices with the truth. It always protects, always trusts, always hopes, always perseveres. Love never fails (1 Cor 13:4–8).

These words are found in the New Testament of the Bible. They deserve a close reading. Certainly when we considered them we began to understand what love was all about. Indeed, so closely did we keep to them that we can remember the phrase that we learned off by heart from the Authorised Version of the Bible: 'Love bears, believes, hopes and endures all things. Love never fails.'

When Mike had stormed out or Katey had retreated into herself and so was non-communicative, these words reminded us of our commitment to love each other and the goal we were heading for. Knowing these things was not sufficient in and of itself. We had to take practical steps in the light of what we knew. This cost us and every time we each had to take a decision, 'Will I take this step or have I had enough?'

At weddings the words quoted above from the Bible are often chosen as a reading by the bride and groom. In the context of the service, white dresses and all the paraphernalia of the wedding day, they are often listened to with a sentimental 'ooh that's lovely' attitude. We smile to ourselves because for every couple who consider what is being said, and are prepared to adopt it as their definition of love, there is a hazardous and hard journey to make.

Wedding anniversaries

Assuming you make it through the first year then it is well worth while celebrating your wedding anniversary. The joke frequently made that husbands don't remember the date and constantly disappoint their wives can easily be circumvented by ensuring one of you write it in his diary. When we get our diaries we always write it in straight away. Mike puts a warning in one week ahead so that he can make suitable purchases if appropriate.

Of all the celebrations in our household (birthdays, Christmas, etc) we make our wedding anniversary the special one. We may not get each other a present but we will do something special to mark the occasion. On our tenth wedding anniversary we found ourselves up a tree house on safari in Zimbabwe. It was more luxurious than it sounds, with electric blankets and hot and cold running water! Many have wondered at the type of tree house this must have been.

Then on our thirteenth anniversary we were shown our very first wild badgers by friends we were visiting. Many memories to enjoy, talk about and reminisce over long into the future.

The difficulty with things like anniversaries is that we can think that we need to spend a fortune. Certainly our cash conscious, prestige hungry society suggests that somehow we should be dining in some exclusive, romantic restaurant supping champagne and indulging ourselves. The inference is that if the men don't initiate at this level then they don't really love their wives. This can generate a sense of guilt, produce a large overdraft or lead us to make unhelpful comparisons with others and the way they 'always' celebrate.

We would recommend that you celebrate in a way that makes economic sense, always remembering that the day is your day. There is no one to impress. It is meant to be for your enjoyment. We would encourage you to follow these guidelines:

Be imaginative. Think of something unique and creative to mark the occasion and to demonstrate your love for your partner. One year Mike literally had no spare cash so he used a promotional photograph of a marquee as an anniversary card. It did have the fact that it was the only such card in the world to recommend it. Katey should have felt special! It's not what you give but the way that you give it that counts.

When deciding how to celebrate together either select one of you to lay on a surprise or co-operate together. The most imaginative treat we have heard of concerned a wife who informed her husband that she was taking him to the races for the day. Not having any money he was suitably impressed. They got dressed appropriately and left to catch the train. Arriving at their destination station the lady concerned marched off away from the ticket barrier and set up stools at the end of the platform. This overlooked the racecourse and with binoculars in hand and a well packed picnic they enjoyed a good day out at the races! And on very much of a shoestring budget.

If you are planning a romantic meal and want to cut corners to remain solvent then allow your imagination to run riot. On one occasion Katey secured a major bargain at the market. Passing a pet stall she spotted some lovely chicken (the dead variety). Enquiring why it was on the pet stall rather than the butcher's the stallholder informed her that as it was bruised it was deemed unfit for human consumption. Pressing him further she discovered that there was nothing else wrong with it and promptly made a purchase. We enjoyed a lovely chicken meal and have been barking ever since!

All the trimmings for that romantic evening can easily be assembled. If necessary, borrow a music machine and cassettes off friends. Make paper flowers or settle for some attractive greenery and unusual coloured plants from the hedgerow. Paint an old milk bottle for service as a candle holder if you haven't any old wine bottles. Katey spied some nice wine bottles in wicker holders hanging from the ceiling of an Italian restaurant and persuaded a waiter to cut her down several. We still use one to this day, the bottle thickly coated in candle wax making it look most appropriate as a table decoration.

A box of wax crayons is a useful investment so that scraps of paper can be decorated by your fair hand and used as wrapping paper or turned into a card with a very personal touch. Unique place mats can also be provided. To be honest, setting up such a meal is so much fun, and has so much of yourselves invested in it, that the whole evening is often more romantic and affirming than the £40 a head job at the local high class restaurant.

Be thoughtful. This is your day. Do be aware that you are celebrating the fact that you have been together. Even if you are returning from a hard day at work make this an occasion. Positively build each other up, and receive with great delight any gift, be it gold-plated cufflinks or bicycle clips. Each of you should find a time to express your appreciation of the other. Think through how you want to express this. It is not a duty to be performed but something you desire to communicate out of the affection you have for your partner.

A further idea is to keep a scrapbook of bits and pieces which reflect the previous year of marriage: stubs from the cinema outing, a postcard of somewhere visited, a slyly taken photo of your spouse. This demonstrates a care and an interest in the year and lays a foundation for building into the year ahead.

Be reflective. Talk through all the things for which you have to be thankful from the previous year. Also note those challenges which changing circumstances have brought, eg deterioration of health or the arrival of children. Take some time to talk around these and stop for a moment of prayer, giving thanks to God and requesting his strength and assistance for the future.

In conclusion, make your anniversary a celebration of marriage. Take time to appreciate one another. Don't lose sight of the event in an orgy of present giving and high entertainment. Rather thank your partner for putting up with you and renew your marriage promises privately to each other. If you are aware of a measure of drift between you both then take agreed steps to change that. In this way anniversaries can provide a wonderful oasis amid the pressures of everyday life and a useful stock take of where you both stand.

As a matter of interest we have reproduced the traditional way anniversaries have been known. The idea is that you purchase a gift of the substance specified.

Anniversary

1st	Cotton	45th	Sapphire
2nd	Paper	50th	Gold
3rd	Leather	55th	Emerald
4th	Silk	60th	Diamond
5th	Wood		
6th	Iron		
7th	Wool		
8th	Bronze		
9th	Pottery		
10th	Tin		
12th	Linen		
15th	Crystal		
20th	China		
25th	Silver		
30th	Pearl		
35th	Coral		
40th	Ruby		

is for
Zero, Blast Off!

APOLOGIES FOR THE CORNY title, but you have made it to the end of the A-Z. Hopefully you are now fully equipped for a life of marriage together. From this point you will be blasting off into your new life together.

Our whole intention with this A-Z has been to provide a practical manual to help and encourage couples like yourselves to set off into marriage on a sure foundation. We realise it is hardly likely you have read this book from cover to cover. It wasn't designed for that. However, we trust that you will keep it by you and make frequent reference to it. It contains a host or practical advice and essential principles to help you in your life together.

Ideally you should pick it up from time to time for a refresher course. Also, when you hit an area of difficulty or some question rears its head, then you will flick through these pages to find some helpful advice.

Our hope and prayer for you both is that you establish a strong marriage and that it provides an enriching experience—not only for you but for those who have the privilege of visiting your home over the years.

God bless you as you set out on the adventure of a lifetime!